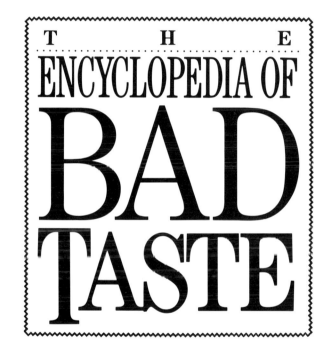

T H E

ENCYCLOPEDIA OF
BAD TASTE

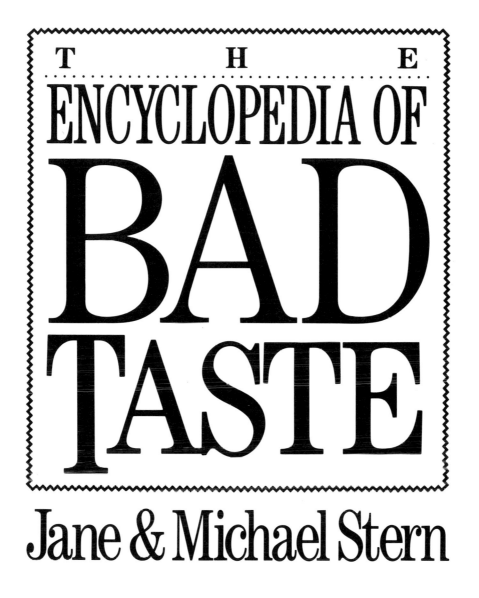

THE
ENCYCLOPEDIA OF
BAD
TASTE

Jane & Michael Stern

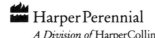 Harper Perennial

A Division of HarperCollins*Publishers*

A hardcover edition of this book was published in 1990 by
HarperCollins Publishers.

First HarperPerennial edition published 1991.

Designed by: Paul and Dolores Gamarello/Eyetooth Design Inc.

LIBRARY OF CONGRESS CATALOG CARD NUMBER 89-46560
ISBN 0-06-092121-8 (pbk.)

91 92 93 94 95 DT/RRD 10 9 8 7 6 5 4 3 2 1

CONTENTS

ACKNOWLEDGMENTS

During twenty years exploring America we have learned much of what we know from a diverse bunch of people we have met along the way. We are everlastingly indebted to those who let us take pictures of their collections of Lava Lites and Elvis souvenirs and allowed us to snoop through closets for vintage leisure suits. We owe special thanks to Rick Kot who, like Sheriff Buford ("Walking Tall") Pusser of Tennessee, speaks softly but wields a forceful stick (in the form of his editor's pencil) that helped whip the unruly contents of this encyclopedia into line. We also want to acknowledge the contributions of copyeditor Patrick Dillon, for whom no reference is too arcane and no fact unfamiliar. And we are especially grateful to Bill Shinker for providing this book such a good home.

To help us get the facts, we relied on the research skills of Cynthia Cotts, Richelle Frabotta, Hillary Ostlere, and Maura Sheehy. Jan Whitaker and Vicky Gold-Levi pointed the way to pictures we needed; Don Preziosi of Preziosi Postcards and Marian Thatos of Petrified Films delivered some remarkable images we could never have gotten elsewhere.

We are grateful to these people who provided information or pictures: Caroline Fee of Nabisco Brands, Inc. (Aerosol Cheese); Steven Levine of Uncle Milton Industries (Ant Farms); Janine B. Kinney of the American Armwrestling Association (Arm Wrestling); John S. Blair of Blair Cedar and Novelty Works (Cedar Souvenirs); Brig Berney at the Jacksina Company (Chippendales); Mark J. O'Brien of General Foods (Cool Whip); Mark Pahlow of Archie McPhee & Co. (Gags and Novelties); Trash American Style (Heavy Metal); Lynn Brinker of Greenwillow Antiques (Hummel Ware); Tom & Bob Figurines (Hummel Ware); John Mundy of Lava-Simplex Internationale (Lava Lites); Joanne Leijon of Gray & Co. (Maraschino Cherries); Al Blalock of Goodmark Foods, Inc. (Meat Snack Foods); Rob Braunfield and Julie Zickefoose (Mood Rings); Jeff Bauer at *Musclecars* magazine (Muscle Cars); Bruce Rosenbaum of the Rosenbaum Talent Agency (Novelty Wrestling); Dr. Steven Zeide (Panty-Hose Crafts); Sharon Bosworth of Barcalounger (Reclining Chairs); Kathi Stiefel of La-Z-Boy (Reclining Chairs); Safari Outfitters (Taxidermy); Ann Marie Murray of the Campbell Soup Co. (TV Dinners); and Phyllis K. Klein of Max Factor & Co. (White Lipstick).

Finally, we thank Putnam Photographic Laboratory for their impeccable work on the original pictures in this book; especially Dawn Singer and Dan Seward, who help make photography one of the lively arts.

INTRODUCTION

Fifty-one years ago art critic Clement Greenberg warned that the spread of bad taste was ''a virulence of kitsch,'' and gasped that it ''has gone on a triumphal tour of the world . . . so that it is now by way of becoming the first universal culture ever beheld.'' Mr. Greenberg's apparition of *vulgaris triumphus* has inflated beyond his worst nightmare. There is more bad taste than good taste—more than enough to fill an encyclopedia. Today the earth brims with billowing moussed hairdos, high-heeled bimbos jiggling in leopard skin Spandex halter tops, cookie jars designed to look like drunks leaning on lamp posts, and ''Your Family Name Here!'' coats-of-arms that give wood-paneled rumpus rooms a baronial touch. For every *GQ* cover boy resplendent in bespoke suits and hand-cobbled shoes, untold numbers of guys waddle through life in velour jogging rompers, sweat socks, and Corfam sandals. While enlightened epicures sing dulcet praise of nasturtium blossom salad, towns full of hearty souls gobble at troughs of fresh-from-the-box Hamburger Helper. As fastidious home-decorating magazines suggest watered silk over goose-down pillows, happy homebodies everywhere lie slack-jawed in their reclining, vibrating lounge chairs made of Naugahyde, wearing T-shirts with an arrow on the chest pointing down to their groins announcing ''Home of the Whopper,'' surrounded by variegated supershag carpet, with big velvet paintings of a matador above electro-log musical fireplaces.

Despite phalanxes of eager lifestyle experts who write books and articles to tell us what to wear, how to decorate, and what to eat in order to prove we are not slobs, bad taste does not go away. It clings like a barnacle, multiplying like some deranged cell, filling the corners of the planet with wall tapestries of dogs playing poker, gift-shop garden gnomes, rubber dog poops, fuzzy dice, and souvenir plates that say ''God Bless Our Mobile Home.'' The strange thing is that although bad taste is ubiquitous, no one has ever paid it much serious attention. No one has investigated the cream of the crop of the cultural underworld; hardly any research has been done into the semiology of such aesthetic bloopers as the vogue for the girl's name Tiffany or the de-evolution of the unicorn and the rainbow from images of uncommon charm to standard mall gift-shop motifs.

That was our goal when we conceived this project: to catalogue bad taste, define the standard masterworks, and inaugurate the annals of the world's favorite faux pas. The way to come to grips with bad taste, we believe, is to study the classics; and they are what we have written about: the pick of the litter, artifacts that never fail to elicit the involuntary groan of horror and fascination that is the true mark of bad taste at its juiciest. Most of the entries in this encyclopedia are things, but bad taste isn't only a matter of material gaucherie; so we explored some of the people who have built careers by offending guardians of propriety, from Jayne Mansfield and Charo to Morris Katz (the world's fastest artist, who prefers toilet paper to a brush). We even thought it appropriate to include places such as the tourist-riddled parts of southeastern Florida and the Smoky Mountains because they are lodestones of vulgarity.

Having relished our travels along America's highways and backroads for two decades, we were aficionados of bad taste well before we began writing this book. When the serious research began, we realized how much there was still to learn. Thanks to years of higher education, we could bend an ear about impressionism's triumph over the academy and the decline of bourgeois realism, but how much did we really know about the glow-in-the-dark paintings of sneering Elvises we had admired for years in truck stops across the country? How had it come to pass that we could toss out a thumbnail biography of Willem de Kooning but knew nothing about Walter and Margaret Keane, the husband-and-wife painting team of the sixties who invented the big-teary-eyes school of painting? The more we looked around at the world of bad taste, the more mysterious it seemed. We began to wonder about things we had always taken for granted. How did professional wrestling ever get so gross? Where did Spam and Cool Whip come from? Who invented the Ant Farm and AstroTurf and aerosol-powered spray-on cheese? What started Jerry Lewis doing telethons and Tom Carvel stammering out his own radio advertisements? Was there really a time when a foot-tall bouffant hairdo didn't look grotesque? What made bowling déclassé? And where does Muzak come from?

We have worked hard to make *The Encyclopedia of Bad Taste* a book of substantial information, not mere opinion. Once a subject was chosen, we tried to proceed with the rigor an anthropologist might use after unearthing some enchanting cultural artifact from a strange civilization. We always dug for facts. Because so many of the subjects are accursed, finding some of the information was a challenge. We could not go to the library and ask for the files on push-up bras or Beagle Puss glasses (the ones that make you look like Groucho Marx). But part of the delight of writing this book was the detective work: engaging in arcane scholarship that led us to discover who devised the outrageous cuts to make French poodles look like topiary ("Miss Cameo" of St. Louis and Tucson), where baton twirling got its start (in Mississippi and Chicago), and which nation makes the world's finest rubber imitation-plucked chickens (Spain).

Deciding what belonged in the book was the most fun of all, because that was a matter of actually defining bad taste. One helpful definition was provided by Hollywood art director Nicolai Remisoff, who went to Las Vegas in 1960 to work on the Frank Sinatra picture *Oceans 11*. Remisoff, a cultivated Russian emigré who was never quite at ease making lowbrow studio movies, gazed at the gaudy lights rising up out of the primeval desert silence and was heard to mutter, "Bad Taste! Bad Taste! Bad Taste!" When a curious bystander asked him how he defined *good* taste, Remisoff thought about it a long time, then answered, "Good taste is what is appropriate."

A devil's advocate will say that "what is appropriate" is entirely relative. After all, flamboyant neon lights and ersatz Arabian splendor can be considered perfectly appropriate for a town built to indulge sleazy fantasies. Still, appropriateness can be a helpful measure of good taste; more to the point, extreme inappropriateness is a sure signal of bad taste. In selecting subjects for this book, we sought things that engender shrieks, belly laughs, or exasperated anger because they are so awfully inappropriate. At its most delicious, bad taste is impudent, and like a lot of strong comedy, it provokes anxiety because it breaks taboos. It is a walk on the wild side of popular culture.

Another useful way to identify bad taste is that it tries too hard to mirror good taste and winds up like Alice through the looking glass, on the wrong side. Bob Guccione, publisher of *Penthouse*, filled his house with fine marble, bronze sconces, and gold fixtures

INTRODUCTION

as well as millions of dollars' worth of famous paintings, but instead of being congratulated for possessing more good taste than the Metropolitan Museum, he gets ridiculed for living in a bogus bordello. Liberace made himself a deity in the firmament of bad taste by turning classical piano recitals into resplendent displays of regal pomp featuring himself in blue fox capes and constellations of jewelry flying through the air like Peter Pan on invisible strings, then alighting to play razzle-dazzle Chopin, Tchaikovsky, and Beethoven.

Bad taste frequently tries to improve on nature. If cotton is good, polyester is better because it doesn't wrinkle and is a wonder of modern science! Similarly, plastic flowers are bad taste's solution to the fact that real ones require so much care, then shrivel up anyway. Fake fingernails are much more fun than ones you grow at the ends of your fingers, which can't be purple with fourteen-karat gold tips and a tiny alphabetical charm on each nail so the fingertips of both hands spell out "Party Hardy." Bad taste argues that if small dogs are cute, then Chihuahuas artificially dwarfed to teacup-size are even cuter; and if large breasts make a woman attractive to men, then a push-up, peek-a-boo, plunging-cleavage brassiere from Frederick's of Hollywood is the dress-for-success look for a woman who wants to make it big in a man's world.

Bad taste is intemperate and impatient. It wants the most out of life. Why settle for a boring clock that hangs forlornly on a wall when you can double your pleasure by building the clock into the stomach of the Venus de Milo, thereby adding beauty to function? And while we are on the subject, wouldn't that Venus de Milo look a lot prettier if she had Raquel Welch's head and two good arms instead of stumps? Why should your salt and pepper shaker look like ordinary kitchen tools when you can buy a set in the shape of John and Robert Kennedy's heads, with holes where the bullets hit them, allowing dinner guests to contemplate the tragedy of the leaders' deaths at the same time they season their Salisbury steak?

Whether created out of innocent fervor or knowingly for shock value, bad taste has mischievous appeal because it breaks rules and flouts decorum. "What is intoxicating about bad taste," Baudelaire wrote, "is the aristocratic pleasure of not pleasing." Artists have cultivated their ability to outrage people since cubism debuted at the seminal Armory Show of 1913, which the *New York Times* declared "pathological" and "hideous" and the *New York Herald* deemed contained "some of the most stupidly ugly pictures in the world." The establishment's distaste was an everlasting thrill for the art world; since then many critics have learned to measure art by its capacity to subvert and upset conventional values. By such a standard, bad taste can be a fount of inspiration because of its insolence. Since the sixties, the tonic power of bad taste has been celebrated by highbrows who see it as a refreshing rebellion against the reign of antiseptic modernism. In a notorious seminar conducted at Yale (with a field trip to Nevada) in 1968 called "Learning from Las Vegas," architects Robert Venturi, Denise Scott Brown, and Steven Izenour, unlike the more dogmatic Nicolai Remisoff, admired the neon vulgarity in the middle of the desert, celebrating "messy vitality over obvious unity" and comparing the casinos to the Acropolis: "polychrome temples [that] stand out proud and clear in the desert." Famous painters from young Andy Warhol to Mark Kostabi have given art patrons big doses of bad taste and dared them to like it and pay plenty to own it.

INTRODUCTION

Lest there be any doubt, this book is about bad taste, American-style. Many of its subjects have roots in other lands (European-bred poodles, Spanish-born Charo, and Danish rubber Troll Dolls come to mind), but it seems fair to say that it is in America where they have blossomed; and it is from America that the greatest tides of bad taste have inundated the world. Consider, for example, designer jeans, heavy metal music, Elvisiana, television game shows, and Spam. Although the American things in this book *are* in many ways the universal pop culture Clement Greenberg feared, it would be chauvinistic to claim that they define the earthly limits of vulgarity, or that our standards of what is uncouth are universal. We Americans ought to tip our hat to other peoples of the world for such heroic embarrassments as the gauche Papal souvenirs of Italy, the propaganda kitsch of Maoist China, the scandal-breathing tabloids of Fleet Street, Brazilian cross-dresser carnivals, misogynistic Mexican postcards, clumsy Russian appliances, asinine Indian musical films, female Japanese James Dean impersonators, and the ungainly mod fashions and bulky twenty-year-old hairdos that still prevail in much of Eastern Europe. An *Encyclopedia of Bad Taste—Worldwide Edition* would be many times longer than this American view of the subject.

Old-fashioned snobs like to make taste a class issue. Clement Greenberg explained that bad taste was born as a result of the industrial revolution, when peasants and petty bourgeois city dwellers learned to read and began to crave "high" culture (which was more infatuating than their old, familiar folk culture) for themselves. Because they didn't have in-depth education and lacked the cultivated sensibilities of the upper classes, formal culture was beyond their grasp. Therefore, ersatz culture, or kitsch, was devised to fill their needs: pictures of naked cupids and busty milkmaids, religious martyrs in excruciating agony, sentimental children, and teary-eyed cows. Greenberg described kitsch as "vicarious experience and faked sensations . . . the epitome of all that is spurious." The emotionalism of kitsch was repudiated by the Impressionists and by virtually all modern art that followed. Early in this century, when the Modernist movement as espoused by the Bauhaus proclaimed form and function one, good taste became a beau ideal that symbolized the triumph of exalted "reason" over kitsch and frivolity in all questions of design and even of behavior. To this day, many a champion of good taste asserts it with the conviction of a religious zealot and is convinced that bad taste in anyone is simply the result of a defective education.

Now that the stingy rationality of modernism itself looks dated, most authorities who tell people how to have good taste have gone back to the time-honored measure of equating it with old, comfortable money. And yet despite the fundamental snobbery of taste vendors from Elsie de Wolfe to Ralph Lauren, for whom good taste has always meant mirroring the upper classes, the equation between class and taste is not so tidy. The lower classes do not have title to all of bad taste's greatest hits. No rational aesthetic of good taste could possibly justify such patrician favorites as corduroy pants appliquéd with spouting little whales, pink Belgium loafers trimmed with piping the color of lime Jell-O, dopey little Bermuda bags and men's slacks made from fifty different swatches of madras plaid.

Bauhaus truths notwithstanding, nothing is naturally in good taste or bad taste. "Beauty is not a quality inherent in things: it only exists in the mind of the beholder," proclaimed David Hume in *Of the Standard of Taste* more than two centuries ago. Things and people and even places become signs of good taste because they embody a set of values considered appropriate in their time. Bad taste is the opposite. Think of it as a warehouse for fashions whose time has vanished, decor gone sour, celebrities who have overstayed their welcome, novelties that make you cringe, pathetic hobbies, ecologically disastrous autos, and pop music that has become more embarrassing than outrageous. But consider the most fascinating aspect of bad taste: When things hang around this collective cultural Warehouse of the Damned long enough, they begin to shimmy with a kind of newfound energy and fascination. Their unvarnished awfulness starts looking fresh and fun and alluringly naughty. They grow beyond mere tastelessness and enter the pantheon of classic bad taste. People start to miss them, crave them, and remember them fondly as signs of devil-may-care exuberance. It has happened to Cadillac tailfins, Elvis Presley, hand-painted neckties, and Lava lamps; given time, it might just happen to everything in this encyclopedia.

And isn't that just grand! We hate to think how drab things would be without bad taste. It is a powerful seasoning; sometimes it is so spicy it makes you gag. But consider the alternative: a world without Roller Derby cross-body dunks, Las Vegas lounge acts, blubbering globules of Tammy Faye Bakker's mascara, and the grandeur of Dolly Parton's breasts. Life would be just too damn polite.

ACCORDION MUSIC

Most things that produce sounds by squeezing out blasts of air are gauche, such as giving a raspberry (also known as a Bronx cheer) or performing the "Colonel Bogey March" by flapping your arm and using a hand wedged in your armpit to control the tone of the flatulated melody. While the accordion is not quite so rude, it is closer in status to a kazoo than to a Stradivari violin. Its gushing major chords make dance floors creak and groan under the boots of sausage-fed revelers as they hurdle round to the "Beer Barrel Polka." Surging bellows wheeze "Oh Promise Me" when a bride puts cake in a groom's mouth, and everybody is compelled to cry. It is the instrument of choice for the pathetic street-corner organ grinder who plays "Mother at Thy Feet Is Kneeling" as his trained monkey passes a tin cup, and of Lawrence Welk pumping out "Lady of Spain" while gliding among champagne bubbles on his television show.

Accordions arouse emotion. It is almost impossible to stay cool while listening to the sounds they make, Marisa Fox advised in a 1988 article called "Polkamentary" in *Details* magazine, calling the music "more like a sweat bath than a symphony." The chronic melodies include such extravaganzas as "Lara's Theme" (from *Dr. Zhivago*) and "Sunrise, Sunset" (from *Fiddler on the Roof*) for nuptials and golden anniversaries, and the rollicking two-steps "Clap and Stomp," "Hinky Dinky Parley Voo," and the "Pope John Paul II Polka" for dance-hall galops.

A good accordion is a finely crafted instrument that produces its characteristic whinny when air is forced through metal reeds, the tones of which are adjusted by buttons on a fingerboard and piano keys. The first ones were developed in the 1820s; the best of them are still manufactured by old-world craftsmen in the small Italian town of Castelfidardo. Despite its pedigree, the accordion has never gotten much respect in the world of highbrow music. Tchaikovsky included four accordions in the score of his Suite No. 2, and American composer

Virgil Thomson tried to write for the accordion in the fifties. In a 1988 article for the *Wall Street Journal* about an alleged accordion revival, Barbara Jepson noted that "trailblazing virtuosos" such as Guy Klucevsek are creating important, large-scale works for multiple accordions; but still, Ms. Jepson conceded, "the classical repertoire remains pretty thin."

It is good-time music that earned the accordion its reputation, starting in the early twentieth century when immigrants from Central and Eastern Europe used klezmers and primitive squeeze boxes to puff out the beat of ethnic celebrations in cities and small towns across America, especially in the upper Midwest. Pietro Deiro, who later opened Pietro Deiro's Accordion Headquarters in Greenwich Village, New York, became known as "the Daddy of the Piano Accordion" when he developed the right-hand treble keyboard, which used piano keys rather than buttons. Combined with a technique known as the "bellows shake" (opening and closing the instrument lightning-fast), the keyboard gave

Sincerely, Frank Yankovic

the accordionist a far greater range than the old-fashioned button box. Bill Palmer's book *The Mastery of the Bellows Shake* suggested using the bellows shake and the triple bellows shake for such show stoppers as ''Accordion Jitters'' and an accordionized version of ''The Barber of Seville.''

In his autobiography, *Accordion Man*, Myron Floren remembered learning his craft in the thirties as a boy in Webster, South Dakota, by listening to such traveling dance-band maestros as Sam and the City Fellers, Lulu Belle and Scotty, and Mike Dosch. After World War II, during which polka music was eradicated in most of Europe, the accordion began to enjoy its halcyon days in America. Floren went on to appear each year at the annual Wurstfest in New Braunfels, Texas, where he was joined on stage by that year's freshly crowned Miss Loverwurst, both of them decked out in full Tyrolean attire. Charles Magnante played an accordion selection every week on radio's ''Lucky Strike Hit Parade''; Frankie Yankovic recorded the memorable ''How Many Burps in a Bottle of Beer?''; and the instrument's most conspicuous champion, Lawrence Welk, became television's preeminent square, hiring Myron Floren in 1950 as his musical family's lead accordionist.

Welk called his early audiences ''wonderful people; a beer-drinking, shirttail crowd; hard-working, respectable folks who enjoyed an evening out and thought that dancing was a good way to have it.'' Starting in 1951 his televised performances from the Aragon Ballroom on the pier in Santa Monica, California, introduced viewers to the joy of polka music, and to an effervescent world of wholesome high jinx for which the accordion supplied the braying melody. Thanks to Welk and Myron Floren, accordion music was enshrined as a symbol of clean, conservative fun. In his autobiography, *Wunnerful, Wunnerful!* Welk remembered the Aragon shows as ''like a Strasburg [North Dakota, where he was born] wedding dance magnified a hundred times, a thousand times. I often strolled through the crowd with my accordion, chatting with the folks.'' The dances were so thundering, he wrote, ''I had the feeling that the whole ballroom, pier included, might just break off and float out to sea, particularly during a strenuous polka number.''

Sales of accordions peaked in the late fifties at three hundred thousand per year; but as popular culture irreconcilably split into hip and square worlds in the next decade, the accordion became an emblem of lowbrow Americana as

Smart Man: "Beautiful!"
Boy: "Who?"
Smart Man: "The Titano Accordion . . . . and the girl"

Ven I tink ouf Gretchen far away
Und songs of luff I've tried,
I feel youst like ein Sausage hot,
All bursted out inside.

evocative as a beer belly in an undershirt or an oversize Chevrolet with an "America—Love It or Leave It" bumper sticker. If you liked the impudent twang of the electric guitar—as all groovy people did—it was de rigueur to laugh at the common man's accordion and its droning sentiment. Accordion music had become the anthem of the hopelessly hokey.

A weird thing happened in the eighties, recognized by a Huey Lewis hit song titled "Hip to Be Square," which noted that avant-garde trendsetters were now taking their cues from low culture. By such inverted standards, the

squares' favorite instrument was suddenly exalted. Rock musicians rummaging through America's folk repertoire for inspiration discovered that accordions had been part of Tex-Mex *conjuto* music (an uncanny blend of Mexican folk songs and Czech immigrants' polkas) since the twenties, and the force behind zydeco (Cajun rhythm and blues) for nearly as long. Accordions were lugged onto the stage by the likes of Bruce Springsteen, Elvis Costello, Paul Simon, and They Might Be Giants—in whose hands the instrument signified not mere hipness but an admirable affinity for the now-venerated common man. A group called Brave Combo from Texas created a sound they called "nuclear polka," which was successful among new-wave listeners and also at old-fashioned polka fests throughout the Southwest. A San Francisco punk band named Polkacide began performing avant-garde polkas wearing studded black-leather lederhosen; and in New York, the all-female Das Furlines appeared on stage in Viking hats and bustiers, playing electric guitars and accordions as their Lower East Side audience learned to cut a caper with the kind of gusto inspired by Myron Floren in his two-step heyday whenever he launched into "Tico Tico." *High Fidelity* magazine proclaimed 1987 the "Year of the Accordion."

For those who have always been loyal to the gusty airs of the squeeze box, its rehabilitation is no surprise. In the sixties Hansen Music Publishers, whose biggest accordion hit was the merry "Who Stole the Keeshka?" (a keeshka is a Polish sausage), also sold accordion arrangements for such contemporary toe-tappers as "The Peppermint Twist," "Unsquare Dance," and "Where Have All the Flowers Gone?" And not to be outdone by such sixties heartthrobs as Freddie of Freddie and the Dreamers and Mick Jagger of the Rolling Stones, Lawrence Welk himself recorded his own mod Champagne Music Maker version of "Winchester Cathedral" and a mind-blowing psychedelic interpretation of *Also sprach Zarathustra* titled "2001 Polka."

See also **WELK, LAWRENCE**

Savings on Accordions

WARDS BUDGET PLAN for Convenient Monthly Payments

34 KEY 48 BASS PIANO ACCORDIONS

Made in Italy

$64.95 CASH
$6 down
$7 A MONTH

- Gleaming White Pearl-Finish Celluloid Covered Frames and Keyboard.
- Usual $125.00 value—or even more!
- 3 Sets steel reeds—Sliding octave coupler for added volume and more brilliant tone
- Extra-deep 14-fold bellows

We shopped music stores in large cities and found this quality selling for $125.00 and more! The photograph shows the beauty of the pearl-finish celluloid covered frames—usually found only in costly professional models! 2% full chromatic octaves—plays all but most intricate scores! A woman can handle it—weighs only 15½ lbs. Size 15 by 6½ in. Nickel-plated bellow corner protectors prevent splitting—Nickel-plated top panel. With 2 shoulder straps, instructions, and 12-lesson certificate giving a special price on a famous course.

551 C 874—Ship. wt. 26 lbs. Cash Price................**$64.95**
Budget Plan Price: $6 Down, $7 a Month.
551 C 898—Form-fitting Black Artificial Leather Carrying Case, lined with soft cotton flannel. Ship. wt. 10 lbs. **$3.95** 71.45

Made in Germany

$49.95 CASH
$5 down
$5 A MONTH

- Plain White-Finish Celluloid covered Frames and Keyboard
- Usual $90 value or even more
- Neat Nickel-plated top panel
- Two sets of steel reeds on separate aluminum plates
- Deep 14-fold bellows, with reinforced edges and nickel-plated corners

Many stores in large cities ask $90.00 and up for this fine quality! A larger model with full rich tone—and a range of 2% full chromatic octaves. The gleaming white frames and keyboard are washable! Carrying weight only 14 lbs. 5 oz.—light enough for a woman to handle with ease. Size 15½ by 7 in.

We include two shoulder straps, instruction book and a 12-lesson certificate giving a special price on a famous course.

551 C 975—Ship. wt. 24 lbs. Cash Price................**$49.95**
Budget Plan Price: $5 Down, $5 a Month. 54.95
551 C 899—Form-fitting Black Artificial Leather Case, lined with soft cotton flannel. Ship. wt. 10 lbs.........**$3.95**

AEROSOL CHEESE

Cheese can be an awful mess: crumbly, runny, or smelly. Even when it is pasteurized and presliced and each slice is individually wrapped, it can still be a bother if you want little snacks, because the square slices are made to fit sandwich-size bread. They are too big and flat for a dainty Ritz cracker or Triscuit.

Nabisco solved the problem in 1966 by inventing EASY CHEESE Pasteurized Process Cheese Spread, also known to supermarket shoppers as Snack Mate Processed Cheese Spread. EASY CHEESE comes in a can with a white plastic nozzle on top. Turn the can upside down, give the nozzle a nudge in any direction, and out spouts cheese spread—American, Nacho-flavored, Cheddar or Sharp Cheddar, or Cheese 'n' Bacon. If sprayed from high above, the cheese slithers out of the can in a smooth Plasticine strand like a well-cooked spaghetti noodle—white, yellow, or orange, depending on its flavor. Experienced EASY CHEESE servers know how to hold the can down low against the cracker or crudité and use its serrated tip to make glistening cheesy rosettes, employing the same techniques a chef uses when squirting fancy icing on a cake with a pastry bag and star tube.

Aerosol cheese requires no refrigeration; in fact, cold will likely plug it up. The only weakness of the design is that if a half-empty can is left on the shelf for several days, it may develop a hard cheese clot in its nozzle that can be pushed out only if there's enough cheese food and nitrogen propellant remaining to bust through from below. Otherwise, EASY CHEESE is trouble-free.

The most surprising thing about this pasteurized process cheese-spread wonder of modern food-manufacturing technology is that it is made in the heart of real-cheese country in a small factory in the village of Wrightstown, Wisconsin, using water from local wells and milk from local cows. Thirty-eight people are employed in the plant, where milk and whey, cream and water, cheese and steam are combined, heated, tested for bacteria and viscosity, squirted into cans alongside the nitrogen propellant, then sealed and shipped all over America.

Approximately six million pounds of EASY CHEESE are eaten every year, the bulk of it during the holiday season, for which the Wrightstown Cheese Plant goes on double shift.

DO NOT REFRIGERATE

NABISCO

EASY CHEESE

PASTEURIZED PROCESS CHEESE SPREAD

Cheddar

ANT FARMS

Ant Farms are sandy slices of life sandwiched between unbreakable and escape-proof transparent plastic walls. At the top of each one is an ant-sized green plastic village, a barnyard, a windmill, and some shrubbery; but the ants who live in Ant Farms want nothing to do with such anthropomorphic habitation. They spend their time in the sand below, *moving mountains right before your eyes*—as promised on the box in which the farm is packaged—and generally doing all the things that ants do, except procreating. (The laws of California, from which all the ants are shipped, forbid mailing queens.) They thrive for about a year and a half, until they die a natural death—at which point the farm's landlord can send away for a new colony of *pogonomyrmex Californicus* (red harvester ants) to recolonize the farm.

Ant Farms have been made by Uncle Milton Industries since 1956. While opening a sandwich at a Fourth of July picnic in Los Angeles that year, Milton Levine found that ants had invaded it. Instead of screaming or thoughtlessly flicking them away, he reflected back on his childhood in Pittsburgh, when he had collected insects and had so much fun seeing ants play in jars. An idea was hatched: ant farming!

A small advertisement for his new product in the *Los Angeles Times* Sunday magazine ("Watch them dig tunnels and build bridges!") attracted hundreds of orders, which was great, but Mr. Levine didn't have enough ants to fill them. Desperate for ant pickers, he offered a penny apiece for good red ants (the only known species that cheerfully digs while on display), and finally signed an exclusive lifetime contract with the Gidney family to supply him. The Gidneys harvested all of Uncle

Milton Industries' ants for many years, inventing a special ant vacuum and hauling their catch to Uncle Milton every Sunday for Monday mailing to customers. (When you buy an Ant Farm, you get no ants because it would be impractical and cruel to try to keep them alive in the Ant Farm box for months on a store shelf. What you do get is a "stock certificate" that is exchanged for ants when you are ready to start them farming.) Now another family, its name shrouded in secrecy, does most of Uncle Milton's ant gathering from their desert home east of Los Angeles.

Steve Levine, Uncle Milton's son, revealed that they employ the old-fashioned

Uncle Milton Levine

picking technique of blowing into ant holes with a straw, then scooping up all the ants that run out and putting them in jars.

Like other small farmers, ants haven't always had it easy. Uncle Milton's brother-in-law and early partner E. Joseph Cossman, author of *How I Made $1,000,000 in Mail Order,* revealed that some of the early farms were held together with glue that polluted the sand and caused all the ants to die within hours of their settling. When an attempt was made to urbanize the farm dwellers in a new style of Ant Farm called "Executive Antropolis" (with Grecian pillars instead of barns and a gold-plated frame instead of green plastic), the $150 toy flopped. Similarly, resettling the ants in a colony built to resemble the New York skyline, where they could crawl in and out the windows of the Empire State Building, proved to be no competition for the charms of rustic farm life. The latest model, "Gigantic Ant Farm," although injection-molded, stays true to the original design and format.

Uncle Milton, who assumed the avuncular name shortly after he got into the ant business, says that ant farming has been successful because they make such good pets. "Ants are very easy to keep," he pointed out. "One big cornflake or a big fly can keep a small colony going for a week." However, there are hazards to ant farming. If a bratty sibling picks up an Ant Farm and shakes it hard, it is likely that its inhabitants will die of shock.

Ant Farm advertising boasts that watching one is like watching TV, but it's better than that. An Ant Farm isn't just something you watch. You possess it. It and all its residents are yours. To those scurrying little creatures, you are more than a landlord. You are a god; or at least you are the lord of their manor. The name of the product—a registered trademark of Uncle Milton Industries—is loaded with ambiguity in this respect. Does owning an Ant Farm make you a farmer? And are ants your crop? Or are you merely a property owner, living a life of leisure, amusing yourself by watching the ants do all the hard work of farming?

Modern Ant Farms are supplied with white tunneling sand, the stock certificate for live ants, an A.W.S. (Ant Watchers Society) membership card, and *Questions and Answers about Ants,* a field guide to the ants' behavior. Late-model farms are connectible, meaning two or more can be strung together, allowing members of different colonies to travel and communicate via clear flexible "Antway" travel tubes. Despite such innovations, the Ant Farm box remains sheer old-fashioned novelty nostalgia, depicting one frolicking, oval-headed ant in a top hat and another with a pitchfork and Stetson. On the side of the box is the Uncle Milton Industries logo—a caricature of Uncle Milton Levine with an egg-shaped head, mandiblelike moustache, and a shock of hair that bears an unmistakable resemblance to a little black antenna.

ARM WRESTLING

Sports events that take place in bars include wet T-shirt contests, women's mud-wrestling bouts, chug-a-lugs, belch-offs, and arm wrestling. What makes them different from normal sports is their spirit of bawdy democracy: Anyone can join in; and the drunker you are (as participant or spectator), the more fun you will have. Arm wrestling has been a favorite way for men to match their strength since big muscles got popular at the turn of the century, but until fairly recently, it was sheer anarchy—guys going up against one another anytime they wanted, willy-nilly, with no respect for rules, sportsmanship, and the moral implications of the game. Schnockered braggarts continue to match muscles for beers in bars across the country; but now there is a higher road. The American Armwrestling Association sponsors matches in the swankiest casinos of Las Vegas, with teams of chiropractic physicians in attendance. While still not yet as refined as dressage, or even bowling or semiprofessional tobacco spitting, arm wrestling is struggling to earn respect.

Like chess, it demands such absolute concentration that it sucks contestants dry. Whereas chess players use brains and arm wrestlers muscles, in neither sport do brains or muscles alone make winners. The conquerors are those who have mastered techniques of psychological harassment and use them to destroy their opponents, which in arm wrestling is accomplished by forcing the other guy's hand down on a table before he forces yours.

To gain the edge, arm wrestlers make themselves as repulsive as possible. They shave their heads or grow feral beards and wear rings in their noses. Many assume fearsome names such as the Hackensack Maniac or Bonecrusher. They bark and drool and speak in tongues as they approach the table where the match occurs. Heavyweight champ Bruce "the Animal" Way is said to gather strength by drinking motor oil straight from the can and eating fistfuls of live crickets. ("Gentleman" Les Clayden of the United Kingdom, who is the only man to have ever arm wrestled twenty-four hours nonstop, inverts these tactics by competing in a British bowler hat, three-piece suit, and Gucci shoes.)

The strategy is to intimidate your opponent. When 290-pound superheavyweight Keith D. Jones was hired by Sylvester Stallone as technical advisor for the arm-wrestling movie *Over the Top,* Jones taught Stallone how to puff out his cheeks and make his eyes bulge as though having a seizure. Reviewers did not appreciate this bit of business (*Films and Filming* likened Stallone's performance to a sledgehammer), but it was absolutely authentic. Arm wrestlers know that a sledgehammer style is what wins, even if it does happen to be bad acting.

Most competitors are manual laborers with huge arms ("the kind of men and women who use Boraxo to get their hands clean after work," according to *Time* magazine), but good technique can whip superior strength. Aside from the psychological strategies already mentioned, good technique means knowing how to imperceptibly curl an opponent's wrist after ''lock-up'' (the initial coupling of hands, with first thumb knuckle visible), thus weakening it for a surprise slam. Heavyweight Moe Motel explained that his tactic after lock-up was to stand stone-still at the table, offering only enough resistance to stay motionless, all the while pumping blood into his arm, readying it for the kill while his opponent grunted and strained and exhausted his strength.

There are two ways to arm wrestle: sitting or standing. American Armwrestling Association rules specify that when standing, an arm wrestler must keep one foot on the floor at all times (the other may be wrapped around a table leg); and it is a foul to use any part of one's body other than the forearm to try to pin the opponent. During a seated match, kicking under the table is forbidden, and athletes are required to keep a minimum of one buttock in contact with the seat at all times. Competitions take place in weight categories that range from ''zero to 135 pounds'' to ''242 pounds and over'' for men and ''zero to 120 pounds'' to ''140 and over'' for women.

Serious arm wrestlers believe the sport has only just begun to grow. When Jay ''the Hulk'' Lyttle, 255-pound heavyweight champ (whose wife, Debbie, was once chosen Female Arm Wrestler of the Year), was interviewed in the Autumn 1988 issue of *Arm Bender* magazine, he said he envisioned arm wrestling as part of the international Olympic games. Bob O'Leary, known as ''the father of arm wrestling'' since he began promoting it in the sixties, recently rewrote the constitution of the American Armwrestling Association in an effort to keep up with the times and elevate the image of the sport. The new bylaws begin with a preamble pledging ''to establish Justice, ensure Tranquillity, and promote Prosperity,'' and include the assurance that ''stickum and resin are permitted.''

ARTIFICIAL GRASS

Whenever Elvis Presley returned home to Memphis after making a movie in Hollywood in the sixties, he traveled by private bus. As he neared Tennessee, he liked to call his favorite hometown radio station and announce that he was coming back to Graceland. In his honor the station repeatedly played one of Elvis's favorite songs: Tom Jones's version of "The Green, Green Grass of Home." Elvis loved green, green grass. He loved it so much that he ripped out all the natural lawn from around his pool because it was not green enough; he replaced it with the greenest nylon grass money could buy. Elvis, who liked to own anything that was futuristic and convenient, was one of the first people to appreciate the advantages of artificial grass.

Manmade grass beats nature's by a country mile. It never surprises you with worms or ants or moles or weeds, and it doesn't smell. It stays bright green—and all that's needed to keep it that way is a vacuum cleaner. It is especially well suited for areas around swimming pools, where chlorine kills all growing things, as well as any place the sun doesn't shine and, of course, heavily trod athletic fields, where frail natural grass with its needs for water and manure means nothing but headaches for grounds keepers. Like a well-made toupee, it is fire retardant (melting point: 500 degrees), and it never needs cutting.

The concept of artificial grass was originally proposed in the early sixties by social planners at the Ford Foundation as a way to remedy the fact that city kids didn't get to play on grass as much as country ones. The first nylon lawn, made by the Monsanto company, was installed in 1964 in an indoor field house at the Moses Brown School in Providence, Rhode Island (where the original, twenty-six-year-old rug is still in play).

The following year Houston built the Astrodome, an air-conditioned stadium made impervious to weather by a clear roof, with natural grass on its playing field. It seemed like a good space-age idea, but baseball players hated it because the glare of the sun on its roof made fly balls impossible to see. To accommodate fielders, the roof was painted. The paint, however, blocked the sun, so the grass began to die. When it withered and turned brown, it was painted green. But green paint could not disguise dead grass, so for the 1966 season the Astrodome's natural grass was removed and replaced by Monsanto's artificial turf. Sports writers named it AstroTurf.

Again, athletes complained. This time they griped that balls skidded instead of bounced (God forbid the ball should hit a seam and go haywire), making the fielding of grounders "like trying to catch rocks as they skip across a lake," according to Dodgers pitcher Don Sutton. Because artificial turf trapped heat in the asphalt below it, field surface temperatures were measured as high as 160 degrees. Players sweated and swooned; plastic cleats on their shoes melted. They testified before a congressional committee on product safety, showing blistered palms, burns, abrasions, and "turf toe" (bruised, purple toenails) which they claimed resulted from sliding and scraping against the plastic lawn's surface. "When a runner plants his cleats," observed Houston Oiler coach Bobby Brown, "he's literally impaled." Such charges were countered by AstroTurf (now Monsanto's trademarked name), which attributed them to "the scapegoat mentality of the football media."

Grounds keepers weren't so happy, either. Having originally welcomed the convenience of eternal grass, they found themselves spending hours removing stuck-on globs of chewing gum, patching holes burned by cigarette butts, and scrubbing with acetone to remove stubborn mustard stains from hot-dog wrappers thrown onto the polyamide playing field by fans.

Nonetheless, by the middle of 1967 sixteen different companies were making their own versions of artificial turf, including American Biltrite's Poly-Turf (which rippled in the heat and split at the seams) and 3M's Tartan Turf (which turned ghastly black in the sun). *Time* called the new surface "Mod Sod" in an article that predicted it would change not only baseball and football but track and field, horse racing, and lawn tennis.

Westchester (New York) County's public golf courses, which used to suffer from bald, baked, brown, and muddy tee areas, were now perpetually green and smooth thanks to a special AstroTurf designed to be pierced by wooden tees. *Business Week* reported that AstroTurf was being used in Hawaii to cover cemetery plots whose Chinese owners were forbidden by religious law from tending grass. By 1971 Monsanto, which had become the country's largest producer of doormats, was confidently predicting an AstroTurfed America covered coast to coast with green, green artificial highway median strips, gas-station tarmacs, shopping-center parking lots, motel breezeways, and entire lawns for private homes. ''Dust will be history,'' rued *Sports Illustrated*. ''We will yearn for the grand imperfect days when a man didn't have to wipe his feet before he ran out onto the field.''

Neither Monsanto's optimism nor *Sports Illustrated*'s pessimism was vindicated. Artificial grass did not cover the U.S.A. As a petroleum product, it was hit hard by soaring oil prices in the seventies. And because it was synthetic, it suffered the curse of non-naturalness that increasingly stigmatized technologically miraculous products,

such as Tang (artificial orange juice) and polyester. Sports fans with a classicist attitude came to think of artificial grass with the same contempt with which they viewed aluminum baseball bats and colorful elastic-waisted uniforms that look like Snoopy pajamas: a material symptom of spiritual rot. Although lots of stadiums have since AstroTurfed, a majority still rely on old-fashioned, aromatic, inconvenient grass. And except as doormats and as novelty indoor-outdoor carpeting around the pools of wealthy connoisseurs of machine-made convenience, AstroTurf has been installed in very few private homes.

Many improvements have been made in the original griddle-hot, linoleum-hard surface; and today's newest AstroTurf-8 is thick and soft, available with a drain-through surface that can process twenty inches of rain per hour. An entire AstroTurf football field can now be retracted and stored by two men, thus allowing one stadium to keep several different playing fields rolled up and ready to unfurl (one with a baseball diamond on it, another with football yardage lines, a third for tennis, etc.). Created out of nylon polymer ribbon dyed green and crimped (to resist flattening), then knitted to polyester tire yarn, then mounted atop a shock-absorbing foam of polyvinyl chloride and nitrile rubber, modern AstroTurf is manufactured in Dalton, Georgia—the ''Carpet Capital of the World.''

ARTISTRY IN DENIM

Tony Alamo was once the king of jeans wear, that dazzling class of leisure clothing that creates finery out of denim. His signature invention was the rhinestone-studded and airbrushed blue jean jacket. The style first caught on with country-western singers and the road crews that accompany them on tour; it was then adopted by glitterati in all areas of show business, and has since trickled down to long-fingernailed teenage girls with credit cards. Alamo's most majestic creations are so completely covered with trinkets, charms, and shiny things, as well as dramatic paintings of wild animals or city skylines, that you barely see any denim at all.

Decked-out blue jean jackets first became popular in the sixties, when outlaw bikers started wearing sleeveless vests ornamented with buttons, insignias, studs, and patches. Hippie fashion pioneers borrowed the idea, which fit the era's penchant for wearing slogan buttons, beads, and exotic jewelry. Soon denim shifted from the fringes of fashion toward respectability; and by the late seventies, when designer jeans rocked the fashion world, it had become the embodiment of chic.

Designer jeans were lean, spare, and streamlined—the sleeker the better. Tony Alamo, who was running a clothing store in Nashville at the time, went the other direction and defined a rococo style of ultradressy denim. He took embellishment to its limit, creating blue jean jackets that sparkled with images of money, fame, sensuality, and sass. He sold the one-of-a-kind, handmade creations from his Music City shop, where they were bought by country-western singers such as Conway Twitty, Hank Williams, Jr., and Little Jimmy Dickens.

Alamo was discovered by the King (Elvis) and Soul Brother Number One (James Brown) in the mid-seventies, when both performers were hitting the pinnacle of their onstage exorbitance. For his new clients Alamo didn't limit himself to denim jackets; for Brown he designed what was known as ''the gorilla'' by the backstage stevedores who had to haul it from theater loading dock to dressing room: a caped ensemble bedizened with forty pounds of rhinestones, chrome studs, and shimmering beadwork. He supplied Elvis with his heaviest high-collar Las Vegas costumes, the biggest of them held together by elephantine belt buckles resembling those worn by pro wrestling's Intercontinental champions.

Browse through the Alamo catalogue, titled *Artistry in Glitz,* and you find merchandise such as the ''Beverly Hills'' blue jean jacket (''one size fits most''), the back of which features an airbrushed Rolls-Royce with a rhinestone grille and a license plate that spells MONEY; the ''United States of America'' jacket, with a multicolored map of the U.S.A. on its back (Hawaii on the right sleeve, Alaska on the left), a fife and drummer, ''In God We Trust'' in rhinestones, and ''The Spirit's Still Alive'' in gold across the bottom; and the ''Atlantic City'' jacket, with a drawing of Trump's Castle Hotel and Casino exploding in a blaze of glory off the planet Earth (the catalogue pictures it with this caption: ''Asked for and ordered by the brilliant and famous actress singer Ann Jillian [who] gave it as a present to her very dear and successful friends, Don and Ivana Trump''). Other popular motifs include skylines of famous cities (San Francisco with the Golden Gate Bridge in rhinestones; Las Vegas with bright lights and show girls; Los Angeles with a freeway); a ''Rich and Famous'' collection with scenes of Saint-Tropez yachts or Palm Springs golf courses; and the ''Moods and Feelings'' series, with wild animals for women (foxes, lynxes, tigers) and men (wolves, leopards, panthers). The price for such a masterwork can be well over a thousand dollars.

Included in the *Artistry in Glitz* catalogue is a list of more than three hundred of the famous people Alamo says he has serviced. They include such superstars as Mr. T, Sylvester Stallone, Brooke Shields, Mötley Crüe, Alfred Bongo (king of Gabon, Africa), Chuck Woolery of ''The Love Connection,'' the Los Angeles Lakers, and world champion lady wrestler Debbie Combs. Perhaps the strangest listing in the roster of celebrity clientele is former President Ronald Reagan, who wore a bicentennial suit (not denim) made by Tony Alamo in 1987.

It is a safe bet that most of the Alamo-connected celebrities would now like to expunge him from their lives and take back the pictures of themselves standing next to him so prominently displayed in his shop and in the catalogue. As of October 1988, when a federal warrant was issued for his arrest as a fugitive from the charge of felony child abuse, Mr. Alamo (formerly Bernie Lazar Hoffman) has vanished. It seems that the king of jeans wear got so carried away with his denim empire that he used the profits to start a born-again ministry known as the Alamo Christian Foundation, whose parishioners he employed to produce the denim jackets. Children snared into the Alamo cult suffered severe spankings with wooden paddles (hence the warrant for his arrest); adult ex-members have told tales of being made to eat food with dead flies and maggots in it, and working as slaves eighteen hours a day, six days a week sewing glamorous denim jackets. With Alamo in hiding, the future of *Artistry in Glitz* is uncertain; but the vulgar style he created will likely live on so long as there are tousle-haired mall rats shopping for the kind of class that glitters.

See also **DESIGNER JEANS**

ASHTRAYS

Before smoking became a bad thing to do, ashtrays were common conversation pieces in everybody's home. There were tasteful ones made of Baccarat crystal, displayed with monogrammed lighters and engraved silver cigarette boxes, that reminded the person snuffing out his smoke how soigné he was; and there were crass ones that suggested what a high-spirited romp it was to be a smoker. Many of the latter category—novelty ashtrays—set imposing standards of gaucherie in home decor. They included genuine stuffed baby alligators designed to hold a lighted stogie in the creature's open jaws, ceramic female rear ends emblazoned with the sentiment "Put Yer Big Butt Here," and musical Statuettes of Liberty that played "The Star Spangled Banner" whenever a cigarette was stubbed out in Lady Liberty's outsized torch.

The earliest novelty ashtrays were manufactured in the 1930s, when smoking was still a fairly manly thing to do. Designed for wood-paneled den or office, decorative ashtrays often came as part of a "smoker's set" with a cigarette box and matchbook holder. Artistic nudes were a popular motif, as were brawny animals such as grizzly bears and barracudas. The Joseph Hagn Company catalogue of 1933 offered ashtrays for card tables (with suits of playing cards engraved on their sides), ashtrays held in the hands of statuary Egyptian slaves and on the upreached trunks of elephants, ashtrays presided over by Scottie dogs, penguins, Humpty Dumpty, and lounging odalisques made of ivory-covered metal. Horseshoes were a popular motif (for good luck), as were comical jackasses, noble palominos with full tack regalia, and bird dogs at point.

In the forties, as tobacco companies launched campaigns to start women smoking, ashtrays became more cheerful. Once cigarettes started getting touted as not only sophisticated but healthful, too (a good way to relax and settle the nerves), ashtrays joined the parade of happy household items that added curiosity value to any room's decor, such as wall plaques of Nubians and Nubianettes and lamps in the shapes of matadors. The 1945 Sears catalogue listed ashtrays in the category "Smart Novelties for Wall or Shelf," along with salt and pepper shakers and a weather-forecasting plaque with a picture of a baby whose diaper turned pink if it was about to rain. Among the Sears specialties that year were "baroque design Syroco wood [pressed and molded wood fiber] trays in walnut or white," and "Baby's First Shoe" ashtrays, for which customers mailed in their toddler's booties, which Sears bronzed ("so that every tiny scuff, every little wrinkle is retained"), then mounted on a two-tone ceramic base next to a removable ashtray—"a thrilling gift for grandparents."

As many Americans discovered the joy of vacationing by car in the 1950s, they also discovered the gratification of bringing home souvenirs, ashtrays in particular. Many a butt was snuffed into ceramic palm trees from California, flamingos from Florida, canoes from the Wisconsin Dells, and hollowed-out Great Stone Faces from New Hampshire mountains. Ashtrays make especially good souvenirs because burning tobacco is supposed to stimulate your imagination. So as you turn to your tray to deposit an ash, your nicotine-saturated brain responds to the tray's motif (the Empire State Building, the Golden Gate Bridge, a bunch of seashells from Myrtle Beach) and you are reminded of the nice place you have visited, and enjoy a pleasant between-puffs reverie about vacations past.

Like so many other aspects of life in the 1960s, ashtrays got extreme. *Playboy* and single-woman magazines such as *Cosmopolitan* scoffed at tiny ashtrays as maiden-auntish, recommending tub-sized butt holders as symbolic of open hospitality. No swinging dude or liberated chick could be bothered with dainty china discs that had to be emptied every five minutes. Young smokers on the make outfitted their pads with trays big enough for a whole night's worth of smoking. Sears featured such elephantine items as the "Pot Bellied Smoker," an eleven-pound ashtray made to look like a

SIP N' SMOKE

stove; the "Bucket Smoker" in the shape of a butter churn; and a hulking "Mediterranean Look" tray with amber glass sunk into black wrought iron, complemented by a decorative beer stein, crossed Toledo fencing foils for mounting on the wall, and Spanish galleon bookends "roughly hewn for an added look of authenticity."

Modern ashtrays fall into two categories. Functional ones tend to be modest and plain, so as to not call attention to the fact that someone is smoking. The extreme example of these is Ronco's battery-operated model, which inhales all stray smoke from cigars and cigarettes that rest in it. Then there are ashtrays that are strictly souvenirs, made only to be admired. After all, it would be a bit vulgar to rest a Tiparillo in the toilet-bowl-shaped souvenir ashtray with the Pope's portrait on the side of the commode that you bought at the Basilica of St. Anthony. And who would dare crush an old Marlboro into the bas-relief faces of John and Bobby Kennedy, pictured inside the memorial ashtrays sold in Dallas souvenir stores?

BAKKER, TAMMY FAYE

Her mascara cakes and globs around her eyelids; and where her eyebrows used to be, two great, startled-looking arcs of eyebrow pencil quiver. Her lashes flutter and stick to her cheeks. Her frosted pink lips, delineated with Emmett Kelly precision by lip liner, turn down and start to tremble. When she blubbers, the pancake makeup erodes, and tears roll down through its crevices. The face of Tammy Faye Bakker is one of the modern world's paramount emblems of mawkishness.

She has so much to be mawkish about. Her husband, the Reverend Jim Bakker, was convicted of fraud and conspiracy for stealing millions of dollars from his own Praise the Lord (PTL) television ministry, including bilking old lady parishioners out of their life savings. The charges were brought in 1988, a year after he was relieved of his duties as president of the PTL and pastor of the Heritage Village Church when former church secretary (now breast-augmented *Playboy* model) Jessica Hahn accused him of slipping her a Mickey, then raping her, then paying her to keep quiet with church money. He admitted that they had had sex; and when Ms. Hahn was asked why he had strayed, she explained to the national press that Rev. Jim's wife, Tammy, a mere four feet ten-and-a-half inches tall, had a vagina that was so big he could feel nothing when they copulated.

Dauntless little Tammy cried long and often, and she stuck by her man, even when new charges, of homosexuality, were brought against him, and when they lost their ministry and lakefront parsonage in Tega Cay, South Carolina, and had to auction off everything, even the air-conditioned doghouse and her own French Provincial desk. When they returned home in disgrace from their Palm Springs seclusion to retrieve what few possessions remained in June 1987, Tammy knelt and kissed the ground and—according to *Newsweek*—"left lipstick smears on a dozen or so cheeks while several hundred disciples shrieked, prayed, and spoke in tongues." Since their long and painful public humiliation, the Bakkers have tried to revive their ministry. Before Jim went to jail in 1989, without a church to back them and with Tammy's perpetually smudged eye makeup ever more suggestive of a maudlin circus clown, they broadcast an hour of religious instruction to a few thousand local viewers from a semiabandoned Shoppers World mall in Orlando, Florida, alongside Nasty Ed's Pub.

I GOTTA BE ME

Tammy Bakker
with Cliff Dudley

Flash back with us for a moment to the salad days of Tammy Faye LaValley, the prettiest little 73-pound coed at the North Central Bible College in Minnesota, and young Jim Bakker, the 130-pound hall monitor, whom she described as ''the handsomest thing I had ever seen.'' They kissed on their first date and married soon after in 1961, spending their wedding night in a pink apartment that Tammy described as ''frosting on a cake.'' After Tammy overcame a bed-wetting problem, the young messengers of God set out to preach and teach, driving their trailer to revival services throughout the Southeast. During this time, Jim bought Tammy a tiny Chihuahua named Chi Chi, and Tammy shaved her eyebrows,

JIM & TAMMY BAKKER

HOW

We lost weight & kept it off!

Foreword by Pat & Shirley Boone

studied new ways to curl and elongate eyelashes, and discovered wigs. ''I love wigs,'' she said.

They began their television career in the mid-sixties with ''The Jim and Tammy Show'' on Pat Robertson's Christian Broadcasting Network, in which they co-starred with a puppet alligator, two floppy dogs, and a puffy-cheeked doll named Susie that they made by burning the ears off a rubber Porky Pig toy and gluing a blond wig on its head. When Jim had a nervous breakdown and was confined to bed, where he drank nothing but heavy cream, for a month, Tammy had to do the show—and all the puppet voices—by herself. To top it off, one evening Chi Chi ate a plate of lima beans, ran into the living room, and died. Tammy prayed to God to raise Chi Chi from the dead, but then realized that God had taken Chi Chi because Chi Chi had been a naughty dog and tinkled all over Tammy's living room. Tammy had once tried to give Chi Chi away, but couldn't; so there she was, burdened with a dog she loved yet who wet on her drapes. ''God knew what was best for me,'' Tammy sighed before burying Chi Chi in a shoebox.

Jim recovered from his breakdown, and in November 1966 he began eight years of hosting the ''700 Club.'' The Bakkers won the hearts of viewers but made many enemies at CBN, where the staff, according to Tammy, was wickedly jealous of their success. Within twenty-four hours of their resignation in 1974 to begin their own ministry, all videotapes of ''The Jim and Tammy Show'' were erased and their giant-size Susie Moppet head was axed and torn to pieces. ''This broke our hearts,'' Tammy cried. ''We did not know there was that much dislike in their hearts for us.''

The Bakkers went to California, where Tammy found a flea market called the Chino Dump to buy bargain ''eyelashes and wigs and all the things that girls need.'' But California ministers denounced their emotionality and their telethons' money lust, and soon they moved the PTL to Charlotte, North Carolina, where they began to create an empire. ''Only the Lord could have foreseen the ensuing growth,'' they wrote in their inspirational book, *Jim and Tammy Bakker Present the Ministries of Heritage Village Church* (recently reduced in price from $100 to $5.95). Their PTL ministry was issued the first-ever private satellite license for broadcasting around the world; and at their peak in 1986 they had the power to reach a billion people. They built Heritage, USA in Fort Mill, South Carolina—a four-hundred-acre theme park, church, hotel, and time-sharing condominium complex (including the relocated, reconstructed, and refurbished boyhood home of evangelist Billy Graham). Tammy Faye, who now had her own signature line of Christian cosmetics, cut a dozen record albums, including *In the Upper Room,* for which Religion in Media gave her a 1985 Angel Award as Best Female Vocalist.

In addition to her duties on "The Jim and Tammy TV Ministry Hour," for which she sang and joined Jim in counseling people with bad marriages, Tammy hosted her own program on the PIL Inspiration Network, "Tammy's House Party." "When I heard that I was going to be able to do a ladies' show, my heart was singing inside," Tammy wrote in her autobiography, *I Gotta Be Me.* "I want to show women how to decorate the home by using contact paper, spray paint, and getting the good deals in the bargain rooms at stores where Jim and I buy most of our furniture . . . how to buy an inexpensive wig for when you can't get to the beauty parlor . . . how to make her face look beautiful even though she feels insecure." It was a merry show with cooking demonstrations, celebrity interviews, studio-audience participation games, and diet advice taken from *How We Lost Weight and Kept It Off,* which Tammy and Jim wrote after she ballooned up from her honeymoon weight to one hundred thirty, then managed to lose it all. "I could actually knead my stomach like dough," Tammy confessed.

When the Bakkers' world came tumbling down, Jim squirmed, but it was Tammy who suffered more. Everybody made fun of her. The month the Bakkers' belongings were auctioned, *People* magazine observed the phenomenon of "Tammymania!," which included Tammy T-shirts reading "Cry Now, Pray Later" and Tammy jokes such as, "What does Tammy Faye Bakker have in common with a good ski slope? Answer: Two inches of face topped by three inches of powder." To accompany the article, *People* doctored up two pages of pictures of famous faces with Tammy Faye makeup: the Mona Lisa with fluttery eyelashes; David Letterman with earrings; and Mount Rushmore with lipstick. "I don't care," Tammy said bravely, "as long as I'm not offending God."

BARBIE DOLL

Barbie is an airhead. She is the material girl par excellence, the original mall rat. Introduced by Mattel at the Toy Fair in New York in 1959 as ''The Barbie Doll: A Shapely Teenage Fashion Model,'' the long-limbed, 11½-inch-tall clotheshorse has no soul and barely a personality but has been the most successful doll in history. Like a handful of other famous women who need only a first name—Madonna, Jackie, Cher—Barbie has been at the vanguard of fashion for years; but unlike her human counterparts, she is a perpetually pubescent girl instead of a woman, and the only things on her mind are what she wears and turning Ken's vinyl head.

Named after the daughter of Mattel's owners, Elliot and Ruth Handler, and styled after a mid-fifties German doll called Lilli (whose molds may actually have been used to make Barbie prototypes), Barbie stunned the world with her bosom. At a time when most dolls were designed as *babies,* a teenage doll—especially one with a pert bust line, shapely hips, and well-turned calves —was revolutionary. Not only was she full-figured (originally marketed as a ''3-D fashion drawing''), she wore plenty of sophisticated makeup. Her eyebrows were arched; her eyes, aimed sideways in a sexy glance, were rimmed with heavy black eyeliner; and her lips and fingernails were bright red. She wore pearl hoop earrings and came packaged (on a posing stand) dressed in nothing but a striped jersey swimsuit and high-heeled shoes. The idea, according to Mrs. Handler, was to provide her own flesh-and-blood daughter Barbie and millions of preteen girls like her with a dream of what they might soon become.

Barbie was a sensation. But what was the point of her wearing gorgeous clothes and looking pretty without a guy around to admire the results? To the rescue came Mattel's Ken (named after the Handlers' son) in 1961, labeled with the exclamation ''He's a Doll!'' In *Here's Barbie— Stories About the Fabulous Barbie and Her Boyfriend Ken,* published in 1962, a fable called ''Barbie, Be My Valentine'' describes their first meeting at a school dance:

''Are you a famous princess?'' asked Ken. Barbie smiled hesitantly. ''I'm Cinderella.''

Ken looked delighted. ''It's about time we met each other. Prince Charming, at your service!''

The music was lovely and she could dance all night, thought Barbie as she whirled around the floor in Ken's arms.

As originally packaged, Ken was a half-inch taller than Barbie, with short, flocked hair that had an unfortunate tendency to rub off on the side of the box, or to disappear completely when wet, leaving him bald. He wore a bathing suit and sandals. He had no genitalia.

There is some question as to whether Ken and Barbie ever married. There were plenty of bride and groom outfits; and they did tour Europe together, without a chaperone, in a 1962 *Barbie and Ken* comic book; but strangely, Ken disappeared in 1967, only to return in 1969 with a new head, a beefier body, and a bright red taffeta ''Guruvy Formal'' Nehru outfit, looking very unattached.

Despite Ken's preposterous attempts to dress hip and, in the rare ''Now-Look Ken Doll,'' even grow his hair into a Neil Diamond pouf, he was incorrigibly dull. Barbie, too, her sexy debut in 1959 notwithstanding, was soon saddled with a squeaky-clean image that her most daring fringe vests and pantsuits of the postmod era couldn't overcome. Even the perfect presidential couple of the time, David Eisenhower and Julie Nixon, were outdone by Ken and Barbie, who had become nothing less than America's two biggest squares. Their odd, sexless relationship, as well as their physical perfection and the fact that they were made of plastic, gave Ken and Barbie powerful symbolic reverberations as a couple. By the mid-seventies, ''Ken'' and ''Barbie'' were names that had come to signify complete and hopeless vapidity.

They weren't the only members of Mattel's family of clean teens. After Ken came Christie, Midge, Skipper, Casey, and Francie; Allan, Ricky, and Todd. There were even Twiggy and Donnie and Marie Osmond and Debby Boone and Wayne Gretzky dolls on the same scale and of the same vinyl plastic species; but Barbie was always the fashion queen. The Barbie Fan Club became the second-biggest girl's organization in America, after the Girl Scouts. There were sing-along-with-Barbie records (with songs such as ''My First Date,'' by Ken Darby and Eliot Daniel, who wrote the theme from ''I Love Lucy''); books, including *Barbie's Fashion Success* and *Barbie's Hawaiian Holiday* (she learns to surf); a Barbie lamp; jigsaw puzzles; board games; trading cards; and Barbie-print bed sheets. In 1976 Mattel introduced the Barbie Fashion Plaza—a complete mall with fashion bazaar, snack patio, bridal boutique, and working elevator to get from floor to floor.

Although her acquisitive personality went unfazed, Barbie's looks changed steadily through the years. Her tarty original expression softened; her hairdo went from ponytail to bubble to flip to the Malibu fall and Quick-Curl cut; she grew a bendable waist and in 1967 had a facelift with an entirely new head. There have been thousands of ensembles, from ''Nighty Negligee'' and ''Disco Dazzle'' to a gold lamé gown actually designed by Oscar de la Renta to the ''Barbie Loves McDonald's'' playshop, including clothes for her to wear as customer (matching striped sweater

and knee socks) or clerk (blue McDonald's uniform, cap, and white shoes).

Like stamp collectors, Barbie collectors prize the rarities. Among the most treasured Barbies are the deformed Miss Barbie doll with silver hair but no lips, Barbie with her first fish, and Ken with mod hair, large-check sports coat, and wide-flared elephant bell bottoms. The rarest Barbies are factory seconds (which at one time were sold cheap to employees), many of which are mutations, thereby offering a rare glimpse of Barbie (or Ken) being not so perfect. These include Barbies with ridiculously small molded heads, Kens with botched mod coiffures that resemble transplant plugs, and Barbies with cheeks sprouting stray clumps of hair that suggest warts.

BATON TWIRLING

atch the prettiest blonde in school leading the Fourth of July parade down Main Street as the tubas and trombones blare behind her. She wears a sequined red bathing suit. Her knees rise high as her feet kick out in a pair of white elk-skin boots hung with big, billowy tassels. On her head is a shako, a tall hat covered in white fake fur known as "polar bear cloth" with a snappy black patent-leather brim in front and a big plume on top. She throws her glittering silver baton high into the bright blue sky, and the marching band behind her marks time as everyone on the street waits breathlessly for her to catch it, cartwheel forward, toss it high again, and continue leading the parade toward the village green.

Baton twirling is small-town glamour of a special kind, the stunt of beauty queens in search of a pageant-approved talent. It is by no means easy to master; but those who do achieve greatness as baton twirlers don't get the same kind of respect given athletes who excel in tennis or basketball. Despite the extraordinary coordination it requires, baton twirling is one of those exotic athletic skills, like bowling-pin juggling or musical spoons, that grow increasingly kitschy as its routines become more elaborate. Twirling one baton is mildly bizarre; twirling three fire-tipped ones blindfolded to an uptempo arrangement of Neil Diamond's "(Coming to) America" is an epiphany of sorts.

The basic twirls are the pinwheel and the figure eight; the high-stepping march that moves the twirler forward is called the strut. The twirler has her choice of a rubber-tipped standard baton; a ribbon baton, with streamers at each end; a hoop baton, through which she can jump; or a fire baton, doused with gasoline at both ends and ignited before the routine begins. Fire batons are traditionally extinguished by an ultrafast twirl at the end of the routine. Twirling prodigies graduate from batons to even more difficult apparatuses, such as the Swiss flag, a streaming banner made to be whipped around in complicated arcs, and the dramatic Samoan Fire Knife, a thirty-inch hooked steel blade designed to be spun around the twirler's neck and body.

In fact, the Samoan Fire Knife may be the true forebear of the modern baton. Baton historians believe that twirling originated on the Samoan Islands, where male dancers did ceremonial sarabandes with swords and knives. Other aficionados of the skill attribute its origins to flag-twirling maneuvers of the armies of Switzerland. In America, baton twirling started as a man's skill, performed by drum majors who juggled heavy batons while leading marching bands. In Chicago in the thirties, Major C. W. Boothe got so big as a twirler that he formed the All Star Twirling Club, for the first time including female "majorettes." Chicago became known as the home of baton twirling, and the first baton-twirling contest was held there in the summer of 1935 as part of the Chicagoland Music Festival.

While some credit Mr. Boothe with fathering modern twirling, others bow to Major Reuben Webster Millsaps, a Confederate officer who founded Millsaps College in Mississippi after the Civil War and introduced baton twirling to the students there, who were eventually also called majorettes. No matter which major was the true father of modern twirling, Mississippi and Chicago still produce disproportionate numbers of champions. And there is no doubt that baton twirling remains a distinctively American sport. "While other nations boast of their ballet masters, we can boast of our baton masters," noted Constance Atwater in *Baton Twirling: The Fundamentals of an Art and Skill.*

In 1959 forty million viewers watched senior champion twirlers Joyce Rice and Claudette Riley on Garry Moore's TV show "I've Got a Secret"; the excitement of their performance was the peak of a wave of interest in the fifties that had led to the foundation of the National Twirling Hall of Fame in 1953 (enshrining such eminent practitioners of the art as Judy Delp of Slippery Rock, Pennsylvania, and Susan Smisek of Minneapolis, Minnesota) and the formation of the Miss Majorette of America Pageant. Dance studios added baton twirling to their roster of tap and ballet classes. Elementary and high schools featured it in physical education programs. Not content with learning the basics, girls flocked to special baton-twirling summer camps and regional conferences, where they were taught the secrets of a perfect Chinese split and a showy reverse cartwheel.

In 1968 a great schism occurred. Strutting and twirling were declared two separate events, and no strutter at that year's America's Youth on Parade Pageant held in Oxford, Mississippi, was allowed to twirl. Strutters, twirlers, and flag swingers each formed their own organizations. ''Strutting really is a whole different aspect of twirling, and it's not for every twirler,'' observed *The Complete Book of Baton Twirling*. Even young twirlers broke off into their own special groupings, such as the Valley Twirlerette Pee Wees and the Little Rebels Twirling Corps, so as to better prepare themselves for lives devoted to twirling. As pictured in the 1969 edition of *Who's Who in Baton Twirling*, the neophytes, many of whom appear shorter than their batons, pose proudly alongside baton twirling's virtuosos, corps of big girls from Ohio, including the Ju-Debs and the Du-Dees.

BEER

Beer tastes fine. It goes well with pizza and hot dogs and pretzels. Beer culture—an oxymoron if there ever was one—is something else. Swilling suds is one of the immemorial ways to thumb your nose at good manners and polite society. Beer is the lifeblood of rowdy party animals tearing up motel rooms on spring break. Big-bellied construction workers gulp it down to prepare for belching contests. It is Hell's Angels' favorite swill. Guzzling it in public is what made Jimmy Carter's brother, Billy, the laughingstock of the nation (and the only President's brother to have a beer named for him). It is the raison d'être for corny Oktoberfests with headache-producing oompah bands. Call it brewski, goon sauce, or cat piss—beer is the beverage of choice among slobs around the world.

Some beer drinkers are true believers; they collect cans (in which beer has been packaged since 1935) and breweriana (signs, labels, coasters, church keys, and anything else made to advertise beer); they brew their own; they fuss like giddy oenophiles over genteel micro-breweries and the distinctions among pale ale, porter, stout, weiss, and bock and the proper temperature for serving them. Most beer aficionados aren't nearly so fastidious. They are happy so long as the suds are cold and flowing, a condition best achieved if they happen to own the beer drinker's hat—a visored cap with an armature around the crown that holds two cans of beer at the sides of the head, with plastic tubes coming out of each can into the wearer's mouth, thus allowing him hands-free sucking, two cans at a time.

A cultural historian has to wonder: Why beer? People do stupid things when they are drunk on any alcoholic beverage, but somehow beer has inspired inane rituals and embarrassing behavior beyond anything conceived by brains pickled in vodka, sour mash, or Chablis. The answer is that beer is inherently more fun to drink. It has foam you can blow off the top of the liquid or wear as a funny white mustache; it is carbonated and produces spectacular burps. Also, beer gives you the most for your money. It is probably the cheapest way to get intoxicated other than by drinking rubbing alcohol, and it is so highly calorific that drinking it is the best known way for men (and women, too) to cultivate a really huge stomach, known as a beer belly. Finally, beer is the most masculine of drinks. It has always come packaged in manly containers, from beer buckets a century ago to elephantine kegs to cans that fit solidly in a big, fat fist; and its power to make drinkers pee prodigiously encourages male bonding at urinals or in gutters.

College students have been perfecting the rituals of chugging swill for at least a century; the culmination of this perseverance is a series of instructional books by Andy Griscom, Ben Rand, and Scott Johnston that includes *Beer Drinking Games* and *Beer Games II: The Exploitative Sequel,* as well as such merchandise as "Boot Factor T-Shirts" (to "boot" is to puke) and "Boot Factor Barf Bags" (fifty for fifteen dollars). The goal of beer-drinking games is to find new ways to get bloated on beer and to enjoy its corollary fun, urinating and vomiting. *Beer Drinking Games* explains the importance of selecting a proper mung rag—a cherished old towel or pair of boxer shorts to wipe up spills. A mung rag is never thrown away; it should be used until it solidifies and grows fur. *Beer Drinking Games* also offers a glossary of verbs to describe vomiting. They include to "ralph," to "blow lunch," and to "blow one's doughnuts." "Losing your lunch can be a moving, spiritual experience," the authors advise. "All at once, your body is poised in a moment of great catharsis. There is a sudden sense of complete abandon to a force greater than yourself, and then a profound quiet." Not all regurgitation is the same, however. In addition to full-fledged vomiting, during which most of the contents of the stomach are upchucked, there is "snarfing," which happens when someone tries to chug a beer too fast and it comes out his nose, and "reverse drinking," also known as "blowing foam," which means spewing out newly drunk, still foamy brew.

Beer Drinking Games suggests many amusing party tricks, such as "Opening Bottles with Your Teeth," "Can Crushing," "Can Biting" (chewing a hole in the side of an aluminum can and drinking the beer from it), and the simple but ever popular "Pouring Beer on Your Head"; the bulk of the book, however, is devoted to more re-fined games. One called "Bullshit" is played thus:

> The Master of Ceremonies asks each player in turn what brand of animal feces he wishes to be. For instance, a player can choose horseshit, dogshit, or even squidshit. The emcee initiates the round by saying, "Someone shit in the parlor." All players respond by saying in unison, "Who shit?" The emcee blames one of the players: "Dogshit," for example. Being accused, Dogshit must reply, "Bullshit!" The emcee then asks "Who shit?" and Dogshit responds with one of the other names, such as "Catshit." Thus the game continues, with Catshit saying "Bullshit!" and Dogshit responding, "Who shit?" and Catshit blaming someone else. Anyone who breaks the rhythm must chug-a-lug a beer.

Some games are not so intellectually challenging but require physical ability, such as "Tending the Teat." For this one, players gather around a keg. One by one, each player affixes his mouth to the spigot as a referee places his fingers on the player's Adam's apple. When the spigot is turned on, the player starts drinking. The rules of the game forbid him to remove his mouth from around the spigot as the beer surges out. The referee counts the number of gulps; the winner is the player who can quaff the most before he begins to drool, snarf, toss his cookies, blow foam, or pass out.

BELL BOTTOMS

Once the mark of groovy and fashionable people, bell bottoms are now the uniform of choice of street-corner weirdos, driveling Dead Heads, and white-trash biker girls who wear their low-slung bells with halter tops that show off their tattoos. Bell bottoms are a signal that their wearer is dangerously out of synch. Burnt-out Charles Manson types tromp around public parks in frayed elephant bells; old love children and street mimes stuck in a time warp wear shrunken jeans with bottoms that flare three or four inches above the ankle, like exploded pedal pushers around a naked shin.

Bell bottoms first became popular in the sixties as hair grew longer and flared outward from the head. Big hair styles of the time—Afros and Caucasian freak-out frizzes—needed an expansive visual anchor down below, such as a wide-flared pair of pants. The two together made for a nice, symmetrical dumbbell look. Originally issued as sailor's pants for men in the navy, bell bottoms were a cheap antifashion statement bought in surplus stores along with pea coats. They announced that their wearer was not the type of conformist square who wore Ivy League stay-pressed chinos.

Sailor pants were worn mostly by bohemians and artists until Pierre Cardin rode into prominence alongside the mod revolution in the mid-sixties. The celebrated Cardin jacket, with its narrow shoulders and nipped-in waist, made an ingenious fit over low-waisted, big-belted, and flared-bottom trousers.

In bell bottoms' early years, a lot of people resisted the idea. In 1964 *Men's Wear* had championed the tight, skinny "continental" look, exulting, "Fat pants have become slim slacks"— a vast improvement over the baggy trousers of yore. As late as 1968 *Playboy* predicted a future of "long lean lines" in men's wear. Clothing manufacturers like H.I.S. marketed Swinger Slacks as "extra slim, extra trim, extra tapered," running ads that showed wrinkle-free taper-legged guys making time with pretty girls.

The revolution happened in 1966, when *Esquire* hailed bell bottoms as a vital addition to every modern guy's wardrobe. They were nonconfining—a noble quality at the time; and if they were big enough, they flapped when you walked. Bell bottoms were a way to say you were free, loose, and literally swinging—which increasing numbers of men and women felt the urge to do.

That spirit of irreverence was what made them exciting, for women as well as men of the counterculture. Bell bottoms were one of the more conspicuous signs (with miniskirts and polka dots) of the fashion revolution that championed letting it all hang out. Teenagers loved them, and nearly every one of *Seventeen* magazine's 1969 National Fashion Council Award winners suggested bell bottoms as her idea of a groovy new fashion look. Kathie Dillon, age nineteen, designed hers in a black-and-white print; Kay Vonderau, nineteen, designed bells of exotic batik; and Jeri Sielschott, eighteen, of Lima, Ohio, designed a pair of wide-leg pants covered with crazy daisies.

Sonny and Cher were the most illustrious bell-bottom pioneers, combining outrageously flared and striped, low-slung pants with funky fur vests, flowered shirts, and pointy boots. Cher fancied ruffle cuffs, with the bells flaring down to great gathered tubes of pleats and ruche or fringe or paisley print cuffs that fell to the floor like twin miniature hula skirts. Janis Joplin was also a bell-bottom style setter. She graduated from the basic hippie look of T-shirt and jeans to a haute thrift shop couture of tie-dyed chiffon blouses and feather boas worn over black crushed-velvet stretch-waisted bell bottoms, tight at the thighs and flaring out dramatically over unshod dirty feet.

Inspired by hippies, stylish people decorated their bell bottoms with ribbons at the cuffs or metal studs up and down the legs. Fringe was also a popular motif, for which the bottom hem of the jeans could be cut, then picked at until a two-inch-long edge of loose threads was created. A book called *Clothing Liberation (Out of the Closets and Into the Streets)*, written by Laura Torbet, offered suggestions for making one's bell

By the mid-seventies bell bottoms were mainstream. Demure ones were now seen on PTA ladies who favored pants suits in no-iron polyester. Bell bottoms were part of neat but natty outfits worn by moms on "The Brady Bunch" and "The Partridge Family."

Like all exorbitant fashions, they became passé almost as quickly as they got popular, and by the end of the decade, gigantic bell bottoms had become a symbol of the seventies' embarrassing cultural extremism, as seen in such painfully overwrought phenomena as *Roller Boogie* (the motion picture), blaxploitation movies (*Cleopatra Jones, Superfly*), and "hip" characters in Norman Lear television sitcoms. Despite the ignominy, they did not vanish along with mutton-chop sideburns and eight-track tape decks. Because of their popularity among people who were loath to throw things out or to keep up with voguish fashion trends, bell bottoms, like many other features of the sunset years of Aquarian culture, have refused to die.

bottoms bigger and grander: cut the seams to the knee, then sew a big triangle of contrasting material into the slit—a red bandana, a frilly organza curtain from the dime store, or patches of leather—and a groovy pair of extra-huge bell bottoms are born.

The style peaked in the early seventies as flares and baggies gave way to voluminous elephant bells, so named because they were cut extremely long to fall completely to the floor and were so capacious they covered the entire shoe, thus making the wearer's big, tubular leg resemble an elephant's foot. The popularity of platform shoes required bell bottoms to be cut in even longer lengths, so the look became one of a grotesquely elongated, ever widening leg with no shoe showing. The perfect silhouette was rather like that of the two-dimensional rubber man Gumby. Some of the widest bell bottoms known to man were worn on stage by Elvis during his final years. His tight satin jumpsuits ended in stiff cuffs the size of man-hole covers.

BIKERS

There are people who ride motorcycles, and there are bikers. Bikers are hairy, smelly, impolite rebels on fat-fendered, chopped Harley hogs with high-rise handlebars who push the envelope of bad taste to nauseating extremes.

Tattoos, nose rings, hobnail boots, and Nazi festoonery are a few of the ways they let the world know their defiance of straitlaced life. Being a one-percenter (a term coined by bikers when the American Motorcycle Association pleaded that 99 percent of all motorcyclists were solid citizens) demands an uncompromisable code of bad behavior. Bikers are proud to wear grimy denim "colors," to have beer bellies that overhang their belts, to barf on a friend's couch —in short, to stomp on all known personal and social standards of good taste.

Bikers first oozed into the public eye in 1947, when a gang of motorcyclists known as the Booze Fighters, many of them misfit army veterans, ransacked the town of Hollister,

California (which was then the garlic capital of America). The event was picked up by the national press and helped create an image of bikers as leather-clad Visigoths who lived to rape, pillage, and revel in an especially odious brand of macho awfulness. Seven years later *The Wild One,* a movie based on the Hollister incident and starring Marlon Brando as a sulky scooter jockey named Johnny, added a new type of romantic goon to the fifties' roster of hoods, juvenile delinquents, and rebels without a cause.

Produced by Stanley Kramer, *The Wild One* showed civic-minded concern for a good boy gone bad; but most of the motorcycle films that followed were content to wallow in biker atrocities. Advertisements for *The Hot Angel,* released in 1958, described motorcyclists as "the menace of the switchblade jungle where the only real crime in life is being chicken . . . teen-agers on the loose . . . leather-jacketed motorcycle maniacs defying law and order, breaking every convention and code of decency."

In the sixties bikers developed a trendy cachet as a special breed of the do-your-own-thing individualist, more symbolic than any garden-variety outlaw or teenage troublemaker. Roger Corman's movie *The Wild Angels* (starring Peter Fonda, Nancy Sinatra, and real bikers from Venice, California) and Hunter Thompson's book *Hell's Angels* helped elevate the California-based rat pack to national celebrity. The Angels, founded in San Bernardino in 1950, as well as lesser clubs lucky enough to bask in their reflected glory, suddenly found themselves exalted as culture heroes. Their freewheeling life was idealized by many in the rebellious counterculture. Bikers rose to the occasion with aplomb, performing a profound metamorphosis from lonesome leather boys to outlaw tribal freaks every bit as outrageous, and twice as dangerous, as the hippies who adored them. It was at this time that biker style came into full blossom.

They ornamented their dirt-caked duds with throngs of swastikas, Maltese crosses, and Yosemite Sam belt buckles. They took the T-shirt

HE'S A Cycle PSYCHO

When he wanted a town...
HE STOLE ONE!
When he wanted a girl...
HE GRABBED ONE!
When he wanted a cop...
HE BOUGHT ONE!

The Company that brought you "HELL'S ANGELS ON WHEELS" now brings you...

ANGELS FROM HELL

THE STARK TRUTH TELLS IT LIKE IT IS!

COLOR

Tom STERN • Arlene MARTEL
TED MARKLAND • STEPHEN OLIVER • PAUL BERTOYA • JIMMY MURPHY • JACK STARRETT • A FANFARE FILM PRODUCTION
BRUCE KESSLER • JOE SOLOMON • JEROME WISH • AN AMERICAN INTERNATIONAL RELEASE

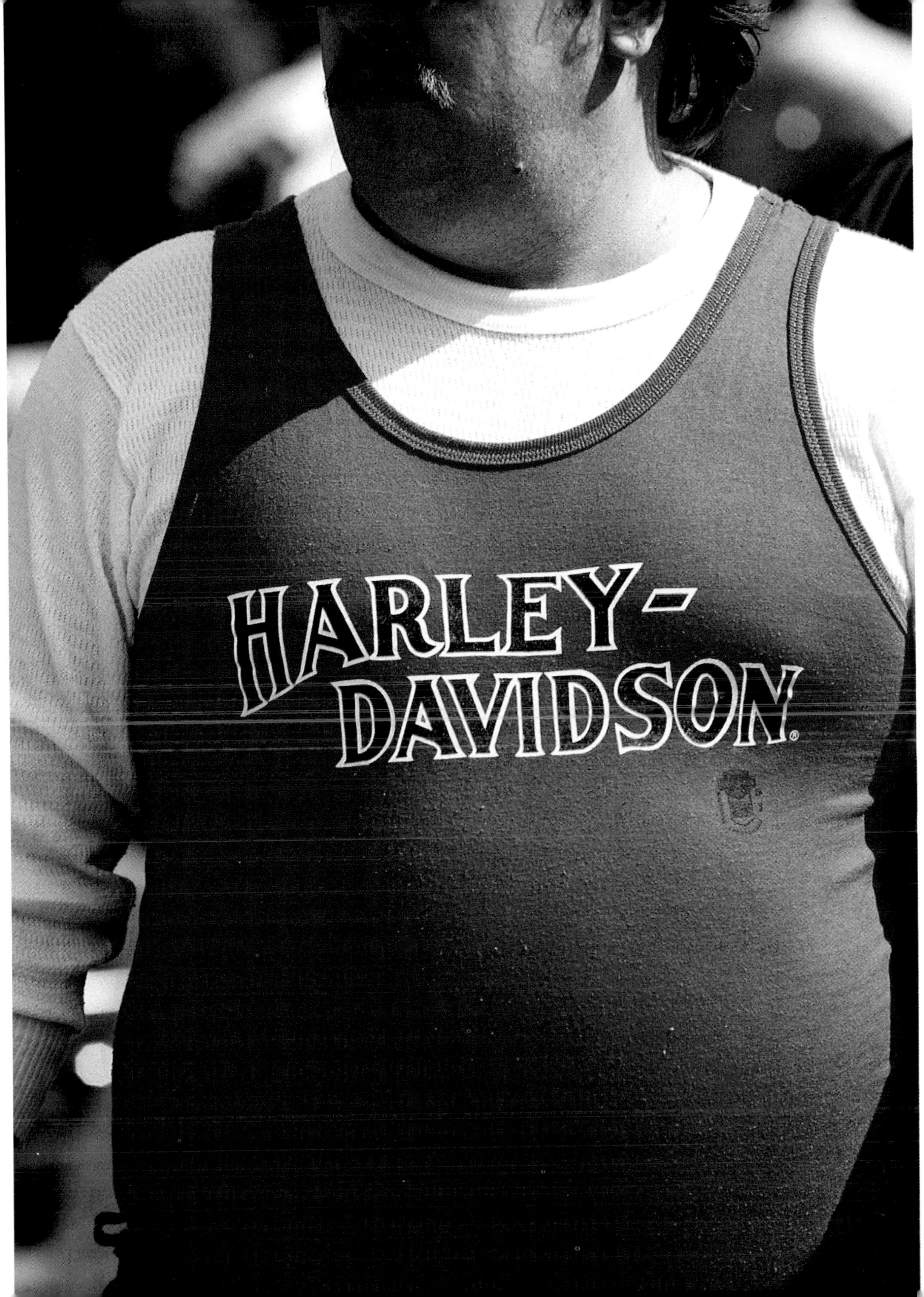
HARLEY-
DAVIDSON

fad to extremes, fancying such slogans as ''If I Wanted to Listen to an Asshole, I'd Fart'' and ''American by Birth—Rebel by Choice.'' They grew their hair long and filthy to match bird's-nest beards that hung halfway to their waists. They tattooed every stretch of available skin with Harley-Davidson eagle wings and death's heads; and when they ran out of their own skin, they had ''This Butt's for You'' tattooed on their old ladies' rumps.

Hell's Angels, Arapahos, Gypsy Jokers, Coffin Cheaters, Charter Oaks, and Diablos created extraordinary fashion shocks as they rumbled two abreast down America's highways. By the early sixties, many of the gangs had begun to forsake their legendary leather jackets in favor of sleeveless denim vests. It was a change of uniform that made them seem more savage: unwashed denim can look much filthier than leather; indeed, biker apocrypha includes an initiation rite in which the novitiate's colors are peed on, shit on, and stomped on by all members of his club. Concurrently, a few Hell's Angel's trendsetters took to wearing earrings and nose rings—further steps toward a rapacious, warlike look.

Bikers lost their status as countercultural heroes at the Rolling Stones' notorious Altamont concert in December 1969. Hired by the Stones to serve as hip security guards in exchange for beer, Hell's Angels turned the event into a Love Generation catastrophe as big a bummer as Charles Manson. Relishing their authority, they allowed their fascist impulses free reign, punching out one of the Jefferson Airplane onstage, beating up concertgoers, and even killing a man. It was very uncool, a terrible embarrassment to all the hippies who had embraced the leather boys, and a symbolic end of the sixties, or at least of the Woodstock Nation that had been wished into existence earlier in the year.

Not everyone who rides a Harley-Davidson is a biker; but all bikers ride Harley-Davidsons. The classic ''putt'' is a low-slung shovel-head Harley with a five-degree rake to its frame and extended front forks; ape-hanger handlebars with a sixteen-inch rise and hog-tail concho fringe grips; a shaved leg (treadless tire) rolling underneath a dresser fender with tombstone taillights; and a Big Bob teardrop purple PolyGly gas tank with a custom airbrushed mural of the Grim Reaper, a stogie stuck in his teeth and a bandanna on his head, riding hard in the wind.

Any biker worth his chromed Heavy Duty Hawg Chain will live in a neighborhood on the wrong side of town, in a ground-level pigsty that allows him to keep his bike in the living room. The digs are a personal toxic-waste dump of crushed Tall Boy beer cans, Jack Daniel's bottles with snuffed-out cigarette butts in their dregs, oil rags, and dirty underpants. The bike, however, is pristine; you could use the fishtail exhaust extension as a mirror.

Bikers are no longer news. Their outlaw life-style has solidified into a familiar ritual of rude gestures designed to show they still have the stuff to shock a solid citizen. Point a camera at a riding biker and he will give you the finger; off his bike, he'll moon you. He attends biker rodeos with the same party-time spirit as any conventioneer, and at the rodeo he enjoys games and sports just like Boy Scouts do at a Jamboree. Biker rodeo activities, however, almost always revolve around Harley-Davidsons, beer, and sex. They include keg derbies, in which contestants

push empty beer kegs to the end of a course using only the front wheels of their bikes; the potato haystack, a free-for-all in which bikers' mamas (not their mothers) fight each other in a pile of hay, trying to retrieve buried red, white, and blue potatoes; and the quintessential biker sport, known as "bite the weenie." Contestants ride, one couple at a time, below a scaffold, the biker driving, his old lady sitting on the seat behind him. Dangling from the scaffold is a hot dog on a string. As he maneuvers slowly and accurately below the suspended weenie, his girlfriend bites off as much of it as she can. Both biker and old lady are forbidden to touch the weenie with their hands as they ride below, and neither is allowed to set a foot on the ground to steady the bike. Whichever woman bites off the most meat from the dangling dog is declared the winner, but any contestant who swallows the whole thing or yanks it off its string is disqualified. "Bite the weenie" tradition demands a foot-long dog, slathered with yellow mustard to make it extra slippery.

A biker is a man of simple wants. He likes to drink beer, look at the boobs on local scooter trash (the name for women who fancy the biker life-style), and ride. When he goes to jail, usually for something dumb like driving his chopper through the window of a 7-Eleven, he spends much of his time writing lonesome letters to *Iron Horse* or *Easyriders*, magazines for one-percenters, looking for pen pals who understand the difference between a '77 shovelhead and a '55 shovelpan. These publications are a vivid distillation of biker style: "There's somethin about skinny chicks with oversized jugs that blamed near drives me bananas," begins the lead article in the June 1987 *Iron Horse*.

"Subscribe or I'll shoot your balls off!" invites the subscription form to *Outlaw Biker,* which offers a five-dollar discount to jailed readers. This magazine wastes no space on subjects that would be boring to bikers. Its table of contents is divided into "Parties," "Bikes," and "Tits." There is a column

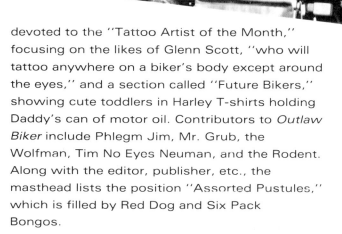

devoted to the ''Tattoo Artist of the Month,'' focusing on the likes of Glenn Scott, ''who will tattoo anywhere on a biker's body except around the eyes,'' and a section called ''Future Bikers,'' showing cute toddlers in Harley T-shirts holding Daddy's can of motor oil. Contributors to *Outlaw Biker* include Phlegm Jim, Mr. Grub, the Wolfman, Tim No Eyes Neuman, and the Rodent. Along with the editor, publisher, etc., the masthead lists the position ''Assorted Pustules,'' which is filled by Red Dog and Six Pack Bongos.

It's been forty years since bikers first made their mark on society, twenty since their heyday in the sixties; and it is amazing how little they have changed. What they aspired to then is almost exactly what they aspire to now. Like members of a cockeyed Porcellian club, they are tenaciously attached to preserving the social status quo. They relish seeing life from the perspective of a born loser, buoyed by the motto ''Born to Ride'' and by the defiant camaraderie among their outlaw pals.

See also **TATTOOS**

BODY BUILDING

Body building is both art and sport, but not quite either. It would be more of an art if everybody who participated aimed for a different kind of body—if, for instance, one body builder created a huge left arm and a minuscule right one with a fabulously well-developed hand, and another one specialized in spindly thighs atop bulked-up calves. That would be interesting art. But the fact is, all body builders aim for pretty much the same perfectly symmetrical look. As art, body building is monotonous.

As a sport, it is pretty silly too, because it is devoted to the cultivation of muscles that have no purpose. It does not demand the talent to run or hit or jump, and there is no test of skill on court or field that requires carting around so massive a physique. Unlike gymnastics or ballet, which also require a fabulous physique, body building involves doing nothing other than standing in front of a crowd and flexing arms, stomachs, and buttocks in synch with music. Participants sometimes justify it as a sport

because of all the hard work that goes into developing a perfect body. But this is strictly conceptual, as it is a process spectators do not see. It would be like showing the car that won Le Mans without showing the race. The activity body building most resembles is dog showing. In both cases, the most handsome wins.

Admiring muscular men has been a popular diversion since antiquity, but it used to be that they were idolized for their strength as much as for their shape. Eugene Sandow, the great turn-of-the-century body builder, was famous for piling nineteen people (including a fat man, a minstrel, and a clown) and a dog onto a board on his back and hoisting them all in the air before an audience. Coiffed in a Samson-like shoulder-length page boy, strongman Louis Cyr hefted hundred-pound weights with one finger. Other popular Goliaths, dressed in loincloths or fig leaves, showed their strength by tearing phone books in half or swimming around Manhattan pulling boats attached to ropes clenched in their teeth.

The father of body building as we know it was Bernarr MacFadden, who in 1903 staged a physique contest open to the public as a way to promote his magazine *Physical Culture*. Subtitled ''The Personal Problem Magazine,'' *Physical Culture* tackled everything from piles and sagging chins to inferiority complexes, recommending a combination of whole-grain diet, sunlight, and exercise to cure all ailments. MacFadden was a naturist (he didn't wear clothes if he could help it) and filled his magazine with ''figure studies'' of men and women in artistic poses, as well as advertisements for sanitariums, colonic cures, and Swedish massage emporiums. Feats of skill remained a popular sideshow. The October 1924 *Muscle Builder* (another MacFadden publication) featured a story by Selig (''Ajax'') Whitman, billed as the strongest policeman New York ever had, titled ''I Pushed 27,000 Pounds Uphill.'' By 1939, a body builder named Charles Atlas (Angelo Siciliano) was taking out full-page advertisements

Your Physique

The Story of Alan Stephan ''MR. AMERICA''

October 25¢

Steve Reeves, 1947

in MacFadden's magazine for his "Dynamic Tension" system. "Here's the kind of new men I build! Do you want to be one?" asks Charles Atlas in a ("actual, untouched") photograph that shows him with his fists clenched, ready for action. Atlas sold thousands of copies of his Dynamic Tension course based on its promise to help ninety-eight-pound weaklings get back at bullies who kicked sand in their faces and humiliated them in front of their girlfriends. Twice winner of the "World's Most Perfectly Developed Man" title, Atlas didn't stop at guaranteeing muscles that grew like magic. He assured people that Dynamic Tension "digs down into your system after such needless, joy-killing conditions as constipation, pimples, and indigestion."

The first Mr. America contest was held in 1939, sponsored by the American Athletic Union in an attempt to organize what was becoming the widespread grass-roots phenomenon of physical culture exhibitions. The AAU was not alone; it had to share jurisdiction with the World Body Building Guild and the International Federation of Body Builders, among others. The International Federation of Body Builders is today the biggest such group, but there is no cooperation among the various organizations, and no single worldwide championship, thus explaining such redundant titles as Mr. Universe, Mr. World, Mr. Galaxy, Mr. Olympia, Mr. U.S.A., and Mr. America.

Although Charles Atlas was a household word and body building had its devotees, the world of physical culture was for a long while tainted by its narcissism, which made it seem unsavory and a little freakish. It was rare for a champion to break out and enjoy the admiration of the general public. Steve Reeves, a Mr. America and Mr. Universe from the late forties, became something of a low-budget heartthrob when he was cast in epic Italian movies as a furious Hercules who grunted and flexed and tore down columned temples with his bare hands. Mickey Hargitay, another Mr. Universe, won a measure of fame when he married Jayne Mansfield in the fifties. But most of body

47

DEMI-GODS

September - 50c

building's superstars, such as Reg Park, Leroy Colbert, and Arthur Harris, were unknown to the public; and body building was still an activity with a certain air of unsavory physicality.

As the glorious Self was discovered in the sixties and seventies, the time was right for body building to make a run for respectability. Along with jogging, aerobic exercise, and health-food mania, it provided wonderful opportunities for people to contemplate their own (and other people's) bodies. Body building demanded that its practitioners look in mirrors often and, at the topmost echelon of the sport, oil their bodies and pose before hundreds of cheering people. To make the big leap out of the musclebound ghetto, however, body building needed a hero. He came in the form of Arnold Schwarzenegger.

The Age of Arnold began when Schwarzenegger (known as ''the Austrian Oak'') was brought to American in 1968 by Joe Weider, publisher of the AAU's *Muscle and Fitness* magazine and wheeler-dealer in the land of big biceps. Arnold had been an undefeated champion in Europe and was rightfully believed to be unstoppable anywhere on the globe. He had more than just a fifty-seven-inch chest, twenty-inch calves, and a smiling head on top; he had star quality and blazing ambition. He seized the attention of an audience that extended far beyond body-building devotees with his featured appearance in the trend-setting 1974 photo-essay book *Pumping Iron* and with a charismatic performance—as himself—in the documentary film of the same name. By the time he retired as six-time-undefeated Mr. Olympia in 1975, body building was out of the closet.

People who never lifted anything heavier than a Twinkie suddenly wanted to know all about iron-pumping shrines like Muscle Beach and Gold's Gym in Venice, California. The Washington *Post* called body building a ''new frontier of ambition and exhaustion.'' Even the flabbiest followers of the newly lionized sport learned to call their white bellies ''abs,'' sloping shoulders ''delts,'' and droopy asses ''gluts.'' Olympic committees were petitioned

(unsuccessfully) to make body building an official event. Women began joining gyms and bulking up right along with the guys. Life-style magazines sprung up with ads for Big Powder Shake (mix it with milk and ''put the new age of weight-gaining technology to work''), French Bronze tablets for that year-round sunless tan, and twenty-four-karat gold Muscle Watches offered by the Gym Rats Company of Texas with faces that instead of numbers sported images of rippling abdominal muscles.

Schwarzenegger parlayed his success into movie stardom, then a fairy-tale marriage to Maria Shriver, a glamorous Kennedy. His successor, Lou Ferrigno, became TV's Incredible Hulk. And new iron pumpers, helped by more sophisticated workouts, have developed bodies that seem to dwarf even the Austrian Oak. Lee Haney, a recent Mr. Olympia, boasts upper arms so massively braided they look like double loaves of challah bread glued together; Rich Gaspari's thighs make you wonder what pair of pants on earth could possibly house them. The only thing that has remained regulation-size are body builder's heads, which have begun to look increasingly inappropriate as expanding trapezius muscles rise up and engulf them.

BOUDOIR PHOTOGRAPHY

In the early 1980s, the notion that everybody is beautiful in his or her own way connected with the trendy psychological chestnut that it is good to act out one's fantasies, and the result was boudoir photography—a disquieting genre of picture taking in which women (and occasionally men) who are not professional models pose wearing slinky lingerie on satin sheets or tiger-skin rugs, squinting into a camera with their own personal version of a come-hither leer.

In most cases boudoir photographs are used as intimate gifts: sets of twelve put together as a cheesecake calendar for thumbtacking above husband's or boyfriend's workbench, or a single grand pose for hanging by the fireplace, with words of unrestrained passion (such as ''Come and get me'') written across the bottom in twenty-four-karat gold. ''Great Christmas Idea!'' advertises Mario Venticinque, Chicago's premier boudoir photographer. ''Present your womanly elegance in a personalized 'Boudoir Portrait'—a gift to yourself or for that Special Someone.'' The ad shows a pasty-faced, bleary-eyed blonde in what could be her driver's license picture, captioned ''Before.'' Next to this ghastly shot is ''After'': the same girl posed in a silk teddy, one strap falling down around her creamy white shoulders, her hair swept back in a glamorous windblown style, her complexion problems eradicated by the magic of soft-focus lenses, colored light gels, fog filters, and makeup.

Clients are expected to arrive at the studio with their own favorite sexy costumes, but savvy photographers stock a tantalizing wardrobe of French-maid ruffles and fishnet stockings, heavy jewelry such as silver snake arm bands and big hoop earrings (for the brazen look), fur boas and cuddly stuffed animals, all sizes of panty hose (to help camouflage stretch marks and cellulite), and assorted corsets and garter belts. Customary studio settings include brass beds and frilly ottomans to lounge on, a hot tub or a shower stall for the ''wet look'' pose, and at least one

bawdy-house backdrop with purple flocked wallpaper and a fainting couch. Small props such as spike heels, champagne glasses, handcuffs, and long cigarette holders are needed too, for seductive bits of business while posing.

introduces her to his stylist (always a kindly woman), sessions begin with corrective makeup, then may last many hours . . . or in the case of a woman who is making a full year's calendar, several days. Novices start with a few fully clothed pictures to loosen up, then gradually most of them get down to the hot stuff. Mr. Venticinque, who wrote the book on the subject *(Boudoir Photography: How to Make Every Woman Look Like Her Dream),* explained that one of the most important qualifications for a boudoir photographer is to be a ''people person able to work (as I have) with clients ranging in age from nineteen to seventy-one.'' The first job of a people-person boudoir photographer is to assure his clients that there is nothing lascivious about posing half-nude on a fur rug in spike heels and push-up bra. When Judy Markey of the Chicago *Sun-Times* wrote about a Venticinque photo session, she observed, ''He uses the word 'tasteful' about eleven times a minute.''

A serious sitting with a boudoir photographer costs at least a few hundred dollars, plus the price of the pictures themselves. They can range from wallet-size peek-a-boo nudies for a few dollars apiece to gilt-framed, airbrushed, canvas-textured, raised-brushstroke ''Old Masters'' portraits for several thousand dollars.

Once a new client is relaxed, which usually happens after the photographer shows her before-and-after pictures of previous clients, gives her a glass of wine, assures her that he will not sell the pictures to *Hustler* magazine, and

BOUFFANTS

The bouffant is a great massive cylinder of hair swirled into a tornado shape rising high above the scalp. In this age of curly perms and feathered shags, it is a shock to see a full-blown bouffant on someone's head; it is monolithic, looking less like a thatch of human hair than like a teetering hassock made of petrified cotton candy. In fact, you don't see many bouffants anymore, except perhaps on a gum-snapping diner waitress stuck in fashion's time warp or a punk musician imitating the impudence of Phil Spector's nasty-girl singing groups of the early sixties.

We suspect that most people who seriously wear bouffants today started wearing them twenty-five or thirty years ago, when they were in high school. Not all girls who wore big, sprayed heaps of hair in those days were wayward, but the ones who cultivated the truly outrageous bubble tops, which made them look in silhouette like Superman's double-dome nemesis Braniac, tended to be the school's bad girls, the slutty glamour queens who hung out with greasy-haired boys in tight black pants, leather jackets, and porkpie hats. The girls' awesome hairdos served as the crowns for faces transformed into macabre masks by profuse applications of white Pan-Cake makeup, iridescent lipstick, and heavy deposits of black eyeliner. Cautionary tales about these bad girls and their prodigious hairdos abounded: they hid knives and zip guns up there; spiders, roaches, and mice made nests inside the sticky towers of varnished hair, feeding on hair spray and growing abnormally vicious, eventually gnawing their way into the wearers' brains.

Creating a bouffant is a strenuous task, begun by wrapping the hair around curlers at least the diameter of a half-dollar, or as big as a beer can, in order to eliminate all kinks and curls. At this stage of construction, it is proper etiquette among bouffant aficionados to wrap the hair and curlers in a scarf tied under the chin and go out in public, thus proudly announcing to the world that you have a bouffant-in-progress on your head. Once unraveled, the hair is infused with gum-thick applications of hair spray, then back-combed (also known as teased), which means combing the hair back toward the scalp while holding it up and away from the head. The result of these operations is clumps of hair that are nearly as malleable as silly putty. When the clumps are brushed upward and smoothed into the shape of a barrel, then sprayed some more, a bouffant takes shape. Once created, a bouffant must be tended, which means wrapping it each night in tissue paper and sleeping in a semiprone position so that it does not deflate.

The bouffant was not always the mark of the sophisticate manqué. When it was first developed in the late fifties, it was truly the height of haute coiffure. The sleek, inflated palisade of teased and sprayed hair symbolized refinement and the utmost in feminine poise.

Bouffants started small, as a French style known as the bubble, which demanded straight (or straightened) hair and was teased only a few inches above the scalp as a kind of halo. To get it up and off the head required some artistry, and the resulting stature made the bubble a soigné replacement for the cute Italian pixie cut that had been fashionable throughout the mid-fifties. The bubble still had a bit of pixie cuteness and was a perky balance for the simple chemise dress, but it signaled the beginning of a drastic upward trend in hair. In 1958, when couturier Hubert de Givenchy introduced the stark, simple sack dress, he realized that for the dress not to look like a potato sack, it required a provocative hairdo as its complement. The recently introduced fat hair roller, as well as newly developed techniques in back-combing, made possible a tour-de-force bubble of formerly inconceivable elevation: The bouffant was born. Givenchy mannequins all sported bouffant wigs specially created by wig-maker Carita; and in one of the key revolutions in twentieth-century fashion, ladies' hats started to become démodé. Big hair, which suffered no hats, had arrived; and the hairdresser soon replaced the milliner as the exalted oracle of women's fashions.

The most famous celebrity champion of the

smaller than the puffed-up base out of which it grew.

The biggest of all bouffants was Priscilla Presley's circa 1963. Priscilla lived at Graceland but was not yet married to Elvis. When it came time to have her hair styled, she consulted with Elvis and decided to put her head in the hands of the girlfriend of his Harley-Davidson mechanic, who moonlighted as a part-time hairdresser. She coaxed Priscilla's hair into an immense conical keg well over a foot high, teased and sprayed with such precision that the sides formed a well-nigh-perfect cylinder and the top a smooth convex cap. It was so big that when Elvis gave Priscilla a Corvair coupe, the poor girl discovered she could sit in the low-roofed car only if she kept her head and hairdo aimed outside through the open window.

The bloated hairdo gauntlet was picked up by Kenneth of New York, who tended Jacqueline Kennedy's relatively modest bouffant, and created glamorous spires for his other clients by using curlers and aggressive back-combing as well as supplementary hairpieces. Soon, however, Kenneth abandoned the extremism of the bouffant and became known for soft, natural coiffures, championing even the close-cropped gamine look of Mia Farrow. ''The lacquered, stiff, glued-together look is outdated,'' he declared in *Kenneth's Complete Book of Hair* in 1969. Worse than outdated, the lacquered, stiff, glued-together, teased bouffant had become a parody of elegance, taken to outlandish heights by overeager hairdressers armed with giant rollers, rat-tail combs, and cans of hairspray.

See also **WHITE LIPSTICK**

bouffant was Alexandre of Paris, who gave Jacqueline Kennedy a brioche-shaped pouf for a Versailles ball in May 1961. When he arrived in America the following year, Alexandre declared, ''I came to make a revolution.'' He piled mounds of hair atop the heads of Elizabeth Taylor, Princess Grace, Audrey Hepburn, and the sisters Gabor, and became known not only for the size of his bouffant but for its intricacy. Looped, beribboned, festooned with jewels, a towering confection created by Alexandre was likened by Marilyn Bender of the *New York Times* to ''a suckling pig dressed by a master chef and laid on a banquet table.'' It was Alexandre who created the most important variation of the bouffant, known as a beehive, in which a single elevated portion of hair appeared to be a separate cone, sometimes considerably

BOWLING

Bowling is the only sport that can be played well while sipping beer from a big wax-paper cup and eating a bratwurst sandwich. Unlike such sports as sailing, tennis, or skiing, all of which demand lean bodies or expensive equipment, bowling requires nothing more than the rental of a pair of used shoes with your size marked on the back.

Newcomers are easily distinguished from pros. The latter own their own shoes, often color-coordinated with the mottled Ebonite ball they tote around in a Naugahyde bag. Their billowing shirts are emblazoned with team names on the back and the wearer's nickname in script on the front pocket.

Ardent bowlers are proud of their game's lineage. The Athletic Institute of New York, publishers of the 1966 book *Bowling,* attests to an impressive pedigree. It says that in the 1930s, British archaeologist Sir Flinders Petrie found bowling paraphernalia in an Egyptian tomb dating back to 5200 B.C. Christian-era bowling began as a religious rite in third-century Germany, where, according to *Bowling,* ''no German man would appear in public without a small wooden club called his kegel.'' Although kegels were designed as weapons, the fun-loving Germans figured out a way to use them for sport: They lined up

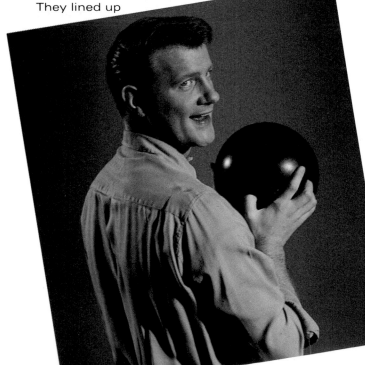

groups of kegels and knocked them over with a round stone in the belief that doing so would purify their souls. (Bowlers with a flair for history refer to the sport by its ancestral name, ''kegling.'')

Kegling became so popular that it spread to cloistered monasteries, where monks competed against one another to see who could knock down the most pins. The winner was declared the most pious. Even Martin Luther took time out from founding the Protestant religion to bowl at home in his own private alley. Luther was an eager kegler who established the standard formation of the game as it was played in Europe for centuries to come: nine pins in three straight rows. An outdoor variation of the sport spread to England, where it became so popular that in 1541 King Henry VIII outlawed it because his soldiers spent all their time bowling instead of honing their military skills. Deeming bowling too rowdy for commoners, Henry usurped the privilege for himself and any aristocrat who could afford a bowling license.

Although variations of the game had been popular in America since Dutch settlers played ninepins upon arriving in New Amsterdam, it wasn't until 1895, when the American Bowling Congress was founded, that rules about ball size and pin placement were standardized. In the thirties, after Prohibition was repealed, bowling as we know it began to take shape. Big midwestern breweries such as Blatz, Pabst, and Schlitz sponsored ''beer teams'' that toured the country to promote their beverages. Henceforth, beer and bowling were forever linked in the public's mind; and a diversion once the province of pharaohs, kings, and blue bloods became the sport of guys with blue collars and gals with brown stretch pants.

After World War II, the look and style of the game took flight as GIs returned from the war in the Pacific and flocked to their neighborhood lanes wearing loud Hawaiian shirts. Their floppy attire created a fashion in bowling alleys and helped inspire the classic flamboyance of the great shirts of the fifties. Bowling soon came

close to being America's national pastime, thanks to the postwar combination of automatic pin spotters, huge new alleys in shopping centers, and air-conditioned lanes where a family could spend a hot summer night in comfort. By 1965, the how-to book *Instant Bowling* called it "the king of family sports," boasting that bowling "combats delinquency" and asserting, "Boredom? Loneliness? . . . Neither is known in bowling."

Like professional wrestling, bowling achieved its early popularity partly because it made such a good television sport. Television showed professional bowlers to be regular Joes —family men with flattops and pleated pants— thus helping to promote the idea of bowling as fun for the whole family. "Bowling Headliners" was the first national bowling show, broadcast in 1949 on the Dumont Network from the Rego Park

Lanes in Queens, New York, and featuring professional bowlers competing for five- to fifty-dollar prizes. Then came big-money programs such as "Make That Spare." "Bowling Stars" (narrated by Whispering Joe Wilson, whose muted, off-screen commentary insinuated tension into every frame), and "Jackpot Bowling" (hosted by Milton Berle and featuring "the world's greatest bowlers" aiming for the $100,000 jackpot).

Television made celebrities out of such humble champs as Buzz Fazio, Ray Bluth, Marion Ladewig (known as the Queen of Bowlers), and Sylvia Wene, the only woman to bowl three consecutive 300 score games. Immortals Don Carter and Therm Gibson thrilled TV watchers as they methodically dried their palms over the

Electric-Aire blower on the ball return and glided to the edge of the lane to lay down a strike. ''TV Bonanza!'' headlined *Bowling Magazine* in 1957. ''Today's leading bowlers have found 'thar's gold in them thar lanes.' ''

Bowling kingpins have always been distinguished from other athletes by their placid temperament and a quiet kind of concentration that could easily pass for dullness. Being able to relax is the foremost requirement of good bowling, wrote hall-of-famer Don Carter in the book *Bowl Better Using Self-Hypnosis.* To assist would-be pros in achieving the mellow state ofsemisomnambulism Carter recommended, Professor Richard Carl Spurney recorded an album in 1961 called *BOWL-A-STRIKE,* which hypnotized listeners, then gave them posthypnotic suggestions to improve their game.

What makes bowling fun, even if you aren't a kegler, is the extravagance of its ornaments, especially the towering wood-look and bronzelike trophies topped with little gold bowlers—perfect to display in the window of the local luncheonette or barbershop, next to the taxidermized trout. Nearly anything with a bowling motif is treasured by collectors of Americana and commands a high price at the type of store that sells Fiesta Ware and pink flamingos: decorative balls with built-in clocks, pin-shaped liquor decanters, strike-'n'-spare ashtrays, and lamps that grow out of the backs of hunched-over ceramic bowlers.

Most prized of all bowling artifacts are vintage team shirts made of Sheen-Glo gabardine or challis with deep-pleated action backs, embroidered with fancy letters, team mottoes, and farfetched insignias. The finest shirts were made by Nat Nast (''Goodbye to score-robbing, shoulder-blade bind!''); George London, maker of the ''All-American'' with red, white, and blue Flex-O-Rib sleeve inserts; King Louie, featuring Coloray Captive-Color Rayon; Hilton (''the aristocrat of bowling shirts''); and the Service Shirts Corporation, inventors of ''the bowling shirt with the built-in deodorant.''

BREASTS, ENORMOUS

Enormous breasts are considered by many people, men mostly, to be just about the sexiest things on earth. Guys who go crazy over them can indulge their fascination by looking at special-interest magazines such as *Boobs, Bazooms, and Bumper Busts,* composed solely of photographs of bare-breasted women usually described in such terms as "astonishingly cantilevered," "gravity-defying," and "tempest-in-a-D-cup"; but there is no need to seek esoteric sources to wallow in acres of giant jugs. They are plentiful in popular entertainment; and it is considered perfectly normal to get excited by them. For the last half-century, it has been common practice to measure a woman's beauty by the size of her chest.

Breasts are like buttocks: soft, round body parts that are technically nonerogenous (women's breasts have no more nerve endings than men's) and therefore much less threatening for the sexually apprehensive male than unequivocally sexual areas. On the proverbial date-score scale, touching breasts is only second base, whereas getting below the panty line is a home run. Please, let us not even discuss the psychological implications of men who lust after the succor of a big, warm, motherly teat; the plain fact is that there are an awful lot of breast men in this world, especially in America.

One thing devotees of enormous breasts like to do is tell jokes about them. Although big-tit humor is without question in bad taste, it is generally considered on the nicer side of obscenity; and it is acceptable at many levels of allegedly polite society for men to snigger over large breasts and for large-breasted women such as Charo and Dolly Parton to use their breasts as part of their act, on stage and off. Boobie humor is a staple of the novelty gift trade, exemplified by such monomaniacal novelties as the Lively One ("A life-sized WALKING BOOBY! Wind it up and watch it do its thing"); Booby Checkers, a checkerboard that, instead of red and black squares, is covered with pictures of breasts; and the Booby Bath Mat, a white foam pad with six life-size breasts bulging upwards to walk on

when stepping out of the shower.

Big breasts have gone in and out of fashion since the Garden of Eden (where Adam and Eve felt compelled to cover only their loins with fig leaves). In the twenties, flappers wore chest straps to reduce their breast size, as had women in Periclean Greece. The origin of the modern era of jumbo-breast obsessiveness can be traced to the debut of Jane Russell, playing a double-D half-breed in the Howard Hughes western, *The Outlaw,* filmed in the early forties. Advertisements asked, "What are the two great reasons for Jane Russell's rise to stardom?" Miss Russell's big breasts were so controversial that the movie's release was delayed for years because of battles with censors; but by the end of World War II, the time was right for enormous breasts to spill forth from low-cut dresses and jut inside tight sweaters.

One of the hallmarks of fifties culture was its fascination with so many things grown abnormally huge, from superwide CinemaScope movies and giant mutant monsters *(Them!, Attack of the Fifty Foot Woman)* to bloated, finned Cadillacs (which featured bosomlike protruding front ends). Exaggeration was a fundamental aesthetic principle of the time, especially when it came to sex appeal: Consider the outrageous sensuality of early Elvis and Brando or the squealing, breathy femininity of Marilyn Monroe. Whopping hooters were not a

57

prerequisite for a woman who aspired to stardom (there was also a slender, sophisticated Audrey Hepburn look), but the fifties were an era when careers could be built upon outlandish measurements (see *Mansfield, Jayne*). *Playboy* magazine began publication in 1953, celebrating distended breasts not only on sexy starlets but on centerfolds, who were presented as fantasy ''girls-next-door.'' Little girls got their big-breast role model in 1959, when the Barbie Doll was introduced, featuring a figure that has been calculated to have the equivalent of a thirty-nine-inch bust (see *Barbie Doll*).

In December 1963 *Newsweek* announced that ''after years of the covered look, the bosom is now fashionable again,'' and reported on the décolleté fashions from Christian Dior in Paris and the new underwire half-bra that made such daring exposure possible. The following year Rudi Gernreich introduced the topless bathing suit, and a teenage cocktail waitress in San Francisco named Carol Doda found a plastic surgeon to fill her breasts with liquid silicone, inflating her brassiere size from 36 to 44D. Doda slithered into one of Gernreich's bathing suits and created a new art form—topless dancing. For connoisseurs of enormous breasts, the millennium had arrived.

The biggest breasts in show business appeared in the late sixties, on stripper Chesty Morgan, who starred in the motion picture *Deadly Weapons*, playing a secret agent who smothered enemies to death with her surrealistic (but genuine and all-natural) eighty-inch udders. Ms. Morgan's modern successor is an actress named Busty Heart, who also boasts an eighty-inch bust (requiring a brassiere with triple-M cups). Heart claims to be responsible for the real-life demise of a member of her audience in a nightclub, a man who died of cardiac arrest when she removed her shirt.

The greatest living champion of outsized jungle drums (his term) is film director Russ Meyer, who began his career in the fifties as a pinup photographer and made his first cinematic study of what he likes to call female pulchritude in 1959 in *The Immoral Mr. Teas* (about a peeping

Tom who lives next door to a stupendously well-stacked woman who spends most of her time dressing and undressing). Meyer made movies with such titles as *Mud Honey* and *Faster Pussycat! Kill! Kill!* starring women with enormous breasts in action-packed melodramas that always involve them doing things that cause their breasts to bounce. By the end of the sixties Meyer had developed some status among cineastes for his uncompromising pectoral vision of life (the New York Cultural Center hosted a retrospective of his films in 1971) and was making relatively big-budget movies such as *Vixen* and *Beyond the Valley of the Dolls* (the latter written by Pulitzer Prize—winning film critic Roger Ebert), still featuring jiggling jugs.

But Meyer's most important movie, to tit men as well as to auteurist critics, was a documentary he made in 1965 called *Mondo Topless*. Unencumbered by a plot, *Mondo Topless* is a paean to the topless craze, and it stars breasts so enormous that in some scenes there is no room on the screen to show the body they're attached to. (One of the movie's featured dancers, Darlene Grey, is described as weighing a mere one hundred twelve pounds, twenty-three of which were ''bra-busting boobs.'') A narrator introduces the location as San Francisco, a city ''situated on precipitous peaks among yawning canyons,'' then warns us that we are about to see girls the likes of which we have only dreamt of. What follow are individual vignettes of eight colossal-breasted women, including ''big-busted Babette Bardot,'' ''protuberant Pat Berringer,'' and ''capaciously domed Darla Paris,'' known collectively as ''the Buxotics,'' each undulating bare-breasted for the camera. They do the swim and the watusi, they drag their breasts through mud pits, they hang from tree limbs, they go-go dance on railroad tracks, they writhe on the floor with their breasts draped in strands of audio tape. Mammillary monomania was never more delirious.

See also **BARBIE DOLL; CHARO; FREDERICK'S OF HOLLYWOOD; GAGS AND NOVELTIES; MANSFIELD, JAYNE; PARTON, DOLLY**

Chesty Morgan

BUMPER STICKERS

The awful thing about bumper stickers is that they stick too well. In the heat of passion, you glue a message onto the bumper of your car or, worse, smack on the paint. Then, long after you have lost your infatuation for Dukakis-Bentsen, the comet Kahoutek, or disco dancing, you are forced to drive around town advertising that you once loved a loser—either that or repaint the car, or sell it. But then, who wants to buy a used car with somebody else's ''I♥Bon Jovi'' or ''Ask Me About My Grandchildren'' permanently attached?

As highway nostalgia, really old bumper stickers can be fun to see—e.g., the elderly hippie in an antique Volvo stuck with a Woodstock dove or a daisy. Such simple, old-fashioned symbols are rare on modern roads, where bumper stickers have become what the CB radio was in the mid-1970s: an easy opportunity for any bellicose dolt to announce his opinions to the world. They began as cheerful proclamations of good will (''Have a Nice Day☺!'') or of ardent concern (''POWs Never Have a Nice Day,'' ''War Is Not Healthy for Children and Other Living Things'') or simply straightforward indications of which candidate you liked, but most bumper stickers of today are cloying, complicated, mean, or obscene.

The age of bumper-sticker creativity started in the sixties, when SANE (a nonacronym for the Committee for a Sane Nuclear Policy) adopted the peace sign from the British Campaign for Nuclear Disarmament. To put it on cars was a break with the original purpose of bumper stickers, to get political candidates' names around, but it was part of the sixties' relentless belief that it was important and effective to broadcast one's feelings as well as one's political preferences.

Bumper stickers were only one of the newly popular means of self-expression, along with lapel buttons, T-shirts, and picket signs.

What made bumper stickers unique among these media was that they were embraced more by the establishment than by the counterculture. (Cars, after all, were an establishment thing.) To counteract SANE's peace symbol, Moral Majoritarians coopted the three-toed insignia for their own bumper stickers, adding their humorous caption: ''Footprint of the American Chicken.'' About the same time Gene McCarthy adopted the daisy for his campaign bumper stickers in 1968, they put flags and ''America—Love It or Leave It'' on their cars.

By 1972, although Democrat George McGovern's campaign bumper stickers featured daisies (again) and the luv-drenched ''Kiss Me—I'm for McGovern,'' bumper-sticker leadership had passed from the antiwar movement to born-again Christians. In fact, the two top-selling bumper stickers in America in 1972 were ''Honk If You Know Jesus'' and ''Smile, God Loves You.'' The proliferation of religious slogans on bumper stickers was mostly the work of an Elkhart, Indiana, man named Elden W. Ferm, who quit his job as a traveling salesman in November 1969 to produce ''Our God Is Not Dead—Sorry About Yours'' and soon became what he described as ''the largest Christian bumper-sticker business in the country.''

The last burst of great bumper-sticker artistry came in the seventies as an expression of Me Decade values: ''He Who Dies with the Most Toys Wins''; ''I'm Spending My Grandchildren's Inheritance''; ''I'd Rather Be Fishing.'' A heretofore unseen belligerence crept into the bumper-sticker repertoire in this era: ''Let the

Yankee Bastards Freeze," seen in the South during the mid-decade oil crisis; "I May Be Slow But I'm Ahead of You," and "As a Matter of Fact, I Do Own the Road." Bumper stickers became an opportunity to unload free-floating hostility, with no purpose other than to give the raspberry to other drivers.

In the eighties, bumper-sticker creativity became like movies, television, and bathroom graffiti—mostly a matter of sequels, spin-offs, and smirking sexual double entendres. The original humane sentiment "I Brake for Animals" led to "I Brake for Tag Sales" and "I Brake for No Reason." "I ♥ NY" begat hundreds of bighearted declarations of love for everything from Doberman pinschers to "Wheel of Fortune's" Vanna White. As on T-shirts, there were thousands of bumper stickers in the naughty-minded "do it" genre, such as "Teachers Do It with Class" and "Divers Do It Deeper." A popular

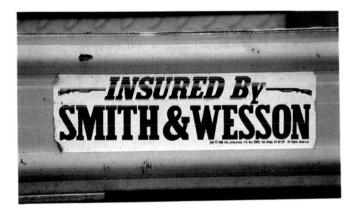

triangular auto-window sign that said "Baby On Board" was the source of innumerable spin-offs, from "Nobody On Board" to "Former Husband in Trunk." The humorous sticker designed for rattletraps, "My Other Car Is a Mercedes," led to the inevitable "My Other Car is a Piece of Shit, Too." And the sign on semi trucks that reads "How's My Driving? Call 1-800-***-****" had its obscene version also: "How's My Driving? Call 1-800-EAT-SHIT."

Many states have wrestled with the issue of bumper-sticker vulgarity. Virginia tried to ban the use of four-letter words, but the bill died in committee because lawmakers worried that it compromised free speech. In Louisiana, the legislature got around the issue by limiting the display of "six specific words describing body functions, body parts and sex acts" to one eighth of an inch high.

CADILLACS

Cadillacs are to cars what Jayne Mansfield was to women: big, flamboyant, brazen, and extreme. She was a sex symbol; a Cadillac is a sex symbol and more. Elvis drove them and gave them away like peanuts. When contestants passed into the big-money range on "The $64,000 Question," their reward was a Cadillac. Blues singers cry for them; lottery winners run out to buy them. "Cadillac" conjures images of rowdy Texas millionaires who mount steerhorns on the hoods, of cruising city pimps who put black-out film on the windows, and of annoying old people on their way to Florida, going thirty miles an hour in the passing lane. Painted pink, white, baby blue, or solid gold, or covered with fish scales and diamond dust, a Cadillac has never been simply a car.

There was a time long ago when to call anything "the Cadillac of its class" meant that it was the best. That cachet shifted in the fifties, when Cadillac, long known for high price and snob appeal, blossomed as not only the most expensive car but the most vulgar. Today regarded as the quintessential gas-guzzling road hog, Cadillac began its long road to the heights of loutishness in 1948 when the once tasteful car first sprouted tail fins on its rear fenders. Cadillacs were the fin leaders of the fifties. Other cars imitated the idea—notably Chrysler Corporation models designed by Virgil Exner (or as he was known to critics, Virgil Excess)—but it was Caddy that made fins a symbol of automotive styling at its most brutish.

Tail fins were the brainchild of General Motors design chief Harley Earl, a six-foot-six Texan known as "the Barnum of Detroit," who had begun his career by inventing two-tone cars in the thirties. Earl patterned Cadillac fins after the P-38 fighter plane. They began as a little design fillip but soon became the supreme talisman of the rococo age when car culture ran amok. During Harley Earl's fantastic reign, he made Cadillacs and other General Motors cars into visions of power and glory. He oversaw such automotive breakthroughs as false air scoops, false gun ports, quadruple headlights, torpedo

taillights, a pointed chrome steering-wheel column (aimed at the driver's chest), and dashboards with rocket-ship-shaped knobs. His philosophy was that getting into a car should be like going on vacation: exotic, fun, and not necessarily practical.

Harley Earl's understanding that people buy cars for reasons other than to get from one place to another helped fashion modern Cadillacs as the personal possession that most aggressively broadcast how much money it cost, even more than jewelry and furs. In keeping with this theme, Cadillacs of the mid-sixties had to pass what advertisements referred to as ''the mink test,'' wherein girls wearing mink coats got into the cars, rolled around on the seats, squirmed and lay down, then got out, at which point lab-coated technicians checked the minks to make certain that all that romping inside the Cadillac had caused no abrasions or discolorations in the fur.

By 1959 the Cadillac had grown into such a monstrosity that awestruck critics called it ''a rolling juke box'' or ''the Batmobile.'' Coming at you, a 1959 Sedan de Ville appeared to be bullying everything in its path off the road. It had a huge grinning face with heavy-lidded dual headlights glaring above a grille that smirked menacingly and seemed to sparkle like a gangster's jeweled fillings. Its two-and-a-half-ton body was draped with chrome, and full fender skirts made it glide mean and low on the road. The rear end was terrifying: twin bullet taillights mounted on colossal pointed fins so sharp that rumors abounded about Cadillacs backing into parking spaces and impaling and killing unwary roller skaters and pedestrians.

Although its fins grew smaller after 1959 and eventually disappeared, Cadillac stayed true to Harley Earl's ideas, even when Earl left General Motors to design Ban Roll-On Deodorant bottles. After all, Cadillac had competition for title of King of the Road. Hot on its rubbery heels were the late-fifties Lincoln Continentals, even bigger than Cadillacs—so long and wide, in fact, that some states required them to be outfitted with amber clearance lights on the front and red reflectors on the rear, like any truck.

In the late sixties, when the cars of the moment were the youthful Mustang (about twenty-five hundred pounds) and the breezy Volkswagen Beetle (about fifteen hundred pounds), Cadillac responded to the trend by introducing a ''personal size'' Eldorado, weighing a mere four thousand five hundred and ninety pounds.

"Is there still a place for FULL-SIZE cars?" wondered *Popular Science* in 1974 as gas supplies dwindled. In the Cadillac design department, there has always been room for full-size cars, so although power was cut and carburetion choked to the point that the big iron boats could only wheeze down the road, the old standard of ever-increasing personal luxury never wavered. In 1974, when an entire Chevy Vega cost $2,788, the same amount of money bought you a Talisman option package for your Cadillac Fleetwood Brougham d'Elegance (base price: $9,537). Even without the Talisman package, the Brougham d'Elegance was an astounding mass of car, including double-decker wraparound parking lights, protruding safety bumpers, vinyl "cabriolet" roof (it looks like a convertible top but isn't), velour-padded doors, deep-pile carpet, sextuple-lighted visor vanity mirrors, and a see-through stand-up Cadillac hood ornament to remind you what you're driving. The Talisman option improved upon this perfection by replacing the ordinary car seats with four separate reclining armchairs covered in a fuzzy synthetic plush cloth Cadillac named "Medici crushed velour."

Today's Cadillacs are still glutted with elegant doodads, expensive-sounding materials, and doughy padded roofs named to bring to mind the noble coach builders of yore. There is a black rubbery "phaeton roof" for the Cadillac Seville; there are lighted "opera lamps" for the C-pillars of the Eldorado; and you can order an electroluminescent Cadillac wreath and crest imbedded in the sponge-soft roof of your Fleetwood. For those who demand maximum ostentation, Cadillac still makes a Brougham d'Elegance. The current model is the longest car manufactured in America and has the biggest engine Cadillac ever built. It weighs over two tons and accelerates only a little faster than a dump truck. It comes with a trumpet horn, carpeted litter receptacle, and gold-plated ignition key as standard features; and it is available with such impressive options as a llama-grain formal padded roof, twenty-four-karat Cadillac grille script and engine plaque, and twenty-four-karat gold Cadillac wreath and crest on trunk and wheels.

CANDLE ART

After the invention of electric light bulbs, candles were no longer a necessity. Instead, they became a symbol of elegance in the home: long white tapers rising from polished silver holders, lit on formal occasions to signify romance or high style. At the very least, they dripped and twinkled poetically in straw-covered Chianti bottles in quaint Italian restaurants. Then the sixties came along and changed the meaning of candlelight. Votive candles began to flicker in crash pads everywhere, creating the proper *misterioso* atmosphere for dope smoking and listening to psychedelic music. Candles were prized as natural light sources in contrast to corporate-made electric bulbs, whose use meant more money for big utility companies. No head shop was complete without a supply of patchouli-perfumed candles in rainbow color combinations.

It wasn't only hippies who made candlelight the preferred way of creating an enchanting mood. How-to seduction manuals taught single girls and swinging bachelors that candles kindled passion; so they dutifully put them in places where no candles had been before: on top of stereo speakers and by the bedside, even along the rim of a bubble-filled bathtub.

By the early seventies candles were turning up in the most grotesque forms and fragrances imaginable, primarily because any ham-fisted craftsman, no matter how badly his brains had been damaged by psychedelic drugs, could still dip a wick and make thick wax tubes in swirling colors. Candles became popular novelty gift items precisely because they were handmade (a big plus in the craft-crazed early seventies). The pure white unscented taper was eclipsed by huge wax tiki gods with wicks coming out of their scalps, by jumbo brandy snifters filled with wads of floral-embossed dark-brown paraffin, by meditating avocado-green Buddhas, and by strawberry-parfait-scented ''chunk'' candles with autumn leaves pressed into their sides.

Home crafts books such as William Nussle's *Candle Crafting: From an Art to a Science* show how easy it is to create candles at home. ''The most difficult part of the art is not in making the candles but in seeing them be consumed when they burn,'' Nussle wrote, pointing out that any receptacle can be used as a form: Jell-O molds, tin cans, toilet-paper tubes, and milk cartons. Nussle's candles ranged from formal jar-lites to great clumps of wax attached to a piece of driftwood. Tandy Corporation's comprehensive *Romantic Candles You Can Make Yourself* offers sample illustrations of a squat kaleidoscopic ''scrap candle'' (made completely from leftover wax stubs) with a postcard of Gainsborough's *Blue Boy* affixed to its surface, and a tall Santa Claus candle with a white ''whipped wax'' beard. The most distressing example of the candle maker's art is *Romantic Candles*'s ''Madonna''— apparently made in an old ham can—with a surface so warty that the Virgin Mary resembles nothing so much as the face of *Nightmare on Elm Street*'s Freddy Kreuger. ''Be proud of your candles,'' this book concludes. ''A glow from a candle always brings a glow to the faces of those who surround it.''

Romantic Candles

$1.50

...you can make yourself

CARR, ALLAN

Being crass is practically a prerequisite for the job of movie producer. So when one stands out as especially vulgar, it is a truly noteworthy accomplishment. Such a man is Allan Carr.

Carr's credits roll like a catalogue of bad taste, from his historic inspiration in 1960 to bring poet Carl Sandburg to the "Playboy's Penthouse" television show (a concept that Carr himself had conceived and sold to Hugh Hefner shortly after graduating from high school) to his production of the notorious 1989 Academy Awards. "The sixty-first Academy Awards ceremony began by creating the impression there would never be a sixty-second," the *New York Times* said the next day, referring to the ceremony's opening act, in which Rob Lowe destroyed all credibility as a movie actor by performing an excruciating duet with a squeaky-voiced actress in a Snow White outfit who strolled among the audience of celebrities, most of whom cringed with embarrassment when she came close.

Born Alan Solomon in Highland Park, Illinois, Carr arrived in Hollywood in 1961. There he met Marlo Thomas and became her personal manager despite the pleas of Marlo's father, Danny, that she not go into show business. "You'll live happily ever after," Carr promised Marlo, becoming what he called a "career doctor" and launching her toward stardom in 1966 in television's perky-girl sitcom "That Girl." By the mid-seventies his clients included Ann-Margret, Marvin Hamlisch, and Won Ton Ton the Wonder Dog.

In addition to his achievements as a professional manager, he was soon acclaimed as Hollywood's grossest sybarite. Creating the neologism "glitterfunk" to describe himself, he sashayed forth in a wardrobe of flowing caftans and kimonos, ankle-length mink coats, and vixenish diamond jewelry, his small, round head ringed with curls permed by Vidal Sassoon. He was photographed lounging odalisquelike on silk pillows or on his huge bed, surrounded by telephones and movie scripts, making deals. Although he was only five feet seven inches tall, his weight swelled to 310 pounds until he had eighteen feet of his intestines surgically stapled

off, and he managed to slim back down to 210. "He was just not pleasant to look at," observed Ann-Margret's husband, Roger Smith.

Carr climbed into the first rank of celebrity as the latest in Hollywood's long line of profligate party givers. "Like P. T. Barnum, he makes the world his circus," *Interview* magazine gushed, calling him "the greatest host since Perle Mesta." He turned his house (built by David O. Selznick and formerly occupied by Kim Novak, Ingrid Bergman, and James Caan) into what he boasted was "the first home nightclub"—creating a private discotheque with a copper floor where embedded lights blinked in synch with music. For one party he filled the house with rented leftover scenery from the movie *Cleopatra* and invited seven hundred of his dearest friends. Another time, he sent out invitations in the form of subpoenas to appear at a party for Truman Capote at an abandoned jail in Los Angeles, where upon arrival each guest was frisked and fingerprinted.

His first successful venture into movie producing was an exploitation picture called *Survive!* in 1976, which *Time* magazine called "the nastiest ninety minutes ever to appear on the screen." The film, which grossed millions, was a reedited version of a cheaply made Mexican movie about a group of survivors of a plane crash in the Andes who get so hungry they eat each other's flesh. He parlayed his success into *Grease,* which despite many bad reviews became the most money-making musical in history and established television actor John Travolta as a big screen star. But these accomplishments were mere prologue to the one crowning achievement that secured Allan Carr top ranking in the pantheon of bad taste, his 1980 disco movie, *Can't Stop the Music.*

The concept of the movie was a fictionalized biography of the Village People, a singing group synthesized by French record producer Jacques Morali as a lineup of macho stereotypes: a cowboy, a cop, a soldier, an Indian, a biker, and a construction worker. The film starred the actual Village People; and to add heterosexual love interest to the beefcake cast, Carr chose Olympic gold medalist Bruce Jenner and Valerie Perrine, selecting Miss Perrine, he explained, because "she saved Superman's life [in the movie *Superman*] and fondled Lenny [Bruce]'s private parts [in the movie *Lenny*]." The twenty-million-dollar extravaganza, directed by Nancy Walker (best known for her role as diner waitress Rosie in television advertisements for Bounty paper towels), featured a gender-reversed Busby Berkeley—like production number with hundreds of men in bikini bathing suits diving into a pool as the Village People belted out their hit song "YMCA," a coquettish anthem about how easy it was for lonely men to meet other men at the Young Men's Christian Association.

Carr spent over ten million dollars promoting the film, but audiences, gay and straight, stayed away in droves. "PLEASE Stop the Music!" headlined critical reviews. "STOP THE FLOPS!" groaned the New York *Post*. "The Village People should consider renaming themselves the Village Idiots," commented *Los Angeles* magazine. The Village People's career died; disco music died; Nancy Walker went back to paper towels; and Allan Carr went on to produce many other embarrassing flops, including *Grease II* and an egregious remake of *Where the Boys Are*. But *Can't Stop the Music* remains to Carr's career what *Citizen Kane* was to Orson Welles's or the Mona Lisa to Leonardo's: the once-in-a-lifetime testament no artist could ever hope to conceive again.

CARVEL, TOM

According to Tom Carvel, founder of the 750-store chain of Carvel soft-serve ice-cream franchises, many Carvel store owners have an acute reaction to the radio advertisements that Mr. Carvel himself records for the company. They say, "Get that senile old goat off the air!"

By his own account, he cannot read a script and cannot work in a studio, and his diction and grammar are deficient. That is just the way he likes it, because Tom Carvel believes that people don't pay any attention to slick announcers with clear voices. "If you say 'uh, uh, uh,' people relate to that," he explained to *Advertising Age*. Saying "uh, uh, uh," mumbling and stammering his way through radio commercials for thirty-five years, Tom Carvel has made himself one of the most recognizable grating voices in broadcasting history.

In addition to the soft-serve, nasal convulsions of his own marble mouth, Carvel is known for featuring the voices of franchisees in his commercials. Many of them don't know the English language well; and even if they do, it is Carvel commercial etiquette for them to be so excruciatingly nervous that they are incoherent, giving at best one-word answers to Tom Carvel's leading questions about the high quality of the ice cream and its on-premises manufacturing process. It is also customary for the sound quality of the interviews to be awful: recorded by Tom Carvel himself, on location, with his portable tape recorder.

Tom Carvel has always been a do-it-yourself kind of businessman. He began his career in 1934 by borrowing fifteen dollars, buying some ice cream, and selling it from the back of a truck. When the truck blew a tire on Memorial Day, he pulled into a vacant parking lot in Hartsdale, New York, and plugged his refrigeration unit into the electrical lines of a pottery shop nearby. Business was so good that he bought the shop and turned

it into the first Carvel Ice Cream store, soon inventing and perfecting (and patenting) the machinery to make his own. In 1946 he began selling equipment to other stores, along with his expertise, for a flat fee and a percentage of the profits. By the early fifties he had twenty-five such stores on the East Coast. The term "franchising" was not yet familiar, but this was one of its earliest and most successful models. (Carvel was approached in the mid-fifties by another entrepreneur who wanted him to get in on the ground floor of a hamburger franchising operation. Carvel thought the entrepreneur, Ray Kroc, was a "dummy" and that his idea, McDonald's, would never work.)

Carvel soft-serve ice cream, which Mr. Carvel calls "gourmet" and "all-natural" in his advertisements, is billed as special because it is made without an air pump. This explains why it is dense and tarry, sodden enough to get extruded into cups and cones, yet so thick it will usually retain its tumid bloat even under sauce, nuts, and whipped topping. When oozed into molds and frozen solid, it changes character completely, turning from a custardlike secretion into colorful bricks of glacial protoplasm whose only

detectable resemblance to food is their vague sweetness. These chunks of frozen soft-serve ice cream are decorated with faces and sold as "ice cream cakes" named Fudgy the Whale and Cookie Puss. At Christmas, the Fudgy the Whale mold is used sideways so that Fudgy's fins resemble the top of a soft hat and Fudgy's torso becomes Santa Claus's face.

The tradition of tormenting advertisements began in 1955 when Tom Carvel heard a radio advertisement for the grand opening of a new Carvel store in Manhattan. He had paid $150 to have the ad read by the radio's disc jockey; but the deejay forgot to mention the borough in which the store was located. Furious, Carvel decided to take control. Knowing that he could never hope to sound like a pro, he wallowed in his inadequacies. "The more flubs, the better," he once said, using his mealymouthed ineptitude to establish what every advertiser dreams of: instant and unmistakable product identity.

CEDAR SOUVENIRS

Cedar souvenirs are knickknacks made of wood, polished and shellacked, and usually embossed with a sentiment, a laminated photograph, or the name of a tourist attraction. Cedar is the most common material, but there are similar mementoes made of pine (knotty or not), compressed wood chips, and even, rarely, redwood.

They come in many forms. The most majestic are wall plaques—oval slices cut from a small tree with a picture in the middle showing such images as Jesus in a crown of thorns, John Wayne in a cowboy hat, a Cheyenne warrior, a unicorn, or a single rose with the inscription ''Love Is Forever.'' On a nice wall plaque, the picture area is ringed with rough bark. Many plaques have mottos or epigrams instead of pictures. One of our personal favorite thought-provoking ones has this poem:

MOTHER-IN-LAW—
How blessed I am
How fortunate I've been
That you are his mother
And also my friend.

Other cedar souvenirs include cuss banks (you must put a coin in the box every time you cuss) and dog shot glasses, which are bar accessories composed of a cedar base that holds a shot glass, with a rubber dog positioned on the cedar base in such a way that he appears to be urinating into the glass. Many cedar souvenirs fall into a category known in the gift trade as ''bathroom knockers,'' meant to be put on the bathroom door. A typical bathroom knocker features a small hammer attached to a cedar plaque illustrated with a picture of a skunk. Another genre of cedar souvenir is the ''bedroom

GETTYSBURG, PA

mood meter," a plaque with an arrow on it. The arrow is supposed to be adjusted by the occupant of the bedroom to point like a compass to one of these categories: "I'm sleepy," "Sure," or "Tomorrow for sure."

Cedar souvenirs got popular after World War II, when gas rationing was lifted and the tourist industry began to prosper. Cedar was the material of choice because it was inexpensive and hardly more than a scrap of it was needed to fashion a little key holder or cuff-link box. In addition, it was readily available throughout the South and the Midwest, particularly in Missouri, North Carolina, and Kentucky. John S. Blair of the Blair Cedar and Novelty Company of Camdenton, Missouri, told us that people took to cedar because it smelled great and had a pretty red color. Blair, whose company is one of the biggest cedar suppliers in the country, added that cedar was especially attractive after the war because it was an American product—something the Japanese hadn't yet figured how to knock off.

Blair told us that just about the only places in America you won't find a full selection of cedar souvenirs are Walt Disney World and Disneyland. Nor will you ever see a Blair artifact with Mickey Mouse or Pluto on it. "Disney is a closed shop," Blair said. Hey, who needs a falsetto-voiced, big-eared mouse when you can have a manly hunk of cedar with a color picture of a twelve-point buck in the cross hairs of a telescopic sight underneath a coat of varnish as clear and smooth as a bowling alley, with a working electric clock just above the antlers?

CHARO

Charo, the dizzy, dancing, singing, joking sexpot, can say "coochie coochie" so exuberantly that her whole body (but especially her bust) convulses like a great big sneeze. A jumpsuited, off-color hybrid of José Jiminez and Gracie Allen, she has a cockeyed way with words that has endeared her to Merv and Johnny on talk shows and to audiences at Caesar's Palace in Las Vegas. ("When I hear whistles, I get bumps all over my goose," she tells wolf whistlers in the crowd.) In her nightclub act, punctuated by the famous coochie-coochie wriggle, she dances the frug (wearing platform wedgies) with male members of the audience while stripping them down to their shorts. Her performance also includes songs with a disco beat and a semiclassical guitar recital. While not generally known as an accomplished musician, she was chosen by readers of *Guitar Player* magazine as the third-best flamenco guitarist in the world, and her recording of "Stay with Me" hit the disco Top 100 charts in 1979.

Born Maria Rosario Pilar Martinez Molina Bazza in Murcia, Spain, in 1945, Charo was discovered by bandleader Xavier Cugat in the early sixties when he divorced Abby Lane and went looking for a new musical "protégée" with a Spanish accent. Early press releases said he found her in a convent, but in fact Charo was playing the juvenile lead in *Night of the Iguana* (at age sixteen) when Cugat decided to bring her back to the U.S.A. to develop her act at the Latin Quarter. When she made her solo debut in his musical revue at New York's Paramount Theater in 1965, the audience stomped and howled with joy as soon as she walked on stage wearing knee-high black boots and skin-tight pants and multicolored ribbons in her platinum hair. She jiggled as the Latin band played their gay-caballero rhythms and beat their bongo drums. Then Charo picked up her guitar and accompanied herself on "La Cucaracha" and "Hava Nagila."

Xavier Cugat was sixty-six and Charo was twenty-one when they married the following year —the first couple to exchange vows at Las Vegas's newly opened Caesar's Palace. Cugie showered her with Chihuahuas, one of which, named Delilah, wore a straw hat and prescription sunglasses; but Charo was not happy being married to the old man. "We were like father and daughter," she recalled. "We never made love all the time we were married. I'd rather have jumped off the Empire State Building." The Cugats were divorced in 1978, after which Charo petitioned a Las Vegas judge to legally lower her age by ten years. He complied, retroactively making her eleven years old when she became the fourth Mrs. Cugat. Four months after the divorce, she married Hollywood producer Kjeil (say "Shell") Rasten in a ceremony that featured Charo in a drastically low-cut wedding gown with a veiled bodice, the exchange of heart-shaped wedding rings, and a heart-shaped "Coupe Charo" wedding cake.

A connoisseur of what she called "extremely natural food," she told a New York *Daily News* interviewer that she liked lettuce and cucumber and salami-anchovy-pepperoni pizza but did not like pesticides. In 1985, she bought the Sandgroper Restaurant on Kauai, Hawaii, and renamed it Charo's. Based on its surf 'n' turf platter, its banana daiquiris and papaya coladas, and Charo's promise to appear on stage every night, the restaurant was awarded three stars by *People* magazine.

At one time the New York *Post* reported that she wanted to try a serious acting career and was planning to lose the farcical Castilian accent that hadn't diminished a bit in a quarter-century of living in America. "Maybe it's too late," she mused. "Maybe I gonna be less funny for people that think I talk funny, which I don't even know, but people say ha-ha-ha you talk funny. They think of coochie-coochie jumping bean, ha-ha-ha-ha."

See also **BREASTS, ENORMOUS; CHIHUAHUAS; LAS VEGAS**

CHIHUAHUAS

A Chihuahua is the smallest purebred dog in the world. Its bugged, watery eyes look sad; outsized bat ears dwarf its shivery domed skull; it is so light its toenails barely graze the floor when it skitters at you, yipping and growling. The American Kennel Club official chihuahua standard lists the maximum acceptable weight at six pounds but suggests no minimum; the smallest of them are one pound. The Kennel Club of Great Britain specifies ''given two equally good dogs, more diminutive preferred.'' ''Cute'' hardly seems an adequate word for a creature so miniaturized it can snooze happily inside a soft old shoe, a lady's purse, or mink muff.

Chihuahuas' ridiculously small size endeared them to what Thomas Hine has called the ''populuxe'' era of the fifties and sixties, when they were the most beloved of toy breeds. (In fact, Chihuahuas reached number three in registrations of *all* breeds in 1960, topped only by poodles and beagles.) The populuxe style reveled in distorted proportion. Tail fins and bosoms: The bigger the better! Ant Farms and sea monkeys: Tiny is wonderful! In this climate, Chihuahuas, the impossibly dwarfed doglets from Mexico, had their heyday. ''The modern Chihuahua has worked its way to a position among the leaders in the American dog world,'' wrote Maxwell Riddle in *This Is the Chihuahua* in 1959. ''Not only in the home, where he is the pet supreme, but in the show ring.'' One-pound specimens were sold by the thousands via mail-order advertisements in the backs of teen magazines that promised they were small enough to live inside a teacup.

If oversized and undersized things were both popular, putting the two together was doubly thrilling. That is how Chihuahuas achieved a glamorous aura—as the favorite cute little pet of big, bosomy starlets. Jayne Mansfield loved to clutch little six-inch Pepe to her forty-six-inch chest; and in June 1967, just weeks before she died, she expressed what might have been her last wish, for ''ten more babies and ten more Chihuahuas and a few Academy Awards.'' Well-stacked song stylist Charo used to have

Chihuahuas, too, although she came to resent them because they were gifts from her first husband, Xavier Cugat, in lieu of sex. (Cugat used to conduct his band with a baton in one hand, a Chihuahua in the other.) Linda Christian was another starlet who had a Chihuahua, named Mousie. In his book *Hollywood Babylon II* Kenneth Anger says that Mousie became so jealous of the bullfighters Miss Christian invited to her penthouse in Rome that he once shredded the ear of a bull that a torero brought her as a present. Anger says that Mousie became so dejected at his mistress's human friends that in June 1964, he jumped off her terrace and committed suicide.

Other than movie stars with enormous breasts, the people who like Chihuahuas best are burly redneck men. Truck drivers often travel with Chihuahuas because they are so easy to stow in the back of a sleeper cab. Rugged and masculine country singer Merle Haggard liked his Chihuahua-terrier mix Pepper so much, he held him close to his chest on the cover of the *Best of the Best of Merle Haggard* album in 1972, and disregarded traditional liner notes to tell the story of the time a whole Merle Haggard tour had to stop for hours so Pepper's mother, WaWe (daughter of Merle's beloved PeBe, and Merle's constant canine companion on tour), could give birth to puppies. The principle at work here is like the one that made Chihuahuas so right for sex queens of the big-bosom era: It is amusing to see a mighty manly person together with a squeaky pint-size dog. With big guys, there is additional fun in the way their machismo is echoed by the bark and bluster of a one-pound pooch.

In fact, Chihuahuas are excellent watchdogs. They love to snarl and yap, and they tend to be bold beyond all reason. Despite their characteristic trembling, they are fearless and will eagerly start fights with dogs a hundred times their size.

It has long been assumed Chihuahuas were first bred by Aztec Indians to be used as sacrifices at funerals. The 1577 journals of explorer Richard Eden mention ''dogges of

LePage

marvelous deformed shape'' that were raised for food by the Indians of Mexico; however, there is some speculation that Eden was confusing little dogs with a small rodent called the agouti. Another theory suggests that Chihuahuas were brought to California by the Chinese as late as the nineteenth-century gold rush. The Chinese ''dwarfed cherry, plum, and maple trees, fish, chickens, and most important for us, dogs,'' notes *This Is the Chihuahua.* Many of the Chinese settled along the Mexico—U.S. border, where the breed originated and got its name (after the Mexican state of Chihuahua).

What is known for certain is that James Watson, an American dog judge and author of the renowned *The Dog Book* in 1906, bought what was described to him as a ''Mexican Dog'' or ''Arizona Dog'' in El Paso in 1888. From that

day on, he wrote, he traveled thousands of miles with the dog in his coat pocket, never noticed by train conductors. A few dozen other similar dogs were imported into the U.S. by breeders, and in 1904 a little red dog named Midget became the first Chihuahua officially recognized by the American Kennel Club. The great early sire was a three-pounder named Caranza, who had a long red coat, a squirrel tail, and big fringed ears. From Caranza came the Meron and Perrito strains—names that became the Cartier and Tiffany of the Chihuahua world—who sired nearly all the champions of the twenties and thirties, and whose distant progeny are still prized today.

The Chihuahua Club of America was founded in 1923, but it wasn't until the fifties that the breed grew from an exotic oddity into a sought-after pet, and long-coated ones were officially distinguished from smooth-coated (the latter being the familiar, naked-looking pipsqueak). Myrle Hale, editor of *Los Chihuahuas* magazine, says the breed is especially prized because it smells less like a dog than like a cat. One unfortunate result of Chihuahuas' popularity was overbreeding, and because the "apple dome" round head is a desirable feature, many hurriedly developed bloodlines became plagued with the problem of hydrocephalic skulls, producing water on the brain. Most Chihuahuas, even healthy ones, have skulls that do not close completely as they grow, resulting in a soft spot on the top of the head.

Chihuahuas can live over twenty years; but longevity requires an adequate wardrobe. Because they are low to the ground, they are in the path of drafts that would go right underneath a normal-sized dog. Because a healthy Chihuahua bounces and barks vigorously, it burns calories way out of proportion to its size and therefore seldom develops a protective blanket of fat beneath its thin skin. Smooth-coated dogs in particular require plenty of clothes. "A sweater and raincoat are essentials," advised *How to Raise and Train a Chihuahua* in 1958; but the well-dressed Chihuahua will also have at least one quartet of booties, a rain hat, a sun hat, a nightcap, and flannel pajamas. Stylish sportswear such as sombreros, miniaturized harlequin sunglasses, and two-piece swimsuits have been ingredients of the basic Chihuahua look since the fifties. And as for formal wear, no dog except perhaps the poodle looks as right in a leopard-skin collar, ermine coat, tiny tiara, and rhinestone leash.

See also **BAKKER, TAMMY FAYE; CHARO; MANSFIELD, JAYNE**

CHILDREN'S NAMES

Several years ago, when droves of parents were naming their daughters Tiffany, they probably liked to envision the future: their Tiffany a ravishing heiress, racing home from yet another deb party, dripping a bottle of bubbly in one jeweled hand while leaning on the arm of a firm-jawed young scion. If you want to go looking for Tiffanys now, however, you won't likely find them at the cotillion or opening night at the opera. Instead, look in the mall, in stores with such names as the Mane Event or Shear Magic, where Tiffany the beautician will most likely be putting the finishing mousse injections into a shag haircut. Unlike Tiffany the store, Tiffany the name has lost all its class.

Other than a twenty-pound goiter, a bad name is about the most embarrassing thing a person can have to drag around all his or her life. It might even be dangerous. When the Circuit Court of Cook County, Illinois, did a study of nearly two hundred criminally deranged people, half of whom had normal names and half of whom had creative ones (Oder and Lethal were given as examples), they discovered that the weird-named lunatics committed four times as many crimes as the Bobs, Freds, and Bills.

At no time was the practice of inventive naming more abused than at the dawn of the Age of Aquarius, when names like John and Mary were replaced by New Age monikers like Sunshine and Sioux (the hippie spelling of Sue), America (Abbie Hoffman's son), god (Grace Slick's kid, spelled humbly with a small g), Free (son of David Carradine and Barbara Hershey, then going by the name Barbara Seagull), and Zowie Bowie (son of David). The nuttiest collection of do-your-own-thing names belongs to the family of actor River Phoenix, whose father (a mere John) named the other children Rainbow, Liberty, Summer, Joy, and Leaf. Frank Zappa blessed his children with the names Moon Unit and Dweezil. Almost as

humiliating as an addled name is a normal name that is spelled creatively—a slightly more subtle attempt to ensure that the child can never consider himself normal. Linda Rosenkrantz and Pamela Redmond Satran, authors of *Beyond Jennifer & Jason,* document this phenomenon by listing such ludicrous variants of Alicia as Alisha, Alysia, Alyssa, Elissa, Elyssa, Ilysa, as well as the oddities Jaysen, Kristoffer, Crystine, Holli, and Malissa.

Plain old ugly names are not really in bad taste, although they statistically guarantee lower grades in school and less respect in adult society. Anyone named Egbert or Clyde or Bertha will be laughed at until death, but people with merely oafish names tend to acquire a certain nobility of spirit by bearing up and surviving despite their handicap. On the other hand, affected names, given by parents who ought to know better, *are* in bad taste—usually the futile effort of people trying to help their children climb the social ladder.

Each decade contributes its own faux pas. The fifties, days of coq au vin and clipped poodles, populated America with such French rococo doozies as Suzette, Fifi, Renee, Babette, and Robespierre—especially spurious-sounding when mismatched with non-Gallic ethnic names, producing such oddities as Mignon Goldblatt and Michelle Caputo. The sixties were responsible not only for harebrained hippie names but for the beginnings of the plague of Jason and Jennifer, which was going full bore by the seventies. Nobody has been able to pin down the absolute beginnings of the popularity of the frightful Js, but equal credit for Jennifer is probably due Erich Segal, whose heroine in *Love Story* was named Jenny, and singer Donovan for the popular ditty "Jennifer Juniper." Jason's origins are mysterious, too; but we suspect it was prized for its aura of Wild West bravado, and because Jason sounded like the kind of rough-hewn guy that a pretty girl like Jennifer would want to marry. About this time, a going-back-to-the-roots spirit caused many newborns to get saddled with names of sturdy pioneers such as Ethan, Lucas, and Shane.

I Love Tiffany

Black parents began paying homage to their roots by giving their children African names such as Ashanti, Camisha, Rashida, and Ajani. Some adults even changed their own names, starting with basketball player Lou Alcindor, who became Kareem Abdul-Jabbar in 1971; and after 1977, when the immensely popular television program *Roots* made a big issue out of slave names versus African names, many proud black parents sought out names that made their children seem African, Muslim—anything but white-bread American. To observe this phenomenon in all its richness, all you need do is study the cast credits of television's ''Cosby,'' which includes a Phylicia, a Tempestt, a Keshia, a Malcolm-Jamal, and a Raven-Symoné.

White babies born in the late seventies and early eighties, no matter what their inherited ethnic roots, had a good chance of getting a Celtic or French name that satisfied their parents' craving to sound sophisticated rather than plain. Kindergartens filled up with Danielles, Nicoles, Megans, Brendans, Ryans, Bryans, Shannons, and Seans. In a similar vein, many eighties names were chosen because they reeked of high finance and good breeding—as it is portrayed on daytime and prime-time soap operas. This was the age of Tiffany and her pals Courtney, Chelsea, Whitney, Morgan, Lauren, and Kimberly, as well as Brittany (''Another World''), Alexis (''Dynasty''), Brandy (''The Edge of Night''), Chase (''Falcon Crest''), Brooke (''All My Children''), and Sloane (the now defunct ''Capital'').

We are now in the midst of a new era of brute names chosen in reaction to the ostentatious ones popular ten years ago. Max, Jake, Harry, and Sam used to be big, smelly men who smoked wet cigars and yelled at people on the telephone. Now they are toddling little boys. Girls are getting off only slightly better in this trend, which is apparently popular because parents want to emphasize that they are unaffected regular Joes. While they may not sound like they were born to run a garment-center business or a cheap detective agency like the boys, girls with such new names as Emily, Hannah, and Molly sound all too ready to spend their lives asleep with cats on their laps.

Girls' names are more faddish than boys' names. In a recent survey done by Dr. Kenneth L. Dion of the University of Toronto, the venerable Michael was still rated the most popular boy's name in America, as it has been for decades. For girls, however, Danielle was number one (after author Danielle Steel?), with such arrivistes as Melissa, Lauren, Jennifer, and Kimberly close behind. Tiffany scored in the seventieth percentile, just below Corinne but way above plain Jane, Abigail, and Florence. At the bottom of the list, the least popular names in North America, were Hortense, Fanny, and Bertha. Yetta wasn't even indexed.

One of the major dangers of choosing a strange name is that like so many fads, it becomes a badge of shame if you keep it around too long. Unlike a Beatle wig, elephant bell bottoms, or a troll doll, a name is not necessarily easy to discard (although Free Carradine became Tom as soon as he had anything to say about it; and Zowie Bowie has renamed himself Joey). One of the strangest phenomena of name evolution is the way some of the names that only a few years ago seemed to signify class and status have now wound up in whorehouses. Sydney Biddle Barrows, ''the Mayflower Madam,'' understood how such names worked as part of her girls' sex appeal. In her book *Mayflower Madam* she suggests prostitutes use names with a high-class image: Brent, Brooke, Avery, Blaine, or Ashley. All formerly classy, such names are now considered by experts to be downwardly mobile, thus allowing male clients to believe they are buying a piece of faded nobility. One name that even the Mayflower Madam rejected, however, was Tiffany. She said it made a girl sound too much like a hooker.

CHIPPENDALES

One of the less elegant spin-offs from women's liberation is male strippers—well-oiled beefcakes who dance on stage wearing little more than tuxedo collars and cuffs, propelling their bulging crotches in the direction of anyone waving a dollar bill. While it is possible to regard this phenomenon as evidence of real equality between the sexes, it also proves the less gladdening fact that given the opportunity, women can be every bit as goatish and vulgar as men.

Rick Dietz of the Los Angeles Chippendales

It began in 1979 when Steve Banerjee opened a Hollywood nightclub called Chippendales, featuring a cast of male exotic dancers and a women-only policy at the door. Before Chippendales, the only place to see men taking off their clothes in a seductive manner was a gay bar. But the Chippendales dancers were something new: They flaunted hetero appeal. Floods of articles and television news features made this novel exercise in sexual role reversal into a gold mine for Steve Banerjee, and he opened branches of Chippendales in New York, Dallas, and Denver. He also began marketing Hot Hunk calendars, videotapes (*Tall, Dark, and Handsome*), greeting cards, and scanty male underwear. ''Girls night out'' at Chippendales quickly became an institution popular among brides-to-be and horny grandmas celebrating birthdays.

Chippendales dancers perform a macho version of the classic burlesque striptease, a muscular bump-and-grind that quickly rids them of whatever stage outfits they wear and enables them to get down to the business of dangling their well-padded G-strings before mesmerized women who have never seen anything quite like this. The power of a Chippendales evening to turn meek ladies into lust-crazed banshees screaming for a grab of tush is legendary.

The most provocative highlight of a Chippendales routine is the ritual called ''kiss-'n'-tips,'' wherein a nearly naked dancer circles among the whooping female spectators, exchanging big wet ones for the folded currency the ladies wave in his direction. Bold members of the audience make their cash deposits directly into the performer's basket; some may even cling to him, wrapping their legs around his waist, riding him around the room like a horse. For a Chippendales star, tips can add up to $1,200 a night, on top of a base salary of between $400 and $600 a week.

Like the singing group the Village People,

Chippendales men come on stage dressed as archetypal studs: a construction worker, a cowboy, a cop, a lifeguard, a chauffeur. The big, muscular soloists need not be trained dancers like the chorus boys who caper behind them. They are chosen to star because they exude a certain breathtaking masculinity and cockiness. Michael Rapp, for example, who has been with the club since 1982 and is known as the Ultimate Chippendale, is a six-foot-four, 210-pound brunet billed simply as "the Sex Symbol."

Chippendales dancers are known by their first names but also by a title. The gorgeous guy who comes out dressed like a priest is Scott, "the Missionary Man"; the humpy hotel servant is John, "Room Service"; and platinum-tressed Eddie, like the eternal goddess Marilyn Monroe, is known simply as "the Blond." In creating soloists' characters, Chippendales borrows a lesson from the golden days of *Playboy* magazine. Just as Playmates were carefully presented as the girls next door (lest they be mistaken for prostitutes), so the "Chips" are bequeathed hale and hearty résumés to make sure the nice ladies in the audience do not think they are being turned on by hustlers.

Programs for Chippendales shows introduce Michael Rapp as a former Catholic schoolboy who graduated from Don's Bock College of Nutrition (sic) while working as a health instructor at Jack La Lanne. Bobby Hill was first runner-up in the 1984 Mr. America Male Beauty Pageant and is an actor in Purina Dog Chow and Aqua Velva commercials. Dean Mammales is a former predental student whose goal is to work hard enough to "retire his father." On a more personal note we learn that John ("Room Service") Rosado is socially conscious and believes that Sally Struthers is the woman who has made the greatest contribution to the world.

This strange upbeat twist to bumping and grinding is what makes male striptease so much more ludicrous than the traditional female variety. Female strippers are what they are: sexy. Nobody came to see Tempest Storm because she had a B.A. in electrical engineering. But it is not enough that the Chippendales look like Greek gods and dance their audience into a frenzy of sexual heat. Their image is carefully crafted to conjure up not only sex but "class." In addition to being hot and horny, they are educated, refined, and love their parents deeply. They are meant to invoke fantasies of champagne and limos, tuxedos and romantic bubble baths à deux in front of roaring fireplaces. It is a view of sex and romance taken straight from game shows like "The Love Connection."

One of the recent Chippendales productions, "Welcome to Your Fantasy," is exquisitely described in its program as "hints and allegations all pertaining to a world of sensuality not yet physically described on stage. It is a show that creates an environment unequalled in the poetic translation of the senses." The theme of the show is a Fantasy Weekend in which members of the audience meet their dream guys, one by one, as the guys perform "I Want Your Sex" and "Dynamite." Producer and choreographer Steve Merritt said that this show differs from previous Chippendales productions in that the performers wear shirts underneath their leather jackets and briefs underneath their pants. "The more you leave to the imagination, the better it is," he explained.

Even *Ms.* magazine seemed to approve of the tasteful male strip shows after a reporter spent a night at Chippendales (for a friend's mother's seventieth birthday) and felt "high off being with so many other women." The article applauded the liberating effect of all that male muscle power on the distaff audience: "Where else could women go out and kick back like that, maybe in a gay women's bar, I don't know."

CHRISTMAS TREES, ARTIFICIAL

Decimating spruce and pine forests and putting the cut-down dead trees in a living room is the ostensibly tasteful way to celebrate Christmas. The bad-taste way is to buy an artificial Christmas tree. Polypropylene trees are well-established indications of vulgarian sensibility, even though the best of them cost far more than once-living trees and leave the forest green. Fake trees' bad standing is simply a matter of the most basic kind of modern product snobbery, which insists that genuine things are always better than their man-made imitations.

Natural as they may be, and as much as right-thinking people rejoice in nature, real trees can be exhausting to maintain and ugly to look at. They are often lopsided, deformed, and dried out by the time they get from the forest to the lot to the living room; they shed needles that clog and destroy vacuum cleaners; sometimes they tilt awkwardly, waiting for the family dog to brush against them and send them crashing to the floor, smashing ornaments and flooding the carpet with water from the stand.

Fake Christmas trees present no such problems. For one thing, they are infinitely more creative than nature's best. J. Callaway's Christmas World stores (headquartered in Tempe, Arizona, but with branches all over the U.S.A.) offer trees in all shades of green, in white and silver, purple, pink, and puce. Synthetic trees come with needles that look just like a Douglas fir's or a Scotch pine's real ones, or with needles that resemble spinach linguine or a spun-sugar croquembouche. Some have no needles at all; they are thick with creative foliage in the form of extruded plastic tendrils, shoots, or rubber tentacles. Many come with artificial snowlike imprints already on the branches, thus saving the owner the trouble of spraying on artificial snow or hanging tinsel every year.

And talk about convenience! Safely stored away in the attic, artificial trees fold up neatly as an umbrella. They don't dry out and become fire hazards. The best of them disassemble completely into color-coded, numbered parts, thus ensuring that when it comes time to screw the tree together, you don't accidentally implant the big branches on the top and the little branches on the bottom. Once the man-made wonder is assembled, you can spray it with aerosol pine scent to give it the holiday aroma that real tree aficionados claim is the reason they would never go fake.

Contrary to their age-of-polyester image, imitation trees have a lineage that goes back to

the mid–nineteenth century, when shopkeepers in Lauscha, Germany, made goose-feather trees as a means of displaying their glass ornaments year-around. Like their modern petrochemical-derived counterparts, the goose-feather trees were dyed in strident pinks, yellows, and blues; unlike contemporary artificial trees, they were carefully hand-crafted, the feathers held together by invisible wires. Feather trees, which were made until the early fifties, are today valuable antiques.

Some modern trees are so sturdy that they are suitable for outdoor use. The Sears catalogue offers "instant shrubbery" in the form of a seven-and-a-half-foot-tall fluffy-limbed Scotch pine made of polyvinylchloride. It comes with a sharp stake at the bottom just waiting to be hammered into the ground; and like its indoor counterparts, it is flame-resistant and insect-proof—"everything wished for in a live tree, and more."

The creative possibilities of decking artificial boughs have inspired many people to use Christmas as the opportunity to let their love of embellishment go hog wild. Liberace decorated his Hollywood penthouse with ten trees, all covered with twinkle lights and fresh flowers in tiny bud vases. At his condominium in Malibu, he had one black-lacquered tree hung with mirrors and crystals and liked it so much he kept it up year-round. Malcolm Forbes once decorated a tree with one- and five-dollar bills folded into origami shapes. If you would like to follow in such imaginative footsteps but don't have the imagination, time, or energy to do so, all you need do is hire a Hollywood company named Christmas Fantasy Ltd. to do your tree designing for you. They have supplied celebrities (including Linda Ronstadt and Candy Spelling) with fifty-thousand-dollar pottery crèches and four-hundred-fifty-dollar porcelain doll's-head ornaments wearing butterfly masks for their trees. And when actress Barbara Carrera said she wanted a Santa Fe look, they supplied her with a

two-thousand-dollar, eight-foot artificial Colorado pine covered with what *People* magazine described as "amber lights and desert-hued balls."

Once your Natural Mountain King "Quick-A-Tree-90 Model AT 84-355-90" has been assembled and staked, it can then be garlanded with a wealth of other unnatural things, such as plastic icicles, glow-in-the-dark spray-on aerosol flocking, fiberglass "angel hair," strands of rubberized reusable popcorn, four-way flashing lights, and electronic microprocessor ornaments that play Christmas music at the clap of a hand. After the tree is decked, only one element remains to complete the Christmas scene; a videotape player with a TV monitor where the fireplace and fire would be. Slap in one of the popular Yule-log tapes (available with a sound track of either cheerful carolers or a crackling fire), and the warmth and good cheer of the Yuletide can be yours. If a video fire is just too phony for you, there is an option: Go to the Christmas store and buy a life-size cardboard fireplace with an electric rotating simulated fire log (crackling fire sound effects not included).

COOL WHIP

Cool Whip may be in bad taste, but that doesn't mean it tastes bad. To the millions of Cool Whip connoisseurs who plop it on instant puddings or add it to baroque gelatin desserts, it is everything that whipped cream should be, but better.

Like artificial Christmas trees and fake fingernails, Cool Whip thumbs its nose at Mother Nature and flaunts industrial superiority. Anything a cow can do, your grocer's freezer case can do better. Whipped cream is fragile; Cool Whip is party hardy. Whipped cream spoils quickly; Cool Whip lasts for weeks. Whipped cream has only one boring ingredient in it—cream; Cool Whip is a chemist's delight, filled with such things as sorbitan monostearate, polysorbate 60, and xanthum gum. Whipped cream comes from a smelly old udder; Cool Whip arrives in a nice white plastic tub that you can use for storing leftovers after the Cool Whip is gone.

Cool Whip enjoys godly status among American homemakers (one out of three buys it regularly, according to the Market Research Institute). Leaf through almost any self-published, spiral-bound cookbook from the heartland and, even if you are a Cool Whip connoisseur yourself, you will be flabbergasted by the many clever uses to which it is put. It serves as topping for icebox cakes, leavener in mile-high pies, glue in "Millionaire's Salad" (combined with a cup each of crushed pineapple, sweetened coconut, mandarin orange segments, and miniature marshmallows), filling for tortes, and mortar for "Rice and Cherries in the Snow." The *Walnut* [Iowa] *Centennial Cookbook,* for instance, is well stocked with recipes such as "Everlasting Desserts" and gelatinized "Prune Salad" that combine eye-popping lists of ingredients, including cheddar cheese cubes, Coca-Cola, Miracle Whip, and Jell-O with tides of Cool Whip.

In old-fashioned days, when a housewife wanted nondairy whipped topping, she had to open a box of Cool Whip's predecessor, Dream Whip Whipped Topping Mix, beat it, flavor it, and chill it. Dream Whip certainly had its advantages over whipped cream: it didn't wilt or separate, and it stayed fresh in its box on an unrefrigerated shelf indefinitely. But it wasn't really instant, and

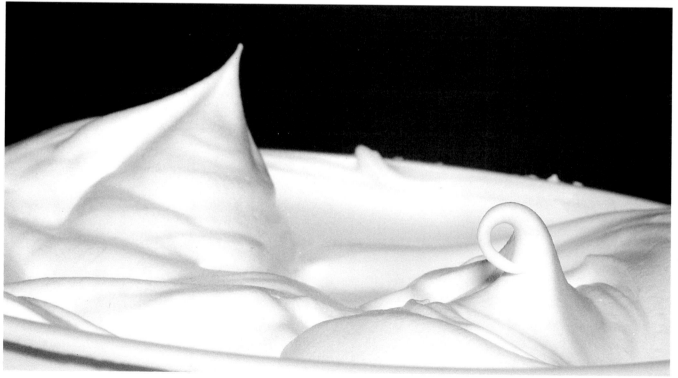

ROCKY ROAD MICROWAVE CAKE

2 eggs
8 ounces (3½ cups) Cool Whip, thawed
30 chocolate wafers, crushed into crumbs (1½ cups)
1 cup semi-sweet chocolate chips
½ cup miniature marshmallows
¼ cup chopped nuts

Beat eggs in large bowl with fork. Fold in Cool Whip, crumbs, and ¾ cup of chocolate chips until just blended. (Batter will be white with specks of chocolate crumbs.) Spread in greased 2 quart microwavable round dish at least 2 inches deep.

Cook at medium (50%) 5 minutes. Rotate dish half-turn and cook at high 4½ to 5½ minutes or until cake starts to pull away from side of dish and is just slightly moist.

Place serving plate on top of dish and invert cake at once. Sprinkle hot cake with remaining chips, marshmallows, and nuts.
Yield: 8 servings

making it soiled mixing bowls and utensils. Cool Whip—ready to defrost and eat—was introduced in 1965, and the following year helped sponsor America's number-three-rated TV program, ''The Andy Griffith Show.'' In 1970 Cool Whip Swiggle was introduced in an accordion dispenser to help consumers create merry swirls of topping on pies and cakes; but it has been the tub packages—allowing open access to big spoons, spatulas, or impatient tongues—that have persevered.

The uses of Cool Whip are apparent to anyone with a sweet tooth; but recently we came into possession of this rather miraculous recipe for a Cool Whip baked dessert, devised by an inventive cook at General Foods. It shows how Cool Whip has entered the age of nuked food with high style.

COZIES

Since the duchess of Bedford originated afternoon tea two hundred years ago, the ceremony of serving it has become encrusted with traditions, including the custom of keeping the teapot inside a cozy. A cozy is a thick jacket, usually quilted, that keeps the pot warm while the tea is brewing. There is a secondary reason for using one: a cozy disguises a gauche teapot and can make even a clunky old iron kettle seem friendly and snug. It is this purpose that has inspired multitudes of American craftspeople to develop a class of household object known also as a cozy, the purpose of which is to camouflage something ugly.

Homes are filled with things people don't want to look at, and it isn't always feasible to hide them in closets or the basement. Case in point: the spare roll of toilet paper. For obvious reasons, you want it easily accessible, within arm's reach of the commode. However, many people find the sight of a roll of toilet paper abhorrent, or at least unpleasant. The solution is to keep it inside a toilet-paper cozy. The simplest toilet-paper cozy can be nothing more than a crocheted muff in rainbow colors, which converts the unsightly roll of bun wad into a festive decorative cylinder atop the toilet tank. A more creative solution to the problem is to secret the spare roll underneath the broad antebellum dress of a Miss Powder Room Southern Belle Cozy Doll, who instead of legs has a single dowel underneath her petticoats, sized to fit inside the roll's cardboard tube and thus keep Miss Powder Room upright and the distasteful roll of tissue hidden where her petticoats should be.

Ideas for toilet-paper cozies have filled crafts magazines since the fifties: angora poodles standing up and begging, macramé angels with robes big enough to hold the roll, scraps-o'-yarn mushrooms, knitted flowers, granny-spare-roll apple dolls with heads carved from fresh, peeled apples (then shrunk and sprayed with fixative), and even red-and-green felt Christmas trees so tall they can shroud two rolls and thus accommodate all the extra use a bathroom gets during the holidays. Our *Burlap Bounty* crafts book from the mid-sixties suggests a pattern for Homespun Hide-A-Boo, a doll made from a stemmed plastic head (available in handicrafts shops) and burlap decorated with velvet ribbon and scraps of old stockings—sufficiently capacious to hide toilet tissue as well as bottles of bath powder or lotion and a battery of hair curlers.

The development of soft-sculpture crafts in the seventies opened new vistas for cozy artisans. People working in soft-sculpture media pioneered the creation of big, lolling heads and swollen faces on cute-ugly gnomes named Gork, Dwork, Nweeb, etc. These techniques were soon grafted onto cozy aesthetics, allowing cozy makers to develop cozies for things no one ever considered disguisable, on a scale heretofore unimagined. Today in any good crafts fair or flea market you will find tall, skinny, banana-headed cozies for plungers, cozies with inebriated faces for shrouding jugs of cheap wine on the table, and even cozies shaped like big, gaping mouths to enclose unsightly telephones. The most striking of the modern creations is the vacuum-cleaner cozy, which completely covers a four-foot-tall upright vacuum or carpet sweeper from floor to handle, making it look like a granny, a gramps, or a witch (your choice). An unattractive appliance is thus transformed into a work of art with dilapidated tennis shoes for feet and a lifelike head made of stuffed, recycled panty hose.

See also **PANTY-HOSE CRAFTS**

A liquor-bottle cozy

DAY-GLO COLORS

When you walk through the woods or along a sunlit stream that seems untouched by civilization, there is one glimmering vision certain to reassure you of humankind's dominion: a flash of Day-Glo color, in the form of a discarded jug of Depend-O Toilet Cleaner or an eye-aching piece of plastic camping equipment. That is the purpose of Day-Glo colors: to attract attention by being more yellow, orange, red, or pink than anything in the real world.

Day-Glo colors did not always exist. With the exception of some exotic parrots and rare fish, the planet earth was home to nothing that resembled the freakish hues first synthesized in the thirties by brothers Bob and Joe Switzer of Cleveland in a series of experiments with dye and resin. The Switzers' incandescent colors were first used to frighten and amaze people in magic shows and for theatrical productions that required a glow-in-the-dark effect even under stage lights (e.g., an eerie speed-skating luminous skeleton in an ice show). The brilliant tints were then adopted by the army for signal work during World War II. In the late fifties, Procter & Gamble discovered the Switzers' fluorescent orange and yellow pigments and put them on a shimmering, spiral-patterned box for Tide. In the world of laundry-detergent marketing, where product names are chosen for their punch, Day-Glo colors gave packagers the opportunity to sock consumers square in the eyeballs.

For a short while in the psychedelic sixties, when it seemed impossible to be too bright or too vulgar, the Switzers' phosphorescent colors —mostly pink, orange, and yellow—were actually fashionable. Acid heads who eagerly embraced any mind-blowing sensory experience used them on rock-concert posters. Op art, which was based on the aesthetic tenet that great paintings ought to seem to shimmy, gave the screaming hues an avant-garde appeal. Mod miniskirts, rain slickers, and vinyl caps were made in riots of yellow polka dots and shocking-pink stripes.

Trademarked as Day-Glo to signify their daylight-fluorescent properties, the Switzers' colors today are sold by the Day-Glo Color Corporation as dry pigment, inks, and paints to the plastics and fabric industries. Day-Glo is used in the production of blow-molded bottles, cartons, pails, Big Wheels bicycles, clothes for hunters to wear so other hunters don't mistake them for prey, and water-sport, camping, and ski equipment. "The great thing about Day-Glo fluorescent colors," company literature boasts, "is that you can't miss them."

DEATH CARS OF FAMOUS PEOPLE

Any fatal highway accident can exude a macabre magnetism when you drive past, but it is a special thrill to see the car in which a famous person died, especially if it is a twisted wreck. You can imagine the famous person tooling along just like you might do, then, *whammo*—the calamity happens—and he or she is dead; the bigger-than-life person exists no more. The shattered vehicle becomes a kind of memento mori with the added luster of celebrity blood.

The first of the famous death cars was Bonnie and Clyde's, a 1934 tan V-8 Ford they stole from Ruth and Jesse Warren. Twenty-three days and seventy-five hundred miles after they took it from the Warrens' driveway in Topeka, Kansas, the legendary bank robbers were eating bacon-and-tomato sandwiches while cruising slowly up a hill outside the town of Gibsland in the pine hills of northern Louisiana. At the crest of the hill, they were ambushed by Texas Ranger Frank Hamer and a band of Bienville Parish patrolmen. Bonnie was hit fifty times by shotgun and rifle fire; Clyde took twenty-seven bullets; both died instantly. Although perforated by 107 slugs, the Ford was mechanically unharmed.

As the police watched, local curiosity seekers stormed the car, gathering pieces of broken glass, tearing away bloodstained upholstery, and snipping locks of Bonnie Parker's hair. One especially eager souvenir-hunter was stopped by the coroner as he tried to saw off one of Clyde Barrow's ears.

Ruth Warren, the car's rightful owner, came to drive it home, horrifying her family when she arrived back in Topeka with the V-8 Ford still in unadulterated death-car condition—whistling full of bullet holes, its interior splattered with Bonnie's and Clyde's brains. Mrs. Warren leased the car to Charles Stanley, the "crime doctor" of Cleveland, who took it on tour around the country throughout the thirties, then put it on permanent display in a Cincinnati amusement park.

The car was bought for $14,500 in 1952 by a showman named Ted Toddy, who displayed it in movie theaters to promote his ganster movie *Killers All;* but by the fifties, according to Carrol Y. Rich, who wrote about "Clyde Barrow's Last Ford" in the *Journal of Popular Culture,* there were at least five phony Bonnie and Clyde death cars making the rounds of carnivals and shopping centers. After the success of the movie *Bonnie and Clyde* in 1967, Toddy put the car on tour once again, telling Rich, "I've seen people kneel before it or do the sign of the Cross. Women have walked away weeping." At last report, Bonnie and Clyde's car was owned by Hollywood stunt man and car collector Jay Ohrberg (who also boasts the *Pink Panther* limousine and a sixty-foot-long Cadillac).

Unlike Bonnie and Clyde's car, which looked pretty good despite the slaughter and its bullet holes, James Dean's death car was a real mess. A silver Porsche 550 Spyder with the number 130 painted on each door and on the hood and "Little Bastard" in red across the rear cowling, it was built as a serious competition vehicle, and bought by Dean for the purpose of racing. Driving it out to a race at the Salinas Airport on September 30, 1955, he got a ticket for doing 65 mph in a 55 mph zone. North of Bakersfield, seventy miles from his destination, Dean decided to exercise the engine. Drivers he passed later estimated he was going at least 130 mph before he slammed head-on into Donald Turnipseed's 1950 Ford Tudor, which was cutting across his lane to make a left turn. Dean broke his neck and died. Miraculously Turnipseed walked away, as

did the passenger in the Porsche, Rolf Weutherich, Dean's mechanic.

James Dean's father, Winton Dean, sold the wreck to Hollywood car customizer George Barris, who in turn sold its usable mechanical components to Dr. Troy McHenry. (McHenry's October 1956 death crash in his own Spyder, built from parts of Dean's car, helped give James Dean's death its ghostly mystique.) Barris took the aluminum scraps of car body that remained, welded them into one big silver glob, and put it on exhibit as "James Dean's Death Car" at the 1956 International Motor Sports Show in Hollywood, along with a placard warning gawkers that this might happen to them, too, if they exceeded the speed limit. All pieces of the metal mass that could be torn or hacked off were filched by onlookers; and to this day, a piece of death car is one of the most sought-after objects of James Dean memorabilia.

To prevent such pilferage, modern-day death cars are customarily displayed behind glass. The worst-looking of them all is Sheriff Buford Pusser's 1974 Corvette, on exhibit at Carbo's Police Museum in Pigeon Forge, Tennessee. Because it was made of fiberglass, the formerly maroon car melted when it crashed and burned, so the remains are nothing but a charcoal mass, resembling licorice drippings atop the steel frame.

Pusser, the club-wielding Tennessee folk hero whose battle against corruption was depicted in the *Walking Tall* movies, had been shot by enemies eight times, stabbed seven times, and run over once. His jaw was shot off in an ambush (which killed his wife) in 1967. But he kept on fighting the bad guys.

On the night of August 21, 1974, after being featured in the Jaycees' dunking barrel at the McNairy County Fair, Pusser sat in the front seat of his Corvette eating two pork sandwiches and a fried fish sandwich from Coleman's Bar-B-Q. He sped off toward home along U.S. 64 at 100 mph, zooming past his daughter Dwana, also heading for home in her Chevrolet sedan. At the crest of a hill, Pusser lost control. The car left the road, skidded onto the gravel shoulder, spun back onto the pavement, tore up a stop sign in front of a small country store, and slammed into a red clay embankment, sending Pusser out through the T-top and onto the highway. As the Corvette burned and Pusser lay on the ground with a broken neck, Dwana approached and found him on the pavement. ''Daddy's dead this time,'' she sobbed. The lumpy black wreck of a car is now part of what is billed as ''the world's largest authentic Buford Pusser exhibit,'' which includes his sheriff's desk, his size 14D shoes, and artifacts from the *Walking Tall* movies.

Another awful wreck behind glass is Jayne Mansfield's death car, a silver 1966 Buick Electra 225 kept in a big see-through box in the backyard garden of the St. Augustine, Florida, Tragedy in U.S. History Museum (just across the street from the Fountain of Youth). Unfortunately, because it is stored outside, the car has developed a severe spotty rust problem; nonetheless, it is easy to see by the way the top of the car is ripped off and peeled back how basically the same thing happened to Jayne Mansfield's head on that foggy morning of June 29, 1967, when the Buick plowed into the back of a truck.

The Tragedy in U.S. History Museum is a lode of death-car memorabilia. Also on display are the ambulance used to carry JFK killer Lee Harvey Oswald to the hospital after he was shot by Jack Ruby, the car Oswald got a lift in the morning he went to shoot Kennedy, and a limousine Kennedy once rode in (but not the day he was shot). Near Jayne Mansfield's death car in the backyard is Bonnie and Clyde's rusting bullet-riddled Ford . . . from the movie. (In addition to morbid automobilia, the museum boasts Oswald's bedroom furniture, two human skeletons from the city's Old Spanish Jail, antique torture equipment, and a beeping video game next to a facsimile of Elvis Presley's last will and testament.)

It is not necessary for someone to have actually died in a car for it to be a valid death car. In the late 1950s,

county fairs in the Midwest featured a 1949 maroon Ford that had been used by Ed Gein, the human cannibal of Plainfield, Wisconsin, whose ghoulish crimes inspired (the considerably sanitized) *Psycho*. Used by Gein to bring home dead bodies dug up at the local cemetery and to deliver friendly packages of ''venison'' to neighbors, as well as to haul various body parts around town for piece-by-piece burial, the Ford was billed as ''the car that hauled the dead from their graves.''

The latest thing in death cars is *near*-death cars, as found at the Country Music Museum in Gatlinburg, Tennessee, which advertises, ''See the Jaguar Barbara Mandrell drove in her near-fatal collision.'' The twisted silver Jag, which Miss Mandrell wrecked on September 11, 1984, in a head-on crash with nineteen-year-old Mark White on Highway 31E outside of Hendersonville, Tennessee (in which White died), was featured in her ''Please buckle up—you may never get another chance'' poster. It is on exhibit along with her 1982 fire-engine-red Ferrari, which she sold as soon as she got out of the hospital. ''Miss Mandrell doesn't hardly drive at all anymore,'' a museum guide informed us.

See also **MANSFIELD, JAYNE; SMOKY MOUNTAINS**

DESIGNER JEANS

Designer jeans are blue jeans that cost extra because they have the name of somebody fashionable stitched on the back pocket. The famous name gives them status and therefore makes the person who wears them feel more important than someone who wears ordinary Levi's.

Before 1978, few people could have imagined that blue jeans would become a status symbol. Denim, which takes its name from *serge de Nîmes* (Nîmes being the city in southern France where indigo-dyed trousers were invented in the 1500s), had always been material for work clothes, especially as purveyed in the American West by the Levi-Strauss company. Jeans were farmers' breeches or miners' overalls, the uniform of lumberjacks and cowpokes. The 1938 Sears catalogue's inventory included such rugged-named denims as "Sturdy Oaks" ("worn by hundreds of thousands of working men on the farm, in the village, and in our biggest cities"), "Hercules" (available in waist sizes up to 56 inches), and "Drum Major" ("Strength, and plenty of it: No skimpy garments from Sears!"). When dude-ranch vacations became popular in the thirties, tinhorns sometimes brought their sturdy Levi's home with them to wear for working around the house.

After World War II blue jeans became a uniform for teenagers, beatniks, and anybody else who wanted to show contempt for the vagaries of fashion. Jeans were *honest,* surly clothes, defiantly anti—middle class, fit for the likes of Wild One Marlon Brando and Rebel Without a Cause James Dean. It was especially thrilling among insolent greasers (girls *and* boys) to wear them skintight, an effect best achieved by squeezing into a wet pair in the bathtub, then going out in the sun to let them dry and tighten on one's legs. A few years later, hippies were virtually living in jeans; and by the late sixties, blue jeans had become the definitive antiestablishment fashion, especially if they were patched and ragged.

In 1969, fast-food hamburger magnate Errol Wetson started manufacturing cotton copies of the faded, tight-fitting jeans he saw on the French Riviera to provide a fashionable blue-jean look without the proletarian associations of ordinary denim. New York's French Jean Shop made a specialty of slim-cut jeans. Jeans manufacturers began supplementing the classic blue, straight-leg design with kinky variations in apricot and zinc, or with flaring elephant bell bottoms. By 1971, *Business Week* declared "blue jeans are the 'hot' pants." Two years later, jeans makers Levi-Strauss received the exalted Neiman-Marcus award for distinguished service in fashion.

The tattered look popular in the late sixties evolved into the "creative denim" look of the early seventies, and soon the pants that were once prized because they were so plain began to get customized with daisy, mushroom, peace-sign, and ladybug appliqués; patches made of velvet, suede, fur; and all manner of silver studs and sequins. The After Six men's wear firm tried marketing denim dinner jackets with plush velvet collars in 1974; and the same year a Levi's-sponsored exhibition of "Denim Art" clothing began touring American museums. Denim was the fabric of the hour: Zenith actually manufactured a "Blue Jean TV" covered in blue denim with copper rivets and a leather name patch. There were "Levi's for Feet," a line of boots and shoes with the Levi's label. However, the Levi-Strauss company rejected applications for license of their name and label from entrepreneurs who proposed a denim-covered mousetrap and a denim-covered, buttocks-shaped ceramic planter.

Although almost universally popular, jeans had still not become quite chic by the mid-seventies. They retained a low-class stigma, even though worn by jet setters as part of what Tom Wolfe identified as the "debutante in blue jeans" look. These high-born ladies could go around in jeans because they had pearls hanging from their neck, or a full-length mink coat to reassure the world of their status. But for anyone who was socially insecure, some clearly visible sign of breeding was required on the denim before blue jeans became correct. In 1977 a couple of New

York garment makers called the Nakash Brothers chose the name Jordache for their new line of jeans because it sounded French and elegant. They began to make French-cut jeans with the Jordache designer label on the back (although there was in fact no designer involved).

Jordache jeans sold very well. By 1979, thirty different companies were making designer jeans, most noticeably Murjani International, whose Warren Hirsh and Mike Murjani had hired Gloria Vanderbilt, along with her patrician name, to identify their jeans. Miss Vanderbilt was not in fact the designer jeans' designer, but each pair had her jazzy, upper-class signature stitched across the right buttock and a small, tasteful swan stitched on the front coin pocket. In a break with tradition, they were cut for women, not men, with room for ample hips and a nipped-in waist that didn't gap. They were advertised on television by Vanderbilt herself, who in a vivacious spiel delivered in a throaty, upper-crust whinny called them "a million-dollar look."

Gloria Vanderbilt's suggestive advertisements, featuring close-ups of shapely jeans-clad fannies, were outdone by Calvin Klein's notorious 1980 ads for his designer jeans, in which a young Brooke Shields wriggled seductively in front of the television camera asking, "Know what comes between me and my Calvins? Nothing."

Designer jeans—or as the *New York Times* called them, "status jeans"—became one of the most visible totems of eighties material culture, especially among brand-conscious mall rats who honed a fine sensibility to distinguish among jeans imprinted with names such as Diane Von Furstenberg, Sasson, Sergio, Ralph Lauren, and Jordache. There were even miniature designer jeans, with "Barbie" stitched across the back pocket, for Barbie and Ken dolls. In the wake of jeans came whole lines of "designer" clothes with fashionable names not only attached but well displayed so everyone could see what brand was being worn. The whole concept of designer clothes, which once meant they were available exclusively to the rich and chic, shifted to mean anything high-priced and prominently labeled.

Now that they are everywhere, designer jeans' elitist appeal is gone; they are no more special than running shoes. They do, however, reveal that their wearer is an attentive consumer who seeks an approved pedigree, in the form of the proper signature on her rump, when shopping for clothes.

DINOSAUR PARKS

Dinosaur parks are half-baked odes to prehistory, most of them created by roadside entrepreneurs who combine their enthusiasm for triceratops with audacious showmanship and a promise that visiting the park is educational. Tourists gleefully pay admission to gape at concrete, Styrofoam, or papier-mâché statues of giant creatures in surroundings designed to recreate the ambience of a million years B.C.

Individual dinosaurs can be spotted lording over gas stations and muffler shops nearly everywhere (in some cases the shops are built inside giant stegosauruses), but it is only in formal dinosaur parks that you can get a full sense of just how hair-raising the Jurassic period can be. At the Prehistoric Forest in Michigan, visitors are issued toy M-16 rifles as they ride among the wobbly animated beasts and a prerecorded voice cries, "Shoot! Shoot!" At the Dinosaur Gardens Prehistorical Zoo, also in Michigan, you can walk up a stairway into the rib cage of a thirty-ton brontosaur, which contains a candy-striped

pink-and-white shrine to "the greatest heart," Jesus Christ. At Prehistoric Creatures in upstate New York, hidden pedals in the walkways cause dinoaurs to roar when visitors approach. The petrified creatures then begin to holler at the customers, shrieking through their tiny hidden speakers that no matter what anybody says about them, being heterothermic lizards, they were in fact hot-blooded, mean sons-of-bitches.

Petrified Creatures is especially interesting because its proprietors are not hobbled by strict anatomical rules when constructing or maintaining their herd. Several years ago, when mice ate the eyes out of the dinosaurs, the management replaced them with Day-Glo red rubber balls. At the same time, they enlarged the dinos' teeth to make them look fiercer; and when the head rotted off the brontosaur, they decided to give the animal an extra-long nape, using so much plaster that the gangly neck scraped the ground and the poor, top-heavy creature then had to have its new head propped up in an iron brace.

Some of the most unusual dinosaurs are the man-size models on display around the parking lot at America's first dinosaur park, National Dinoland in Massachusetts, where Carlton Nash tends a quarry filled with genuine fossilized dinosaur tracks. Nash's monsters are cute, stubby, waist-high critters, made from what look like globs of mud painted with fanciful colors. Signs advise visitors how much each one weighed, as well as what its nickname is among dinosaur connoisseurs: the allosaur is known as Ally; the stegosaur is Stego. Nash sells fossilized footprints from what seems to be an endless supply of imprints of toenails, toes, and whole feet embedded in the rocks behind his souvenir shop. *Yankee* magazine reported that Dale Carnegie once bought a footprint from Mr. Nash because, he said, it reminded him of his own insignificance.

Carlton Nash's Dinoland started selling footprints in 1939, the same year Mammy Gas (a gas station in the shape of a black mammy) opened for business in Mississippi and Gutzon Borglum completed his sculpture of four

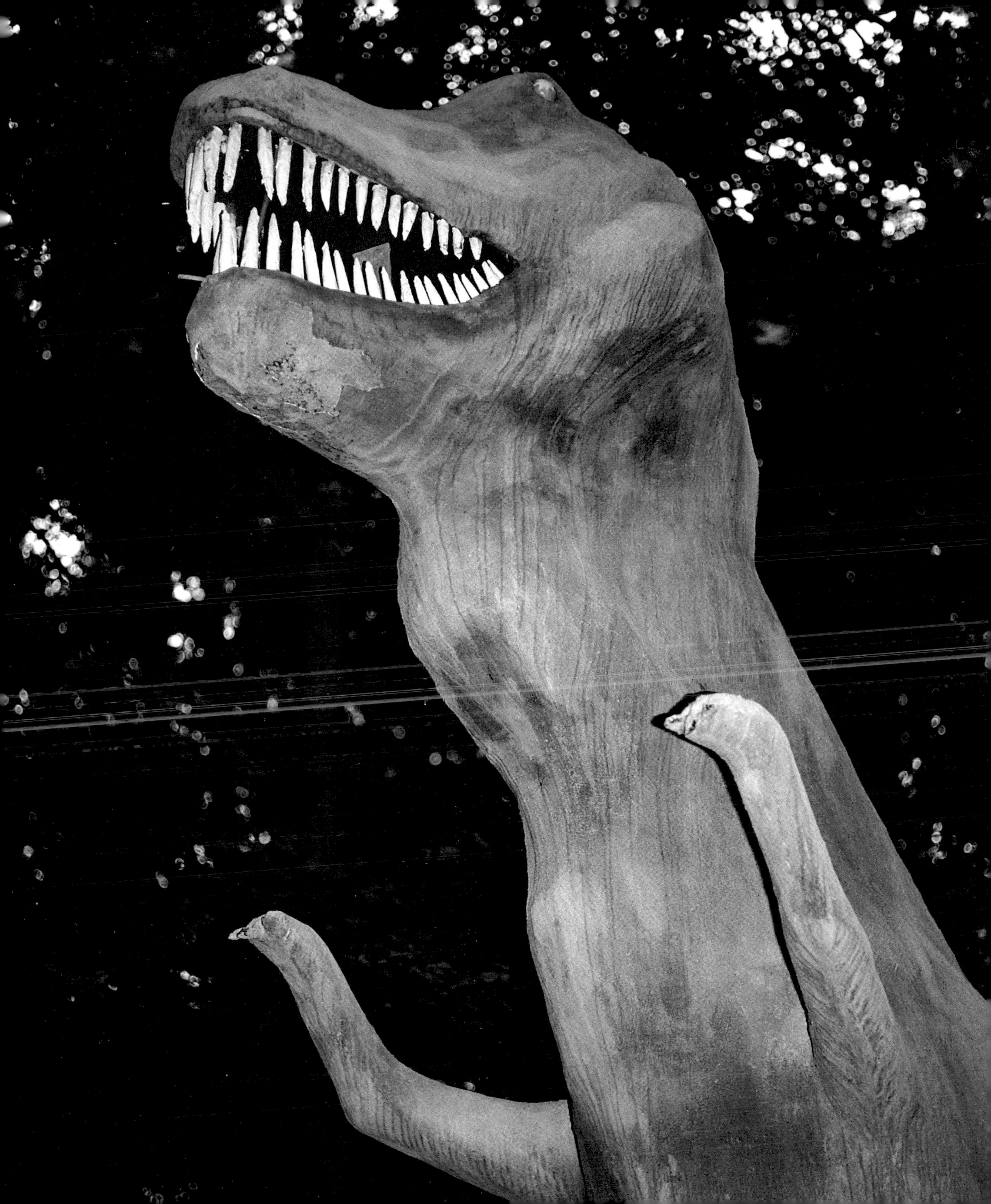

American Presidents in the granite face of Cathedral Cliff on Mount Rushmore. The affinity of these three events becomes clear if you consider another event of 1939, the unveiling of the Futurama exhibit at the New York World's Fair. The Futurama predicted a wondrous tomorrow of endless highways. As the prediction came true, and as highways covered the land, marvelous roadside attractions were built alongside them. Mount Rushmore—an entire mountain made into a sculpture—was the most unabashed, but there were hundreds more Mammy-like oddities constructed to attract people's attention, the bigger and more awesome the better.

So the modern age of dinosaurs began, and paleontology became the favorite science of American motorists. Only one other scholarly discipline can boast so many silly places to study life-size reconstructions of its subject matter, and that is criminology, in the form of wax museums with effigies of famous murderers; but wax museums rarely evidence the zeal of a good dinosaur park.

Dinosaur parks purport to be accurate and instructive; but the best of them offer more than just erudition, in the form of rock and fossil shops, paleozoologically themed miniature golf courses, jungle water slides, video game arcades, and ear-piercing salons where the piercing is free if you buy a pair of Black Hills gold and diamante pterodactyl earrings. Land of Kong in Arkansas, which advertises sixty-five acres of dinosaurs, used to include Hollywood glamour as part of the package, billing itself as John Agar's Land of Kong until Mr. Agar (the male ingenue in John Ford's *She Wore a Yellow Ribbon*) severed his business relationship with the big lizards. Land of Kong still augments its dinosaur collection with a stupendous statue of King Kong holding a life-size Fay Wray in his upraised fist. Dinosaur Land in Virginia (formerly the Rebel Korn'r) boasts likenesses of a sixty-four-foot shark, a ninety-foot octopus, a cave man, a cave woman, and a ragged Egyptian mummy who stands up and waves a Confederate flag in front of a velour wall tapestry of a moose. Dinosaur Land's shop stocks an impressive array of take-home sculptures—none, sadly, of dinosaurs. But it did feature a very nice bust of Michael Jackson in his Sgt. Pepper jacket, and several Elvises with gray skin and crimson lips.

DISCO

Disco wasn't always loathsome. Before the slick vested suits and slit-legged polyester dresses with platform heels, before there were dances with names like the freek and the lust hustle, and before the word *discotheque* conjured up images of writhing coke freaks with social diseases, "disco" meant a nice lively bar with a record player and a selection of records on hand where you could go for a drink and a listen, and maybe a few twirls around the dance floor.

The word was originally French, from *discothèque*, a neologism coined to describe a place with a good library (*bibliothèque*) of records (*disques*). In Paris during World War II, clubs deprived of live entertainment set up makeshift sound systems to play jazz records (which the Nazis despised as decadent) for their clandestine audience of partisans. One such club, dating back to the thirties, was called La Discothèque.

Discotheques thrived in Europe after the war, beginning with Paris's Whiskey Club (later Whisky à Gogo) in 1947, and a club in St.-Germain-des-Prés called Chez Castel, which featured a dance area in its cellar favored by jazz-loving bohemians. Chez Régine opened in 1960, with a "Disco Full" sign on its door to turn away *all* customers. For weeks curiosity-seekers wondered about this boîte that was so hot nobody was allowed inside; finally the sign was removed, customers flooded in, and Chez Régine was an instant success. The marketing strategy was the work of a former ladies' room attendant at Whisky à Gogo, Régine (last-nameless), who became queen of disco life, playing an important role in the international success of the twist, the notoriety of the jet set, and the rise of a new class of club society that included rock stars, slumming socialites, and shiftless hangers-on who craved to rub elbows with the rich and famous.

New York had a lively disco scene at this time in places such as Arthur, the Cheetah, the Peppermint Lounge, the Dom, and the Electric Circus. It was disco's penultimate moment, an exciting era when popular music seemed to be on the cutting edge of cultural change, and when the groovy sixties mind-set about the new "meritocracy" of creative, beautiful people had not yet been entirely replaced by the hallmark of seventies discos—goons installed at the front door to separate the hip from the un-.

It was in the early seventies, well after the idealistic Aquarian myths had crumbled and been discredited, that disco suddenly rose up with a vengeance. The very word *disco* came to mean much more than a club or a way of dancing. It became a life-style of gold neck chains and splay-collared shirts, hair mousse and awful synthesized music, runny-nose street hustlers and star fuckers: decadence incarnate. Once young and sexy, discos turned steamy and grotesque. Poppers and Quaaludes replaced the mellow hallucinogenic drugs of the Love Generation. From the time the twist burst out of the Peppermint Lounge in 1960, popular clubs had been hard to get into; but by the late seventies, lines of pleading discomaniacs craving

The Village People,
circa 1980

to get inside
Studio 54 or Xenon gave
the whole experience an aura of supreme
degradation. If one did gain admission to the
truly hard-core clubs such as New York's
Sanctuary or the all-gay Aux Puces, the humping
bodies and blinding stroboscopic lights presented
a hellish vision of carnal freakishness that would
have embarrassed Dionysus himself.

Something calamitous happened to the
music, too: The rocking songs that made people
want to get up and dance lost their momentum
and were replaced by what sounded like one
endless industrially synthesized Afro-Latin pop
tune, punctuated on occasion by a novelty
number such as ''Macho Man'' or ''YMCA''
performed by the Village People. The disco throb
was so dominant on the pop charts that some
people started saying rock and roll was dead.

It's a tough call to decide exactly which in

the disco phenomenon
created the more abominable legacy:
the celebrity-sucking freak-show scene at the
clubs, which motivated such fashion triumphs as
Spandex tube tops, designer jeans, patent-leather
hot pants, and rhinestone-studded denim urchin
caps, or John Travolta's suit in the 1977 movie
Saturday Night Fever.

Originally a 1976 New York magazine article
by Nik Cohn about a group of lower-middle-class
Italian kids in Brooklyn who frequented a
neighborhood disco, Saturday Night Fever took
an already-big phenomenon and made it
monstrous. While Cohn's article was an
exploration of a punky subculture, the movie was
basically a rousing come-and-get-it guide telling
viewers how to disco dance, how to disco dress,
and how to score with disco girls. It was wildly
successful. Disco franchises (2001, Tramps, and
Boeing 747) sprang up in small cities; Hilton
hotels quickly converted many of their bars to
discos; Halston marketed a line of loose and
clingy disco wear; airports announced plans to

attach discos to passenger terminals for jet-setters with an hour to spare for dancing. Albert Goldman concluded *Disco,* his 1978 study of the fad (''where it's all at today''), with a chapter called ''Is Disco God?,'' answering the question thus: ''Of disco one could say exactly what Voltaire did of God: 'If [He] did not exist, it would be necessary to invent Him.' '' The *Saturday Night Fever* sound-track album by the Bee Gees and others sold more copies than any other album in history (until Michael Jackson's *Thriller* in 1984).

Playing Tony Manero, the hottest bum-wiggler in town, John Travolta wore a white suit with vest, shiny black shirt open wide, gold neck chains, and black flamenco-style ankle boots. Because the movie presented him not as a jet-setter or beautiful person but as a regular nose-picker from the neighborhood, Travolta inspired millions of men without movie-star physiques to wear tight white suits, style their hair in a borough pouf, sulk like Tony Manero sulked, and strut like he strutted. A new, truly odious macho style was created. And although disco as a fad petered out and Travolta as Tony Manero was laughed off movie screens in the execrable sequel, *Staying Alive,* remnants of the polyester peacock look created in *Saturday Night Fever* can still be seen in small-town motel disco clubs throughout the land.

DRIFTWOOD (Including Cypress Knees)

Collecting driftwood is a craft that demands a keen eye but no manual dexterity. Wander along a beach until you see a piece of wood that has been modeled into an interesting shape by waves, sand, wind, or worms. Shake off the dirt. Bring it home and put it on a bamboo mat on a sideboard. *Voilà:* Art has been created. And you have a conversation piece that broadcasts your creativity because it was you, walking on that beach, who noticed that the protruding knob at the end of the piece of wood resembles Jay Leno's jaw.

That is the aptitude driftwood collecting requires: the ability to find beauty where other people see only mundane things. If you look at the knot in a tree and see a knot in a tree, you will never make a great driftwood collector. If, on the other hand, you look at the knot and see a sailing ship, a sad clown in floppy shoes, or Elvis at the gates of heaven, you just might have the makings of a driftwood artist. To the advanced driftwood collector, the shape needn't be representational. An abstract driftwood arch or boomerang might

suggest graceful movement and be perfectly suited as an end table knickknack alongside a lamp with a base in the form of a ballerina's toe shoe.

Driftwood gathering became the craft of choice among many offbeat do-it-yourselfers in the fifties. Driftwood was appealing because it was natural and rudimentary, two qualities much admired at the time for their ability to serve as a foil for ultramodern home design. Sleek Danish modern living rooms required the presence of a primitive element or two, such as African masks on the wall, a native American rug, a collection of geodes . . . or a twisted piece of driftwood, combined in a tableau with dried palm sprays and a few black pebbles with interesting shapes. Driftwood also fit nicely into the kind of older modernistic homes inspired by Frank Lloyd Wright's notions of bringing nature indoors in the form of rough-hewn stone and wood.

Prospecting for driftwood can be done on beaches and along mountain streams, and in deserts (whose yield the connoisseur knows as "ghostwood"). It is possible to buy it in a souvenir store or roadside shop, sometimes already made into a lamp or clock; but to a devotee, that's too easy: The hunt and the discovery give the finished piece its meaning and allow its discoverer to tell admirers how it was found, and at what point and in what form its physiognomy became apparent.

The big issue among driftwood collectors is whether it is ethical to tamper with a found piece of wood. Purists believe all the work must be done by nature. Their job is simply to discover the beautiful pattern, then to bring it home, find a well-lit place for it, and admire what nature has wrought. Others set off on a driftwood hunt with saw and pruning shears in hand, ready to sever any likely-looking root, then bring it home, sand it, gouge it, stain it, varnish it, paint it, attach it to other pieces of driftwood, and combine it with ceramic bucktoothed squirrels or tragicomic macramé owls in a diorama that tells a story.

Although the doyenne of driftwood collecting, Mary E. Thompson, once considered it "well-nigh sacrilegious" to tamper to such a degree with nature's handiwork, she had lowered her standards by the time she wrote *The Driftwood Book* in 1960. Miss Thompson, whose biography identifies her as "a nationally accredited flower show judge," has many suggestions to augment the gnarled wood she extols as "the living beauty of the rugged, enduring life force" with other materials, including wrought iron, shredded aluminum foil, and scraps from old venetian blinds. One amazing creation she presents began as a four-foot-tall driftwood stump. She topped it with an automobile spring and wires rising eleven feet in the air, which were mounted on an electric turntable that caused two strelitzia flowers on top to wriggle in a circle. Another fascinating example of mixed media is a sculpture called *Transportation,* which includes a sea-sponge basket filled with scrap iron ("suggests cargo") and a dried papyrus plant ("propeller").

In 1934, before driftwood collecting became popular as a source of conversation pieces and inspiration for flower arrangements, Tom Gaskins of Arcadia, Florida, started experimenting with cypress knees—an extraordinary form of driftwood. Knees are the conical shapes that form on the bottoms of cypress trees in swamps and grow upwards to supply air to the roots when the ground is flooded. To Gaskins, who was raised in the Florida swamps, they contained revelations of such magnitude that he devoted his life to them. He started harvesting cypress knees, experimenting with forced growth, and making cypress knees into lamps and urns. In 1937 he moved to Palmdale, Florida, where he has been curator of the Cypress Knee Museum for the last fifty-three years.

Cypress knees are funnier, weirder, and

103

more shapely than any other kind of driftwood. They range from just a few inches high to man-size. The knees in Gaskins's museum, cleaned and polished but otherwise unaltered, tell many chapters' worth of human history. Exhibits include knees in the shapes of Joseph Stalin, Franklin D. Roosevelt, and Adolf Hitler, Flipper the television dolphin, and a hippopotamus wearing a Carmen Miranda hat, and a knee with a smile as sweet as the Mona Lisa's.

There are cypress-knee shops throughout the swampy parts of the South where one can purchase small paperweight knees for a few dollars all the way up to giant glass-top coffee tables for many hundreds; but Tom Gaskins's museum is the center of the cypress-knee world. Announced by series of signs along Highway 29

with words spelled out in free-standing letters on the branches of leafless trees (such as ''NEVER WAS NEVER COULD BE NOTHING LIKE IT NOWHERE'' and ''LADY, IF HE WON'T STOP HIT HIM ON HEAD WITH SHOE''), this most amazing roadside attraction offers a catwalk through a cypress swamp and a videotape of a presentation by Mr. Gaskins showing how the knees are peeled. We watched the videotape along with Mr. Gaskins himself, who was barefoot and wore a wooden hat fashioned out of a cypress knee. The demonstration's most dramatic moment came when Gaskins licked the stripped knee to demonstrate that its spongy lining is virtually the same as the edible wood fiber used in bakery bread.

ELEVATOR SHOES

Men in all walks of life, no matter how tall they are, are recognizing the important advantages of being taller," reports the Richlee Shoe Company catalogue. Should you be seeking those advantages, two extra inches are available if you wear Richlee shoes, three inches if you wear boots. Other companies sell shoes that make men bigger, but it's Richlee that owns the trademark "Elevators," and it has been selling its product through the mail in little advertisements in the backs of magazines (as well as from a showroom in Maryland) since 1939.

The superiority of genuine Elevators over booster shoes with immense heels and extra-thick soles is that the height accretion happens *inside the shoe.* Soles on Elevators do not look orthopedic or bulky. Scrutinize an Elevator and you will see that the quarter (the part of the upper directly above the heel) is especially generous. That's because it's encasing not only a foot but the Elevator's urethane foam inner mold, which is what makes short men tall and tall men taller. Although removable and replaceable, the inner mold will not work in ordinary oxfords, because it would lift the soles of the wearer's feet nearly outside of the shoe.

Elevators come in all styles, including sneakers, boating moccasins, tasseled wing tips, work boots, western boots, chukka boots, dress boots, and jean boots. There are even classic service oxfords in shiny man-made material for stubby military men. The mail-order form assures nervous buyers that shoes are sent in boxes marked "Richlee Shoe Company"; the telltale word "Elevators" does not appear anywhere—not even inside the shoe. (Steady customers, however, know the contents of a box if they spot the Richlee Shoe Company emblem on it: a silhouette of a man standing on what appears to be an orange crate.)

ELVISIANA

Elvis Presley was as famous for his personal style as for his music. In matters of taste, he was a true fanatic, not satisfied with what was merely right or polite. He liked everything he did to be the ultimate, the most, the richest, and the best.

Propriety never constrained him. In the beginning, he was the kid with pink Cadillacs, a gold lamé suit, and greasy sideburns—so threatening to good manners that his swiveling hips had to be censored out of the picture when he sang on Ed Sullivan's television show. When he got rich, he did not hire some snooty interior decorator to make his mansion look like the home of someone with good taste; he personally went to one of Memphis's tackiest furniture stores and created a Polynesian-themed "Jungle Room" complete with running waterfall and colored lights.

Everything he did was extreme. He wore ermine capes, drove Harley-

Davidson trikes (because he got too fat to balance on a two-wheeler), ate bacon by the pound and banana pudding by the tub, and got addicted to Feenamint laxative chewing gum. His extravagant life peaked in the seventies at the Las Vegas Hilton in glittering performances that ranged from "Hound Dog" to "My Way," and ended in death from heart failure triggered by straining to overcome constipation while sitting on his toilet.

At each stage of his career, Elvis had an unfailing ability to appall and upset everybody except the tens of millions of fans who loved him whatever he did. In the beginning, critics condemned his bump-and-grind singing style as indecent. In the sixties, he caught hell for betraying rock and roll to sing ballads and make a series of happy-go-lucky Hollywood movies. And in the seventies, when he took his sound-and-light musical revue on the road, he got blamed for being too slick and too maudlin and not like he used to be. Elvis was always doing something other than what he was supposed to do. If the role of art is to upset the status quo, music has never known a truer artist than him.

When he was a living person, his voice was so inspired that many who might otherwise have been exasperated by his behavior could always excuse him as an idiosyncratic virtuoso. When he died, however, shocking new levels of vulgarity turned the Elvis phenomenon from a story of eccentric genius into the quintessential saga of bad taste, American style.

The postmortem outrageousness began at his funeral, when the *National Enquirer* snuck a photographer into the wake and nabbed a front-page picture of Elvis lying in his coffin. A few weeks later, three men were arrested for plotting to steal his body from the Forest Hill Cemetery, where it had been buried. It was later revealed that the grave-robbing story was a hoax, trumped up by Elvis's father, Vernon, as a way to get Elvis's corpse dug up and reinterred in the backyard of Graceland, where it would be safe (and where it remains today).

Even before he died, Elvis had been picked at like buzzard's meat by three former bodyguards who wrote a book called *Elvis, What Happened?* (with *National Enquirer* reporter Steve Dunleavy), describing him as a deranged junkie. Suddenly what had been a very private life was opened up and pored over by sensationalizers who realized that Elvis was a gold mine. In 1980 Albert Goldman came out with the exhaustively repulsive *Elvis,* a compendium of scandal meant to discredit not only Elvis but his family and his fans. Goldman plumbed never-before-tested depths of bad taste in his painstakingly detailed descriptions of Elvis lying semicomatose in a drug-induced stupor, and in comprehensive accounts of his bowel habits.

Then came the impersonators. Not content to merely idolize Elvis, they *became* him, some going so far as to have sideburn implants and plastic surgery and take speech lessons from Memphis vocal coaches who taught them how to mumble and stutter as Elvis did when he was nervous. Virtually all impersonators become the Elvis of the seventies, because it was then that Elvis attained his most kingly demeanor, both in personal size (big) and in the folderol of his wardrobe and stage show. Most don't really look like him, but that doesn't matter, because the iconic Elvis has by now been reduced to a few basic and instantly recognizable elements: sequined white jumpsuit with elephant bell bottoms and a high collar with shoulder-wide wings, girder-sided silver glasses, and masses of glittering rings on the fingers. Connoisseurs of impersonatorology evaluate Elvii on the subtlest details: Do they wear Brut cologne like Elvis did? Do they make their hair blue-black with Clairol Black Velvet, his chosen brand of hair dye? The phenomenon of men (and even some women and children) remaking themselves in his image, and fans

receiving these living effigies as avatars of Elvishood on earth, has no precedents outside of arcane fetishistic religions.

When he was alive, there was always an embarrassment of riches in Elvis souvenirs, including record albums containing scraps of his clothing, Love Me Tender lipstick, and sweaty scarves that he threw into the audience while singing, ''Are You Lonesome Tonight?'' Posthumous exploitation includes liquor-decanter statuettes, memorial candles (to be burned only on August 16, the anniversary of his death), vials of his sweat, bags of dirt taken from the lawn of Graceland, scraps of rug taken from the floors where he walked, Elvis-faced panty shields, and virtually anything and everything he ever touched or even came near. Exhibits in Elvis museums around America include his checkbook stubs, his underwear, photocopies of his weekly shopping list, his electric razor, and X-rays of his sinuses.

Those who don't believe he is actually gone have had a ghoulish heyday spotting the undead man in the local K Mart or at a hamburger stand. Some have seen him reborn in a cloud or in the blob inside their Lava Lite. In 1989 the Weekly World News reported on a tribe of ''wacky savages'' in Brazil who all wear Elvis wigs and perform tribal rituals that involve beating on bongo drums and singing ''Blue Suede Shoes.'' The Elvis-worshipping natives were themselves not surprising; other sensation-seeking newspapers have regularly told stories about grass-skirted savages on Pacific islands who have been praying to Elvis since he made his movie Paradise Hawaiian Style nearby in 1966. What was startling about the Brazilians, according to Henri Bonjean, the French anthropologist who discovered them, was that they claim to have been visited by Elvis in 1981, four years after he was supposed to have died. ''He called himself King Elvis and strummed an old wooden guitar,'' Bonjean told the Weekly World News, which described the savages hopping up and down and swiveling their hips when they sang.

There is some crazy logic in the trajectory of Elvis from teen idol to the world's looniest lodestone of publicity. In the fifties, he represented all the frightening indecencies of the emerging youth culture, including but not limited to rock and roll. Critics said he foreshadowed the end of Western civilization. Western civilization has not yet ended, but to those forever worried about it going down the tubes, the outrages of modern Elvisiana are exemplary symptoms. The king of rock and roll has gone on to become the god of excess.

See also **FAKE FUR; LAS VEGAS; SHAG RUGS**

EPIGRAMS

It is not easy to always think of something clever to say. The good news is you don't have to, because the world is full of ready-to-think thoughts in the form of epigrams. Epigrams appear on varnished wall plaques, in greeting cards, strung together in inspirational books with such titles as *Our Flag* and *What Is a Truck Driver?*, ironed on rubbery promotional visored caps, embossed onto novelty ashtrays, and branded into cedar hope chests.

Traditionally, an epigram is terse and piquant and bristles with irony. The kinds of epigrams we are talking about—the ones you can buy in souvenir stores and T-shirt shops—tend to be witless. They are public-domain aphorisms made to express commonly held opinions about such topics as annoying mothers-in-law, the price of beer, or the joys of fishing. They might strive to be clever ("There are three stages to a man's life: Stud, Dud, Thud"), or they might express the kind of maudlin sentiment that even the most bathetic person would be too embarrassed to actually say out loud ("Anyone can be a mother, but it takes someone special to be a Mommy").

Instead of being witty, a large number of modern epigrams are cranky. Designed to be posted for public view (or worn on a hat or T-shirt), they announce a grievance about housework or bills or sloppy teenagers or people who spend too much time in the bathroom. There is no immediate objective for complaining; it is simply a convenient way to let people know you are exasperated and have a cynical view of life, without your having to think of any original reasons why you feel that way. On the job, for instance, you could get a pencil holder that says, "It's hard to soar with eagles when you work with turkeys." At home, you can amuse guests in the rec room with a bar lampshade that announces, "Those who think they know it all are very annoying to those of us who do."

Not all trite epigrams express irritation. Some are inspirational. Most moccasin shops sell wooden plaques and souvenir plates with this "Great Spirit" prayer: "O Great Spirit, grant that I may not judge my neighbor until I have walked a mile in his moccasins." For expressing love of other family members there are "Father: someone we can look up to no matter how tall we get" and "Grandmother's heart is like a rose: always blooming, always caring, always sharing."

Drinking is a major theme on plaques, glasses, and bar accessories; and it is always treated pugnaciously, as an amusing sin for which the proprietor of the epigram has no remorse: "I'll tell you why I came home drunk. I ran out of money." Or: "A man's got to believe in something. I believe I'll have another beer."

Golf and fishing are extremely popular subjects of epigrams. Like drinking, they inspire belligerent aphorisms charged with hostility toward responsible life, as in the classic "A bad day of fishing is better than a good day at work." There is also a self-mocking theme that runs through many golf-fishing epigrams, as in the "Fisherman's Code": "Early to bed, early to rise, fish like hell and make up lies." Golfers make fun of their sport with the "Primitive Man" epigram: "Primitive man screamed and beat the ground with sticks. They called it witchcraft. Modern man does the same thing. They call it golf."

Before racist jokes became taboo, Confucianisms used to be an extremely popular form of epigram in which leering wit is attributed to the Chinese philosopher Confucius. A Confucianism begins with the words "Confucius say," then delivers a proverb similar to the slip of paper in a fortune cookie but with an ironic and usually sexual twist. For instance: "Confucius say wife who put man in dog house find him in cat house." Or: "Confucius say man who farts in church sits in own pew."

Because sitting on the toilet is a time for reflection and contemplation, many epigrams are designed to be placed in or around the bathroom —on the door, explaining, "How long a minute is depends on which side of the door you're on," on the wall as a toilet-paper holder ("If you sprinkle when you tinkle, Be a sweetie and wipe the seatie"), or the ever-popular sign for bathrooms near swimming pools: "We don't swim in your toilet. Please don't 'P' in our pool."

Today is the first day
of the rest of your life.

°The Pipeworks, Inc. Boston, Mass. 1971

Epigrams have been around since biblical times and cross-stitched on wall samplers for hundreds of years, but their boorish modern era began in the early 1900s, when the interior decorator Elsie de Wolfe (known as ''the chintz lady'' and also as the person responsible for making leopard-skin upholstery fashionable—*and* as the inventor of the Pink Lady cocktail) began embroidering sofa pillows with her own clever words of wisdom rather than biblical or time-honored ones. De Wolfe's sagacious epigrams include ''Failure only begins when you give up trying to succeed,'' ''Today is the tomorrow you worried about yesterday,'' and ''The large intestine is the mainspring of youth and beauty.''

Most advances in modern epigrammology were the work of anonymous novelty and gag merchants, but after Miss de Wolfe, there was one other notable creative artist who applied his intellect to epigrams. He was E. Joseph Cossman, Uncle Milton Levine's brother-in-law and business partner (see *Ant Farms*) and the distributor of such products as the Jivarro Shrunken Head, the Spud Gun, 100 Toy Soldiers for a Dollar, and the Fly Cake. In the fifties, Cossman pioneered a whole new venue for epigrams by taking them out of books and off pillows and putting them by the side of the road. Cossman had a two-sided sign by the road outside his offices in Hollywood. It was the kind of sign that had movable letters; so instead of just leaving the name of his company on it, Cossman decided to emblazon it with a different epigram every week. The bywords he invented include: ''Middle age is when your broad mind and narrow waist begin to change places.'' ''A friend is a gold link in the chain of life.'' And ''It is better to tighten your belt than to lose your pants.''

Cossman's idea was adopted by churches, who reached out to passersby with attention-getting sermon boards such as ''This Sunday: Meet Jes s. What is missing? 'U' are.'' So many motels and businesses have adopted the idea that it is now impossible to drive far in America without experiencing this form of grass-roots wit, in the form of epigrams on mobile billboards (often accompanied by a smiley face) in front of gas stations and convenience stores everywhere. For drivers who cannot haul a billboard with them but nonetheless want to let the world know that they, too, are in possession of a clever thought, there are bumper stickers.

See also **BUMPER STICKERS; CEDAR SOUVENIRS; T-SHIRTS**

FACE-LIFTS

Skin sags as it ages. Wrinkles, jowls, turkey neck, crow's feet, and baggy eyelids are the results. In order to stay looking young, about a hundred thousand people every year spend between three thousand and ten thousand dollars per operation to have a face-lift. The skin of the patient's face and neck is cut away from underlying muscle and tugged back so that it is smooth as an adolescent's. Excess skin is cut off, and the newly taut skin is stitched behind the hairline and around the ears in such a way that the scars don't show. Depending on the skill of the surgeon, the resulting face will look either like a young version of the patient or like a freeze-dried fright mask of the patient with epicanthic eyes and a tightly drawn fissure with exposed teeth where the mouth and lips used to be.

The alternative to being cut is being burned, in a nonmedical procedure known as the chemical peel or chemabrasion. A patient's face is swabbed with a caustic solution of phenol, croton oil, and soap, which creates a controlled second-degree burn. The cauterized skin is then covered with tape that stays on for hours or days, depending on how deep the wrinkles are, while new skin grows below it. When the tape is removed, old hide peels off too, leaving skin that looks sunburned but new and smooth and pink.

Chemabrasion was perfected in the twenties by a French nurse named Antoinette La Gasse, who devised it by watching her father, a physician, use phenol solutions to treat soldiers with burned faces. La Gasse brought her chemicals to Hollywood, where, despite charges of malpractice by doctors, she was known to have secretly rejuvenated aging movie stars in the days before plastic surgery became readily available. When she died in 1952, the formula was passed on to her apprentices, including Miriam Maschek, whose son, Francis, opened the thriving Derma-Lift Salons of Hollywood and Miami, where his wife Jacqueline Stallone (Sylvester's mother) supplemented the Derma-Lift process with advice concerning false-eyelash application.

Although crude cosmetic plastic surgery was performed in the twenties (before the foundation of the American Society of Plastic and Reconstructive Surgeons in 1931), it is only in the last thirty years that the operation has been refined enough to produce patients who don't look numb and rubber-headed. It is now a common operation, but still not without dangers. The widower of comedienne Totie Fields said it was a botched face-lift that caused her to develop gangrene, then have to get her leg amputated, then die. Liberace's plastic surgeon removed so much wrinkled skin from the aging pianist's face that when Liberace took off the bandages, he realized with horror that he was unable to keep his eyes closed. Unless squeezed tightly, they wanted to spring open, even when he slept, requiring him to use drops throughout the night to keep his eyeballs from drying out.

No one ever used to admit to having cosmetic surgery, and it is still a taboo subject among many celebrities, from young de-Africanized Michael Jackson to lift-and-peel veteran Lana Turner. That great confessor First Lady Betty Ford admitted she had had her face lifted in Palm Springs in 1978, which suddenly made it okay to admit to an occasional nip and tuck; and Phyllis Diller joked about her new face for years. But it is the Gabor sisters and their mother, Jolie, who deserve credit as the women who made the world aware of the marvels to be wrought by plastic surgery. Their "total lift count is probably exceeded only by their collective total of husbands and lovers," according to Norma Lee Browning's book *Facelifts*. Jolie had her first lift half a century ago at age forty, and regularly thereafter staged unveiling parties to introduce her new face and the doctor (usually young, handsome, and expensive) who had sculpted and/or chemabraded it. "The face lift does not hold so perfectly as you get older but still it is always a plus," she wrote in *Jolie Gabor (As Told to Cindy Adams)* in 1975.

Thanks to social-arbiter clients such as Jolie

and her daughters, ''lift men'' have enjoyed celebrity status among the rich and the vain. The hot ones are revered by patients as artists or gurus; getting an appointment with one is like booking a table in a snobby restaurant: If you are a nobody, they don't want to know you. In the seventies, Dr. Ivo Pitanguy of Rio was the superstar of plastic surgeons, providing patients with not only new faces but newly shaped breasts, buttocks, and thighs. He was joined in the pantheon by Dr. Jean-Paul Lintilhac of Tahiti when it was revealed that Dr. L. was the artist who had remodeled Catherine Deneuve and Sophia Loren. His most famous patient was his wife, Simone, on whom he had resculpted everything, including buttocks, thighs, stomach, breasts, and face—but not the nose, which he considered perfect. In fact, it was such a pretty nose that Dr. Lintilhac developed a nice little business among Tahitian women, giving them nose jobs that reduced their broad, flaring noses to pert little bobs like Simone's.

According to Norma Lee Browning, Palm Springs, California, had become the face-lift capital of the world as of the early eighties, with dozens of doctors specializing in aesthetic plastic surgery, many of them operating out of their own private clinics (away from hospital hoi polloi and the scrutiny of other physicians) and providing luxurious recovery ranches for their exclusive clientele. ''The Palm Springs social season is a continual round of parties always scintillating with choice face lift critiques,'' Miss Browning wrote, adding, ''Most lift-watchers agree there is a definite 'look' to a face lift done in Palm Springs. It's known as the hatched in Palm Springs look: too tight, too tucked, too young, and too frozen or terrified (it's hard to tell which) to smile.''

See also **GABORS; LIBERACE; NOSE JOBS**

FAKE FUR

It used to be that fur was something that only rich and classy people wore. No doubt there are still some well-bred old ladies who have swank mink coats, and a few faded glamour queens holding on to that once chic, now tattered leopard; but most of the people you see swathed in fur these days (men as well as women) are nouveau-riche vulgarians. Wearing the skins of dead beasts is like driving a gold-trimmed Cadillac or putting lots of gaudy rings on your fingers: a crass way to let the world know you have plenty of money.

If you don't have money yet still want to appear ostentatious, there is fake fur. Fake fur is humane; many otherwise refined animal lovers laud it because bad taste is a lesser evil than killing animals. Made from a stew of coal-tar derivatives, pretend pelts relieve the wearer of the moral burden of feeling responsible for the deaths of God's creatures (except slowly, via pollution created when the fake fur is manufactured); also, fake fur can be considerably cheaper than the real thing. In addition, because it is not directly dependent on God, fake fur can be made in any color, in any length and nap, and thus become what is known in the garment industry as "fun fur," like the pelt of no known creature.

The story of fake fur (a version of what the textile business knows as "high pile fabric") begins with a Yankee inventor named Herbert J. Hope, who was described by Jody Shields in *Details* magazine as "fake fur's folk hero and patron." Before Hope, clothiers were selling coats made of what the 1928 National Bellas Hess Department Store catalogue described as "pressed and sheared plush fabric, skillfully constructed to look like real and expensive fur." The problem with the furlike coats was they had no nap. In 1931, Hope figured out a way to weave a shaggy plush cloth from Angora goat hair in such a way that it vaguely resembled the pelt of a raccoon. He called it Koongora, and within a few years perfected "Ra-ra-coon" and an imitation ermine called "Erminpelz": They were warm but not very stylish, and were used for coffin lining and

stuffed-animal covering as well as for coats. By the late thirties, there were alpaca pile fabrics, lusher and tougher than Koongora; and middle-class department stores were selling wool coats that looked like lamb, rayon coats that looked like caracal, and cotton pile coats that looked like leopard—each for about ten dollars.

Fake fur leapt toward verisimilitude in 1944, when knit pile fabrics first became available. The new materials were denser and furrier than woven ones; and because they could be made on a mechanized sliver knit machine, they were cheaper. By 1953, the Montgomery Ward mail-order catalogue offered ''fur-effect'' fabrics in all the usual animal patterns, plus the newest high-fashion simulation, poodle—a tight, curly pile of wool and rayon. Two years later, *Life* featured a cover story that marveled at ''the $125 Man-Made Mink,'' manufactured from different-length fibers of Orlon and Dynel to approximate the varmint's ''guard hair'' look.

When fashion went to hell in the late sixties, fake fur was at the front lines of bad taste. Creative clothiers seemed to reason that as long as the fur was fake, what was the point in slavishly imitating nature? Why not liberate fake fur? In addition to faithful reproductions of leopard and silverblu mink, fake furs were made with polka dots and Day-Glo colors and with pile that ran in op-art squares and circles. Different naps of fur, some resembling animals' skins,

some like nothing in nature, were combined in sculptural effects as coarse as macramé, or on Leatherette clothing surfaces that sometimes took on the appearance of a hide suffering severe ringworm infestation. Glenarctic hi-pile modacrylic fake fur was advertised as lustrous and iridescent, available in frosted black, navy blue, and wine colors. Poodle fur was now available in scarlet and loden green as well as the traditional black and gray. The technology was such that these wonder fabrics could be made cheaply in abundance—and they were, for trim on boots, hats, and hot pants.

Fake fur was so popular, and so fake, and so cheap, that the line between it and utilitarian bathroom carpeting began to blur. Every truck stop sold tiger-skin seat covers, and cheap fabric stores sold great rolls of furry fake stuff to staple around the inside of swingers' vans and onto the walls of rec rooms. ''How would you like an African room?'' asked *A Groovy Guide to Decorating Your Room* in 1969, suggesting, ''Cut a rug out of fake fur zebra (no hemming is needed). Make a mane and tail with black yarn and hang it up with a staple gun.'' The result? ''Instant z-i-n-g.'' One of the most impressive collections of fake-fur room decor was amassed by Elvis Presley in Graceland's Jungle Room, which was filled with zebra-skin furniture and bunny-fur pillows, complemented by a furry green rug that ran up the walls and onto the ceiling. Elvis enjoyed the sheen of fake fur so much, he even put it on the top of his bathroom scale.

Like polyester, fake fur got a horrible reputation during the seventies, when it was used as liberally and as repulsively as shag rugs. ''Critter fur,'' as some in the clothing industry prefer to call it, has left behind those days of synthetic intemperance; but in many people's minds, it still evokes images of slovenly house-wives in harlequin glasses and fake leopard-skin hats, or of Sonny and Cher circa 1965 looking sullen and in love, wearing bell bottoms and matching shaggy-haired ''bobcat'' vests.

See also **LEOPARD SKIN; SHAG RUGS; TAXIDERMY**

FEMININE HYGIENE SPRAY

Vaginal odor was an almost unheeded problem until 1966, when it was attacked by a new product called FDS. Known as a feminine hygiene spray, FDS was designed to be applied to the external areas of women's vulvae as a deodorant. Tests showed it reduced odor from 38 to 78 percent better than soap and water. Within a year, at least thirty similar brands were competing with FDS for a piece of the market. They included Pristeen, Vespré, Naturally Feminin, Demure, and Feminique.

The time was ripe: More and more women were wearing panty hose made of synthetic fibers that didn't breathe, as well as taking birth-control pills—two things that can encourage vaginitis and its accompanying unpleasant odor. In addition, miniskirts were at an all-time high, on the verge of exposing women's vulvae and thus disclosing any untoward smell. Three years after feminine hygiene sprays made their debut, *Women's Wear Daily* assessed the development as an inevitable result of the sexual revolution: "The pill is just not enough. It might give the American girl sexual freedom, but getting the man is still an art. What could be more artful than a sweet-smelling vagina?"

Once aerosol cans were perfected in the early sixties (for deodorant, mouthwash, and foot spray), the scientific breakthrough that made feminine hygiene spray possible was the development of fluorocarbon 12, a propellant that produced a warm, nonsticky spray rather than an aerosol chill. Hexachlorophene (an antibacterial agent) and perfume were added, and a vaginal deodorant called Bidex appeared in Switzerland. In America, Warner-Lambert began test-marketing Bidex, and Alberto-Culver scientists developed their own version of the product, named FDS to sound scientific (although one executive worried that it sounded too much like FDR, and critics later complained it was deceptively close to FDA, the Federal Drug Administration).

Advertising vaginal deodorant was a dilemma. Nearly every manufacturer beat around the bush. Pristeen, which had a "pink chiffon smell," promised to take care of "worry-making odors" and was billed as "essential to your cleanliness, and to your peace of mind about being a girl—an attractive, nice-to-be-with girl." Original advertising copy spoke only of "the most girl part of you"—a line later boldly changed to read, "the most girl part of you—the vaginal area." FDS advertisements advised, "A woman, if she's completely honest about it, realizes her most serious problem isn't under her arms."

As tasteful as the spray makers tried to be, it was a product destined to be controversial. Feminists condemned it because it reinforced primitive sexist ideas that women's sexual organs are shameful and need deodorizing. "The way they're advertised presents a horrendous image of women as being inherently smelly creatures," said psychoanalyst Natalie Shainess in Nora Ephron's 1973 article "Dealing With the, Uh, Problem." Ephron also referred to Ralph Nader's condemnation of the "why-wash-it-when-you-can-spray-it" ethic.

Furthermore, there were questions about safety; in 1972, the FDA banned the active ingredient hexachlorophene because it could cause seizures. The year after, feminine hygiene sprays fell under the gun of the FDA once again, when the government demanded warnings against spraying more than once a day or spraying on itchy, irritated skin. The words "hygienic" and "hygiene" were stricken from labels and advertising, as was any implication that the sprays had medicinal value.

Once the perceived need was established, however, there was no way feminine hygiene sprays would go away. In fact, they were only a beginning. In their wake came "private deodorants" for men's penises, such as Pub's Below the Belt and Bill Blass's Man's Other Deodorant. "If there's a part of the human body to exploit, you might as well get into it," Mr. Blass said. Alberto-Culver went head-to-toe with their Light Touch, the "all-over body deodorant," not only for vaginas and penises but for armpits, feet, anuses, scalps, scrotums, and any other part of the body (except teeth) likely to cause embarrassment because of its aroma.

FINGERNAIL EXTREMISM

Too much makeup and overcoiffed hair have always been sure signs of a slut, or of someone who wants to affect a slutty look. In the last three or four years, developments in fingernails have made them the new frontier in trash cosmetology. If you want to say "I'm cheap," there are few more effective ways of doing so than displaying a hand with ten long nails that have been embellished with an airbrushed paint job, precious metal appliqués, decals, gold charms, fake or real diamonds, birthstones, and filigree.

In more polite times, conscientious nail care was simply a matter of cuticle management, oily-nail-bed treatment, breakage control, shaping, painting, and polishing. Now, manicurists, once the lowly buff-and-file girls in the corner of the beauty salon, like to present themselves as licensed nail technicians; and in their hands, manicuring has become one of the liveliest of the vulgar arts.

Nails provide the beautician with an unprecedented opportunity to be creative. Unlike skin, which is a living thing, and hair, which, although dead tissue, must in most cases remain at least semiflexible, nails are hornlike plates that don't need to breathe or move. And if a woman breaks or bites her nails or doesn't want to bother cultivating lengths of expired epithelial cells at the ends of her fingers, artificial ones are easy to apply—in working length, sophisticated length, fashion length, or curved-square extra-longs. Using these ten ovoid canvases, modern nail art has gone absolutely wild with daring new possibilities.

Once the nail is in place, nail art begins with color, which can range from old-fashioned polish in a variation of traditional red to detailed freehand acrylic designs, such as sky-blue nails with a different fleecy white cloud painted on each, or shimmering pearlescent nails with S-W-E-E-T spelled out in fancy metal-flake letters across the fingers of one hand and S-A-S-S-Y on the other. And if one has made the commitment to fake nails, it then becomes possible to select a single nail for special treatment in a contrasting motif. For example, if nine fake nails are all tinted with a simple Nail Glass Peach Tawny color, you might choose to have the tenth, an index-finger nail, be a diamondized Spirit of Love nail, which gives the appearance of polished gold encrusted with stripes, rows, or amoebic fields of what the Spirit of Love artificial nail catalogue calls ''multi-diamonds.''

After color, embellishment can be as simple as a tip, which is a cap, either square-cut or round, in gold or silver, that fits over the end of the nail. It can be plain metal or, like the Spirit of Love nails, it can be ornamented with starlites (opaque imitation rhinestones, made of plastic) or with a monogram. For accenting the body of the nail rather than the tip, there are silhouettes, which are gold or silver patterns that are secured on the nail with either polish or a post. A company called Sweet Lady Jane offers silhouettes that show champagne glasses, spider webs, or palm trees, as well as tiny mottos such as ''99% Bitch,'', ''I ♥ Travel,'' or ''Like a Virgin.''

To attach something with a post, it is necessary to pierce the nail, which you will do anyway if you want danglies or chain rings. Danglies are miniature hoops, charms, hearts, and unicorns that hang from holes in the nail like earrings. A chain ring is a gold-link ensemble that connects a gem or dangly on the nail to a ring on the same finger. The dressiest nail treatment of all is a hand with some of everything, including a super chain ring that connects the nail not merely to a ring on its finger but to a bracelet on the wrist.

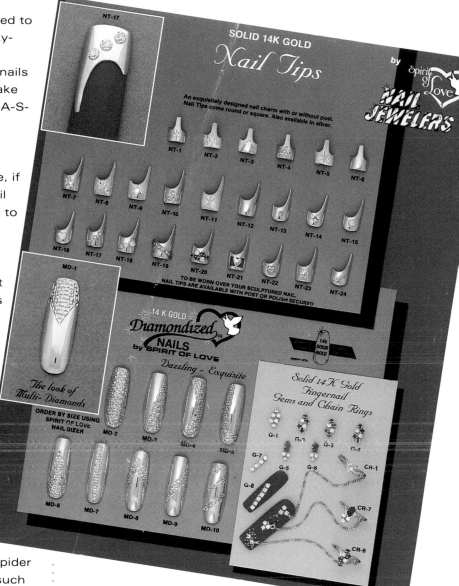

Once the design is complete, the finishing touch to an artistic manicure is brush-on nail fragrance, available in familiar scents such as Giorgio and Opium, as well as ever-popular musk. However diverse the art on the various nails, most nail technicians recommend using the same fragrance on all fingers and toes.

FISH STICKS

If you agree that the sight of a fish on a plate is repulsive, especially if it's still got its head or tail, then you understand the raison d'être of fish sticks. A stick of fish, as opposed to a whole fish or part of one, eliminates so many of the gruesome problems of eating seafood: having to look at a dead animal or, even worse, eviscerate and scale it, then fillet it; worrying about choking on fish bones; having hands that smell like fish; and disposing of the skeleton in a place where the cat can't find it. Fish sticks also pretty much eliminate the other awful thing about fish: the taste. Those pleasant golden-crusted logs with snow-white insides have only the gentlest hint of fish flavor, which is easily disguised by a good dollop of sweet tartar sauce.

Despite these many admirable qualities— actually, because of them—fish sticks are way down low on the ladder of culinary respectability. Epicures turn up their noses at them because fish sticks deny fundamental gastronomic assumptions with impunity. A fish stick says bake 'n' serve is as good as spending an afternoon making court bouillon for poaching. A fish stick says industrially formed and flaked Alaskan pollock compares to king salmon in its natural form. To those people who actually like eating fish, the closer it is to its swimming, living state, the better it is. (Hence such shocking culinary concepts as sushi [raw fish], ''rare'' fish, and whole fish that you have to pick off the bones to eat.) To the fish frowners of the world, however, fish is tolerable only when someone else has cleaned it, filleted it, cooked it, and covered it with Newberg sauce; or better yet, frozen it, whitened it, and miter-cut it into handy little sticks.

In the days before technology made cooking easy, people dealt with the fish problem by making their own fish balls, fish croquettes, and fish loaves. This was fine if you had leftover fish, and it did yield a main course that at least looked like a respectable piece of meat; but it didn't address any of the annoyances that make fish

BAKED FISH STICKS

24 frozen fried fish sticks
Tartar sauce

Place frozen fish in single layer on a cookie sheet. Bake at 400 degrees 20 minutes or until fish flakes easily when tested with a fork. Serve with tartar sauce.

Yield: 4–6 servings

preparation so daunting. A solution was stumbled upon in 1946 by Edward Piszek of Philadelphia. Piszek made crab cakes for a local tavern every Friday night. One Friday he found himself stuck with a batch of unsold crab cakes. Rather than throw them out, he decided to try and freeze them. He defrosted them the next day, heated them up, and sold them to happy beer drinkers.

Piszek opened a store where he sold just-cooked crab cakes to individual consumers and frozen ones to local grocery stores. As more private homes got freezers, he expanded his operation beyond the crab-cakes-to-go business. This was the beginning of Mrs. Paul's Kitchens (named for one of Piszek's partners). In 1952 Mrs. Paul's introduced its million-dollar idea— fish sticks. No longer was it necessary for the homemaker to fuss with fish, or the diner to pick at them. Fish sticks came ready-cooked. They only needed to be heated and strewn on a plate, from which they could be eaten effortlessly with fork or fingers. Fish sticks transformed fish from something frightening into a meal perfectly suitable for school lunch rooms and clean-smelling suburban kitchens: easy to make, easy to eat, and utterly innocuous.

The above recipe, adapted from *Let's Cook Fish!*, published by the U.S. Department of the Interior, demonstrates just how effortless fish sticks are.

FONTAINEBLEAU HOTEL

The Fontainebleau was the biggest, costliest, and most luxurious hotel on Miami Beach when it opened in 1954. It established standards for architectural extravagance that have never been matched.

A 550-foot-long masonry-and-glass arc built atop the remains of the Firestone mansion in an area once reserved for the homes of the elite superrich, the Fontainebleau changed the image of Miami Beach from an inaccessible strip of patrician land into a glamorous and sophisticated resort available to all prosperous people, if not to the common man. "Everyone will feel like he is being carried around on his own little silver platter," a hotel spokesman said when it opened. Although rooms were expensive (a minimum of thirty-three dollars a day), the hotel's whopping size abjured exclusivity. One dining room, with a hydraulically controlled dance floor, seated eight hundred; the Grand Ballroom accommodated three thousand. The main lobby was seventeen thousand square feet. "Gigantic?" asked Joan Neilson of the Miami *Herald* after opening night. "There must be a bigger word."

No one architectural style is big enough to contain it; but the characteristic design elements of architect Morris Lapidus's work, which he had been

perfecting ever since he began building what he called "wild and wooly modern" stores in New York in the twenties, were the "woggle," the boomerang/palette shape, usually affixed to walls or dangling from the ceiling; the "cheese hole," the nonfunctional free-form opening in any surface, particularly in a dangling woggle; and the "bean pole," thin rods hanging from the ceiling, attached to a wall, or coming up from the floor. Bean poles were sometimes functional, used to hold woggles; but often they were attached to things simply to create a sleek effect.

"I want that nice modern French provincial," Lapidus was told by builder Ben Novack when he was given the Fontainebleau commission; he obliged by filling the fourteen-story hotel with flamboyant chandeliers, red velour draperies by the ton, rococo mirrors, ennobling statuary, babbling fountains, formal gardens, dramatic jutting canopies, cantilevered staircases, platoons of bellboys in paramilitary uniforms, and a million and a half dollars' worth of European antiques. What a far cry from the reigning contemporary

standards of architectural good taste, which glorified clean lines, open space, and rational reasons for every element of the design! Even the name "Fontainebleau," which had dawned upon the builder's wife when she visited France, seemed ornamented with French provincial vowels.

"A hotel should be no place like home," Lapidus was fond of saying. Nor was the Fontainebleau much like any hotel that had preceded it. It was a building that did more than make guests feel comfortable. It entertained them in nearly the same manner as Disneyland, which opened the following year, by creating exotic tableaux and farfetched illusions wherever you looked. People who lunched on the patio had underwater views of swimmers in the pool; for dessert they ate a dish called "La Rosée Poetiques Gourmandises Le Plaisir d'Empire" (baked Alaska), carried through the room by white-gloved waiters in a flambé parade. Lapidus explained the architectural logic: "People are looking for illusions. . . . And, I asked, where do I find this world of illusion? Where are their tastes formulated? Do they study it in school? Do they go to museums? Do they travel in Europe? Only one place—the movies. They go to the movies. The hell with everything else."

For years, the Fontainebleau was the standard bearer of Floridian opulence, condemned by cultural elitists as kitsch but beloved by sybarites from Elvis Presley, who went straight to the Fontainebleau when he got out of the army in 1960, to Liberace, who made it his home away from his Las Vegas home whenever he visited Miami Beach. It hosted the Miss Universe Pageant for eleven years, and added a rock grotto lagoon, including man-made mountain and waterfalls, in 1978, when it became the Fontainebleau Hilton.

"Your building is your stage set and your actors and your audience are one and the same," Lapidus told The New Yorker when the Fontainebleau opened. He described the goal of the place as "Step inside the door, and zingo! Euphoria!"

FOREST LAWN CEMETERY

There is something missing at Forest Lawn Memorial Park in Glendale, California: a happy Jesus Christ. For years Forest Lawn's owner, Hubert Eaton, searched the world to find an image of a smiling Jesus for his cemetery. In Italy, he offered a million lire to any artist who could paint the Savior with a smile. All he got, according to the definitive book about Eaton's life and works, *The Forest Lawn Story* (1955), were the usual gloomy-Gus Christs and a few Christs with "sickly grins." This was not good enough for Eaton, who had a vision when he first saw the little cemetery in the rolling foothills of the Sierra Madre mountains. It was a vision of a burial ground that would be a sunny place.

Except for the smiling Jesus Christ, Hubert Eaton's vision did come true. "Nineteen centuries had to pass before Christians in any number accepted the fact that beauty and joy could take the place of ugliness and sorrow in association with death," observed Ralph Hancock, Eaton's biographer. Nearly two millennia after Jesus Christ, the joy of death was realized at Forest Lawn.

Eaton first got into cemeteries in St. Louis with partners who pioneered what is now known in the interment business as the "before need" system: selling people graves before they die, so the resting place is ready when they are. In 1913, eager to light out on his own, Eaton took the idea to the tiny Los Angeles suburb of Tropico (now Glendale), and a cemetery that was having a hard time selling space. After three years as sales manager, Eaton became a partner, and eventually sole owner of Forest Lawn Cemetery, the name of which he changed to Forest Lawn Memorial Park. He then set out on his life's work of creating the happiest, most flamboyant burial ground in the world.

He imported ducks and singing birds and built babbling fountains. He banished "misshapen monuments," allowing only magnificent mausoleums and memorial gardens. He went to Europe twice each year, bringing back genuine and imitation tapestries, statuary, stained glass, paintings, and antique furniture—all cheerful, none sad—to fill the grounds. Eaton built three imitation European churches, including the Wee Kirk o' the Heather (where the folktale of Annie Laurie is told in its stained-glass windows), a tenth-century Church of the Recessional (just like the one Rudyard Kipling used), and a Little Church of the Flowers, inspired by Thomas Gray's "Elegy Written in a Country Churchyard." He built a Hall of the Crucifixion, boasting the largest religious painting in the world, Jan Styka's *Crucifixion*—195 by 45 feet—which happens to be covered (before its unveiling every hour, on the hour) by the world's largest curtain —thirty-five hundred pounds of hand-hemmed velvet.

Hubert Eaton

124

Eaton battled with California's Board of Embalmers and Funeral Directors, who hated his bombast and in fact lobbied to deny him a mortuary license in 1933; but movie stars and show-offs of all professions fell in love with the pomp and prodigality. It was, after all, *so Hollywood.* Ronald Reagan was married (to Jane Wyman) at Forest Lawn; a million tourists visit every year (and shop in the on-premises souvenir store); and here are buried more stars than you could ever hope to spot alive if you go celebrity hunting around town, including W. C. Fields, Jean Harlow, Buster Keaton, Humphrey Bogart, Liberace (along with his brother, George, and their mom, Frances), and Freddie Prinze. Here, too, are buried Theodore Dreiser (in the Whispering Pines section), Gutzon Borglum (Mount Rushmore's sculptor), evangelist Aimee Semple McPherson, Joseph Baerman Strauss (designer of the Golden Gate Bridge, whose bronze tablet is a bas-relief of the bridge), William Henry Rowe (inventor of the cigarette vending machine), and John Ball (who wrote the novel *In the Heat of the Night* and who, as "Donald Johnson," was one of America's leading advocates of social nudism).

Other great Forest Lawn attractions: a collection of replicas of every coin mentioned in the Bible; a thirty-foot mosaic of Turnbull's *The Signing of the Declaration of Independence;* a full-size Old North Church; Hubert Eaton's personal rock collection (he was a metallurgist by trade); and the pride of the collection— Michelangelo's *David.* "World travelers are thrilled to find Michelangelo's *David* in a setting far more inspiring than the original in Florence," biographer Ralph Hancock enthused, not mentioning the relief prudish travelers must experience when they find that this David, although an exact reproduction of the original in every other way, has no penis.

See also **LIBERACE**

FREDERICK'S OF HOLLYWOOD

I love women. I love their curves. I love looking." So wrote Frederick N. Mellinger, founder of America's foremost purveyor of naughty negligees, Frederick's of Hollywood. Whatever a woman needs to make herself sexy in an old goat's eyes, Frederick's sells it. If you are in the market for Riot Squad Bikini Panties and Sheik's Choice slave-girl harem pajamas, this is the place. If you need shoes, perhaps you want to consider Cuddle Puff lucite slippers with marabou-trimmed vamps. Or Dagger-Dance five-inch spiked heels. Or Conquistador knee-high white calfskin boots ("You'll need a whip to beat the men off!"). All are classics from more than forty years of Frederick's mail-order catalogues.

In addition to flirty nighties, pinup-girl swimsuits, bewitching evening wear (in crepe, satin, metallic lurex, and taffeta), and a boundless assortment of scandalous scanties (including Back-to-Nature panties with lace-edged derriere cutout), Frederick's of Hollywood has been the nation's number-one specialist in prosthetic fashions that help make a woman's figure perfect, whatever its flaws. To correct flat fannies, Frederick's has offered the Living End girdle with foam rubber padding in the seat

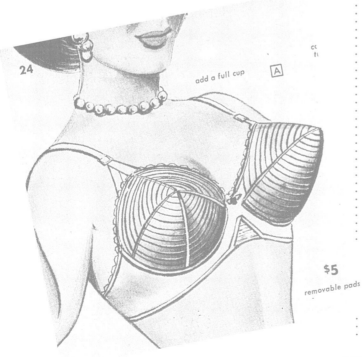

24

add a full cup Ⓐ

$5
removable pads

("feels real!"); for fannies that droop, there was the Secret Helper, which lifts the bottom of the buttocks and separates the cheeks "for that natural look." Bust problems could be alleviated with all kinds of padded bras, from the push-up Oo-La-La and Hollywood Hi-Dive to the Light 'N' Lovely Air-Lite Inflatable, which allows the wearer to choose whatever bust size she wants on any particular day, then blow up her brassiere cups using a hidden straw. Prosthetic jutting nipples on pads designed to fit inside brassieres, at three dollars a pair, were available for women who want to achieve the pointy look.

No anatomical problem is beyond a Frederick's fix. Large waists can be corseted; skinny calves can be turned into plump drumsticks with padded panty hose; even a flat head can be rounded by the proper choice of a Frederick's of Hollywood domed wig. Mr. Mellinger, who appears as the dapper "Mr. Frederick" throughout Frederick's of Hollywood catalogues in little cameo pictures with bits of advice about such topics as "the difference between *sag* and *surge*" and "the Hollywood look he'll love," wrote, "There is no 'perfect woman,' but a perfectly proportioned woman with a balanced figure is a real attention-getter."

Perfectly proportioned women were Frederick's of Hollywood's goal from the beginning. All the time Mr. Mellinger served in the U.S. Army in World War II, he dreamt of perfectly proportioned women. But when the war ended and he was discharged, he worried that his dream might never come true. Later, he recalled the frustration: "Where were the satin and lace nightgowns and slips that went with every mental picture I'd had of girls who did turn me on when I was in the Army?" He determined to correct the dearth of nightgowns and slips. "I studied anatomy. Why breasts drooped. Why fannies or hips were flat. Why waists were thick. Why legs were 'piano legs.' I knew there had to be ways to reproportion women and give every

loveable one of them EQUAL OPPORTUNITY in the eyes of men." In 1947 he started a mail-order business with a Hollywood address; and postwar America, frisky and eager for fun and enraptured with a new curvaceous ideal of feminine beauty, made Frederick's of Hollywood a grand success.

In 1952, Mellinger began opening retail stores, first in Hollywood, then all across the country. By the mid-eighties, there were 148 Frederick's stores specializing in sexy "outer fashions" and "body sculpting" foundations. The flagship, on Hollywood Boulevard, was—and still is—a grand lavender palace with an almost quaint air of naughty-but-nice titillation. (Recently, efforts have been made to modernize Frederick's image by putting the more respectable teddies and camisoles up front, and raunchier items, such as musical and edible panties, in the back.)

The regalia of feminine beauty sold by Frederick's of Hollywood are seducers' fundamentals: leopard-skin-patterned sheaths; ruffles and lace; fluffy powder puffs attached to shoes and bodices; see-through and peek-a-boo. Likewise, the ideal Frederick's woman is a party girl who now seems like an artifact of another time. She has long, curly hair (or fall or wig), swelling buttocks, extra-long legs, tiny waist, and, of course, the pièces de résistance—full, pert, pointy, pink, perfectly symmetrical, and neatly separated breasts.

Although Frederick's idea of feminine pulchritude—the hourglass figure—was established in the bosom-worshiping forties and fifties, the mail-order catalogues have always been quick to offer glamorized versions of currently popular street fashion. For example, when hippie style was in vogue, Frederick's offered buyers a chance to "DO YOUR OWN THING! B.P.'S (BEAUTIFUL PEOPLE) DO . . . WITH FREDERICK'S, OF COURSE"—in the form of Ring-A-Dinger hip-hugger pants with frantic suede fringe flowing out from the knees, and crepe culottes covered with daisies and known as Flower Child ("lovely to look at and ripe for the picking!"). A few years later, when platform shoes were the rage, Frederick's sold "the newest, the nowest, the highest" shoes, with cork platforms and glittering gold straps. The latest catalogues offer Dynamic Denims and crotchless panty hose, as well as a supply of novelty briefs for men (flamingo-faced G-strings, tear-away thongs).

Frederick's mirrors changing tastes, but its fashions have always been unique. The clothes are frilly and feminine, if not downright flimsy; and they are cheap. (These are low-ticket items; even the most expensive things in the catalogue —the fake furs—have always sold at prices that are less than half of what Sears has charged for its more demure equivalents.) Most of what Frederick's has offered over the years are clothes unaffected by contemporary fads. "Dumb fashion trends are not for us or our customers," Mr. Mellinger wrote. "We change fashions for one purpose. To glorify and re-glorify a woman's figure." The Frederick's look, unlike clothing found in boutiques and department stores, only reluctantly changes from year to year and season to season; and despite efforts at modernization, Frederick's vision of ideal beauty has remained constant. The result of this rock-steady philosophy is a collection of apparel that in at least one way compares with the fashions of Coco Chanel or Brooks Brothers: It is timeless. Bad taste never goes out of style.

See also **BREASTS, ENORMOUS**

FUZZY DICE

The best fuzzy dice are sold by the kind of mail-order automotive catalogues that list such wonders as instant Engine Overhaul Pellets (drop them in the crankcase for thousands of miles of trouble-free driving), the programmable musical horn (it plays "La Cucaracha," "Strangers in the Night," etc.), and the incredibly realistic imitation cellular phone ("Only YOU will know it's a replica"). The dice, which come in pairs, are covered with plush fake angora fur and have a built-in string so they can be attached to a rearview mirror, where they dangle and bounce like dice in play as the car cruises through town. Fuzzy dice are available as 2½-inch cubes or 4-inch cubes in a variety of color combinations, including white with black dots, black with white dots, light blue, dark blue, red, brown, and gray. The time-honored color combination is pink with black dots, although a salesperson at J. C. Whitney & Co., Chicago's 65,000-item mail-order auto parts supply house, told us that he felt pink dice were too effeminate and that the J. C. Whitney inventory had been pared to the indisputably masculine color combination of white with black dots.

The origin of fuzzy dice, like the origin of casino dice, is obscure. Archaeologists have proven that gaming cubes were invented before the written word; but it seems safe to speculate that fuzzy ones for cars did not exist until at least the thirties, when gambling was legalized in Las Vegas, or possibly the forties, when teenage drivers first began making hot-rod cars from plundered junkyard parts. Many early hot rods were designed to combine a look of extravagant luxury with outlaw ferocity; fuzzy dice perfectly fit those aesthetic criteria. They provided a time-honored sign of devil-may-care sinfulness; but their munificent size and softness made them voluptuous enough for a lush show car.

In the old days, fuzzy dice were only made in black-and-white and were covered with felt rather than the more luxurious imitation goat fur. Fuzzy dice sales soared in the fifties when colorful variants became available; they became a popular decorative touch in ordinary hardtops and convertibles as well as custom dragsters. Improved plushness in recent years has ingratiated them with low riders who prefer nearly everything inside their vehicle to be soft and woolly. And, along with pink flamingo lawn ornaments, fuzzy dice have also garnered fans among retro-hip sophisticates, to whom the outré lucky charms are a symbol of the gloriously gauche era of big tail fins, leopard-skin seat covers, and making out on Lovers' Lane.

Although dice alone make it perfectly clear that the person behind the wheel marches to the beat of an uncouth drummer, our J. C. Whitney salesperson convinced us that they were only half the answer if what we sought was a truly opulent interior. He suggested we complement the dice with an Angora Look Fun Fur Dress-Up Kit, which includes a long-nap dashboard cover with self-sticking tape (trims easily to fit any dash), an elasticized short-nap steering-wheel cover, and a rearview-mirror muff. The Dress-Up Kit comes in colors that exactly match the dice, and looks especially sharp, our shopper advised, when used in concert with a foot-shaped accelerator pedal (complete with chrome toes) and a black plastic 8-Ball Shift Knob.

GABORS

Diamonds, mink coats, and rich husbands: Zsa Zsa and Eva Gabor have never gotten enough of any of them. The two Gabors, abetted by their sister, Magda, and their mother, Jolie, are voluptuary beauty queens known less for their abilities as actresses than for their voracious self-indulgence. Notoriety is what the Gabor women have spent their careers amassing, even more than men and money.

They have always been the epitome of glamour—in the old-fashioned and slightly promiscuous meaning of the word that suggests a life of ribboned gift boxes from handsome suitors delivered to the penthouse suite, lavish nights on the town, fabulous divorce settlements, popping champagne corks, and pink bubble baths. When the Frederick's of Hollywood catalogue marketed Zsa Zsa's book, *How to Catch a Man, How to Keep a Man, How to Get Rid of a Man* (which was printed on powder-blue paper), it described the author as "Hollywood's most glamorous femme fatale." The Gabors' feminine charms have been enrobed in an exotic and remarkably undiminished Hungarian accent that manages to make any remark sound provocative.

Eva was the first Gabor to arrive in America from Budapest, at age eighteen in 1939. She married a Hollywood gentleman she lauded as "a Norse god, the handsomest man in the world"—Eric Drimmer, alternately described in contemporary accounts as a psychiatrist, an osteopath, and a masseur. In 1941 she began her career as an actress in the B movie *Forced Landing*. The New York *Post* summarized her early acting career as "an array of stage flops from La Jolla, California, to Broadway, New York." Eva recalled one early such production, staged in a tent in Hollywood: "I was in my dressing room and I leaned against the wall and found myself in the street. There I was in Ventura Boulevard in my panties."

Although her show-business career went nowhere until 1950, when she played an acrobat-turned-maid in the Broadway play *The Happy Time,* Eva was soon a millionaire, thanks to marriage number two, to realtor Charles Isaacs. She married three more times and had some notable dramatic successes, in Noël Coward's revival of *Present Laughter* in 1958 and, most memorably, in television's hit series "Green Acres" from 1965 to 1971, in which she played a socialite living reluctantly on a hillbilly farm outside the hick town of Hooterville with, among others, Arnold the pig. She reached a cosmetological climax of sorts in the mid-sixties, when *Celebrity Register* author Earl Blackwell noted that her blond bouffant was "as blinding as Mont Blanc on a sunny day."

Eva shared glamour secrets with her readers in an autobiography called *Orchids and Salami* (because they were the two things she always had in her refrigerator), the dust jacket of which promised the book would "break through the mink curtain." Among the revelations was its author's reliance on a long cigarette holder. "Some men will swoon over a woman wearing hip boots and carrying a sack of dead mackerel, provided she smokes a cigarette in a long holder," Eva advised. Other beauty secrets, from the chapter "Me and My Glamour": "My routine includes weighty conflicts over the right dress, the right jewelry. I ask myself more questions than Hamlet as I ponder over which pair of shoes to wear."

Eva had the reputation as the serious actress in the family and, according to *Esquire* in 1953, "the shrewdest of these careeristinas"; but to her dismay she was often upstaged by older sister Zsa Zsa (formerly Miss Hungary, or first runner-up, in 1938, or 1933, depending on whether you believe Zsa Zsa or the facts). Zsa Zsa divorced her first husband, a Turkish diplomat named Burhan Belge, and landed in New York in 1939. "I arrived in the morning and had lunch in '21' in the afternoon," she recalled. A few weeks later, she joined Eva in Hollywood, where she went on a blind date with Conrad Hilton.

Hilton and Zsa Zsa married, had a daughter (Francesca), played house (as when Zsa Zsa burned the rug in their Plaza Hotel apartment

trying to cook a Turkish dinner at an indoor campfire), and divorced. Hilton said he enjoyed his marriage despite what the lawyer testified were "indiscretions that would result in her deportation as an undesirable alien." After the divorce, Hilton cheerfully commented, "I did not begrudge a penny of it."

Zsa Zsa was so busy with romance, she didn't have time for show business until her third marriage, to actor George Sanders. In his autobiography, *Memoirs of a Professional Cad*, Sanders described his role as a husband to Zsa Zsa as being "a sort of paying guest," recalling little other than desperately trying to get his wife's attention while she was under the hair dryer or being interviewed and photographed by the show-business press. When Sanders went to Italy to shoot *Voyage to Italy*, Zsa Zsa appeared on a television panel show called "Bachelor's Heaven" and wowed the audience with such witticisms as "Men I can do without—but not for long" and (when asked about her jewelry) "Oh, these—these are just my working diamonds." Director Mervyn LeRoy was so impressed he gave her a part in the movie *Lovely to Look At*.

Although Magda was an actress, too (the *Post* described her as "the talented one"), and all three sisters did a nightclub act together in Las Vegas in the mid-fifties, she seemed not to have her sisters' enthusiasm for publicity. "Magda has tried," said one former husband (she had four), "but has never had the success the others have as far as being written about." By the late fifties, when Eva and Zsa Zsa were in their heyday, Magda had been eclipsed, becoming what *The Complete Directory of Prime Time TV Stars* described as "a society figure in New York."

The Gabor saga is not complete without mention of the career of Mama Jolie. In her book *Jolie Gabor (As Told to Cindy Adams)*, she compared herself with her daughters: "No matter how much aggressiveness and competitiveness and desire to succeed and be gorgeous and famous that they may have, I still have more." Jolie liked to say that she arrived in America in 1946 with only a hundred dollars and a mink coat, after divorcing Papa Vilmos Gabor and fleeing Budapest when the Russians marched in. She used her hundred dollars to tip the crew of the ship, and the mink was stolen; nonetheless, she managed to start Jolie Gabor, Inc., on Madison Avenue in New York, a costume-jewelry store that boasted nonexistent branches in the glamour capitals of the world and a staff of European pseudoaristocracy. Jolie herself began playing the field, was named corespondent in the splashy 1949 divorce case of Baron Stephen Kelen D'Oxylion, and settled down in marriage for a short while (just long enough to obtain U.S. citizenship) with ex-G.I. Peter Christman, an employee of the Hamburger Heaven across the street from her shop.

In her book *Facelifts*, Norma Lee Browning described an "unveiling party" given for Jolie Gabor in the early eighties in Palm Springs, California. The thing being unveiled was Mrs. Gabor's new face, a mere eighteen days after its lift, performed by Dr. Borko Djordjevic using the then-radical tuck-and-peel technique that left octogenarian Jolie's skin as smooth as chrome. "Jolie's new face was the talk of the party," Miss Browning wrote. "It was, to put it mildly, rather spectacular."

Of all the Gabors, it was Zsa Zsa who established the gold standard for marrying and divorcing rich, getting into highly publicized fights, and making outrageous remarks to the press. "I wasn't born," she used to say. "I was ordered from room service." Zsa Zsa was especially adept at attracting attention when she feuded with sister Eva, which she did often and spitefully.

Their most vicious sibling row occurred in 1945, after Zsa Zsa had a fight at El Morocco with the club's owner, John Perona, with whom Eva was cohabiting at the time. Zsa Zsa threatened to expose Eva's shameful living arrangements. According to Zsa Zsa's lawyer, Eva had had Zsa Zsa shunted into the West Hills Sanitarium for the mentally ill. Zsa Zsa said she spent seven weeks getting shock treatments and drugs and having insulin injected into her thighs.

When she got out, Zsa Zsa made up with Eva—temporarily—but sued her own lawyers for "misplacing" her furs and jewels while she was incarcerated. John Perona barred her from El Morocco in perpetuity.

Zsa Zsa's feuding wasn't only with her sister. She was famous for her public fights. In 1945, for reasons now lost in the mists of time, she attacked Hildegarde, the singer, who dispatched her friend Louis Ritter, a New York furrier, to beat up Zsa Zsa. That same year she appeared at '21' with a bandaged nose, which she says she got fighting a duel over a man with a Washington hostess. (Skeptics tracked the bandages to the I. Daniel Shorell Hospital for Plastic Surgery.) The next night, when people laughed at her bandaged nose at a New York nightclub, Zsa Zsa doused them with champagne.

Among her juicier sorties was one with French-accented actress Corinne Calvet that began when Zsa Zsa said Corinne was born in the slums of London (not Paris, as Corinne claimed). Corinne countered with a $1 million slander suit and a challenge that both actresses strip to the waist to prove who had the bigger bust.

Zsa Zsa's fight with playboy Porfirio Rubirosa in 1953 was the most notorious of her career. Rubirosa first ran into Zsa Zsa in the elevator at the Plaza Hotel. "Her blonde hair was swept up," he recalled. "She was wearing a mink coat and leading two poodles. She was a staggering sight." To make husband George Sanders jealous, Zsa Zsa dated Señor Rubirosa and abandoned herself to a life she described as "polo, nightclubs, and parties." Some time after Ruby dumped Zsa Zsa for heiress Barbara Hutton, the two ex-lovers confronted each other in a Las Vegas dressing room, and hell broke loose. He said he merely pushed her and she hit her forehead on a door. She said he hauled off and punched her. Whatever the choreography, Zsa Zsa emerged from the battle and appeared at the press conference that followed it (Gabor fights are customarily followed by press conferences) wearing a low-cut gown and a black eye patch to cover an ugly shiner.

In June 1989, Zsa Zsa had one more headline-grabbing fight, this with a police officer who stopped her for driving with expired license plates and having an open bottle of liquor in the car. She slapped the officer, breaking two fingernails, and was arrested. "It's getting so you cannot drive a Rolls-Royce in Beverly Hills anymore," lamented Zsa Zsa at the postarrest press conference, reminding reporters that she now prefers to be called Princess Zsa Zsa, since her most recent husband, Frederick von Anhalt, purchased a European title. Convicted on all counts after a fifteen-day publicity bonanza of a trial (during which she tried to explain that the birth date and weight on her driver's license had been altered by Mexican vandals), Zsa Zsa proclaimed herself a Hungarian freedom fighter and announced that she had been found guilty only because the members of the jury were not her class of people.

See also **FACE-LIFTS**

GAGS AND NOVELTIES

WHOOPS!'' says the headline of an advertisement that shows a chunky puddle of lifelike vomit heaved on the floor as shocked and embarrassed people gather around to inspect it. ''Place this disgusting mess of plastic in the bathroom, near the refrigerator, on a rug—anywhere! Watch the fun begin when your friends try and figure out who got sick. Great at parties, banquets, conventions . . . only $1.00.''

This particular advertisement appeared in the back of a 1962 issue of *Rhythm and Blues* magazine that featured a very young Miss Aretha Franklin on the cover. Unlike Miss Franklin, who is a modern American original, artificial vomit is practically an antique, dating back perhaps a hundred years; it will no doubt last as long as people think practical jokes are funny. Faux vomit and its partners in mirth—rubber dog doo, black soap, red-hot chewing gum, joy buzzers, flies in plastic ice cubes, fabric ''snakes'' that fly into your face when you open the candy jar, and squirting lapel flowers—have been around so long that if there were clubs for awful things, theirs would be the equivalent of the DAR.

It is a mystery even to the people who operate the novelty trade where many of the classic items originated. Some gags have been around for as long as they, or even their grandfathers, can remember. Mark Pahlow, who runs a large gag and novelty company in Seattle under the names Archie McPhee (retail) and Accoutrements (wholesale), is about as close to a historian as we found. Pahlow, labeled ''der Kitsch Kaiser'' (the Emperor of Kitsch) by the German press, believes that many well-known gags and novelties originated in Germany. As an example, he points to the Spud Gun, a toy pistol designed to shoot hunks of raw potato after the barrel is plunged into the vegetable and withdrawn, which he says was invented in Germany in the 1800s. On the other hand, E. Joseph Cossman, popularizer of the American Spud Gun, contends it came from England, where he bought his original tooling. Cossman, an early TV pitchman and brother-in-law of Uncle Milton (manufacturer of the fabled Ant Farm) sold a million and a half Spud Guns in the fifties, as well as other classic novelties such as half-size big-game wild-animal-head trophies molded of pliable skin-textured plastic. (Spud Guns are now listed in the Archie McPhee catalogue as Potato Guns, for $2.95 each.)

Pahlow thinks that most of the now-familiar novelties made their American debut early in the century, when traveling carnivals were popular and large quantities of cheap gags were in demand as prizes for midway games and penny-arcade claw machines. He also speculates that the sometimes nefarious life-style of the carnival barkers set the tone for the wholesale novelty trade of today, which is run mostly by secretive family businesses with much intrigue, rivalry, and counterfeiting of hot items.

The novelty business boomed in the twenties and thirties, when the Pressner and Nadel companies of New York traveled to the Orient and set up factories to have merchandise made cheap in Japan and China. Catalogues from those years show many of the same sorts of things popular today, but with their sharp racist themes undisguised. One ten-cent novelty listed in a vintage catalog from Pahlow's collection is a movable disk with a "cullud lady" on one side and a "cullud man" on the other: flip it around fast and you see them "spooning." In those days, the glasses with big bushy eyebrows and big noses that make everybody look like Groucho Marx were known as "Jew Nose"; big wax lips were "Nigger Lips."

World War II was a near disaster for many in the gag and novelty business. The Pressner and Nadel companies, which were riding high selling dirt-cheap Japanese merchandise before the war, almost went out of business when Americans refused to buy Japanese goods. They were stuck with warehouses full of whoopee cushions that they could not sell. (Both companies survived and are now run by the sons of the founders.)

Today, most novelty companies have specialties; and individual countries are known for making certain things best. For example, the Franco-American Company of Glendale, New York, run by Bob Oumano, makes the best Jew Noses, which they have copyrighted under the less offensive name "Beagle Puss." Spain— Barcelona in particular—is known as home of the

world's finest rubber chickens; Germany is famous in the trade for stink bombs and noise makers. Italy produces superb fake foods, such as rubber joke hamburgers and inedible chocolates.

One of the best-known and biggest marketers of gags and novelties is the Johnson-Smith Company of Florida, formerly of Mount Clemens, Michigan. Their catalogue *2000 Novelties* includes such enjoyable jokes as rubber bats with suction cups, high-voltage electric chocolates, awful-tasting cola drink, bleeding daggers ("wear on your back"), bony hands (clip on dress, tie, coffee cup, etc.), gory horror rubber feet, giant horrible rubber hands, comic bald heads, X-Ray Spex ("see your legs right through your pants!"), and a beatnik disguise ("real gone, man").

Good taste is a surprisingly big issue in an industry that trades in bad taste—at least to Mark Pahlow. Both his Archie McPhee and his

"WHOOPS"

GREAT FUN AT HOME • PARTIES • OFFICE

THE MOST DISGUSTING LAFF GETTER!

SPRINKLE WITH WATER TO MAKE IT LOOK MORE REALISTIC.

PERFECT FOR THE...
• BATHROOM
• REFRIGERATOR
• AUTO SEAT
• SIDEWALK

#689 "WHOOPS" Reg. U.S. Pat Office ©1985 FISHLOVE/FUN INC. Chicago, IL 60614

Accoutrements pride themselves on their selection of "neat stuff": all-in-good-fun items like fake cigarette burns for the carpet, plastic ants, eyeglasses with eyeballs attached to Slinky springs, and glow-in-the-dark cockroaches. They do not touch "adult" and X-rated gags. For those, the place to go is Forum Novelties of Elmont, New York.

Forum's catalogue includes perfectly respectable chattering teeth, plastic potato chips, and battery-operated beating hearts; but it also contains so much dirty stuff that the merchandise is divided into distinct categories such as Novelty Underwear, Box Gags, and Eye Accessories (eyeglasses with attached penis-nose, eyeglasses with temples shaped like female legs, etc.). Here is where you find Fundees

underwear made for two; Potty Pot Shots toilet-bowl targets for men to pee on, and the Shove-It desk set which includes a pen holder shaped like an upraised pair of butt cheeks with an anus sized to hold the pen.

The variety of jokes involving breasts and genitalia staggers the imagination. There is Mister Peter, a plastic mold to make penis-shaped ice cubes; a Ball with Boobs golf ball to help your favorite bachelor keep his eye on the game; penis-shaped ice-cream cones; "Booby" teething rings; a rubber hot-dog bun holding a two-headed rubber penis; a big nipple that fits on the top of beer cans; and a gift box "for the girl who has everything," featuring a three-cupped bra.

Bowel movements are also a popular gag theme. The Shit Head Hat is a bonnet made with a pile of lifelike rubber turds on top; Deluxe Doggy Doo (made in Spain) is "so real it fools other dogs"; the Party Pooper is a turd shaped to look like it is drooping off the toilet seat ("someone missed!"); and there is also a "good gift for expectant parents": an imitation dirty diaper "so real you can almost smell it."

Who buys gags and novelties? Mark Pahlow says that a disproportionate number of orders come from the wealthy suburbs of Washington, D.C. Now, there's a good laugh: thinking that the people who run the United States government are well supplied with Mr. Spock ears, rubber brains, and Magic 8 Balls.

GAME SHOWS

What are people willing to do in the pursuit of money, valuable free gifts, or the thrill of being on television? They will push walnuts across the floor with their noses ("Truth or Consequences"), they will wear chicken suits, flap, and cluck ("Let's Make a Deal"), they will reveal intimate details about their sex lives ("The Newlywed Game"), they will tell the studio and viewing audience how their husband lost his job and his wooden leg got eaten by termites and all they really want is a new iron lung for their crippled sister ("Queen for a Day").

Not all game shows involve abject humiliation and bathos; but even the tests of intelligence, such as "The $64,000 Question," "The $25,000 Pyramid," and "Jeopardy!," have been built upon an unholy alliance of avarice and exhibitionism. They are television distilled to its purest form—an amalgam of money lust, sponsor plugs, preposterous suspense, and relentless gaiety.

It is an ingenious programming formula. Game shows are cheap to produce. In most cases they celebrate the joy of acquiring products, then offer advertising time to people who have products for sale. In the case of "The Price Is Right," the longest-running game show of all time, the whole point is to canonize buying things and to reward those contestants who prove themselves most familiar with products and prices. Nearly every show features breathless announcers extolling the giveaways, pretty women in gowns fondling merchandise (known in the business as "teasing the prizes"), and players noisily jumping up and down with the thrill of acquisition.

No matter how complicated the game itself, the basic win-or-lose formula of all game shows can be grasped by anybody one IQ point above brain death. Slack-jawed viewers can vegetate in the comfort of their homes and wallow in a strike-it-rich world of glittering prizes earned by people not much smarter than themselves! Of all the things television does well, it does nothing better than game shows, which have been a

"The Price Is Right"

programming staple since "Missus Goes A-Shopping" on New York's WCBS in 1944 and "Cash and Carry" (the first national show) on the Dumont network in 1946.

There were plenty of game shows on the radio in the thirties and forties, at first brain-teaser types such as "Uncle Jim's Question Bee," "Quiz Kids," and "Pot o' Gold," in which the format wasn't much more complicated than basic Q-and-A. After World War II, Bert Parks began hosting a show called "Stop the Music," produced by Mark Goodson, which offered not just money but *valuable prizes.* The thrill of suddenly winning THINGS (many of which were scarce during the war years) inspired movies such as Preston Sturges's *Christmas in July* (1940), *People Are Funny* (1945), *Champagne for Caesar* (1950), *The Jackpot* (1950, starring Jimmy Stewart), and *Queen for a Day* (1951, based on stories by Faith Baldwin, John Ashworth, and Dorothy Parker). After bright, shiny things became the stock-in-trade of game shows, it was natural for the shows to move to television so the things could be seen (and advertised).

In 1950 "You Bet Your Life," the civilized Groucho Marx show in which humor counted more than prizes, moved from radio to television. Another gentle-spirited game show premiered the same year: "What's My Line?," with high-tone celebrity panelists Dorothy Kilgallen, Louis Untermeyer (replaced by Bennett Cerf), Arlene Francis, and Franklin P. Adams sitting behind a long desk on which was painted a giant-size bottle of the program's sponsor, Stopette spray deodorant. They chatted wittily with host John Daly while trying to guess guests' offbeat professions (snake handler, human cannonball).

Nineteen fifty was a landmark year in the annals of television bad taste. That was when two of the most infamous game shows got their start. One was another long-lasting transplant from radio, "Truth or Consequences," on which contestants got buzzed by Beulah the Buzzer when they were unable to answer silly questions, then had to perform "the consequences"—an embarrassing stunt that involved getting shaving cream sprayed into their pants or having to carry a grapefruit across the stage balanced on a spoon held in their clenched teeth. "Beat the Clock" featured married couples performing nearly impossible tasks such as "Bal-Lingerie" (can wife stuff twelve balloons into hubby's long johns, while he's wearing them, without popping any?) and "Spuds in Your Eye" (hubby lies on his back on the floor with an empty ice-cream cone in his mouth, while wife stands overhead and drops scoops of mashed potatoes, trying to land them in the cone).

It wasn't until 1956 that "Queen for a Day" moved to television from radio, where it had premiered in 1945 as "Queen for Today." Like other game shows, "Queen for a Day" gave away prizes, but the twist was that the prizes went to a contestant selected by audience applause. To earn applause, contestants had to tell what they needed and why. Some wishes were frivolous; but the one who invariably received the loudest ovation was the woman who told the most heart-rending story about the suffering in her life.

Broadcast from Hollywood's Moulin Rouge theater-restaurant, "Queen for a Day" set standards of toe-curling tastelessness that have remained unequaled in game-show history. In order to win, it was almost always necessary for the contestant to whimper and moan as she enumerated her miseries, and thereby made herself seem even more wretched than any of the other sad ladies hoping to be crowned. As she

wailed her tale of woe, host Jack Bailey told jokes to keep the mood of the show light. (A contestant sobbed that her house had been robbed on New Year's Eve. "Happy New Year!" laughed Mr. Bailey.)

Adding to "Queen for a Day"'s stunning tactlessness were the prizes. Women whose lives had collapsed around them were awarded trips to the hairdresser and lunch at a movie studio, plus prizes to fit their particular dilemma. A woman whose husband was paralyzed and lay dying in the hospital was given a new car to go visit him and a year's supply of men's deodorant to bring him as a present. One contestant whose husband had died in bed pleaded for a new mattress. The end of each program was a dazzling coronation scene, during which the chosen Queen, always crying hysterically, was swatched in ermine and crowned, given a bouquet of red roses, and led to her velvet-covered throne by scantily clad courtiers, as Jack Bailey showered her with gifts, which were always announced by their brand names.

"Queen for a Day" set the benchmark of bad taste, but in the sixties Chuck Barris productions came close by devising new formats to provide contestants with heretofore unknown opportunities to make fools of themselves. On "The Dating Game" (starting in 1965), unseen bachelors were quizzed by a potential date, who had to select one of the guys based on his answers. The fun of the show was seeing the

expression on the questioner's face when she finally met the date she chose and compared him with the ones she didn't get. Barris's "The Newlywed Game" (starting in 1966) had four sets of newly married couples answer questions that tested how well each pair knew each other. This game provided all sorts of entertainment: watching the adorable newlyweds get red in the face when forced to answer risqué questions about how they "made whoopee" (the show's code words for sex) or about former boyfriends and girlfriends; seeing them club each other over the head with cardboard signs when they got questions wrong; and gaping at the amazing wide-collared pastel leisure suits that virtually all male contestants wore.

In a more self-conscious mode Barris created "The Gong Show" in 1976, based on "Ted Mack's Original Amateur Hour," on which talented amateur performers were interspersed with terrible acts such as a man who played the flute with his nose or one who made fart noises with his armpit. Even more egregious was Barris's "$1.98 Beauty Pageant" (1978), in which a panel of celebrities watched as cheap-looking babes paraded around in skimpy swimsuits and gave displays of their dubious and usually lewd talents.

Although "The Newlywed Game" always peppered its repartee with double entendres and the word "whoopee," it wasn't until the new "Match Game," premiering in 1973 (based on a show that first ran in 1962), that game shows got really ribald, as celebrity panelists began using what are strangely known in television as "adult words," such as "tinkle," "ding-dong," "bazooms," and "fanny." On "The Match Game," celebrity panelists had to fill in blanks in sentences such as "When I get married, I want a man with a big *blank*." There was no "correct" answer in games such as this; players won by guessing how their teammates or a celebrity panel would respond.

Traditionally, though, it has been acquisitiveness, not sex, that has made game shows such pinnacles of bad taste. One of the finest examples of this principle was "Supermarket Sweep," produced in 1965 by none other than the very cultured David Susskind, which sent men speeding into grocery stores with shopping carts to see who could grab the most stuff in a five-minute run, while their wives stood at cash registers trying to guess the prices of merchandise. The show's high point was watching the husbands battle it out at the butcher case over the most expensive roasts and turkeys. *Variety* called it a "daytime paean to human greed."

In 1982, several great game-show themes were combined in "Fantasy," a tour de force that attempted to recreate the magic of "Queen for a Day." On each show, co-hosts Peter Marshall and Leslie Uggams read a letter from a viewer in which the viewer described some terribly sad people who needed a fantasy to come true. The "Fantasy" truck was dispatched to find the needy people, who were taken by surprise when the "Fantasy" crew (accompanied by a Minicam to record the action) barged in and started showering them with valuable free gifts. On one memorable occasion a family of stunned Cambodian boat people were rendered speechless when they were awarded a brand-new microwave oven.

"Fantasy" concluded each program with a test of skill in which an impoverished contestant was sealed inside a glass-walled closet filled with dollar bills. When the buzzer buzzed, powerful fans inside the closet started blowing the dollars all around. The person inside the closet had sixty seconds to grab and keep as many dollars as he or she could hold. The trick to getting the most was to stuff them into your shirt, pants pockets, brassiere, underpants, waistband, and mouth. Such is the essence of game-show greatness.

GUCCIONE, BOB

Bob Guccione, founder and publisher of *Penthouse,* has been known for many gifts to world culture during his career, including exposed female labia in men's magazines; sexually explicit letters to the editor; a thriving sexual prosthetics and body-oil business; deposing the first black Miss America; and showing pictures of Jimmy Swaggart's favorite prostitute posing in the positions the Reverend Jimmy enjoyed most. But there is one thing for which he is best known: his chest. He did not invent the fashion, but Bob Guccione perfected male décolletage.

Guccione has frequently flaunted his chest in public on television talk shows and for interviews defending what he considers to be his First Amendment freedoms, the righteousness of "sexual candor," and his own broad-minded attitudes. Dangling on his chest are many gold chains with charms and amulets, including a small penis. The chest, wellspring of Guccione's manly sandpaper voice, is broad and hairy, visible at least to the sternum but sometimes to the navel underneath shiny peek-a-boo shirts.

The peritoneal exhibit of gold is just a peek at the valuable things that crowd Bob Guccione's life. He lives in an East Side New York townhouse (actually two townhouses made into one) with Carrara marble floors, an indoor pool with blue tiles laced with pure silver grout, a twenty-four-karat-gold mosaic whirlpool tub, a toilet carved from a single solid block of marble, walls made from bricks hand made in Italy according to an ancient Roman formula, bronze sconces shaped like women feeling their bosoms, millions of dollars' worth of famous paintings, an Icelandic goat-fur rug, and a private hair salon. "The furnishings look as if they came intact from a Neapolitan bordello," *Time* scoffed; but Guccione and his companion, Kathy Keeton, designed it all themselves, room by room, to reflect the same kinds of good-taste-be-damned sybaritic fantasies that have been *Penthouse*'s ticket to fortune.

The man who lives like a king started life as the son of a New Jersey accountant. He attended Brooklyn's Blair Academy, where his nicknames were "Maximus" and "Modest," and where the yearbook said he was "noted for his masterful bull-throwing, magnetic personality, hearty wit, and especially, his colossal egotism," then earned a living designing greeting cards and producing a syndicated humor column for college magazines. Dissatisfied with his modest career, he moved to London in the late fifties and got a job managing a small chain of dry-cleaning shops. Even in the dry-cleaning business he went too far; he was fired when he tried to make the shops London's only twenty-four-hour cleaners. Guccione then worked as a cartoonist for the *London American,* of which he eventually became managing director. The *London American* folded; and while Guccione scraped by selling pinup pictures and back issues of American dirty magazines through the mail, he conceived *Penthouse.* When it debuted in England in 1965, he was prosecuted and fined for sending indecent matter through the mail—which earned the new magazine priceless publicity.

His first promotional brochure described *Penthouse* as "a magazine that separates the men from the boys." When it debuted in America in 1969, that same macho strut distinguished it from *Playboy*—the magazine Guccione was out to beat. "We're going rabbit hunting," early *Penthouse* advertisements boasted, referring to *Playboy*'s rabbit logo. (In 1975, *Penthouse*'s circulation did top *Playboy*'s.) *Penthouse* always went further than *Playboy.* Whereas *Playboy* was known for coy girl-next-door cheesecake, *Penthouse* offered spread-legged nudes in erotic poses—"girls enjoying their sensuality" is the way Guccione once described the Pet of the Month motif. The steamy pictures, many of them taken by Guccione himself, were characterized by sensuous soft-focus effects, filmy negligees, and captions that suggested little sexual fantasies to have while viewing them. In the magazine business, the poses became known as "crab shots" because they so often showed women who seemed to be examining their genitalia for cooties.

Playboy had fashioned itself as an upward-striving service magazine showing readers how to have urbane parties, intellectual badinage with prominent smart people, and expensive stereo equipment. *Penthouse* wasn't concerned with giving advice about fitting into polite society. It featured an advice column from Xaviera Hollander (''the Happy Hooker''), steamy porno letters in the ''Penthouse Forum,'' and ads for sex aids—just the kinds of things Hugh Hefner's *Playboy* had scrupulously avoided in its quest to prove that nude girls could be part of a high-class life. Hef always tried to show that sex is in good taste; Guccione came swaggering along, made the girls spread 'em, thumbed his nose at good taste, and earned a fortune.

In recent years, Guccione has established *Penthouse* as a spoiler, printing nude pictures that embarrass people and/or expose their hypocrisy. The most famous was the Vanessa Williams photo session—three separate issues in which he ran nude photos (including leather strap and handcuff bondage shots) of the newly crowned Miss America. The pageant committee dethroned her. Williams sued Guccione, claiming she didn't really sign photo releases. Guccione blamed the ugly scene on hypocritical pageant judges and offered to finance Miss Williams's case against them. (She did not accept; nor did she win her suit.) Hugh Hefner, who had earlier refused to publish the naked pictures of Miss America, called Guccione immoral. Guccione called Hef ''an unmitigated hypocrite,'' and said the pictures were the best thing that ever happened to Vanessa Williams' career. He subsequently offered Oliver North's secretary Fawn Hall a half a million dollars if she would expose herself in his magazine after testifying before Congress.

Sex expert Dr. Ruth Westheimer is nuzzled by Bob Guccione

141

HAMBURGER HELPER

The annals of cookery bulge with imaginative treatises that suggest new things to do with ground beef. This is a fundamental kitchen skill, because ground beef is cheap, nearly every family member likes it, and most recipes require no talent and little time. As a casserole ingredient, it is even more popular than canned tuna, starring in such hearty man-pleasers as Hamburger 'n' Tater Tot Casserole (from the *Walnut* [Iowa] *Centennial Cookbook)*, and canned-corn-and-canned-mushroom Oklahoma Casserole (from *The Oral Roberts University Family Cookbook)*. Home economists have devised untold ways to glamorize ground beef—as the stuffing inside a flaccid green pepper, in hobo stews cooked inside a coffee can on the backyard grill, and in recipes for the rude-named school-lunch staple, sloppy joe.

But even a "Hamburger Can-Can Casserole" (beef combined with six assorted cans of vegetables and condensed soup) or the sloppiest of sloppy joes requires foresight (assemble the ingredients) and a modicum of skill (open the cans; stir frequently; arrange buns to hold the cooked meat). In 1970 General Mills eliminated the last shreds of such drudgery from hamburger cookery by introducing Hamburger Helper—a box of prosthetic foodstuffs that when combined with meat in a skillet create instant dinner.

Hamburger Helper was the zenith of the convenience-food revolution that had been gaining momentum through the sixties (see also *Aerosol Cheese; Cool Whip; TV Dinners)*. No longer would pebbly ground meat need to loll repulsively in a puddle of its own grease in a frying pan while the chef hunted for a can of Veg-All or lima beans to disguise its oily nakedness. With a box of one of the five original kinds of Hamburger Helper at the ready, the beef could instantly become Potato Stroganoff, Beef Noodle, Rice Oriental, Hash, or Chili Tomato. (Now there are Lasanga and Cheeseburger Macaroni, too; and Chili Tomato was reformulated in May 1984.)

Hamburger Helper was no easier than many other instant meals, but the name—Hamburger *Helper*—gave it special resonance. Any cook who needed help even for hamburger meat was de facto admitting sloth, incompetence, and defeat in the kitchen. To growing numbers of gastronomes in the seventies, for whom the mere suggestion of convenience cookery was anathema, Hamburger Helper was conclusive evidence of how abysmally far the American dinner table was from civilized and sophisticated cooking. Hamburger Helper became a pop-culture bad joke as familiar as Spam and Twinkies—and not only among the epicurean elite. Chevy Chase's hopelessly vulgar in-laws in *National Lampoon's Vacation* (1983) serve up a meal that the budget-minded host (played by Randy Quaid) describes with gusto as "Hamburger Helper without the hamburger."

Should a regimen of Hamburger Helper start to seem monotonous, look to the right or left of it on the shelf at the supermarket and you will find General Mills's lower-profile but equally synthetic other Helpers, Chicken and Tuna. Tuna Helper was introduced in 1972 and is now available not only in the traditional skillet-dinner formulation but also as a box of Tuna Pot Pie, which includes Bottom Crust Mix, Top Crust Mix, and Sauce Mix. Other Tuna Helpers include Cheesy Noodles ("Now with Twice the Cheese!"), Tomato Macaroni, and Buttery Rice. The cheesiest-tasting of all the Tuna Helper formulations, Macaroni Newburg Tuna Helper, was introduced in 1973 in an apparent attempt to move the product upscale in competition with Stouffer's luxurious frozen Lobster Newburg; Tuna Macaroni Newburg, alas, became extinct in 1978.

HAMBURGER HELPER

Despite its ignominious reputation among food snobs, Hamburger Helper has many friends. The self-published *Mom and Me* cookbook by Viola Miller and Evelyn Pflugshaupt of Shelby, Iowa, features a recipe called "Garden Cheeseburger Dish" which uses a box of Cheeseburger Macaroni Hamburger Helper as one ingredient in a skillet meal that also includes ground beef, tomatoes, onions, and green peppers. Also included in *Mom and Me* is the testimonial to just how much some cooks love Hamburger Helper: a recipe that tells readers how to make their own "Hamburger Helper Seasoning Mix" for those times when they need a Helper (the word is trademarked) but find the cupboards bare. The formula consists of bouillon granules, dried onion, onion powder, nonfat dry milk, salt, dried parsley, condensed tomato soup, and macaroni—but no dried corn syrup, disodium phosphate, or hydrolyzed vegetable protein, as listed on a box of the real McCoy.

HAPPY FACE

The happy face first seized people's attention when it appeared as a lapel button in the sixties. Wearing buttons was a fad; some had a political message, such as the peace symbol or "America—Love It or Leave It"; others, particularly those worn by the counterculture, sported funny epigrams: "Legalize Brown Rice" or "Don't Take Drugs—Give Them to Me." They were bought by hip people at groovy stores like the Psychedelicatessen on Avenue A in New York or the Print Mint in San Francisco. Among the most popular ones was a yellow circle with no words on it at all: just two black eyeholes and a curved smile line, denoting happiness.

Unlike buttons that broadcast strong personal sentiments, the happy face was an enigma—a grin for no apparent reason. To hippies, it seemed mischievous, and it captured the dopy, glazed feeling of being stoned. And yet precisely because of the button's ambiguous message, it made a specatacular leap from counterculture obscurity to widespread popularity among the silent majority, who saw it as an embodiment of upbeat values.

In the years before the happy face went big time, it had a nice, quiet life. Charlie Alzamora, program director at New York radio station WMCA, says that his station originated the happy face in 1962, using it on sweatshirts given away as promotional items to publicize its disc jockeys, known as the "WMCA Good Guys." David Stern of Seattle claims his ad agency invented it in 1967 for a local savings and loan in search of a genial image. Stern revived it in 1989 when he ran for mayor, announcing, "Behind the happy face, there's a thoughtful, committed, caring human being."

It can be argued that the happy face was rooted in public consciousness long before the sixties. For years, Kool-Aid advertising featured a frosty pitcher of America's favorite bug juice on which was drawn a happy face consisting of a linear smile and two dots for eyes (plus a little nose and two arched eyebrows). Prototypical happy faces appeared in the film version of *Bye Birdie* (1963), in which Dick Van Dyke sings "Put on a Happy Face" while dancing about, drawing happy faces in the air through the magic of animation.

It was at the end of the sixties that happy faces became a national obsession. Among the early documentation of the phenomenon is *Mr. Natural #2*, an underground comic by R. Crumb published in 1971 in San Francisco. Mr. Natural, a grumpy guru recently released from jail, walks the streets of the city, finding happy faces painted on all the store windows and plastered on T-shirts, balloons, and bell bottoms. Perplexed, he mutters as he walks down the street: "Hmmm . . . everything's changed while I was in prison . . . keep seein' that dum' face! Th' goddamn things are everywhere." He stops a girl on the street who has happy faces on her T-shirt and on each back pocket of her jeans. "Er, excuse me . . . could you tell me what that face on your shirt is all about?" he asks. "Don't you know?" she beams. "It's th' happy face. It means have a nice day."

The astonishing ascent of the happy face can be credited to N. G. Slater, a New York button manufacturer, who in 1969 began churning out dozens of happy-face items, which were actually named Smilies. By 1971, Slater and a Philadelphia company called Traffic Stoppers were selling happy-face novelties by the millions to dime stores and specialty shops across the country. Smilie had gone through the roof.

Sunny yellow cookie jars leered from kitchen counters; Smilies appeared as chain links on hip-hugger belts, on note pads, bath mats, toilet seats, and neckties. Swank stores such as Cartier offered smile pins in precious metals. Elvis Presley's daughter, Lisa Marie, wore a fourteen-karat-gold Smilie ring with diamond chips as eyes. Rock City, a Tennessee tourist attraction, advertised with a sign it claimed to be the world's largest happy face. In 1972, presidential candidate George McGovern appropriated Smilie to join the daisy logo on campaign bumper stickers. Manufacturers of the popular tranquilizer Miltown gave their physician clients a coffee mug bearing an appropriately stupefied happy face on its glazed surface.

People began incorporating Smilie into their signatures, dotting *i*'s with little happy faces, cheering up memos with smiles in the margin. Teachers accented a good grade by inscribing a smile on the student's test; conversely, a bad grade was accompanied by Smilie's alter ego, the unhappy face (mouth downturned). The happy face became inextricably linked with the salutation ''Have a nice day,'' with which it often appeared on bumper stickers and buttons. Conspicuous success soon led to ironic meanings for the happy face, as it began to beam from bumper stickers that said ''Don't Eat Yellow Snow'' and ''Eat Shit.'' By the mid-seventies, however, overexposure had killed even the satirical connotations of the Smilie. It had become a symbol of mindless optimism, representing the most offensive kind of blandness and conformity.

In the late eighties, the happy face staged a comeback. It began turning up on clothing of downtown types and club kids in New York, Chicago, London, and the Balearic Islands off the coast of Spain. ''Acid house'' music, a postmodern gloss on acid rock, was attracting a crowd who dipped deep into the retro fashion trunk and come up with a new mix of old sixties symbols: peace signs, flowers, tie dyes, and—most conspicuous of all—the beaming yellow happy face, occasionally augmented by a bleeding bullet hole in its forehead. British manufacturers Pink Soda and Boy London turned out clothing imprinted with the happy face, while Macy's in New York opened the ''Happy Faze'' boutique and Bloomingdale's the ''Don't Worry, Be Happy'' shop, named for Bobby McFerrin's Smilie-lyric song. Fashionable people have

rekindled interest in the happy face; but as with anything trendy, it is only a matter of time until the enchanting yellow disc is again pushed to the back of the closet.

For at least two friends of Smilie, however, he'll never go out of style. Duane and Janet Muse of Jefferson, Ohio, began collecting in 1974 and never lost their enthusiasm, amassing over seven hundred specimens, including an embroidered happy face, a five-hundred-piece jigsaw puzzle, and photographs of water towers and billboards that were too large to carry home. ''We now have an entire room devoted to our smile collection and eventually plan to renovate the room to accommodate more smiles and display those we have better,'' they told the *National Enquirer*. Mr. and Mrs. Muse's motto is ''If you meet someone without a smile, give him one of yours.''

HAWAIIAN SHIRTS

Hawaiian shirts have long been known as the uniform of loudmouth tourists, racetrack touts and gangsters in movies, soldiers with a weekend pass, and anyone who wants to show the world he doesn't have to dress for work. Loose-fitting and worn not tucked into pants, brilliantly colored and splashed with pictures of flowers, hula girls, leaping marlins, or the interesting sights of Honolulu, a Hawaiian shirt worn anywhere other than near a beach or swimming pool is the classic way a vulgarian announces that he is unbounded by the livery constraints of polite society.

On the islands of Hawaii, where Hawaiian shirts are known as aloha shirts, the style originated when Christian missionaries insisted that the naked natives put some clothes on. The abashed westerners introduced shirts and muumuus so large and loose they didn't need to be sized, which the residents decorated

with Polynesian designs applied with bright vegetable dye. The dye faded with age, however; so it wasn't until 1924 and Du Pont's introduction of rayon (which holds colors fast) that the production of Hawaiian shirts as we now know them began. The twenties were when the Hawaiian tourism industry began, too; and Hawaiian shirts, tailored by small island shirtmakers with orchid or palm-tree patterns or pictures of steaming volcanoes and sandy beaches, became obligatory souvenirs. Travelers in those days were of the taste-conscious classes, so once they got their shirts home, many were too embarrassed to wear them. They were put away and worn again only on vacation (if ever)—which explains the supply of mint-condition old ones for sale in secondhand-clothing stores.

During World War II, thousands of American soldiers went to or through Hawaii, and many came home with a Hawaiian shirt to commemorate the experience. Wartime restrictions on the clothing industry created sportswear as drab as a GI's uniform, so when the war was over, those bright Hawaiian shirts looked mighty good to color-deprived civilians as well as guys who had been wearing uniforms. After the war, to promote wearing the shirts in public, Hawaii initiated an "Aloha Week" celebration in September, which encouraged businessmen to wear them to work.

Hawaiian-shirt sales boomed, and not only in Hawaii, as more people took to wearing sport clothes at places other than the beach. The fifties had a penchant for exaggerated ersatz exotica in the form of such far-flung caprices as sweet-and-sour Polynesian cuisine and African-inspired tribal shields and masks on rec room walls. Hawaiian shirts filled that bill perfectly. The 1952 Montgomery Ward mail-order catalogue offered an eye-opening array of rayon short-sleeve shirts in "Tribal and Tropical prints in the newest and coolest Hawaiian designs—an asset to any man's wardrobe," including a "Vacationland Print" that employed a photographic process to cover the shirt with lifelike scenes of tropical sporting events such as deep-sea fishing, water skiing, and natives banging on drums.

Although most people still thought of them as vacation clothing, there were conspicuous exceptions who wore them out of context and helped define the style as irreverent and somewhat boorish, if not downright vulgar. Lawrence Langer, in a book called *The Importance of Wearing Clothes* (1959), complained about a "laxity creeping into the male attire in the U.S.A." He cited brilliantly colored beach robes, Bermuda shorts, and Hawaiian shirts—once strictly weekend summer wear for rich people— now being worn by "factory workers without the restraining influence of the conventional standards of middle-class taste." Nouveau-riche guys, gigolos, and that idle class of males known as "sportsmen" also found the Hawaiian shirt perfect raiment for their lives of leisure—as opposed to the work clothes or prison uniforms they might otherwise be wearing.

Celebrities helped make the Hawaiian shirt acceptable, if not respectable. Sticky-voiced television personality Arthur Godfrey was known for his Hawaiian shirts and ukelele. President Harry Truman wore one on the cover of *Life* for an article titled "The Evolution of a Wardrobe," which described how uncomfortable the man from Missouri was in starched-collar shirts and presidential suits. Elvis Presley, who loved all things Hawaiian, relished Hawaiian shirts not only for their gaudy colors but because their boxy, outside-the-pants cut covered up his love handles.

In the posthippie era, many men came to believe that fashion should be a matter of self-expression and doing your own thing. Hawaiian shirts' go-to-hell quality made them a favored costume among those who wanted to make the fashion statement that they were contemptuous of conservative dress rules. They scoured secondhand-clothing stores and junk shops to find a gabardine or rayon beauty for two or three dollars that would proclaim the wearer a proud member of the counterculture, thumbing his nose at the dictates of the clothing industry.

"Why should I, or anyone, love an old shirt?" asked Jeff Weinstein in his antiestablishment paean to Hawaiian shirts in the *Village Voice*. He said an old shirt, notably one that still smells in the seams, was a way to understand the past. He explained that shirts are "advertisements" and wondered, "What kind of man will a shirt with flowers be selling?" His answer was: "The shirt may be a tent. The shirt may be a skin. The shirt may be a flexible painting. The shirt may be a condom. The shirt may be a business card. The shirt may be an invitation. . . ." Et cetera.

The awestruck rediscovery of Hawaiian shirts climaxed in 1984 with the publication of H. Thomas Steele's book *The Hawaiian Shirt*— the definitive work, loaded with color photographs of classic patterns. The *New York Times* recently reported that the ranks of Hawaiian-shirt aficionados include such tastemakers as Bill Cosby, Steven Spielberg, and Mick Jagger. A connoisseur will pay hundreds of dollars for a genuine shirt with buttons made of coconut shells or wood, matching pockets that don't interrupt the design, or an original "Aloha" label. Any genuine rayon original from the thirties, forties, or fifties is a precious collectible, much too rare to be the mark of the unrefined lout it used to be.

HEAVY METAL

Combine Wagnerian opera, satanism, Nazi chic, Kabuki theater, bad cosmetology, and sadomasochistic fetish clothes. Add cheaply cast skull-and-bones jewelry, yards of tattooed skin, and sneering mouths full of toothpicks. Amplify with mega-volume loudspeakers. There you have heavy metal.

Heavy metal has been a popular form of rock and roll since the late sixties. The name was taken from the line ''heavy metal thunder'' in the hit song ''Born to Be Wild,'' recorded by Steppenwolf in 1968. They had borrowed it from William Burroughs's novel *Naked Lunch*. Despite its popularity for more than twenty years, heavy metal has few friends in polite society. Unlike rhythm and blues, Elvis, the Beatles, or Bruce Springsteen, all of whom have attracted more than their share of intellectual apologists, nobody of any refinement has stepped forward to champion heavy metal. Because of this fact, metal remains in its own way the purest sort of rock and roll—an audacious

exercise in kicking out the jams and grossing out the squares.

The driving force of heavy metal is the beat, more important to the listener than the usually unintelligible lyrics. The brash sound of guitar strings taking maximum abuse was a sound first developed by mid-sixties English groups such as the Kinks and the Yardbirds and by America's exhibitionist-guitarist Jimi Hendrix. Mablen Jones, rock historian and author of the book *Getting It On,* suggests that the first true heavy metal group was California's Blue Cheer (named after a particularly potent brand of LSD), whose 1968 album *Vincebus Eruptum* and the group's outrageous stage act created the ''ponderous, pseudo-Gothic flavor which is the cornerstone of the heavy metal sound, attitude, and imagery.''

Deep Purple and Led Zeppelin led the way, followed by Black Sabbath, Alice Cooper, Blue Öyster Cult, and Kiss, who helped make metal the potent commercial force it remains today. To the ear-rending music these groups added a repertoire of monstrous stage behavior such as chopping baby dolls in half and biting the heads off live bats. Their costumes were outrageous, too, featuring chains and tight leather or ripped jeans and little else. The clothing pioneers include Ozzy Osbourne, among the first to go topless on stage, and Ted Nugent, who went even further, turning himself into a virtual nature boy in only a flapping loincloth. Following their heroes' lead, male fans of heavy metal often go around town without shirts, flaunting their scrawny teenage chests and exposing arms covered with the obligatory tattoos of snakes, skulls, and daggers.

Heavy metal's main appeal is to adolescent white boys who take pleasure in monsters and dungeons, want to be as tough as nails, and have fantasies of doing to their parents and sisters what the musicians do on stage to their props. It is all about Sturm und Drang and braggadocio, drinking lots of Jack Daniel's, having a gigantic penis, and taking so many drugs your head explodes.

Like its fans, who call themselves headbangers, heavy metal is always in big

trouble, getting blamed for teen drug use, satanism, and suicide. Senator Albert Gore's wife, Tipper, head of the PMRC (Parents' Music Resource Center), proclaimed metal songs "vulgar and dangerous to the children of America" at U.S. congressional hearings about the menace of rock and roll. It is hard to think of nice things to say about Mötley Crüe, a band that sings about devil worship, or grand old metallurgist Gene Simmons of Kiss, who wiggles his outsized tongue at every tender teen girl in the audience. (The inanity of heavy metal musicians was the inspiration for Rob Reiner's hilarious pseudo-documentary, *This Is Spinal Tap,* in 1984.) The nasty mien of singers such as Dee Snider of Twisted Sister or "Dizzy" Dean Davidson of Britny Fox, with their explosive manes of overprocessed hair and gobs of blue eye shadow, inspired one critic to compare the appearance of a group of heavy metal rockers to a convention of alcoholic housewives. And these guys are the polite side of the metal scene, disdained by hard-core fans as "poodles" and "lollipops" whose oeuvre is so benign it can sometimes be played on the radio. Queensrÿche

and Megadeth, on the other hand—known as thrash metal rockers, as opposed to the pansy poppers—are always much too loud and rude for public airwaves. James Hetfield, lead singer of Metallica, one of the most repulsive of all trash metal groups, once said the only love songs he wants to sing are about beer.

Fan magazines *Metalshop, Rip,* and *Metal Edge* show pictures of heavy metal stars looking as mean and repulsive as they know how. Axl Rose, lead singer of Guns 'n' Roses, is shown bathed in sweat on stage, his teeth as yellow as an old dog's; Ratt's Bobby Blotzer chews on the neck of a guitar; one of the Bulletboys appears with a bare chest, his jeans unzipped and his pelvis thrust toward the camera. Articles offer sympathetic profiles of such celebrities as W.A.S.P.'s lead singer, Blackie Lawless, who was forced to respond to "modern day witch hunters" by excising the part of his stage act in which a naked woman was strapped to a torture rack and appeared to have her throat slashed. Blackie is also famous for throwing raw meat to his audience and drinking blood from a skull. *Metalshop* magazine advised that Blackie often feels "misunderstood."

See also **TATTOOS**

HELLENIC DINERS

Diners used to be made of radiant machined steel and pastel Formica, with Art Deco tile patterns on the floor and slick vinyl cushions in the booths that hissed gently when you eased down onto them to eat your ham and eggs. Some of them were dazzling and futuristic, but no matter how bright the silver gleamed and the neon shone, there was always a blue-collar probity about the old diners. They were eminently functional, designed to serve square meals fast and cheap. Diners like that are history.

The new style of diner, which we call "Hellenic" because the great majority of them are decorated in ways that refer to the glories of the ancient world (and are also Greek-owned), are light years beyond the once-basic hash house. Hellenic diners bubble over with overblown luxury, style, comfort, and convenience. They are sybaritic pleasure palaces with capacious booths big enough for families of six hefty people, counters with upholstered captain's chairs instead of stools (for beefy truck drivers), video games in the vestibule for kids to play, Muzak to relax you, mirrored lounges with free shoeshine

machines, hostesses in floor-length gowns at the reception podium, and service bars with more brands of creamy-sweet liqueur than there are nations in the world.

Their dining areas are shockingly big, always featuring at least one tableclothed room in addition to the traditional counter and booths. This special room invariably has a decorative theme, or perhaps a few decorative themes combined, such as "Antiquity," which is expressed by displays of busts of ancient Greek philosophers and wall plaques of goddesses in profile; "La Belle Epoque," done in multicolored organic-glass Tiffany-like lamps and flocked purple wallpaper; "The Great American West," with wagon wheels, barbed wire, and ox yokes; and "Executive Modern" —suede walls with wood-grain-laminate accent panels, pin-striped fabric in the booths, and a muted mauve-and-gray color scheme reminiscent of a Lincoln Town Car's upholstery.

The exterior of a Hellenic diner, which may or may not match its interior, is a pageant of architectural enthusiasm that tramples upon such trifling academic notions as integrity of design and form-follows-function. Neoclassical Ionic columns, trellises, and ornamental balustrades are popular, as are festive Byzantine wall mosaics interspersed with Bauhaus windows lifted straight from Mies van der Rohe or brown timber and white stucco panels to evoke Tudor England. Many of the most lavish of the Hellenic diners are finished in a grottolike veneer, their exterior walls stuck with terrazzo, their windows arched and edged with heavy stones, their mansard roofs topped with Spanish quarry tiles. Statuary gardens and dancing fountains dress up the parking lot.

The L & M Diner in Ocean Township, New Jersey, is a paradigm of such a place. Lauded by diner historians Richard J. S. Gutman and Elliot Kaufman in their book *American Diner* as an example of "the most recent, and now most popular, historical, revival style: the Mediterranean," the L & M is plastered outside with arched stucco bays supported by tail fin—like projections, each lit at night with its own spotlight. The interior of the L & M features a colonnade filled with statuary (muses) and Roman busts and lit by crystal chandeliers. No Las Vegas casino is more majestic.

These structures are so far removed from the old shiny dining cars it's fair to ask why they are classified as diners at all. In fact, many owners prefer to advertise them as "dinoraunts" or "rest-o-dines" or some other tricky name that evokes higher culinary ideals than the simple beaneries of yore. The answer is that, like their stainless-steel ancestors, Hellenic diners

are not built the way ordinary buildings are built —on the spot. They are made by diner factories in big modular segments that include nearly everything but the dishware, food, and staff. The segments are trucked to their location and fitted together, thus explaining how a mega-diner can suddenly appear in a lot that was empty when you drove past it last week. Also, there is a historical continuity to the Hellenic diner, in that the best of them are made by the same factories that made the best of the streamlined classics, most notably New Jersey's Kullman Dining Car Company and De Raffele Manufacturing Company. It was Kullman that inaugurated the era of posh diners in 1962 when it constructed its first "colonial-style restaurant" out of brick, stone, and wood-grain Formica and erected it in New Jersey.

Even more extravagant than the decor of a Hellenic diner is its menu. We have yet to see one that is smaller than two feet high and three feet wide when opened up and eight to ten plastic-encased pages long. Whole sections are devoted to such circumscribed culinary topics as "Bagel Fantasies" and "Happy Waitress Omelettes." You can order triple-decker sandwiches with names like Mt. Olympus and Zeus; there are a hundred pastel-shaded after-dinner cordials waiting to be mixed with heavy cream or coffee; choose from among rafts of Greek dishes from moussaka to stuffed grape leaves, or Jewish matzoh ball soup, or full-course Sunday roast-turkey dinner with all the trimmings. Order a Hellenic diner's "Fruit Fantasy" and you get a bushel of produce in a pineapple shell covered with maraschino cherries stuck with paper parasols. Nothing is ever out of season or unavailable at a Hellenic diner. If you want Italian spaghetti, truite au bleu, souvlaki, Texas T-bones, New England clam chowder, or quiche, it's probably on the menu.

The test of a true Hellenic diner is the boast of "on-premises baking," which grabs your eye as you enter by making you pass a spotlighted rotating pastry case near the front door. Here are examples of the baker's art often better to admire than to eat: mile-high cream pies with meringues as perfectly rhythmic as the waves in the ocean, spun-sugar croquembouches, eclairs as big as salamis, napoleons packed with pounds of creamy goo, white cake swans with white chocolate caramel-tipped wings, and mammoth pans of multileaf phyllo dough pastries stuffed with nuts and honey. Like everything else about Hellenic diners, the outlandish lineup in the pastry case is a study in restaurant ecstasy unchecked.

HOME SHOPPING NETWORK

Everything is happy on the Home Shopping Network. The handsome hosts and pretty hostesses are gay twenty-four hours a day, and they are always extremely nice to one another and to all the television viewers who call them on the air. There are wondrous products to buy, always at unimaginable bargain prices. The best thing is that you can fill your house with appliances, semiprecious jewelry, and artistic figurines without once going to the mall or having to speak with a clerk or get out of your easy chair and put on shoes. As long as you have a working television in front of you and a telephone by your side, you have access to the treasures of the world—at least to the kinds of treasures that get incredibly, unbelievably marked down.

Home Shopping Network is one of many cable-TV and UHF networks, stations, and extended programs that show products on the air and coax viewers to call in immediately and buy them. It started in the late seventies, at a time when special television record offers (for the greatest hits of Slim Whitman or Tchaikovsky) were making quick, big bucks for advertisers. Lowell Paxson and Roy Speer, two broadcasters in Florida, figured out that they could give the same kind of sparkle to their advertising and keep the money rolling in all day by replacing whole blocks of programs with long, chatty commercials, run like a telethon with operators standing by to take orders. Their concept was so successful that they went national in July 1985, as the Home Shopping Network on cable TV.

The idea was an immediate sensation, spawning imitators as well as alarming predictions that in the future all television programming would weave ads right into programs, not only into talk and variety shows but into comedies and perhaps even the news. There was a classy network—QVC—which featured blond wood sets, well-spoken hosts, and merchandise sold by categories such as "What's New to Make Your Life Easier"; and there was a Crazy Eddie World of Home Entertainment Shopping Network hosted by Jerry Carroll, who became famous for acting like a screaming maniac on behalf of Crazy Eddie appliance stores.

So far, the home shopping concept has not spilled into regular programming, but nearly every cable system has at least one network devoted to selling bargain-basement merchandise round the clock. The format is a kind of hybrid talk and game show, with a synthetic studio audience on the soundtrack ready to laugh and applaud and gasp at the beauty of the cubic zirconia or Black Hills gold on display and at their unaccountably low prices. As a stopwatch in the corner of the screen counts down the remaining few minutes to call up and buy, the host and/or hostess extols the merchandise, at the same time keeping track of how many of the particular item remain. "Only forty Magic Dusters left. Good luck getting to your phone. We now have less than thirty-five. Two more minutes or sellout!" As the clock ticks down and the merchandise sells out, viewers' calls are taken on the air, so they can echo the host and hostess in testifying how good and cheap the merchandise is, and that they would expect to pay at least fifty dollars in the store for the Eternity Ring now going like hotcakes for $16.70.

The original Home Shopping Network, which claimed to reach twenty-five million homes by the beginning of 1987, took a middle-of-the-road approach to selling. One of its first hostesses was Carmella Richards, known for tooting a

rubber-bulbed bicycle horn when she got excited and for being exceptionally chummy with caller-fans when they phoned in to buy the gold-toned tablewear or hand-painted ceramic rotating musical clown (plays "Send in the Clowns") she was advertising. HSN viewers always got a generous three to five minutes to call in when a new product was presented; if the phones were so busy that some callers were unable to get through, the time to buy might even be extended.

Watching HSN, QVC, or CVN is educational. Nowhere else will you find so concentrated a course in making small, cheap, unfashionable things sound big, valuable, and necessary. Ruby and sapphire chips are measured in large-sounding points rather than in fractions of karats; gold and silver is sold by the gram, or described as the "thick, sumptuous ten-karat coating" on a base metal; and new faux-semiprecious wonders are paraded forth incessantly, from diamanté pins to wax-filled fish pearls. The cloying air freshener you walked right past at K Mart last summer (where it was on the close-out table reduced from K Mart's regular low price of $19.95 to $5) is now marketed on television as a medical-breakthrough air-purifier health aide, recommended by physicians, reduced from an MSR (manufacturer's suggested retail price) of $49 to $25.

It isn't enough for a home shopping hostess to be merely enthusiastic. She must also have a first-rate manicure, well-scrubbed ears, and pretty skin, because it is often her job to model the merchandise—to wear the jewelry, to pedal around the stage in a child's toy car, to pretend to be tanning under a sun lamp. In the case of semiprecious stones, which are always infinitesimal, it also helps for a model to have petite fingers or earlobes. Sapphire earrings are shown in the ear in extreme close-ups, the image blown up so big that even the daintiest ear appears to be elephant-sized.

The main quality hosts must have is the ability to rhapsodize nonstop about one mundane thing after another, with no diminution of energy or enthusiasm. From camcorder to toilet brush to personal computer to inflatable hemorrhoid pillow, the buy-now-or-forever-be-without-it pitch never ends. And although certain selling points about items are scripted in advance, an impressive amount of creativity is required to keep the patter going without a break. Recently we were mesmerized by a Cable Value Network hostess's spiel about a ring: "made of marcasite [like fool's gold]—that incredible stone from that incredible tribe in American history, the Indians, who valued it more than diamonds." She then topped herself three minutes later when a sterling silver necklace came up for sale, reduced from $900 to $299.92: "It says in the American Constitution that you have the right to free speech, freedom of religion, and the right to invest in sterling silver jewelry."

HOT PANTS

Tramps and hookers in most cities of the world are recognizable by a universal uniform: short shorts made of satin, leather, or snakeskin, low-waisted and tight around the buttocks, slipped on over glittering tights; and silver-sequined platform shoes. The short shorts are known as hot pants. With the possible exception of crotchless panties, there is no other article of clothing as irredeemably cheap.

In January 1971, when *Women's Wear Daily* coined the term "hot pants," they were on their way to becoming high fashion. Marlo Thomas wore them on the streets of New York, and Jackie Onassis was stocking up on Halston hot pants for yacht wear. Furriers sold hot pants made of ranch mink for two hundred dollars per pair; white lace hot pants were worn by trendy California brides; Italian designer Valentino showed all-sequin hot pants in Rome; black tuxedo hot pants, with satin stripes along the thighs, worn with tasteful black suspenders over lace blouses, appeared throughout the spring and summer of 1971 at gallery openings and formal balls, right alongside more traditional floor-length gowns. By September, hot pants were so stylish that the Miss America Pageant was forced to rescind its prudish rules against them, allowing hot-panted contestants in the talent competition.

Hot pants were originally perceived as a rebellion against the tyranny of clothing designers and fashion magazines, which had tried to create a market for the midi skirt in 1970. The midi was a mid-calf fashion that was supposed to replace the miniskirt's youthful look with a more mature, womanly style. Maturity, however, had no appeal whatsoever to trend-setters in the early seventies, and the midi skirt was a thunderous dud. Hot pants, which showed more leg than the shortest micro-miniskirt, first appeared as boutique-made street fashion in London and in Paris in late 1970. At first, no well-known designers or fashion editors were pushing them, so they had special appeal to fashion-conscious iconoclasts. Within weeks of their appearing in American stores—even in the dead of winter, which required they be worn with knee-high boots—they were an immediate smash. *Time* reported that when Bloomingdale's put them on sale in January they were mobbed. Many customers turned out to be clothing manufacturers from Seventh Avenue, eager to get their hands on pairs from which they could make instant copies.

Hot pants were ideal attire for discotheques, allowing free movement and maximum sex appeal. They offered none of the difficulties presented by the miniskirt, such as how to sit down, bend over, walk up a flight of stairs, or cross your legs. The "tarty look," as this fashion trend was called, inspired Soul Brother Number One, James Brown, to record his hit single "Hot Pants," a crotch-throbbing song with the primal lyric "Hot pants . . . make me want to dance."

Two of America's most outrageous fashion authorities, Sammy Davis, Jr., and Liberace, jumped on the hot-pants bandwagon with zeal. Davis appeared on stage in Vegas in a hot-pants version of a Three Musketeers outfit that featured a voluminous shirt, thigh-high boots, and hot pants. He and his wife Altovise entertained at home wearing his-and-her matching tuxedos with hot pants instead of trousers. Liberace wore patriotic red, white, and blue hot pants on stage, which he showed to the audience by marching around to the music while twirling a drum majorette's baton.

Nowadays hot pants remain in polite society only as the standard uniform of half-time football cheerleaders. The Dallas Cowgirls' snug white shorts, combined with calf-hugging vinyl boots, are a standard wet-dream motif for many men.

Roller Dancing for fun and fitness

Bonus instruction book inside with over 100 photos. If you can walk, you can skate—and roller dancing is simply moving on wheels to the musical beat. The illustrated instruction book teaches you the fundamentals, and the record provides the ideal music to develop your roller dancing style. The album-size instructions can be propped up for easy viewing, and you can practice indoors or outdoors on any smooth surface. The music selections begin with simple disco beats, then progress to more complex rhythms that will have you whirling on wheels in no time! And for the grand finale, there's a choreographed routine. Skating works wonders for your body. While you're having fun, you're burning 600 calories per hour, and as an aerobic exercise, skating ranks with running and swimming. According to Olympic team medical advisor Dr. Max Novich, "No other sport provides the agility with the fun element...you will be rewarded with a sound heart for a lifetime."

HUMMEL WARE

Hummel figurines, greeting cards, bells, decorative plates, wall calendars, and dolls are among the world's most popular collectibles. And why not! Who couldn't use another rendering of a red-cheeked, tousle-haired, big-eyed child engaged in precious antics?

Like many things that have become bloated and unconditional examples of bad taste, Hummel ware started in a humble way. The big-eyed kids were the creation of Sister Maria Innocentia Hummel, a Franciscan nun. Born Berta Hummel in Bavaria in 1909, she was an artistic young girl who liked to sketch the world around her. Her favorite subjects were schoolmates, birds, flowers, and the gentle animals of the forest. After earning a degree in fine arts, she joined the Franciscan Convent of Siessen in Germany in

Sister Maria Innocentia Hummel

1934, where the mother superior encouraged her to continue drawing pictures of happy children. Her original drawings and occasional watercolors and oils are truly cute in a robust way, and show none of the drippy sweetness that has come to be associated with her name and art. Sister Maria Innocentia drew and painted until her death from tuberculosis in 1946.

More than a decade before she died, her nunnery contracted with the W. Goebel Company of Rödental to produce three-dimensional ceramic figurines based on her sketches. To this day the Goebel factory is the only authorized maker of M. I. Hummel figurines, commemorative plates, bookends, plaques, holy-water fonts, candle holders, annual bas-relief bells, and wall vases. The convent at Siessen, which receives all royalties from Hummel ware, publishes an official "Story of the M. I. Hummel Figures" which informs the reader in no uncertain terms, "You will delight in the beauty of *The Holy Child* or *The Little Shepherd*. Yes, you will love them all with their round faces and big, questioning eyes."

The names of the many Hummel figurines suggest their charm: *Puppy Love, Bashful, Boy with Toothache, Merry Wanderer*. Add to the roster of cuteness twenty-seven different models that all begin with "little," including *Little Tooter, Little Bookkeeper, Little Goat Herder, Little Thrifty,* and *Little Helper*. Some of the "little" figures share a theme with nonlittles. *Little Fiddler*, for example, is virtually identical to *Puppy Love*, but involves a fiddle instead of a dog.

Except for the occasional Madonna, Hummel statues all depict one, two, or three children with puffy pink cheeks and wind-tossed hair, sometimes dressed in lederhosen, doing something delightful: playing an instrument, engulfed in outsized grown-up work clothes, feeding an animal, singing, or huddling under a big umbrella. Although they do share big eyes with the children in the paintings of Walter and Margaret Keane, Hummel figures are happy moppets; their eyes are wide with wonder and joy, and they never brim with tears. Some figurines are free-standing, but many are attached to ashtrays, candy dishes, and table lamps.

Because collecting Hummel ware is big business (some of the rare figurines sell for a thousand dollars), it should be no surprise that there are many Hummel imitations on the market, all hoping to capture the lovable, serene, and innocent qualities of the genuine wares marketed by Goebel. Sister Maria Innocentia's own mother won a lawsuit to merchandise all images of her daughter's work from before she entered the convent. Schmid Brothers, the original American importers of Hummel ware (since 1935), was cut off by Goebel in 1968 when Goebel set up its own Hummelwerk distributors; and since then Schmid has specialized in ''authentic art of Sister Berta [not M. I.] Hummel'' plates, bells, trinket boxes, candles, and key chains. Arnart Imports of New York sells an ''Original Child Life Series'' made in Japan; National Potteries of Cleveland sells ''Our Children,'' also made in Japan: Both require sharp, Hummel-savvy eyes to distinguish them from the real thing. Likewise, the Ars Sacra company has put out a raft of Hummel stuff, including canvas wall calendars, gift wrap,

souvenir spoons, and jigsaw puzzles, as well as a replica of an original Sister Hummel drawing showing a boy trying to hide a bunch of apples from his pet dog called *There for Mom's Pie*.

Hummel lovers on vacation can visit the Goebel factory in Rödental or the Goebel Collectors club headquartered in Tarrytown, New York, both of which feature a gigantic *Merry Wanderer* statue on the lawn outside. It depicts a little boy with an umbrella over his shoulder, his mouth half-open, and big clunky shoes and bell-bottomed pants reminiscent of those on the figure in R. Crumb's ''Keep on Truckin' '' cartoon. Every June in Eaton, Ohio, the world's largest festival devoted to Hummel art attracts up to twenty thousand collectors (200,000 people belong to the Goebel Collectors' Club).

The most dramatic celebration of Hummel art is the annual look-alike contest held in West Germany each year, for which children from two to eight years old dress and pose for photographs meant to replicate well-known Hummel statues. A recent winner was a little girl wearing a bandanna and apron, down on her knees with a bucket and scrub brush, looking just like Hummel #363, *Grossreinemachen*, or as collectors know it, *Big Housecleaning*.

JELL-O

What a dull world it would be without Jell-O. It shimmers in Crayola-crayon colors that put all of nature's fruits to shame. Watch it wiggle; hear how it sucks at the serving spoon and plops onto the plate; then feel it slide down your throat without needing so much as a nudge from tongue or teeth. Any properly made gelatin dessert behaves that way, but we're going to call the stuff Jell-O, which is General Foods' brand name, because Jell-O has attained the status of Kleenex and Band-Aid: a brand so paramount it has made the generic term seem small and inadequate. In fact, Jell-O is the largest-selling prepared dessert on earth.

It comes in many forms. There are humble plain cubes served by hospitals to sick people. In the South, it is made into ornate "congealed salads" jazzed up with cream cheese, studded with pecans, and laced with sweetened coconut.

What Mrs. Dewey did with the NEW JELL-O!

48 FASCINATING NEW RECIPES

In the Midwest (Ohio in particular) Jell-O is customized with constellations of nuts, fruits, and berries, making jiggly edifices that look like stained glass. Probably the most famous formula for elaboration is the one actually called "Broken Glass Dessert": three kinds of complementary-colored Jell-O, Cool Whip, and crumbled vanilla wafers, all assembled in such a way as to suggest multicolored panes of glass in lead casement. Virtually without exception, the biggest sections in cookbooks published by PTAs and fund-raising groups in the heartland are their recipes for Jell-O, best described in the words imparted to us by one artistic-minded Jell-O-loving chef from Iowa: "the baroquer the better."

More than any other food, Jell-O symbolizes how America really eats. We say *really* eats because you wouldn't know Jell-O exists if you read only gourmet magazines, where a dessert so easy isn't welcome among the complicated tartes and tortes that snooty people like to eat. Fastidious epicures John and Karen Hess have scorned Jell-O desserts as "sugary, gummy messes, chock full of synthetic flavors and colors," pointing to the beginnings of Jell-O in 1897 as "a fitting close to the late nineteenth century with its steady decline of taste." Patricia Nixon gave herself away, the Hesses once wrote, when she contributed a recipe for "Continental Salad" to a Republican fund-raising cookbook. The salad was made with lemon or orange Jell-O, canned grapefruit juice, and canned beets, with a whipped cream cheese and mayonnaise dressing. To be fair to Mrs. Nixon, by any reasonable standards of Jell-O cookery, her recipe, which used no nuts, no miniature marshmallows, no canned coconut or bing cherries or mandarin oranges or fruit cocktail, was positively demure.

The division between Jell-O lovers and Jell-O haters is not a right wing/left wing distinction; nor would it be fair to say that liking Jell-O is patriotic and despising it is tantamount to admitting you eat black bread and borscht, if you catch our drift; but let this be said: Jell-O is Americana in a mold. It is unsophisticated, fast,

BROKEN GLASS DESSERT

4½ cups hot water
1 3-ounce package lime Jell-O
1 3-ounce package orange Jell-O
1 3-ounce package strawberry Jell-O
1 packet unflavored gelatin
¼ cup cold water
1 cup pineapple juice, heated
4½ cups thawed Cool Whip
25 pulverized vanilla wafers
¼ cup melted butter

Divide water into three 1½-cup bowls.
Dissolve each flavored Jell-O in a separate bowl.
Chill each in a flat square or rectangular pan until
thoroughly set. Cut into ½-inch squares and put
all the squares into the refrigerator.
Dissolve unflavored gelatin in cold water. Stir
in pineapple juice. Chill. Fold in Cool Whip.
Mix vanilla wafers with butter and press half
the crumbs into a 9 x 13-inch pan. Gently fold
Cool Whip mixture into cubes of Jell-O and
spoon atop the crumbs. Sprinkle remaining
crumbs on top. Chill overnight.
Yield: 18 servings

pretty, and sweet. There isn't another foodstuff in the pantry that so readily lends itself to rules-be-damned, mix 'n'-match, tear-the-box-open-and-be-creative cookery.

From the beginning, Jell-O was sold as a nearly magic powder that yielded spectacular results from minimal effort. Add water and chill: Dessert is served! When the idea for gelatin dessert was patented by Peter Cooper in 1845, no one paid any attention, because no one had a refrigerator; besides, most people still thought of making gelatin as an all-day affair requiring the processing of crushed calves' feet or the membranes of fish bladders. Charles B. Knox came up with a prepackaged mix in the 1890s and started Knox's Gelatine Company selling unflavored instant powder to make aspic. About the same time, Pearl B. Wait, a cough-medicine bottler in LeRoy, New York, decided to get in on the ground floor of the burgeoning packaged convenience food business with a similar idea, but his packaged gelatin was *flavored*. Wait had no luck selling his product, so in 1897 he unloaded the company for $450 to Orator Francis Woodward of the Genesee Pure Food Company. It was named Jell-O, after Woodward's popular coffee substitute, called Grain-O.

Woodward decided he might pep up sales if he advertised it as "America's most famous dessert"; after a slow couple of years, Jell-O sales surged and Woodward renamed his business the Jell-O Company. Early advertising featured the Jell-O Girl, a pretty maiden drawn by Rose O'Neill, inventor of Kewpie dolls, and boasted of the Safety Bag inside the box—purchasers' assurance that the contents "will remain for years as pure and sweet as on the day it was made." Knox tried to halt Jell-O's ascent by running ads scoffing at "sissy-sweet salads" and stressing Knox Gelatin's purity; but it was

New JELL-O *Recipes made with the new flavor* Lime

no contest. Jell-O's emphasis on pretty, dainty food made it the household word.

Daintiness was a preeminent goal in the early years of the twentieth century, when many homemakers were determined to leave coarse immigrant recipes and hayseed ways behind them; and Jell-O, at a dime a pack, placed fragile, pastel, nonethnic dainties within reach of anyone. Fannie Farmer's *Boston Cooking School Cookbook,* a stated goal of which was to "put gaiety into housekeeping," embraced the new product as a way for ordinary housewives to create meals with the kind of color and panache heretofore attainable only by professional cooks.

To encourage experimentation the Jell-O Company (which joined with Postum to become General Foods in 1925) published hundreds of booklets over the years with titles such as *Want Something Different?, Quick Easy Wonder Dishes, Thrifty Recipes to Brighten Your Menus,* and *What Mrs. Dewey Did with the New Jell-O!* (she made Hawaiian Sunset Mold, Mystic Fruit Layers, Emerald Fruit Cup, Charlotte Russe Imperial, Manor House Salad, and Marvel Lemon Pie). The goal was *something special;* and for the cooks who love it, that's what Jell-O has always provided: *novelty.* "Gelatin, no matter what it's in, always gives a gay party air to things," observed Edith ("the dingbat") Bunker, Archie Bunker's wife on television's "All in the Family." Even the most déclassé of all Jell-O flavors, lime, has become the basis for myriad ocean-colored

salads and a pistachio-flavored post-Nixon novelty known as Watergate Mold.

Among the basic techniques of modern Jell-O makers are "opaquing" (mixing Jell-O with cream cheese, thereby muting its hue), "layering" (Jell-O alternated in a glass with Cool Whip), "ribboning" (multiple layers of different-colored Jell-O), "poke-caking" (pouring unset Jell-O on top of cakes pricked with fork holes), and "pinstriping" (inserting a straw into dark-colored molded Jell-O and letting white cream settle in the tunnels). One of the most influential recent developments in Jell-O-ology has been the introduction of Gummi Bears and similar translucent candies to the Jell-O maker's tool chest, thus allowing for such creative showpieces as Jell-O molded in a fish tank with gold Gummi Bear fish and parsley "seaweed," as well as sunset forest dioramas rendered in wine-tinted Jell-O containing Gummi Bear fauna, broccoli and cauliflower bushes, and a marzipan setting sun emanating egg-noodle rays.

See also **NOVELTY WRESTLING**

JOGGING SUITS

The uniform of people who abjure dry cleaners and ironing boards, jogging suits (also known as warm-up suits) include any combination of soft-textured, baggy-fit, stain-resistant, elastic-waisted long pants and top (or sometimes a single-piece jumpsuit), usually in a dusty pastel color and always manufactured of at least 50 percent miracle fabric. They are as common as blue jeans; and in suburbs, where moms and dads perform so many different kinds of errands every day around town and mall, they are especially prized, because they are acceptable as suitable attire for anyone doing anything anywhere.

A jogging suit is the all-purpose solution to all clothing problems. Step out of it at night and step into it in the morning; or sleep in it and never take it off. Spill Tang down the front and drip a jelly donut on your lap and let baby spit up on your shoulder. Wear it the next day and the next. Finally, when it becomes too grimy, throw it in the hamper and wear another one. No need to treat it well: Jogging suits are cheap and easy to replace. Their only flaw is that when they finally become too fetid to wear anymore, they are no good as rags, because the slick, close-knit fibers of which they are made will not absorb anything but the odor of perspiration.

Sweatshirts and sweatpants, first devised in the late teens for track and field athletes, were designed to be sweated in, at a gym or running track. They were big enough to pull on over spikes, and utterly utilitarian, as gray and drab as mechanics' overalls. Until the sixties, wearing such gym clothes to a restaurant or any polite place would have seemed as ill bred as appearing without a shirt. The astonishing thing to consider, particularly when you look at the frumps who ferment themselves for days on end in velour or terry-cloth rompers today, is that only twenty years ago, wearing jogging suits in public was actually fashionable!

Jogging itself was trendy then, embraced not only as an exercise to improve the body but as the key to a *life-style* that would make you an all-around Good Person—noncompetitive and in

touch with your own vibes, or at least your pulse. A book called *Jog for Your Life* raved, "There is no more joyous experience than finding yourself totally off the ground—momentarily airborne—step after step." In 1968, when the cinder path around New York's reservoir in Central Park was officially declared a jogging track, the *New York Times* announced that jogging had become "the in sport." *Cosmopolitan* suggested it was one of the best ways to meet eligible men.

At the same time jogging blossomed into what *U.S. News & World Report* called "a national cult," professional athletes were helping to create the peacock revolution in men's fashions. "We're psychedelic, man!" announced Tommy Hart of the San Francisco 49ers, who was known for his twinkle-toe white cleats. Earsell Mackbee appeared at the Minnesota Vikings training camp in 1970 wearing a red lace jumpsuit, a fake-fur maxi vest, and a slouch hat. When not dressed to kill, such fashion plates as Joe Namath (football), Walt Frazier (basketball), and Derek Sanderson (hockey) were seen around town wearing their team's bright, mod warm-up suits instead of drab old gray sweat clothes. The fashion immediately jumped from pro teams to amateur joggers.

To demonstrate that they were athletic, joggers and many who were nothing more than *simpatico* with the stylish idea of exercise started wearing expressive paraphernalia such as running shoes, headbands, and warm-up suits. (*Forbes* magazine actually suggested that men who were real running aficionados ought to wear ladies' panties rather than athletic supporters under their sweat pants because panties helped prevent chafing.) Velour became the shiny, plush-textured star of a new kind of clothing known as active wear. Such life-style gurus as Robert Redford and Farrah Fawcett-Majors frequently exhibited their allegiance to fitness by wearing fitness clothes even on occasions when they didn't exercise. And so began the fashion known as jock chic, the basic point of which is *always* to look like you are on your way to or from the gym.

The trend was marked by *Sports Illustrated* in June 1972, when it declared, "The hottest thing around may be the warm-up suit. . . . Civilians of all ages, sexes, and shapes are now wearing them everywhere: they turn up on tennis courts and basketball courts, on the golf course and the beach, at the supermarket and in the city streets." Ralph Lauren offered velour suits in bright red, deep purple, and peach. Head made bell-bottom double-knit nylon warm-up pants with a matching white-zippered top that featured slash pockets. Bonne Bell, which began manufacturing "sports cosmetics," announced a policy of allowing its employees to wear warm-up suits to work.

Jock chic is a style that never went away, but the look today has evolved into Lycra leotards, scanty workout shorts, and skintight tights borrowed from bicycle racing. As fashion, the voluminous running suit long ago hit the racks of the lowest-end and least fashionable discount stores; and it is now sold not for any connotation of running prowess but for its cheapness and convenience. Notice, the next time you see a surprise drug bust on television news: Chances are good that the perpetrators being led from their apartment to the paddy wagon are wearing jogging suits.

KATZ, MORRIS

What miracles I can do with a full roll of toilet paper!" said Morris Katz, who uses ten thousand rolls per year defending his title as the fastest painter in the world. In 1956, while studying at the Art Students League in New York, Mr. Katz discovered that brushes were too slow, and so turned to a pallet knife and wads of rolled, folded, and feathered double-ply toilet paper as his instruments for applying paint to canvas. The pallet knife, he says, "speeds up production." Toilet paper "adds depth and subtlety." Scented, extra-soft toilet paper, which he uses for his more expensive paintings, makes the studio smell better. Katz holds the *Guinness* world's record for creating a finished 12-by-16-inch work of art faster than anybody else (thirty seconds, plus eight seconds to frame it); and long ago he surpassed Picasso as the world's most prolific artist, having completed and sold 181,818 paintings as of July 1, 1988.

Katz began painting at age thirteen in a displaced persons' camp in Germany after World War II. He came to America in 1949 and was soon able to support himself from the proceeds of outdoor art fairs, where he sold impressionistic pictures of thoughtful rabbis, Moses receiving the Ten Commandments, and romantic landscapes. According to the mimeographed brochure available at the Morris Katz Art Gallery in New York, "Katz felt he had added directly to the tradition of the old masters who emphasized four dimensions: proportion, color, light and shade, and perspective. His paintings had all four. Yet he was not content to emulate their great example. Katz wanted to be an innovator. He added a fifth dimension: money."

Katz stages painting shows at Catskill resort hotels, private parties, conventions, and charity auctions. The shows consist of him creating works of art while telling jokes before an audience. ("People ask me, do I date my paintings? I say yes, that's why I'm single. Van Gogh cut off his ear when he couldn't sell. Me, I cut my prices.") His output is then sold or auctioned off, the prices starting at one hundred to two hundred dollars per painting, but usually bargained down to about fifty dollars. "Put them on a gallery wall on Madison Avenue under a spotlight with a refined woman saying sophisticated things about them," Katz once told an audience, "and they'd sell for three thousand dollars apiece."

Among his recent accomplishments is the world's fastest mural—an eight-by-four-foot seascape on the wall of the Cadillac Bar in Manhattan, painted May 10, 1988, in 20 minutes, 44 seconds. On July 15, 1987, he painted twelve hours nonstop at the Penta Hotel in New York City, creating one hundred and three paintings (of which fifty-five sold that day), and donated the proceeds to the Boy Scouts of America. In December 1976, when Katz and Bing Crosby were guests on Joe Franklin's television talk show, he began painting a snowy forest scene at the same time der Bingle started singing "White Christmas." The song and painting were finished simultaneously.

It is not necessary to be a collector of genuine oil paintings to own a piece of Morris Katz's oeuvre. At his studios in Manhattan and Jerusalem, he markets all of his finest works as postcards, five dollars per set. There are action sports scenes, still lifes, landscapes, and Mediterranean village tableaux, as well as great moments from the Bible, funny-looking dogs, and a picture of Pope Paul VI that Katz did in 1965, making the painter, in his own words, "the first Jewish artist to paint a pontiff." (More than three million prints of the Pope painting have been sold.)

Recently, Katz completed a series of pictures of each American president with the flag draped behind him. All are available as postcards. Ronald Reagan, like the Pope before him, was actually painted with brushes in what Katz called his "old master style," and the painting took three whole weeks to execute (the Pope took only nineteen consecutive hours). Even on the postcards, you can almost feel the original and never-duplicated Morris Katz slashed-on and toilet-papered impasto, created with gobs of paint mixed to a consistency he likened to heavy sour cream.

KEANE, MARGARET AND WALTER

The Keanes are the artists who originated the Big Eyes school of painting: pictures of gaunt children with eyes three times normal size. The children are portrayed in a dark alley or a lonely tenement hall, in a somber world so shrouded in gloom that its windows, doorways, streetlights, and even the moon above could all be mistaken for mournful eyeballs. Sometimes the children clutch a puppy dog or a kitten. Their goggle eyes, which stare out from the picture and seem to follow a viewer around the room, brim with tears; in some paintings, one will overflow, sending a massive droplet running down a cheek; in rare instances, both eyes spout tears, and both cheeks glisten with the discharge.

Big Eyes paintings were the best-selling art of the early sixties. While critics and museum curators extolled pop, op, and hard-edged abstractionism, hordes of people who didn't know art but knew what they liked fell in love with saucer-eyed children. At the height of Big Eyes popularity a Keane original sold for as much as a hundred thousand dollars; but Keane reproductions and other artists' imitations were available in dime stores everywhere for twenty-five cents and up. Big Eyes wall plaques, decorative plates, and postcards —all in the Keane style—were sold by the millions in souvenir stores, at outdoor art shows, and from the pages of trading-stamp redemption catalogues.

"My paintings ask the eternal question, 'Why?'" Walter Keane said to explain his success. "I am able to express this universal questioning through the eyes of an innocent child facing an unknown destiny. I want my painting to clobber you in the heart and make you yell, DO SOMETHING!" He hit upon the formula when he quit his job as a real-estate agent in California and went to Paris to study art in 1947. He painted the streets of Montmartre and lounging nudes, as did any dutiful aspiring artist; but he couldn't get the sight of Europe's war waifs and street urchins out of his mind. When he returned to America, he set up a studio in San Francisco, where he began painting children with big eyes.

Keane met his wife, Margaret, in the mid-fifties at an outdoor art show in Sausalito, where they were astonished to see each other's work: Both of them painted Big Eyes! Margaret had been doing it since she was eleven, starting in school notebooks that she filled with Big Eyes doodles. As an adult artist, she specialized in elongated maidens reminiscent of Modigliani with heads so shrunken they barely had room for eyes. A catalogue description of her painting *Escape,* which shows a Big Eyes girl with a low-cut, fur-collar dress and a windblown flip hairdo walking through a sinewy landscape fraught with Edvard Munchian horror, explains that the girl is "walking in pursuit of her desires. She goes forward, her eyes wide open but looking inward, leaving behind the city with its false nocturnal lights, confusing fog, and pale men." Within a few years of their marriage, the work of the Keanes seemed almost to mesh; and although knowledgeable Keane collectors prize her work over his, it became difficult for the casual observer to distinguish a Walter from a Margaret.

In San Francisco's North Beach, Keane took delight in playing the part of an eccentric artist, complete with beret and tousled hair. He wasn't the van Gogh type, who suffered for his art, but was more Picasso-like, relishing his world with robust appetites. He drove a white convertible and bought four white toy poodles which he named Rembrandt, Gauguin, Matisse, and Degas. An early self-promotional brochure called "The Painting Keanes" said that he "romps through life with the evident enjoyment of a terrier rolling in a clover patch. Of all the artists in San Francisco, Walter is the most carefree bon vivant."

After a few years of romping through life but not selling many paintings, the Keanes decided to make an end run around the art world, which refused to "discover" them. They opened their own gallery in San Francisco. Before a show opened, they plastered lithographs of their work all over town; Walter gladly touted himself on television and bought space in major daily papers as well as *Pennysaver* newsletters, brazenly promoting his and his wife's unique style. They made a deal with the First Western Bank so that buyers of modest means could use a special time-payment plan to get themselves a Keane original. However abhorrent all this was to effete guardians of art-world etiquette, the strategy was a whopping success. When he opened his first New York show in the newly created Keane Gallery at Madison Avenue and Sixty-fifth Street in 1959, everything on the walls sold immediately (for prices between $600 and $1,500), including his young daughter Jane's painting of a Big Eyes *Mr. Potato Head,* which went for $6.

By 1964, Keane was such a phenomenon that one of his biggest Big Eyes paintings, *Tomorrow Forever,* was selected for the Hall of Education at the New York World's Fair. Art critic John Canaday of the *New York Times* could not allow such an affront to good taste in his own hometown. Although he never had seen the painting in question, he wrote a column howling that Keane "grinds out formula pictures of wide-eyed children with such appalling sentimentality that his product has become synonymous among critics with the very definition of tasteless hack work." His denunciation so intimidated world's fair planners that they quietly asked Keane to withdraw *Tomorrow Forever.*

Although art experts were put off by Big Eyes, as well as by Keane's aggressive publicity seeking, there was never a shortage of movie stars and celebrities to give the work a glittering aura. Jerry Lewis paid Margaret Keane ten thousand dollars to paint a portrait of him, his wife, his children, and his three dogs and four cats all with big eyes and wearing clown costumes. Joan Crawford said "Keane paintings are my friends" and commissioned Walter to do a life-size portrait of her, which she hung above the couch in her Hollywood home. On his television show, Jack Paar held up a Keane original called *Our Children,* depicting Big Eyes around the world, and declared it "the greatest painting I have ever seen in my life." Columnist Earl Wilson

called the Keanes "the find of the twentieth century."

In 1965, at the peak of their fame, the Keanes divorced and disappeared from the public eye, leaving an artistic legacy that Lawrence Alloway, curator of New York's Guggenheim Museum, called "heroic bad taste . . . incredibly vulgar, weird, but gorgeous." For that body of work alone, the Keanes earned their place in the pantheon. But then in 1970 a new, painfully crass dimension was added to the Big Eyes story. Mrs. Keane went on a San Francisco radio talk show and declared that it was she who had painted all the Keane paintings—hers *and* Walter's—but that he had threatened to kill her if she told the truth. In an attempt to prove her point, she dared her ex-husband to fight it out in a painting contest. He refused. But fourteen years later he told *USA Today* that she was taking credit for the paintings only because she thought he was dead and couldn't fight back. Margaret Keane sued Walter Keane for slander.

During the trial in 1986 in a Honolulu courtroom, Margaret claimed that the Big Eyes idea was originally hers—contrary to all the early catalogues' and press releases' assertions that Walter had created his style in Europe. She explained that after marrying Walter, the eyes in her paintings got bigger and sadder to express her own misery as his wife, and therefore it was her pain—not Walter's brush—that made "Keane" paintings so successful. Her testimony reached a dramatic climax when she set up easel and canvas before the jury and in less than an hour created an unmistakable Walter Keane original—a giant-eyed waif peeking over a fence. When the judge asked Walter to do the same, he said his shoulder was injured, preventing him from painting. The jury awarded Margaret four million dollars; and as the freshly painted waif looked on with eyes full of tears, Walter Keane said he couldn't pay because he was penniless.

LAS VEGAS

The most fun place on earth since God incinerated Sodom and Gomorrah, Las Vegas is a testimonial to the power of compulsive behavior. It exists to satisfy the cravings to gamble, drink, fornicate, gorge, spend, bully, binge, grovel, and engage in every other form of narcotic debauchery that is known as pleasure. Henny Youngman described it as "the only town in the country where you can have a wonderful time without enjoying yourself." Sammy Davis, Jr., called it "instant swinger."

Like any hardworking harlot who is in the business of taking money from people so they may indulge taboo desires, Las Vegas makes itself outrageously seductive. There isn't another place on earth that beckons so relentlessly to gamble! feast! ogle nude girls! Everywhere you turn, scintillating signs shimmer with glad tidings, from "$2.99 PRIME RIB!" to "LOOSEST SLOTS IN TOWN!" The great, giddy neon proclamations are everywhere, begging for your favor; they are more conspicuous than any of the city's buildings; they block the sky above and the mountains in the background and obliterate the darkness of night. Visitors are cajoled by flashing promises of huge jackpots and easy odds; inside the casinos they are flattered by obsequious personnel fawning for tips and by scantily dressed cocktail waitresses (who, when Caesars Palace opened, were instructed to approach gamblers and say "I am your slave" and respond to drink orders with "Yes, master").

The famous casinos such as the Flamingo, Bally's, Caesars, and the Hilton are built on a superhuman scale that can make anyone who enters feel small and insignificant. But feelings of inadequacy are easily countermanded by would-be big shots who know that Las Vegas is the most equal-opportunity place on earth: Any slob,

however low his social standing, however ugly his clothes, and no matter how uncouthly he may behave, gets treated like royalty if he has money to spend. Waving cash in the form of tips (known hereabouts as ''green grease'') or at the gaming tables turns anyone into a superior being—a king, a sheik, an emperor, or a cattle baron, depending on the theme of the casino. (The serious gamblers' favorite gambling house in downtown Las Vegas, Binion's Horseshoe Club, doesn't bother with theme window dressing: Its leitmotiv isn't Araby or the Barbary Coast; it is CASH, and each customer is offered the opportunity to have a photo taken in front of a wall papered with one hundred genuine ten-thousand-dollar bills.)

Nothing about Las Vegas is subtle. It aims to dazzle for the simple reason that dazzled people gamble more. And it *is* dazzling to take a midnight cruise past the big-name casinos on Las Vegas Avenue (''the Strip'') or downtown in ''Glitter Gulch,'' where the neon pyrotechnics and the bonging bells of slot machines debilitate any sane sense of scale and perspective. Enter a casino, and you are relieved of the burdens of the turning of the earth: Because they have no windows and no clocks and never close, you could spend eternity inside not knowing if it is day or night. We once passed a merry afternoon on the verge of great wealth at the roulette tables in Caesars Palace and discovered only the next day that a tornado had come through town, uprooting trees and flooding streets while we were reducing our bankroll.

Las Vegas turns somersaults twenty-four hours a day to get your money, but because the easy money comes from gambling (the house *always* wins), everything else is cheap. Being in Las Vegas is like finding yourself in a city staffed entirely by Crazy Eddies and rabid used-car salesmen, hollering ''Cut rate!'' at you from all directions. Hotel room prices are half what any other popular vacation or convention city charges; every casino boasts copious all-you-can-eat buffets where bargain hunters stuff themselves for anywhere from ninety-nine cents

(for breakfast) to eight dollars (for Caesars Palace's Olympic feast, advertised as ''Roman decadence at its very best''). Casinos regularly engage in prime rib and shrimp cocktail wars, undercutting prices to lure customers. The Lady Luck boasts that it loses $360,000 per year giving away FREE shrimp cocktails that are six inches high and three-quarters of a pound, served inside the fluted plastic glasses ''made popular by Dairy Queen sundaes,'' with free lemon wedges and saltines besides.

Despite the bargains, and even if you don't lose money gambling, there are plenty of places in Las Vegas to get your wallet lightened fast. ''Sex-tease joints,'' which cater to people who are extremely naive or unfamiliar with American currency, are notorious for selling customers champagne at a thousand dollars per bottle in exchange for the promise of sex. Suckers get no sex (unlike other parts of Nevada, Las Vegas has outlawed prostitution), and the champagne doesn't even get them high. According to the *Las Vegas Review-Journal* (August 1989) Terry Gordon, owner of such places as Pigalle and Alley's, explained that he sold bogus, nonalcoholic champagne as his way of helping solve the drunken-driving problem.

Other opportunities to blow big bucks are provided by the many galleries that sell the works of such people-pleasing artists as Erté and Leroy Neiman as well as huge and expensive bronze sculptures of noble Indians to decorate the homes of the newly rich. For less refined pleasure seekers, a business called the Gun Store (two convenient locations!) offers customers the opportunity to purchase not only guns and ammo but silencers, camouflage clothing, handcuffs, and billy clubs. The Gun Store's brochure advertises, ''Stop by and shoot a live SUBMACHINE GUN on our air-conditioned indoor range.'' Renting a machine gun costs ten dollars, plus ammo, but the Gun Store does give a free Gun Store hat to everyone who pays to pump lead. If buying time behind an Uzi or a tommy gun is not your idea of fun, you might want to spend your cash at a shop called Bonanza, which has a

ATOM BOMB BLASTS

COURTESY

Benny Binion's Horseshoe Club

ACTUAL PICTURES PHOTOGRAPHED FROM VANTAGE POINT HIGH ATOP MOUNT CHARLESTON, NEAR LAS VEGAS

DOWNTOWN LAS VEGAS, NEV.

blinding sign on the strip exulting that it is the world's largest souvenir store. Need an inflatable, life-size, naked Wayne Newton? A farting rubber ball? A ceramic mug that has a small hand affixed inside with its middle finger upraised, giving the bird to the coffee drinker? Bonanza's got 'em.

Las Vegas's title as the supreme source of bad taste has been heralded around the world by a legion of well-known entertainers who embody what everyone recognizes as the Las Vegas style. To say an act or a human being has Las Vegas style is to say it or he or she is unctuous, sanctimonious, all hyped up, and even possibly hip in the old-fashioned, early-sixties sense of the term that was personified by a group known as the Rat Pack. The Rat Pack consisted of Las Vegas regulars Frank Sinatra, Dean Martin, Sammy Davis, Jr., Joey Bishop, and Peter Lawford. They were much glorified at the time as the era's prototypical swingers—always a little

looped, always partying with big-bosomed bimbos, always supremely cool. Their brand of vaguely gangster-connected, lounge-lizard savoir faire was even sprinkled with political stardust in the form of Lawford's marriage to one of John Kennedy's sisters. (During the 1960 presidential campaign, JFK was photographed hanging out with the Rat Pack in Las Vegas as they filmed the movie *Ocean's Eleven*.)

Remnants of the laid-back Rat Pack style still infuse some threadbare lounge acts in Las Vegas, but the one trait that makes someone a big name today is perspiration. "If you sweat," Jerry Lewis said, "you'll be really successful in Vegas." All major Vegas performers are known to work hard and give 110 percent. Among the hardest-working people in show business, the superstars who have been able to make Las Vegas a lucrative venue include Elvis, Liberace, Ann-Margret, Charo, Tom Jones, Don Rickles, Lola Falana, Engelbert Humperdinck, and Julio Iglesias —all of whom are known not merely as singers or comedians but as total entertainers who work

174

their hearts out. The greatest of the Vegas acts, known variously as Mr. Las Vegas Show Business, King of the Strip, and the Midnight Idol, is Wayne Newton, who does *two full hours* instead of one, plays the violin at lightning speed for "Orange Blossom Special," sings both "When the Saints Go Marching In" and Elvis's "Suspicious Minds," and has never in recorded history done a show that does not conclude with him saying, "Ladies and gentlemen, you have been a very special audience."

It took a long time for class acts of the Wayne Newton caliber to get to Las Vegas. For years after its beginnings in 1905, Las Vegas (which means "the meadows," not—as Milton Berle used to say—"lost wages") was nothing but a jerkwater cowtown along the rail line. In hopes of reviving a depression-pinched economy, the state legislature legalized gambling in 1931, but most of the places that thrived weren't much more than cowboy saloons, known as "sawdust joints." Some dude-ranch hotels were built in the early forties, but it was not until 1946 that the town began to cultivate its unique mixture of gangster sleaze and show-business sparkle. Benny (Bugsy) Siegel, who already controlled illegal gambling in southern California and on ships offshore, created the first deluxe casino, which he named the Flamingo for his redheaded girlfriend. Siegel built a chartreuse suite with palm-tree wallpaper for himself at the Flamingo, planted grass in the desert all around the building, and imported live flamingos from Florida for the opening, which featured Xavier Cugat and Jimmy Durante on stage.

When Bugsy Siegel was murdered in 1947 by his investors (as depicted in the movie *The Godfather,* in which he is "Moe Green"), the rubout proved to be great publicity for Las Vegas; the Teamsters Union Pension Fund financed new casinos on the Strip: the Sahara, the Sands, the Dunes, and the Riviera (which paid Liberace the unheard-of sum of fifty thousand dollars to perform on opening night in 1953). By the early fifties, tourists were coming not only to gamble but to watch atomic bombs go off in the desert

northwest of the city. In 1952, proprietor Wilber Clark of the Desert Inn told *The New Yorker* that his pit men were instructed to announce each impending blast; but he said most players didn't go outside to watch—they just played more furiously and drank more heavily at detonation time. The *New York Times* called the blasts "the greatest tourist lure since the invention of the nickel slot machine," and local casinos began to offer "Atomic Cocktails" (vodka, brandy, champagne, and sherry).

Other significant moments in modern Las Vegas history include the debut of toplessness in 1958, in the "Lido de Paris" show at the Stardust, and the opening of Caesars Palace in 1966. Caesars—no apostrophe, because owner Jay Sarno said the possessive "would mean it was the place of only one Caesar," whereas he wanted every paying customer to feel sovereign —was conceived as a temple of self-indulgence. Forgoing the Wild Western and North African desert motifs that had become customary, Sarno went for what he called "a little true opulence" in the form of a Roman orgy theme. The entire facility, including the craps tables, was built as a series of curves and ellipses, because, according to the hotel's in-room promotional film, "the Greco-Roman oval shape was designed to promote relaxation." The antique orgy theme still infuses Caesars, where toga-clad "wine goddesses" massage male customers' backs and pour wine into glasses from shoulder level in the Bacchanal dining room. Full-size marble replicas of statues of Venus, Bacchus, and Sabine women being raped decorate the grounds; and stationery in the rooms appears burnt around the edges (suggesting that patrons be as dissolute as Nero was when Rome went up in flames). Caesars today, augmented over the years by such wonders as a porte cochere that is the world's largest cantilevered structure of its kind (illuminated hot pink at night, in contrast to the hotel's aqua lights) and a replica of a Roman temple with laser holographs inside that show ancient Romans partying, remains Las Vegas's gold standard of gaucherie.

One of the more delicious attractions of Caesars is known as Cleopatra's Barge, midway between the Olympic Casino and the Circus Maximus, just west of the entrance to the Appian Way. To walk through the hallway past Cleopatra's Barge—which is, in fact, the front end of a good-size ship floating in real water— you walk beneath the prow. If it is night, and revelers on the barge are dancing on deck, the ship bobs up and down in the water and the prow nods and waves above. The bobbing causes the figurehead, a topless Cleopatra, to dip down over the hallway so that her large, full, golden breasts plunge up and down over the heads of passersby. Newcomers to Caesars tend to duck as the giant breasts swoop toward them. Veterans don't even look up. And because the breasts are just out of reach of all but the tallest people, no one tries to rub them, as is practiced regularly on the nearby statue of the Capitoline She-Wolf, whose nose as well as udders are kept shiny gold by superstitious gamblers looking for luck.

There is more to Las Vegas than gambling, however. There is also getting married, which is just about the easiest thing to do other than lose money. The same bill that legalized gambling in 1931 also changed the law to allow instant, no-blood-test, no-wait marriage and nearly instant divorce (after only six weeks' residence). Being so near Hollywood, Las Vegas became the favorite marrying place for impetuous stars, including Elizabeth Taylor and Richard Burton, Steve Lawrence and Eydie Gormé, Paul Newman and Joanne Woodward, Jane Fonda and Roger Vadim, Elvis and Priscilla Presley, and, in recent years, Joan Collins and Jon Bon Jovi—but not to each other. In his book *Vegas Live and in Person*, Jefferson Graham says that stripper Lili St. Cyr had to postpone her Las Vegas wedding three times in February 1955 because she wanted to get married at the exact moment a much-delayed atomic bomb was being detonated in the desert.

If you want to get married in Las Vegas, all you need is twenty-seven dollars for the license and a potential spouse. Beyond that, each of the thirty-eight chapels in town offers its own special amenities and unique ambience. Most of them are open round-the-clock, every day, and look like adorable miniaturized churches, with neon signs of bells or angels outside and two or three rows of pews inside for friends and press agents. Services are generally offered à la carte: ten dollars for recorded music at the ceremony, twenty-five dollars for a living organist, ten dollars for a bride's garter, etc. Ministerial fees are taken care of as "donations." The requisite witness is free of charge. Some chapels also offer whole packages. The $125 Economy Package at the We've Only Just Begun Chapel includes use of the chapel, candlelight, recorded music, one eight-by-ten glossy photograph, two five-by-seven photographs, four wallet photographs, a bride's corsage, and a groom's boutonniere. The $500 Deluxe Special adds many more pictures, flowers, a video recording of the event, a cake, champagne glasses (but no champagne), and a leather-bound marriage-certificate holder. All We've Only Just Begun wedding packages include free limousine service from your hotel to the marriage license bureau to the chapel and back to your hotel again. If you want to set the date, just dial 1-800-322-LOVE.

Additional tidbits: Not counting wedding chapels, there are more churches per capita in Las Vegas than anywhere else in America; Las Vegas has the most unlisted phone numbers; and tourists have a greater chance of suffering a heart attack than in any other American city.

See also **CHARO; ELVISIANA; LIBERACE**

LAVA LITE

Behold the Lava Lite: a low-hipped glass urn with a long, tapering neck. Inside the urn is liquid, which can be clear, Listerine yellow, or Scope blue. Lolling in the liquid is a waxy ball, either white or red. The liquid-and-wax-filled jar roosts on a satin-finish gold base that mirrors the conical formation of the glass. The whole thing is a foot and a half tall, and the base is large enough to contain the controlling mechanism: a forty-watt light bulb and a metal coil.

When the bulb is switched on, the liquid inside the globe glows and the coil below it begins to warm. When heated, the wax expands and its specific gravity decreases. As it lightens— a process that can take hours from start-up time in a particularly phlegmatic Lava Lite—the wax rises. And as it rises, it dilates, stretches, and slithers; appendages appear and protrude, then recede; it multiplies by fission like some immense new amoebic life form. Tiny pustulations break away and drift up fast; big ones, gliding toward the top of the liquid, begin to cool and decelerate, then plummet, occasionally rejoining with other waxy globs taking part in the hypnotic slow-motion ballet.

So it was in the beginning. So it shall always be inside a healthy Lava Lite . . . unless some idiot replaces the forty-watt bulb with a brighter one in hopes of speeding up the action. Run too hot, a Lava Lite will suffer ball-out: The wax hovers an inch above the bottom like a somber wad of mud.

It is a sensitive mechanism, this phenomenon of modern lighting technology. Manufactured by Lava-Simplex Internationale of Chicago, Illinois, Lava Lites are made according to a top-secret formula involving a balance of eleven chemicals measured and mixed to the nearest ten-thousandth of an inch to create the proper equilibrium of wax and liquid. ''Every batch has to be individually matched and tested,'' Lava-Simplex president John Mundy said. ''Then we have to balance it so the wax won't stick. Otherwise, it just runs up the side or disperses into tiny bubbles.'' Although mysterious, the chemicals are not noxious. When one distraught

mother contacted Lava-Simplex (via postcard) about the prognosis for her child, who had unscrewed the top of the living-room Lava Lite and drunk the insides, Mr. Mundy told her not to worry—the lad would be all right . . . although he might not feel too well.

The Lava Lite was invented in 1964 by an Englishman named Craven Walker, who called it the Astrolight and designed it as a cylindrical vase (without the pronounced conical bulge) to be shown at a Hamburg, Germany, novelty exposition in 1965. Two Americans, Adolph Wertheimer and Hy Spector, made a deal to manufacture Astrolights in America. Rechristened Lava Lite, the device was expected to be another hula hoop—a lucrative fad that would peak, then fade away. Lava Lite sales did peak in the late sixties, when the slow-swirling colored wax happened to coincide perfectly with the undulating aesthetics of psychedelia. Like water beds, Lava Lites were handy ways to feel the surging vibrations that nearly everbody wanted to experience at the time. They were advertised as head trips that offered "a motion for every emotion."

Although they are essential sixties artifacts, Lava Lites are actually a variation on a lighting tradition that began in the fifties—the TV light. TV lights, shaped like poodles, fish, elves, and various woodland deities, were designed as mood-inducing little nimbuses that provided TV viewers in an otherwise darkened den just enough illumination to read the television listings and switch channels, but not so much light as to spoil the dreamy television-watching frame of mind. Likewise, Lava Lites aren't for lighting up a room or reading. Their function is to set a mood. Indeed, their "classic place in the home,"

according to Jack Mundy, "is on top of the television."

When Mundy, who used to stare at Lava Lite displays in the window of a store when he was a college student in Chicago, took over Lava-Simplex Internationale in 1976, sales were on the downslide. But as style makers began to ransack the sixties for inspiration, Lava Lites came back. Formerly dollar-apiece flea-market pickings, original Lava Lites—particularly those with paisley, op art, or homemade trippy motifs on their bases—became real collectibles in the late eighties, selling in chic boutiques for more than a brand-new one.

You must beware of old Lava Lites. Even if well cared for and switched on regularly, most of them get cloudy as the precisely balanced chemicals inside begin to decompose; and once that happens, they cannot be repaired. (Globes on models made after 1976, when the design of the base was changed, can be replaced.) New Lava Lites are available in five models: the Century (the original design), the Enchantress (it's slimmer), the Aristocrat (a perforated base creates a starlite effect), the Midnight (it has a black base), and the Coach Lantern (a copper-finish bail and base capture what company literature calls "the elegance and mood of Old World England and modern Americana").

In addition to Lava Lites, Lava-Simplex Internationale also manufactures Gemlites—plastic tubes with thousands of flecks of swirling, glittering confetti inside—and the Wave—a see-through rectangular box containing extruded acrylic matter that rocks back and forth and gives the impression of a slow-moving ocean surf. Deluxe Waves are filled with black-light-responsive fluid and emit the sound of the ocean.

LAWN ORNAMENTS

Lawn ornaments are plaster, concrete, or plastic statuettes designed to brighten up a yard or garden. They include happy green frogs reclining on toadstools, dwarfs pushing wheelbarrows, and gnomes snoozing under mushrooms, as well as such irrefutably tasteless effigies as black jockeys (hitching posts), lazy Mexicans with bare feet, cherubs with fountain-spout penises, and comical drunks leaning on lampposts.

Most lawn ornaments are sold from sprawling garden shops by the highway: acres teeming with fauna begging to beautify your life. Few lawn-ornament curb markets, however, sell only things for the lawn. It is a good bet that if you see plaster deer and all-weather Elvis busts, you will also be able to stock up on wall tapestries of unicorns, velvet paintings of matadors, giant plush stuffed animals, firecrackers, and bottle crafts (7-Up bottles with their necks stretched grotesquely long and thin to accommodate a single rose). Find a big lawn-ornament store and you have found a gateway to the world of bad taste.

Although many modern lawn ornaments are profane, the world's first ones were religious, in the form of altars to pagan gods set up by ancient Romans around their villas. In this century, many devout Christian immigrants renewed that ritual when they moved from city tenements to homes with yards. Suddenly they had a marvelous opportunity to create permanent shrines to biblical figures or saints as well as dramatic Christmas scenes of Jesus or Santa or both of them together once each year. It was a custom that began early in the 1900s and continues to this day in tradition-conscious neighborhoods, fed by year-round Christmas stores and reliquary manufacturers such as L. J. Campanella & Sons of Brooklyn, which sells nine different Blessed Mother statues in various sizes, Holy Family groups, and dozens of saints. Anthropologist Joseph Sciorra has found that today's religious front-yard shrines had

progenitors in medieval Italy and observed, "To the popular mind these shrines are tacky, déclassé; but they have so much to tell." Many of them, Sciorra explained, are built as part of a deal a homeowner makes with a saint: If you cure my lumbago, I will erect a statue of you. A devotional lawn display may remain in place for years after its plastic flowers have shriveled and turned to polyethylene dust, even if a new owner moves into the house. In certain neighborhoods, a well-maintained shrine adds to the value of a piece of property.

Secular statuary meant to suggest the denizens of the forest primeval was used in some eighteenth-century English gardens, which were designed to look like nature-in-the-wild with an occasional concrete sylph, faun, or similar woodland creature hiding in the brush for inspiration's sake. When tacky plaster versions of such concrete garden ornaments began appearing in front of modest American homes in the twenties, they celebrated nature's whimsy, too, but on a budget and on a forty-foot building lot. Suburbanites could not afford to live on a remote estate with genuine forest animals running around, or to buy sculpted statues of beasts or garden nymphs for grand gardens; so they bought plaster-cast reminders of what nature—and sculptures of nature—are like for their lawn. Painted plaster animals gave

even the most modest front yard a bucolic touch in the form of deer and rabbits. And for the aesthetically adventurous there were lawn balls: short Grecian columns with a bright silver (or other metallic color) ball on top, suggesting some Druid monument from before the dawn of time.

After World War II, as new suburban streets, housing developments, and mobile-home parks blanketed the land, the lawn-ornament industry stood ready to beautify them. Small manufacturers around the country and in Mexico began to sell plaster statues and wooden cutouts either bare or garishly prepainted, in dozens of shapes, including the all-time favorite pink flamingo.

Hot-pink flamingos joined the grass menagerie about the time Florida was popularized as a vacation destination and retirement spot in the fifties. The exotic-looking bird became an emblem not only of Florida but of the era's stylistic excess (visible also at the Flamingo resort built by Bugsy Siegel in Las Vegas): like a tail-finned car, it was both sleek and ungainly; and although natural, it seemed wondrously synthetic. The earliest flamingo lawn ornaments were enamel-painted plywood cutouts; then in 1957 Don Featherstone, working for Union Products in Massachusetts, designed a hollow plastic, three-dimensional pink flamingo with long, straight black legs that stuck neatly and easily into the ground. For years Featherstone's creation reigned as the lawn ornament nonpareil —not the most popular (it was regularly outsold by birdbaths and plaster Santa's helpers), but the ornament of choice among hard-core vulgarians. John Waters's merrily repulsive movie Pink Flamingos, featuring a dog-doo eating scene, showed its heroine, played by the late drag queen extraordinaire Divine, living in a mobile home with plastic pink flamingos on the lawn outside and struggling courageously to prove herself the filthiest person on earth. By the late seventies, the flamingo had become

one of the elementary icons of bad taste, so delectably naughty that it was adopted by many cultural subversives—along with Hawaiian shirts and loud ties—to signify their defiance of propriety.

Like many affectations championed as counterculture regalia, pink flamingos seeped into mainstream culture, joining unicorns and rainbows as a favorite souvenir motif. *People* magazine credited their popularity to the appearance of live flamingos in the credits of the television show "Miami Vice," and wrote, "Sales began to rise in the early eighties, when 'retro' became hip." America, *People* gasped in 1987, was "in the middle of a flamingo boom." That year, for the first time since the pink plastic flamingo lawn ornament was invented, it outsold the eternally popular plastic lawn duck.

We are now living through what future archaeologists will surely see as the lawn-ornament renaissance. Emerging from its years as a despised and depressing form of low-class landscaping, lawn ornamentation is enjoying glory days, spurred by the invention of new kinds of statues made of new materials. The most successful modern lawn decor is not refined by any means, but neither does it have the white-trash stigma of the old plaster icons. Featherstone's blow-molded plastic pink flamingos are selling better than ever (about 250,000 per year), as are relatively tasteful flocked-n-fuzzy pigs and sheep, wooden Tweeties and Sylvesters, and behemoth California Raisins. Some even wind up as retro-hip living room decor.

In Maine, blessed with more lawn ornaments per capita than any other state, Bryce Muir (author of the definitive book on the subject, *Lawn Wars*) has created such original wooden patterns as a cutout Elvis with whirligig hips, a flamingo wearing sneakers and playing a guitar, and the figure of Christina from Andrew Wyeth's painting *Christina's World*. It is believed that Maine is where the Granny Fanny first took hold, brought down by vacationers from Nova Scotia (where much of Maine's wooden statuary is cut

and painted). Without question the most popular lawn ornament since the pink flamingo, the Granny Fanny—also known as Betty Bloomers and the Bend-Over Lady—is a two-dimensional plywood cutout that resembles a rear view of a chubby old lady bending over and exposing her underwear. Although first spotted down east about five years ago, Granny Fannies are now everywhere. A customer we met shopping for fannies at an outdoor-ornament store in North Carolina explained that because they come in so many colors and with different-shaped buttocks, they're addictive. "Once you've got one fanny planted, your lawn just seems to call for more," she explained.

LEISURE SUITS

Spun out of springy synthetic polyester fibers, with pockets that look pasted on and exaggerated welting patterns that make the fabric appear vulcanized, the leisure suit became an eternal symbol of lounge-lizard low fashion in the mid-seventies.

When you look at one today, perhaps the most shocking aspect is the color. Leisure suits came in a jaw-dropping array of Easter-egg pastels, including pink, powder blue, saffron, and tangerine, as well as earth-tone mocha, burnt orange, poison green, crimson, cinnamon, and umber. They had a bizarre shape, too. Designed to appear less formal than a suit jacket or blazer, the top half of a leisure suit is sometimes lapel-less, sometimes even sleeveless, often cut long and belted like a tunic, resembling a shirt more than a jacket. It has decorative stitching, occasionally in a color that stands out against the suit; and if it does have sleeves, the cuffs unbutton and turn up, allowing the wearer to display a shirt in a floral or abstract pattern or contrasting darker color, customarily a silk-textured synthetic worn with its wide collars outside the suit, spread like vestigial wings flapping in the wind upon the shoulders, the ensemble gilded by a hefty medallion on a gold chain gleaming on the chest.

Although they became the sure sign of a rube, and the uniform of virtually every male contestant who ever appeared on television's "The Newlywed Game" as well as countless characters on "The Love Boat," leisure suits were first introduced after World War II as high fashion, strictly for rich people. Louis Roth Clothes made the earliest leisure suits out of wool gabardine. They had belted jackets with an inverted pleat in back and came in bright colors. They cost a hundred dollars—four times what Sears was charging for a good wool suit—and they were designed as vacation wear, to be worn by sporting gentlemen on golf courses in Palm Springs and Miami.

Leisure suit sales took off in the early seventies, when they were suddenly available in hundreds of variations, thanks to the miracle of

The earliest known leisure suit

polyester knit fiber. It was a time when men's clothing designers were still riding a wave of optimism based on the belief that in the postmod era, guys were eager to shuck stodgy tradition (such as neckties and pin-striped suits) in favor of a groovy kind of uniform. Men had just landed on the moon in shiny silver spacesuits; and Elvis Presley had returned to the stage in a great white jumpsuit and cape. Futuristic movies such as *Rollerball* (1975) showed the people of tomorrow in regimental lapel-less, two-piece garments and no ties. And on the television program "The Six Million Dollar Man," Lee Majors played an astronaut with mechanically implanted super-human powers and a wardrobe full of leisure suits, which he wore while performing great feats of jumping and running.

Formality was considered square, but sloppy dressing (like hippies) was passé. A groovy guy was one who did not have to stuff himself into a suit and tie every morning but still managed to look natty. "Can an executive wear at work what he wears at play? Can a lawyer meet with a client dressed like a client? Can a white-collar worker work with his collar open?" So asked a Macy's television commercial in 1975, answering, "Yes—thanks to the leisure suit revolution." Macy's second floor, according to *The New Yorker* in a 1975 article about the leisure suit phenomenon, was filled with "leisure suits as far as one's eye

can see." Some models had names suggested by their color or cut: the Apple Jack, the High in the Sky, the Top Cat; Barney's offered "New Yorker," "Imperial," and "European" leisure suits.

Leisure suits were sold by department stores and men's wear shops as the ultramodern answer to every wardrobe problem—the garment equally at home behind a desk, in a swank restaurant, and at a country club. The marketing strategy did not work. While they did acquire a modicum of standing among entertainers, athletes, and street hustlers, few genuinely classy guys were willing to trade their nice navy-blue wool worsteds for a rubbery copper-colored leisure suit with gold stitching and a complementary black crepe shirt. Because it was so easy to manufacture the coarsely cut polyester suit cheaply, bargain-basement models flooded discount stores, job-lot outlets, and street-corner flea markets.

Leisure suits never had a chance at enduring respect because they denied one important function of clothing—to separate the classes. John T. Molloy's *Dress for Success* (1975), which told people what to wear to get ahead in the business world, warned that leisure suits were "terrible: They snag and bag and stretch and shrink. They are also hot, and all but the most expensive are ugly." Commenting on their proliferation in 1975, Jack Hyde of *Men's Wear* said he thought leisure suits made everyone look like a bus driver.

The great promise of the leisure suit revolution—that men could be comfortable and dressed for business at the same time—never came to pass. Instead of becoming acceptable wear in correct society, leisure suits turned into an emblem of the churl, the bumpkin, and the cheapskate vulgarian. Just to make sure no such interloper crossed the line into the world of good taste, in 1977 Lutèce, New York's most famous four-star French restaurant, posted a small, elegant sign on its door, reading "Please! No Leisure Suits."

See also **POLYESTER**

LEOPARD SKIN

Leopard skin is a paradox: It is swank and it is tacky. Formerly a sure sign of glamour, it has become a caricature of glamour. It conjures up a silly image of a Hollywood beefcake Tarzan in a spotted bathing suit, swinging through studio trees, or of a pinched-faced trailer-park woman in hair curlers and fuzzy slippers wearing a synthetic leopard-skin housecoat while she gobbles chocolates, smokes cigarettes, and watches Roller Derby on TV. Tobacco-chewing long-haul truck drivers drape leopard skin in their sleeper cabs to impress female hitchhikers with their sexy, high-class demeanor. Chihuahua breeders make leopard-skin sweaters to keep their shivering one-pound bantams from catching cold.

At its most basic level of meaning, leopard skin makes the person who wears it look like a leopard—wild and exotic. Unlike mink, beaver, or chinchilla, which lose their animalistic qualities when stripped away from flesh and sewn together to become plush fabric, a leopard's spots ensure that it will always look like the skin of an animal, and therefore connote primeval qualities. Whether as a coat, a lamp shade, or automobile seat covers, leopard skin—genuine or fake—is an enduring statement that its owner wants to be perceived as "different."

For as long as men have hunted, leopard has been one of many pelts used for warmth and decoration, and by sportsmen to cover ottomans in their dens; then in the twenties it became a preeminent mark of avant-garde fashion. In an era with a penchant for danger, ferocious cats meant power and sexuality. When Metro joined with Goldwyn, it was the Goldwyn lion, not the Metro parrot, that became the company mascot; next-to-naked exotic dancer Josephine Baker was famous for walking her pet leopard (as well as a pet cheetah and a swan) on a leash and in a diamond collar along the Champs-Elysées. In 1925 Elsie de Wolfe, the woman who once said, "I think that I may say that I created the profession of interior decorator," took leopard skin out of the man's den and shocked guests to her Villa Trianon dream house in Paris by spreading it everywhere. She used dozens of animals' worth for carpeting, cut it up to upholster chairs, and wrapped it around lamp shades.

Inspired by Miss de Wolfe's daring flirtation with savagery, clothing designers began to use leopard skin for coats that made a statement that mink did not. Wearing leopard said that you were not only rich, you were audacious. Couturière Elsa Schiaparelli designed a leopard-skin hat in 1938. Coco Chanel matched a leopard-skin hat with a leopard-trimmed coat. Leopard coats and ensembles became the sportiest high-fashion apparel, suggested by Nina Ricci fashion house directrice Madame Geneviève Antoine Dariaux only "for the lucky few who can buy themselves a different fur coat for each hour of the day."

Genuine leopard skin was always expensive; but because the simple black-on-gold spot design was easy to counterfeit even in a crude way, fake-fur makers, whose business was thriving by the thirties, made the wild-animal look available to everyone. "Looks like leopard!" boasts the

BRING OUT THE ANIMAL IN HIM

[A] #2–7145   VEE-DEEP
He'll never forget you when he sees you in this slither of acetate jersey with French cuffed, long slim sleeves. The neckline topped with a semi-shirt collar above a deep, deep "V"! Little boy leg romper. Leopard animal print. Misses Sizes 8 to 16.   **$17**

[B] #2–7530   L'IL LEOPARD
You can be queen of the jungle . . . or anywhere you wear this little leopard tank top. So close-fitting, it looks like the spots are your own. Simply stunning when worn with our leopard skirt. Acetate jersey. Small (6 to 8); Medium (10 to 12); Large (14 to 16).   **$8**

[C] #2–7097   HEP CAT
For the prettiest kitties, this 8-gored swing skirt in wild leopard print GOES with your leopard tank top (see #7530)! A blast to wear with a see-through blouse, a bare midriff topper. In Acetate jersey, just 17'' long, it's a real swinger. Misses sizes 6 to 16.   **$10**

[D] #2–7748   JUNGLE TOP
Awakens his primitive instincts in a clingy, curvy leopard print top. V-neck styling, and long sleeves. Wear it with our leopard skirt for greatest effect. Acetate jersey. Small (6 to 8); Medium (10 to 12); Large (14 to 16).   **$10**

[E] #2–7527   CALL-OF-THE-WILD
Here's leopard . . . to bring out the tiger in him! Turtle-neck playsuit has a zipper front, so you can wear it open or closed. French leg for perfect fit. In close-clinging acetate jersey. Sizes 8 to 16.   **$15**

[F] #2–7528   FEMALE ANIMAL
Going on a hunt? Wear a leopard print skirt . . . and maybe he'll track you down first. Wear it with your leopard play-suit or a favorite blouse. Acetate jersey. Sizes 6 to 16.   **$10**

[G] #2–7755   JUNGLE JUMPER
G-r-owl, pussycat, and catch yourself a tiger! You'll be fit to pounce in this Leopard print bonded acetate Jersey that fits like your second pelt. Jumpsuit zips up the back, with a turnover cowl neck, animal-print. Misses Sizes 8 to 16.   **$19**

[H] #2–7144   THE LEAST ONE
Run-around from morning till night! The least is the most in this hug-me tank shift.   acetate jersey. Sleeveless! Pullover! And-how scoop necked! Leopard animal print. Misses Sizes 8 to 16.   **$13**

jersey knit

[A]

zip front
wear it open
or closed

jersey knit

regular 19''
length skirt

1937 Sears, Roebuck catalogue about an $8.98 Trotteur Swagger coat in thick, furry cotton pile fabric with "the same tawny gold tones, the same rich black markings!"

Leopard skin became one of the primary patterns of the fifties (with boomerangs and rocket nose cones) because of advances in synthetic fibers. No longer was it necessary to try to replicate nappy fur to get the leopard-skin effect. Rayon, Dacron, and modacrylic fabrics could simply be printed with a cream tan background and tawny spots to create the look, if not the feel, of a feral cat. Once used strictly for outerwear and upholstery, the leopard-skin look was adopted by designers of naughty lingerie for its untamed, hedonistic implications. Hollywood sex goddesses (Elizabeth Taylor, Lana Turner) wore leopard skin; theirs was a look that trickled down fast now that the pattern was so easily manufactured. "Turn him on with an ANIMAL ACT!" suggested a Frederick's of Hollywood lingerie catalogue in reference to the Go Native deep-V-plunges, slinky leopard-skin negligee (with elastic waistband). Leopard skin was rampant in the Frederick's catalogue, used for the Gay Topper jungle-print hide-all hat ("wonderful for covering up untidy hair or rollers"), for Jungle Music swimsuits, and for the Cozy Up blanket, which featured leopard spots on one side and smaller ocelot spots on the reverse.

As tacky as the spotted pattern became, real leopard skin hung on as the regalia of high fashion. The autumn 1959 *Fashions of the Times* supplement featured a majestic model in an enormous leopard-skin cape-coat and matching hat on its cover. When First Lady Jackie Kennedy wore her Somali leopard coat on a trip abroad in 1962, she set off such fashion shocks that the price of leopard coats tripled from $6,000 to $18,000; within five years Somali leopards were officially declared an endangered species, and the modern era of endangered-animal consciousness began. *Elegance (A Complete Guide for Every Woman Who Wants to Be Well and Properly Dressed on All Occasions)* suggested in 1964 that leopard was especially chic because mink, particularly mink jackets, stoles, and cape-stoles, "has become so banal." Bad minks, *Elegance* observes, "make you look like a seventy-year-old lady who just got off the train from some provincial home town." Leopard, on the other hand, "has probably become the most coveted fur in the world . . . very chic for sports and sophisticated city wear, stunning as a hat or muff." For the cover of her first book, *Every Night, Josephine* (1960), Jacqueline Susann posed with her toy poodle, Josephine—both of them outfitted in leopard skin.

By the sixties leopard skin was ensconced as the banner of the trashy, ersatz-glamour look— simulated on everything from terry cloth to linoleum. Rather than being a sign of sophistication, leopard-skin decor and clothing fell into cultural perdition. The ridiculous Douglas family (played by Eddie Albert and Eva Gabor) of the television sitcom "Green Acres" kept a leopard-skin couch in their living room: a perfect sign of their futile striving for sophistication in the hick town of Hooterville.

In recent years, couturiers have begun to use the leopard-skin pattern as a tongue-in-cheek exercise in *nostalgie de boue* on everything from hats and shoes to silk and lycra body suits. Leopard skin is high fashion again—but this time with a postmodern smirk. "Now more amusing than risqué," according to *Vogue*, leopard skin—anywhere other than on a leopard—is a joke.

See also **FAKE FUR**

LIBERACE

People criticize me," Liberace once told Hollywood's Mr. Blackwell, "but when they meet me, they can't help liking me." We hate to disagree, but we bet that most people's reaction when confronted with Wladziu Valentino Liberace was not love or hate but stupefaction. Until his death in 1987, Liberace reigned supreme as the personification of show-business kitsch. He began as a pianist, but early in his career his substantial musical abilities were upstaged by the world's most flamboyant wardrobe, blinding batteries of jewelry, gilded pianos, and musical programs of such stunning mise-en-scène they put the stars in heaven to shame.

Liberace was born in West Allis, Wisconsin, on May 16, 1919, the son of a Polish mother and an Italian father who played the French horn in the Milwaukee Symphony Orchestra. He was a prodigy and began playing the piano at four. When he was seven he met the great pianist Paderewski and wowed him with selections by Liszt and Beethoven. At nineteen, Lee Liberace was a soloist with the Chicago Symphony Orchestra.

He toured the Midwest playing classical music at small-town concerts, but in 1938 in La Crosse, Wisconsin, his future was cast. For an encore request, he chose the popular Kay Kyser tune "Three Little Fishes" and played it with much winking and grinning at the audience to let them know that it was a daring thing to do in front of the local music critic, who was a highbrow and a snob. The novelty of a pop tune played with classical flourishes made local headlines and became a wire-service story that gave the young pianist his first taste of notoriety. "I realized after that incident that my heart was not in concertizing but in entertaining," Liberace recalled, and at once he surrendered his classical aspirations to take a job at the Wunderbar, a tavern in Warsaw, Wisonsin, where he performed using the stage name Walter Buster Keys. ("Buster" had been selected by the Wunderbar management to signify Liberace's joie de vivre.)

Liberace's career soared in the forties.

Success at New York's Persian Room in the Plaza Hotel, after which *Variety* predicted, "He should snowball into box office," was followed by appearances on KLAC-TV in Los Angeles; and soon television made him a star. In June 1952, he substituted for Dinah Shore and was so popular he got his own fifteen-minute network show in July. Liberace believed the secret to his success was the way he flirted with the camera. "I looked it right in its one big eye just the way I'd look you in the eye. When I winked, everyone in the whole television audience could see for themselves that I was winking right at them."

Until 1952, Liberace performed in traditional pianist's garb: full-dress black tails. For a performance at the Hollywood Bowl that year, however, Liberace was worried that the twenty thousand fans would not be able to see him against the black tuxedos of his orchestra, so he wore all white. It was a sensation, and he declared that for his next performance he would wear gold lamé; and from that day on, Liberace's stage wear spiraled up, up, and away to include such famous outfits as a 40-pound rhinestone jacket, a 175-pound fox cape lined with jeweled brocade, and black velvet dress tails with "LIBERACE" spelled out in jet beads and diamond-on-diamond buttons.

Critics rankled at Liberace's overly white teeth, his wavy hair, his dimples, his abundance of gaudy jewelry and frilly clothes; they were appalled by the ornate candelabras atop his polished piano, and most especially by the sentimentality and cleverness of his embellished playing style. His own list of favorite condemnatory adjectives included "winking," "sniggering," "giggling," "snuggling," "scent-impregnated," "fruit-flavored," "over-sweetened," "over-flavored," "over-luscious," and "sickening." After a Carnegie Hall performance, John Crosby of the New York *Herald Tribune* fumed, "If women vote for Liberace as a piano player—and I'm sure they do —it raises questions about their competence to vote for anything." Liberace responded with one

of the great show-business quotes of all time: "I cried all the way to the bank."

Despite the critics, Liberace became a nationwide craze in 1953. As Sinatra had done a few years before, he made audiences faint and cry for joy when he performed. But his audiences were not bobby soxers; they were gray-haired ladies—mothers and grandmothers. They formed fan clubs and sent Liberace five thousand pieces of adoring fan mail every week. They thought he was a dreamboat, so clean and polite—and he never failed to say something nice about his one real sweetheart, his mother. (Another performer who was also nice to his mother, Elvis Presley, struck up a lifelong friendship with Liberace when they met in Las Vegas in 1956. Elvis studied his act and learned incalculable secrets from the man known as Mr. Showmanship. He and Liberace shared a rare gift of making each member of the audience feel singled out.)

As Liberace's fame grew, so did his appetite for glitter. His private homes as well as his concerts were paeans to profligacy. He said that automobiles signified "the glamour that was Hollywood," and so ordered his first Cadillac with wall-to-wall mink carpeting, upholstery made to look like piano keys, and gold trim everywhere. His fleet of cars grew to include a red, white, and blue star-spangled Rolls-Royce (made for his

bicentennial show at the Las Vegas Hilton), a diamond-studded dune buggy, a gold gull-winged Bradley GT, and limousines whose insides were swathed in acres of blue and white velvet.

Perhaps his most remarkable acquisition was the face of his companion, Scott Thorson. Thorson's book *Behind the Candelabra* recounts that Liberace instructed plastic surgeon Dr. Jack Startz of Beverly Hills to restructure Thorson's cheekbones and chin and give him a nose job. Liberace's goal was to have a lover who was his own mirror image, a live-in Liberace look-alike. It worked: When the bandages were removed from Thorson's face and the swelling receded, Liberace gazed upon a physiognomy that was a younger version of his own and declared, "A beauty—a star is born."

He maintained homes in Las Vegas, Palm Springs, Los Angeles, and Malibu, each decorated by him personally. When making a home his, Liberace's first order of business was to disguise the toilet. He hated seeing a naked commode so much that he told one reporter that he was working on plans for a disappearing one that would pop up only when needed. Lacking this ultimate facility, he had the toilet adjacent to the master bathroom at the Cloisters, his Palm Springs home, remodeled to look like a royal throne.

The Cloisters also featured glass garage doors that swung open as the master's car approached, exposing an interior outfitted to look like a ballroom with crystal chandeliers. The master bathroom was awash in Baccarat glass, hung with baroque chandeliers and sunken Jacuzzis. The bedroom in Liberace's Las Vegas home featured a replica of the ceiling of the Sistine Chapel including Liberace's own face among the cherubim; the living room had an all-mirrored piano with a Lucite bench; and the bar in the adjacent Moroccan room was overlooked by a full-sized stuffed peacock and bedecked with hundreds of tiny twinkle lights. Liberace loved showing off his homes to groups of admiring lady friends. So they wouldn't soil the carpets, he asked each visitor to remove her shoes and put on a pair of the gold stretch slippers he bought by the bushel for just such occasions.

Lee, as his friends called him, liked to go antique hunting and to mix such genuine treasures as Tsar Nicholas II's desk with ample amounts of fakery and kitsch picked up while scouring tag sales. He was an inveterate trickster and loved to boast that the roaring fire in his baronial hearth was gas-fueled, that the logs were cement, the ashes ground asbestos, and the wood smell and crackling sound created by a special product he found to sprinkle over the fake logs.

Liberace acquired so many things in his life, he filled three warehouses in addition to his homes. Many of his possessions were put on display in the Liberace Museum in the Liberace Shopping Center (also including Liberace's Tivoli Gardens Restaurant) on Tropicana Avenue in Las Vegas. After he died, the museum expanded into three marble-floored, chandelier-lit buildings in the shopping center: one holds his most famous pianos and automobiles; one holds costumes and statues; and a third includes a replica of his bedroom and study, the George Liberace Gallery (things that were his brother's), and a gift shop. Among the museum's impressive holdings is a set of gold hands—exact life-size replicas of Liberace's (but without any jewelry on them), resting upon a purple velvet pillow with a gold rose.

In performance it was a challenge for the man known as Mr. Showmanship, the Candelabra Kid, and the King of Diamonds to steadily top himself. Audiences came not so much to hear him play "Ave Maria" or "Kitten on the Keys" as to bask in his ever-increasing resplendence. He arrived on stage like Peter Pan dangling from invisible wires, or stepping forth from a mock Fabergé egg wearing a cape made from a hundred pounds of pink turkey feathers, or—for a command performance before the Queen of England—wearing a velvet coronation robe trimmed with sixty thousand dollars' worth of chinchilla pelts. For less formal performances, he wore red, white, and blue hot pants with fringed

jacket and knee socks—a kind of patriotic Woodstock Nation ensemble with a dash of traditional lederhosen. (A photo of Liberace performing in hot pants at Caesars Palace in 1971 was the most widely run wire-service transmission ever to come out of Las Vegas.) Oddly enough, in his private life Liberace claimed he dressed rather modestly, bragging that he bought many of his clothes at K Mart.

All his life many people assumed Liberace was gay, but he denied it. In 1959 he won a libel lawsuit against Cassandra, the London *Daily Mirror*'s gossip columnist, who implied he was a homosexual. In 1982 the *National Enquirer* headlined "Liberace Bombshell—Boyfriend Tells All"; and again Liberace was embroiled in a lawsuit, this time with Scott Thorson, who wanted to sue him for palimony. The suit ended quietly in 1986 with Thorson receiving a settlement of $170,000, a gold Rolls-Royce, a white Auburn, a Doberman pinscher, and an English sheepdog.

As he got older, Liberace tried not to change. Plastic-surgery tucks and lifts made his face as tight and immobile as a Kabuki mask. His toupees took on the appearance of taxidermic pelts, perched high atop his powdered and painted face. Despite the attempts at preservation, after a final triumphant performance to a sold-out crowd at Radio City Music Hall in November 1986 nearly everyone commented that he looked terrible. He explained that he had lost too much weight on a watermelon diet. But in January, the Las Vegas *Sun* finally revealed the secret that shocked his most devoted fans but few others—Liberace had AIDS. A month later he died in bed, watched over by a Shar Pei named Wrinkles, one of the many beloved dogs he always called "my children." Liberace was interred in the Court of Remembrance in Hollywood's Forest Lawn Memorial Park, in a six-foot-tall white marble sarcophagus decorated with images of a piano and his signature in gleaming brass, flanked by trees shaped like candelabras.

LIMOUSINES

Could there really have been a time when limousines were the height of elegance and good taste? There is evidence to support this theory: old Rolls-Royces, even old Cadillac and Lincoln limousines, are refined black cars with tasteful gray upholstery and a few quiet amenities to make the rich people who owned them comfortable on their way to stockholders' meetings or the opera.

Today's limos are another story. Sold not to private owners but to a burgeoning segment of the economy known as the livery market, most limousines are basically nothing more than big, vulgar taxicabs. They are hired by foursomes who want a swanky Friday-night ride to the Atlantic City or Las Vegas casinos; by party-hearty high-school students as a place to drink, have sex, and puke on prom night; by corporations too penurious to own their own who want to make a sale to a client; and by anybody who thinks the world will treat him

with respect if it sees him stepping out of an extra-long car driven by a man in a chauffeur's hat. When the *New York Times* did a story about Jack G. Schwartz, the limousine king of the South Bronx (who manufactures, sells, and leases more limos than anybody else in the country), reporter Douglas Martin described Schwartz's customers as ''pot-bellied sexagenarians with miles of gold chains,'' who rode in limos to pick up bimbos. (One Schwartz customer purchased a limo with no seats in back, just a deer-skin bed.)

Because they are rented by a different parvenu every day, most limousines operated by livery services age very fast. There is only so much spilled pink champagne and crushed honey-roasted cashews a carpet can absorb before it begins to smell like a leaky trash compactor. The usual high-roller amenities such as VCR players, refrigerators, and cellular telephones may indeed all be in working order, but once an ardent pair of newlyweds has carved their initials into the zebrawood vanity table, it's hard to forget that you are renting your luxury by the hour.

As for automotive excellence, the majority of rental limos are made by a process no more complicated than taking a factory-fresh Cadillac or Lincoln and slicing it in half with a carbide saw. The drive train is extended, new body panels are attached with a welding torch and putty to stretch the car four or five feet, and the interior is made sumptuous. In almost every case, the engine in the finished three-ton showboat is the same pokey one that barely pulled the normal-weight sedan around; the suspension offers the same marshmallow ride, which magnifies road bumps into seasickening boings and bounces once the vehicle has been stretched. When *Car and Driver* tested an ultrastretch Lincoln limo (thirty-six feet long, with two bars and two televisions) in 1986, it reported a 0–60 mph acceleration time of 19.4 seconds (two to three times slower than normal). It also said that stopping was a problem ("The brakes faded instantaneously") and that trying to turn a corner resulted in "an eerie feeling that the car is sliding sideways . . . like a minute hand on a clock."

The ridiculous elongation of deluxe limousines was a paradoxical result of the oil crises of the seventies. For the sake of fuel efficiency, Detroit downsized its cars; the factory-made Cadillac limousine shrunk by half a ton. But as cars were shrinking, super-rich people were getting richer, and their automotive whims were getting grander. King Khalid of Saudi Arabia, who had plenty of oil money to spend, hired Wisco Corporation, a Detroit customizer, to stretch his '76 Cadillac three feet—an event that made a small sensation in the American press because it ran so contrary to prevailing belief that cars ought to be getting smaller.

In 1982, a newcomer to the stretch limo business, the Ultra Limousine Company of Orange County, California, built a ridiculously long—thirty-two-foot—limo as a show car to drum up customers. Hollywood stunt man Jay Ohrberg (owner of Bonnie and Clyde's bullet-riddled death car) topped them when he built one fifty feet long; and the stretch limo wars began in earnest—fueled by an entry for Ohrberg's car in the *Guinness Book of World Records*. Ohrberg's supreme masterpiece was a sixty-foot, sixteen-wheel, twenty-thousand-pound Cadillac with slot machine, putting green, water bed, helicopter pad, and room for fifty passengers. Ultra retaliated and grabbed back *Guinness* recognition with a 104-foot Cadillac that featured eight television sets, ceramic-tiled swimming pool with diving board, and a complete kitchen, including food processor and microwave oven.

Ultra has recently designed a hot tub small enough to bolt into the trunk of any Lincoln, stretched or not. It also informed *The Robb Report* that it has plans to build a mini-limo that will travel on the back of the super-stretch limo and be used in the same way a dinghy is used from a yacht—to ferry passengers back and forth to places the big boat cannot go.

LOUD TIES

Tie styles are always changing, and almost any tie that is not in fashion at the moment can seem gauche; but it was American ties of the late forties that became the archetype of all ostentatious neckwear. Their flamboyance has never been seen again, not even in the mod era of wide, polka-dot, lobster-bib ties. For a few years after World War II, when six hundred different companies were making a combined total of two hundred million ties per year, tie designers went wild, creating a chromatic riot on silk: twirling tornadoes and dripping amoebic blobs and geometric friezes, flying saucers and boomerangs, blossoming hibiscuses and hunting dogs at point and bucking broncos, and ties with cheesecake pictures on the front or secreted in the lining.

Before the war, the Duke of Windsor had set a dry style in men's clothing, to which most fashion-conscious Americans subscribed. When the war was on, patriotic men who weren't in uniform dressed modestly, because old or at least conservative clothes didn't require the diversion of precious war resources toward frivolous fashion. (In fact, some men who wore flashy zoot suits and loud ties got beaten up by overzealous patriots to whom garish apparel symbolized a treasonous incontinence.)

When the war ended, floodgates opened. It was assumed by nearly everyone

who manufactured anything that Americans were hungry for color, innovation, and luxury. Car and appliance makers frantically retooled and hired fashion experts to guide them. And the fashion industry itself, reined in by wartime austerity, burst forth with apparel meant to signify leisure, comfort, and a bright future ahead.

Wide lapels, broad shoulders, and voluminous pleated pants, once the hallmark of the disreputable zoot suit, became the height of fashion. Hawaiian shirts appeared on city streets. Even conservative Sears offered ''light-as-a-feather lounging shoes made of cotton novelty fabrics in the leisure style that is sweeping the country.'' Dignified Botany offered a startling collection of neckties that boasted geometric scrolls and figures; Cheney Brothers sold ties with pinwheel prints, feathered prints, circles, rectangles, all-over scrolls and squares. In 1946, the *Saturday Evening Post* said, ''Most men like their ties wild today.''

In their comprehensive book *Fit to Be Tied: Vintage Ties of the Forties and Early Fifties*, Rod Dyer and Ron Spark observe that tie manufacturers began postwar extravagance by leapfrogging the conservative thirties and reaching back to the stylish twenties for ideas— Art Deco patterns and a palette of lime green, chrome orange, and cobalt blue; futuristic zigzags and sunbursts on ultra-sheen

rayon and silk. Tie maker James Lehrer hired surrealist artist Salvador Dali to design ties with images of women becoming trees and skeletons dancing in pools of blood. There were hand-painted ties of hunting scenes created (and signed) in limited editions by Countess Mara; there were photographic ties depicting famous scenery (great souvenirs!); and "ties to tease your eyes" in three-dimensional patterns from Van Heusen, which boasted that "the longer you look, the more you see." Even Liberace tried his hand at painting ties in his spare time, creating gaudy images of piano keys, musical notes, and his own swirly signature.

Although some garish ties were worn by perfectly refined people, the authors of *Fit to Be Tied* estimate that no more than 15 percent of the ties bought in the late forties were the "ham and eggs" style (named because they were so busy you could drop your breakfast on them and no one would notice). For most people they were novelties that were given as gifts or bought as souvenirs, then relegated to the closet.

Tie manufacturers soon relented, and the explosion of design and color that bubbled up after the war faded fast. By 1948, *Apparel Arts* reported that "the east has already taken back conservative tie styles"; and in 1951, *Apparel Arts* created a character named Mister T ("T" for tapered), whose ties were narrowed down to a conservative 3½-inch-width and were nothing but solids and stripes.

By the time Eisenhower was elected, loud ties had become the sure mark of an oaf who was ignorant of what polite men are supposed to wear. "Show me a man's tie and I will tell you who he is, or who he is trying to be," wrote John T. Molloy in *Dress for Success,* advising readers who want success NEVER to wear a tie with any kind of picture or garish pattern on it. Except in their role as campy thrift-shop antifashion or kitsch collectibles, loud ties are a chapter of clothing history that no one has been eager to revive. They remain, like automobile tail fins and bouffant hairdos, one of the awe-inspiring modern examples of design enthusiasm gone berserk.

LOW RIDERS

Low riders are Hispanic men who drive cars with their springs cut down to make them ride so close to the pavement that they create sparks as they move. A low rider calls his car a "scrape." In the pidgin English of the barrio, scrapes are also known as "caruchas," "ranflas," or simply "rides." Scrapes are not made to go fast; low and slow is how they cruise. Most of them are big 1949–51 Fords or Mercurys or early-sixties Chevrolets that have been "chopped." That means the roof is removed with an acetylene torch, its pillars are shortened six to eight inches, then it is welded back onto the body. The result is a pinhead silhouette with narrow slit windows for driver and passengers, who sit as low in the seats as possible, to peer out as they glide along the favored low-riding boulevards of East Los Angeles, Santa Fe, and San Jose.

Riding low means having a custom paint job in shades of iridescent purple, glitter-flecked lime, or something equally eye-catching, the paint enhanced with an original piece of airbrushed art work, such as a burst of flames around the wheel wells, or a door mural of an Aztec warrior carrying a swooning virgin to the top of an erupting volcano. All chrome is thickly replated and polished to a military shine. Front headlights sport metallic visors. Wheel flaps bedizened with reflector lights adorn each wheel well, and the back two wheel wells are covered over with "skirts" that intensify the low appearance. A scrape's tires will be many sizes too small, making the car seem even more enormous and closer to the ground.

The inside of a well-outfitted scrape is a playpen of tuck-and-roll crushed-velvet upholstery, leopard-skin velours with metallic piping, fringe baubles around each window, thick shag rugs on floor and dashboard, and funny horns that play "La Cucaracha" at the press of a button. The paltry light bulb on the roof will have been upgraded to a small crystal chandelier or a discotheque strobe light. A television set, giant loudspeakers, and CD "jukebox" programmed with nothing but golden oldies are all in place.

The steering wheel has been ripped out and replaced with a circle of welded metal links so small in circumference that it could be driven by someone wearing handcuffs. (The alternative is a big "no holes" padded wheel that resembles a velvet dinner plate attached to the steering column.)

Low riders pay little attention to the ordinary car buff's concerns about horsepower, drive train, and transmission. The single most important mechanical feature of a low rider's car is its hydraulic lifts. These are affixed to the front end (sometimes also to the back) and operated by four to six heavy-duty batteries in the trunk. At the push of a button, the driver shoots a jolt of power to the lifts that sends the carucha's front end hopping from its squat position. Expert hoppers use the jolts and momentum from the springs to make the car start bouncing up and down, higher and higher. Standing still, side by side with another hydro carucha in a hopping contest, a really loco scrape can bounce its front end two feet off the pavement. Cruising, whole lines of scrapes can undulate like jumping beans.

The men behind the wheels and their dates (low riding is a study in machismo) are as thoughtfully put together as their scrapes. There are fancy pachucos in effulgent zoot suits looking like Hispanic Cab Calloways, many of whom belong to official car clubs; and there are more basic cholos, homeboys who belong to gangs instead of clubs, and whose slow-moving cars tend to suggest menace as much as pride.

Cholos never go by their Christian names. They take street names like El Dopey Loco, Mr. Taco Vesta, or El Mr. Joker Loco Wino. The way they dress is so consistent as to constitute a uniform. Calvin Trillin, in a 1978 article about low riders in *The New Yorker,* concluded that the cholo's chosen outfit is in fact a street version of what prisoners wear in jails. It consists of starched khakis pulled high above the waist and falling loosely over the shoes, a white T-shirt or slingshot-strap shirt, a baggy plaid Pendleton shirt always fastened at the neck button but open the rest of the way down, and clunky Stacy

Adams black shoes. To this standard ensemble, cholos add a bandanna tied so low around the forehead it almost looks like a blindfold. A pair of black wraparound sunglasses and a stingy-brim hat pulled low on the head, or possibly a baseball-style cap with the brim flipped up, complete the look. Nearly all cholos grow a skinny mustache.

A low rider's posture is as stylized as his clothing. He stands with one or both hands in the pockets of his pants, knees slightly bowed, the feet touching at the heels and spread in something like a ballet dancer's first position. A low rider does not smile. He cultivates an impassive, blank look, staring ominously at a camera or looking up and away with an expression of streetwise hauteur. Low riders tend to like tattoos. Those who have spent time in jail sometimes have a small tear tattooed on their cheek near the eye. Others prefer pictures of glamorous long-haired women on their arms.

Low riders' girlfriends try to look as much like the tattoo dream girl as possible. Ideal beauty consists of long dark hair puffed and feathered all around the face and falling over the shoulders, dark eye makeup with extra mascara, and bright red lipstick. "Las homegirls" pluck their eyebrows to a fine line and wear "chola" bands on their hands: thin black rubberized ribbons that extend all the way from finger to mid-forearm, tied in complicated knots and semiotic designs. Cholas also like halter tops and tight jeans worn with high heels, and often wear stingy-brim porkpie hats that match their boyfriends'.

To study low-rider culture at a distance we direct you to two remarkable magazines: *Low Rider* and *Teen Angel.* Both contain swell pictures of cars and lots of candid snapshots of homeboys and homegirls assuming the cholo

LOW RIDER

★ JANUARY 1981

pose. *Teen Angel* is the funkier of the two, more like reading a wall of graffiti than reading a magazine. It contains endless lists of dedications from lovesick homeboys to their cholas, each sentiment expressed by selecting an appropriately named oldies hit record. Homeboy Mr. Penguin sends La Shy Girl the following message: ''Angel Baby.'' Mr. Stranger de E.S.J. tells La Giggles ''Confessing a Feeling.'' Like the song from which it takes its name, *Teen Angel* is full of passion and morbidity; it is packed with handwritten love laments, jailhouse drawings of pretty girls, and sad poems like ''Forget Him'' by homegirl La Angelita de San Pancho about a boyfriend killed in a gang war.

Low riders' very elaborate way of looking and acting owes a great debt to the blossoming of American teenagers after World War II. As youth seceded from adult society and established a precise counterculture with its own music, fashions, and hairstyles, even its own kinds of (hot rod) cars, values of coolness and rebel-without-a-cause insolence were established that still inform low-rider life. They listen only to golden oldies music and drive nothing but big, old low-and-slow cars. The uniforms they wear, from zoot suits to the cholo's khaki-pants-and-undershirt, and the racy hot-mama attire favored by their ladies are flamboyant, time-honored barrio style that gives the raspberry to mainstream fashion.

Low riding is now at least three generations old. *Low Rider* magazine regularly prints pictures from the early fifties of men with thin mustaches wearing white T-shirts, wraparound sunglasses, and baggy khakis, their hands thrust deep in their pockets and their feet turned out at the familiar cholo angle. They stand sullenly in front of what were then brand-new Chevys and Pontiacs—polished to a gleam—waiting for someone to notice.

See also **ZOOT SUITS**

Two simple knots—the clove hitch and the square knot—are macramé's foundation. From them, a snarl of hanging plant holders, cloche hats, ponchos, caftans, herbal pouches, net guitar straps, and rough cord place mats have spread across the earth. Wherever there are craftsmen wearing sandals, there is macramé. In flea markets with used eight-track tapes and bargain boxes of Hamburger Helper, there is a booth selling macramé toilet-paper cozies and macramé hoot owls with big ceramic saucer eyes. In retired high-school art teachers' homes, you will find the macramé on the wall, its knots exquisitely interwoven with driftwood twigs and stalks of desiccated pussy willow.

You'd think it would have gone away by now, along with such other totems of the Age of Crafts as pop-top vests, felt-trimmed burlap tote bags, and macaroni flowers; but macramé has refused to fade into oblivion. Like candle crafts, which came into vogue about the same time, macramé is a menial activity that yields a thing of beauty that can be sold to shoppers looking for something personal. It is still made in abundance, because, although monotonous, the work requires little skill. Acid heads whose brains got stuck looping and beading can make macramé and be proud that they are creative. Ugly as the

finished product may be by any objective measure, it is the result of human hands at work and therefore, to admirers of all things natural, more interesting than something made by a machine.

In principle as old as looms and sailors' knots, macramé comes from either the Turkish word *makrama,* meaning a fringed napkin, or the Arab *migramah,* meaning embroidered veil. It was used for church garments in medieval times, and for drawing-room fringe and dress decoration in Edwardian England; but it was not until the mid—twentieth century that macramé, along with other tactile crafts such as knitting, crocheting, embroidering, and denim patching, rose in status from ladies' handwork to what was finally called *Art Fabric* (in Mildred Constantine and Jack Lenor Larsen's 1974 book, *Beyond Craft: The Art Fabric*).

No matter how skillfully it is done, macramé almost always seems ingenuous, which is just what the modernistic fifties home needed. The rough and nubby texture of a macramé wall hanging gave a human dimension to severe contemporary interiors (see also *Driftwood*). An elaborately knotted hemp lamp shade or a set of burnt orange place mats had the honest, handmade connotations of peasants making ceremonial sashes and Greek fishermen mending their nets.

In the sixties, macramé was the ideal craft for hippies who wanted to express their back-to-nature values. It was primitive; it allowed the knotter to get his hands into such nontechnologically named fibers as hemp and jute and sisal cord—so much more honest than nylon or polyester. In addition to using it for decoration, hippies found dozens of uses for macramé as clothing. A knotted hat, a stringy vest made from gold rug yarn, a white bib necklace, or a knotted tunic to be worn over hiphuggers looked natural and at the same time snubbed establishment factory-made clothing.

The most popular use for macramé, other than to make clothes, handbags, and coarse entanglements of beaded jewelry, was the creation of elaborate slings for hanging potted plants. Even after hippies were history, hanging plants in macramé cradles filled the air in brick-walled restaurants and in city lofts and suburban porches throughout the seventies. Bruce Morrison, staff artist at Craft Course Publishers and author of *Macrame Hang-Ups* (1973), was correct when he surmised that ''macrame flowerpot holders [are] a craze that will be around, we think, for many years to come!'' He explained their appeal: ''They truly add the decorator accent and can be hung from every ceiling of every room in your home! They bring a touch of outdoors indoors when you add the colorful potted plants. Or place a fishbowl in a hanger with a little greenery.'' (This last project was called ''Aquitaine.'')

For people without space to hang pots from every ceiling of every room in their home, another helpful Craft Course book called *Macrame Hangers for Small Spaces* (1975) contained knotting plans aimed at ''*you*, the dorm dweller with the study cubicle [or] the visionary decorator who thrives on kicky new ideas like mini

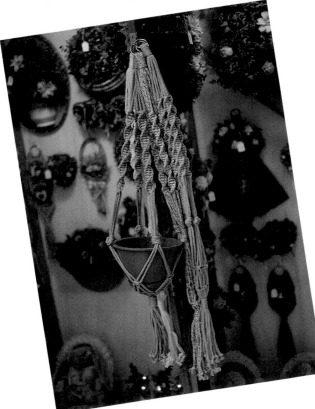

macrame pot hangers between the staircase railing banisters [or] the little great grandma who finds big bold macrame too large to handle.'' Among the miniaturized ideas are a seven-inch angel for a Christmas tree and a tiny jute replica of the 1962 world's fair Space Needle. Going in the opposite direction was a 1974 macramé book called *Knots and Pots* by Thelma Lee (author of *Safety Pins in 3-D* and *Mobiles in Beads*), which features plans for a pot hanger called ''Nebuchadnezzer's Delight,'' knotted to resemble the Babylonian king's fez, eight feet from top to bottom, with a berth for a two-foot-wide pot, requiring 490 yards of five-ply natural jute.

It's a little sad to read these old, enthusiastic books about the joys of macramé, large or small, knowing how the whole idea of string crafts has sunk into ignominy during the last ten years. In the fifties, coarse knotting seemed exotic; in the sixties it was groovy; in the seventies macramé turned trite, hackneyed, and utterly prosaic. Once the sign of an artistic hand, macramé is now more likely the work of a bored motorcycle mama or a part-time astrologer for whom a tangle of hemp is as challenging as life can be.

MALLS

Malls make life easy because they are predictable. You know when you go to one that there will be no surprises, nothing different or weird or odd to upset you. Virtually every shop is a branch of a familiar chain, stocked with predetermined merchandise. All the food is vended in sanitary paper and Styrofoam by uniformed employees of well-known franchises. And the consumers in the mall are all docile (with the exception of some hyperkinetic gangs of teens), lulled into a serene state of spendthrift apathy by a combination of hypnotic Muzak, the numbing assault of merchandise crying out to be purchased, and the sensory deprivation of being enclosed within a mazelike asylum that has no windows. Thus detached from reality, oblivious shoppers roam blissfully in packs through the cavernous courtyards, their unblinking eyes dazed and dilated, their arms loaded with bags of merchandise, their jaws chewing rhythmically on clumps of barbecue popcorn or a sodden, freshly baked chocolate-chip cookie.

Malls are where people go to fantasize about what things they will buy if they win the lottery, to observe fashion trends, to exercise (there is an organized sport known as mall walking), and to alleviate boredom. Malls' food courts offer a bigger variety of snack foods than you could ever find in a single city neighborhood, plus the thrill of such unique mall cuisine as stuffed baked potatoes and doughy hot cinnamon buns. All the current hit movies are playing in one jumbo multiplex (half of America's movie theaters are in malls). Being private property, they are patrolled by security personnel empowered to evict rowdy troublemakers and raving mendicants who are at liberty to run rampant on public streets. Parking is free. And the weather inside is always fine.

For young people studying how to be enthusiastic consumers and how to behave the way everyone else behaves, malls offer an education in material culture that no well-meaning parent or teacher could ever hope to give. At the mall, which they cruise with the same cliquish panache used to swagger through the halls at school, teens learn the crucial distinctions among clothes labels such as Esprit and Benetton; they learn to covet the most popular records and shoes; they can study and buy all the products they see advertised in magazines and on TV; they learn to talk alike and have the same opinions as their peers. And when they have learned all these lessons, they become what the rest of the world knows as "mall rats," and proud of it. Teenager Ramona Lee told *Seventeen* magazine that she loved going to the mall because it had the "things we need and want and dream of." Ramona's list of dreams included "one perfect pair of jeans, a hamburger just the way we like it, and some other things too big to fit in a plastic shopping bag." What Ramona was referring to by "things too big to fit in a plastic shopping bag" was romance. She explained that she was one-half of a mall couple, and that she and her mall boy had taken their first romantic walk together underneath the metal arch of the tag detector at the mall's record store.

Although they are designed to always seem familiar, not all malls are alike. The big ones have at least two major department stores, one at each end (known in the mall trade as "anchors"), so that shoppers who want to visit both are forced to walk past all the stores in between. The West Edmonton Mall in Canada—the world's largest—has 11 department stores, 821 other shops, an amusement park with twenty-two water slides, and more spaces than any other parking lot on earth. (Mall parking lots are striped and restriped according to how good business is. A mall in a slump offers fewer parking spaces, making the lot appear full, and thus attracting customers who crave to be where everybody else is—the exemplary mall shopper's mentality; a mall doing booming business cuts down spaces to a minuscule 8 x 17½ feet to squeeze in more customers.) Mini-malls, also known as pod malls, are anchored only by a 7-Eleven or Stop-N-Go convenience store and are at best a stopgap measure for any shopper who craves the neurological bombardment of a full-featured mega-mall. In an attempt to lure customers back downtown, some cities have tried to revitalize their dead and dying parts by turning them into "festival marketplaces," such as Faneuil Hall in Boston and Horton Plaza in San Diego. These emporiums offer a mall-like panoply of shops, but they tend to have too much architectural character to provide the sense of stupefying conformity that makes a modern mall pleasant and soothing. To work its magic, a mall must always seem brand-new, prefabricated, isolated, and impersonal, with all the physical charm of a prison or factory.

Shopping centers are nearly as old as the automobile, but the first fully enclosed mall, named Southdale, was not built until 1956 in Edina, Minnesota. Malls grew with the suburbs and the highways; their success was fed by money from a generation that perfected heretofore unimaginable skills of product discrimination and acquisitiveness. But more than just cathedrals of consumption, malls have become what Southdale's designer, Victor Gruen, had predicted they would be: town centers to which people come to socialize, exercise, dine, have a mammogram or a blood pressure test, and get a tan (in a tanning salon), even attend church —all in surroundings designed to make buying things the supreme pleasure. The latest improvement on the formula is condo-malls, with living spaces attached, thus making it possible for residents to stay in a shopping environment their whole lives.

"Every day will be a perfect shopping day!" early Southdale advertisements promised; and the promise has come true. Malls contain nearly all the approved, advertised, fashionable things a person is supposed to want; and malls make them available to buy in a controlled habitat where it never rains, but where a hundred-string version of "Raindrops Keep Fallin' on My Head" gets piped out of the sound system at regular intervals throughout the shopping day.

See also **MUZAK**

MANSFIELD, JAYNE

Poor Jayne Mansfield. Everybody paid attention to her forty-six-inch bust instead of her 163 IQ. Miss Mansfield, who said the "y" in "Jayne" was given to her after an especially exciting party at Yale, was the bosomiest dumb blonde of the fifties, known for a curvaceous, cantilevered figure variously measured at 40-18-36, 42-20-36, and, at its biggest, 46-24-36. Instead of talking, she purred and squealed and sighed seductively. Instead of walking, she perfected an astounding, stiletto-heeled gait that hurled her hips sideways and started the famous breasts jiggling like a brace of pink dirigibles filled with flaccid Jell-O.

Her livery was pink, signifying flesh; her crest was a heart, meaning love. She slept in a heart-shaped bed, bathed in pink bubbles in a heart-shaped tub, and lived in a Sunset Boulevard home known as the Pink Palace, featuring a heart-shaped fireplace, fluffy pink carpet on floors, walls, and ceilings, a purple couch and gold piano in the living room, a white marble fountain that spurted pink champagne, and a heart-shaped swimming pool out back that had "I Love You Jaynie" written on the bottom. When she signed her name, she dotted the "i" in "Mansfield" with a big, bosomy heart. She even had a heart-shaped satin crib (in powder blue) for her baby boy, Miklos (Mickey), Jr.

She was a queen many times over. Early in her career she served as Queen of the Chihuahua Show, Queen of Refrigeration Week, Queen of the Palm Springs Rodeo, Nylon Sweater Queen, Gas Station Queen, and Princess of the Freeways. She held the titles of Miss Tomato, Miss Direct Mail, Miss Lobster, Miss Negligee, and Miss Third Platoon. She was crowned Playmate of the Month in the February 1955 *Playboy* and was pictured each February for Valentine's Day in the magazine through 1958, and again in 1960. In 1958, after divorcing Paul Mansfield (whom she married when she was in high school), she wed Mr. Universe Mickey Hargitay, whose fifty-two-inch chest was even bigger than hers.

All her life, she said she wanted to be taken seriously as an actress, a mother, and a violin player. She once even dyed her hair back to its natural brunet, hoping that the change from platinum blond would encourage people to appreciate her brains. But things always happened to Jayne. Mostly, her bosoms popped out of her dress, and damned if there weren't photographers around to take pictures of the mishap. That was how she got her big break in show business in January 1955.

Jayne had made her first trip from Texas to California in 1953, kissing the ground as soon as she crossed the state border, sobbing, "I am home." In Hollywood, before she unpacked, she found a phone booth and started calling producers and press agents. Despite impressive readings from the balcony scene of *Romeo and Juliet,* no one gave her a job until she met Jim Byron, who was then famous as the press agent who had gotten starlet Marilyn Maxwell photographed with a leopard in her swimming pool. Byron found a place for Jayne on a publicity junket to Florida for Jane Russell's new film, *Underwater.* The film's producer, Howard Hughes, had arranged to have the press see the movie under water, providing each reporter with an Aqua-lung and setting up an in-the-pool screening room. Before the screening began, and before Jane Russell arrived, Jayne dove into the pool in a bikini. Somehow, her top came off; and by the time Jane Russell arrived, the photographers had used all their film on Jayne and her struggle with the swimsuit. One tabloid headline read "Jayne Outpoints Jane."

Her first big acting role was on Broadway in George Axelrod's *Will Success Spoil Rock Hunter?* in 1955, where her scant costume in the opening scene—a bath towel—caused a sensation. In Frank Tashlin's *The Girl Can't Help It* in 1956, her first big movie role (and one of her best), she is introduced walking—as only she could walk—along a city street. Men's eyeglasses shatter as she passes; caps pop off of overflowing milk bottles on the front stoops of brownstones. The part could have been Jayne's autobiography: she plays a woman with the sexiest body in the world who wants only to be a wife and a mother. "I really understand this character," she said.

She announced that she wanted to marry Mickey Hargitay wearing a white satin bikini; and although that wish did not come true (she wore a pink dress), the outsized couple were wed on January 13, 1958, at the height of Jayne's career. After a honeymoon in Miami Beach (during which one of the city's small streets was named for her), Jayne and Mickey went to Las Vegas, where they performed as a singing and dancing duo in Sid Kuller's "House of Love Revue," Jayne in a see-through net dress with sequins over her nipples and Mickey in dancer's tights, picking her up and twirling her around the stage.

In 1960 *Playboy* magazine lauded Jayne for not getting spoiled by her success. Whereas other starlets "have usually disdained any further display of their charms *au naturel*" after they became famous, "our Jayne continues to disrobe at the snap of a camera shutter wherever she may be." Jayne, however, soon became a victim of the sixties. Her problem was simply that she was just so *womanly.* In an era that began to prize lithe, winsome girls with boyish figures, her well-upholstered body began to look positively dinosauric. Bosoms were passé. "She really is an old bag," Beatle Paul McCartney announced in 1965.

Jayne struggled valiantly to be an actress in the sixties, making many movies, including *Spree* (a documentary about Las Vegas, in which she strips and sings "Promise Her Anything"), *Promises, Promises!* (which featured nude scenes previewed in *Playboy* but cut from the theatrical release), *Las Vegas Hillbillies,* and *Primitive Love* (a documentary about mating practices of humans and animals around the world). One of the last motion pictures she made, in 1966, was the autobiographical *The Wild, Wild World of Jayne Mansfield,* which featured a guided tour through the Pink Palace and Jayne judging a Jayne Mansfield look-alike contest for transvestites.

She was killed on June 29, 1967, while driving to New Orleans for a TV talk show to promote her engagement at the Gus Stevens Supper Club in Biloxi, Mississippi. Her Buick, driven by Ron Harrison of the supper club, collided with a truck in the fog at 2:25 a.m. Her children, Mickey, Jr., Maria, and Zoltan, sleeping in the backseat, survived the accident. Her business manager, Sam Brody, and Ron Harrison were thrown from the car and killed. Jayne Mansfield was decapitated. And the miniature Mexican Chihuahua she had been holding in her arms died, too.

See also **BREASTS, ENORMOUS; CHIHUA-HUAS; DEATH CARS OF FAMOUS PEOPLE**

MARASCHINO CHERRIES

Maraschino cherries are exciting because they are so special. Who doesn't look for the maraschino cherry half when canned fruit cocktail is served, and who doesn't feel privileged if he gets it? And when a fancy Polynesian drink arrives at the table in a tiki-god mug, wouldn't it be disappointing if the decorative parasol, orange slice, and pineapple chunk speared on a plastic sword above the libation weren't accompanied by a glamorous maraschino cherry?

Nothing in nature is as red as a maraschino cherry, and few thing are as sweet—two big reasons the syrupy baubles aren't taken seriously by food snobs. Maraschino cherries also suffer guilt by their association with Cantonese sweet and sour pork, unsophisticated Manhattans (in lieu of a tasteful twist of lemon), and a thousand happy-housewife recipes for candied duck in cherry sauce. Some brands are packaged with this peculiar warning on the label: "REAL CHERRIES—MAY CONTAIN PITS"—apparently necessary because it is so easy to mistake the contents for factory-made candy.

Shocking as it may seem, there really is such a thing as a maraschino cherry tree. It is called the marasca, and it grows along the Adriatic coast in Yugoslavia and northern Italy, yielding bitter little dark-red cherries that have been used by vintners for centuries to make a clear, delicately flavored cordial called maraschino. Like kirsch, maraschino is an ingredient in sugary desserts such as nesselrode pudding and fruitcake. Italians began preserving white, sweet cherries in maraschino liqueur to give them color and to augment their sweetness with maraschino's zest. These became known as maraschino cherries, and were first exported from Italy to America during the gilded age of extravagant gastronomy at the end of the last

century. Maraschino cherries, with a powerful alcoholic kick, were a delicacy available in the finest restaurants and hotel dining rooms.

In the late 1890s, American food manufacturers began making their own maraschino cherries, using native Royal Anne cherries from California and Napoleons from Michigan, both of which are naturally sweet, with pale meat and yellow skin. The amount of maraschino liqueur used to preserve the cherries was lessened and eventually eliminated, replaced by similar-tasting oil of bitter almond.

By 1900, Fannie Farmer was suggesting recipes for maraschino sauce, frosting, and cream. In the twenties, when virtually all maraschino cherries were the liqueur-less American kind, many recipes for ladies' lunch salads called for one-half a maraschino cherry as a crowning touch; and help-for-the-hostess booklets advised that the soigné way to serve a half grapefruit, chilled or broiled, was with a half cherry at its center, covering the unsightly core. In 1930, *The Cherry and Its Culture* reported "increasing demand for a special sweet cherry product known as 'Maraschino' . . . used in salads, by cake and pastry bakers, and by ice cream and confectionery manufacturers."

To get maraschino cherries red and sweet, they are mechanically harvested, transported in a cushioning solution of water and gaseous sulfur dioxide, bleached, brined (which firms up the meat and strengthens the stem's attachment), pitted, sorted by size, dyed luminous red, then soaked in a constantly resweetened sugar solution for five to seven days until they reach 40—55 Brix, which is food-manufacturing terminology for sweetness. This is about half sugar. (Glacé maraschino cherries, used for fruitcakes and cookies, are soaked in the sugar solution until they reach 70—75 Brix.) Finally, the maraschino flavor is added in the form of oil of almond.

Maraschino cherry lovers had a scare back in early 1976, when their coloring ingredient, Red Dye No. 2, was determined by the Food and Drug Administration to be carcinogenic. Because Red Dye No. 2 was ubiquitous in manufactured food and cosmetics (used in packaged gravies, lipstick, pills, ice cream, hot dogs, dog food, and cake mixes), some stories predicted that suddenly nearly all foods would change color. *Time* warned that instant chocolate pudding would henceforth be greenish and grape soda would be blue. In fact, red M&Ms disappeared for over a decade. Might the same fate befall maraschino cherries, the brightest red food on earth? Red Dye No. 40 came to the rescue, then Red Dye No. 3, which since 1984 has been the subject of further controversy, because it gives rats thyroid cancer when they ingest the equivalent of a hundred bottles of cherries per day. The maraschino cherry industry, however, says that No. 40 is the only way to get cherries their happy red hue, and pooh-poohs its tumor-creating powers. For now, maraschino cherries are every bit as red as they ever were . . . except for the bright green, mint-flavored variety marketed alongside the traditional ones during the Christmas holidays.

See also **POLYNESIAN FOOD**

MEAT SNACK FOODS

Prehistoric Indians dried bison and venison meat to preserve it long after the hunt. They called the thin, air-dried strips *pemmican*—a Cree word for "little food, much nourishment." Modern Americans buy meat snack food in shrink-fit plastic packages at the convenience store. They call the snacks Slim Jim, Chubby Sausage, the Big Jerk—manufacturers' words for sorbitol, sodium erythorbate, sodium nitrite, hydrolyzed vegetable protein, monosodium glutamate, corn syrup, and lactic acid starter culture combined with chunked, ground, and formed beef and mechanically deboned poultry. The term "meat snack," like "cheese food" and "creme filling," is food-industry poetry, used to evoke thoughts of meat (or cheese or cream) about products that contain little or none of the substance in question. In fact, meat snacks always do contain parts of animals, but they must be called meat snacks because the tissue has been so prodigiously refabricated.

We cannot confirm that any person has ever actually gone shopping with the specific intent to purchase a meat snack, or whether a meat snack has ever been purchased by anybody who was sober; but like other seemingly inexplicable bar foods such as eggs in brine and CornNuts, meat snacks serve a role in the contemporary diet. When six to twelve or more steins of beer are sloshing their way down into the bladder and out, they take a lot of salt with them. Meat snacks are saturated with salt, and also MSG, which helps give vegetable protein a brackish smack. They are also very chewy; gnawing on them activates an alcohol-numbed digestive system.

Best of all, a meat snack is convenient. To eat one requires no difficult manipulation of

silverware; nor need you fear the embarrassment of aiming a hamburger or a bologna sandwich at your mouth and missing the mark, thus smearing condiments on chin or cheek. Because they are long and slim and dry, meat snacks are easy to steer toward an open mouth. If you should happen to miss, they aren't messy; and they are pliable enough (unlike a pretzel stick) so that they will bend when accidentally mashed against your face.

Although techniques for jerking (air drying) and smoking beef are hundreds of years old, beef jerky was considered cowboy or hillbilly food until shortly after the turn of the century, when Upton Sinclair's *The Jungle* terrified readers with tales of "embalmed beef" being processed by tubercular workers. Beef jerky, in contrast, is *supposed* to seem embalmed, and you could feel relatively certain that any tuberculosis germs were killed by the drying process; so when meat consumption fell off by one-third in the wake of Sinclair's book, meat packers offered dried, jerked beef—the unadulterated predecessor of manufactured ground-and-formed beef snacks—advertising it as "the ham of the beef animal" (Armour) and boasting of its purity.

Today's meat snacks are packaged in see-through plastic that assures consumers there is nothing to hide. They come in various shapes, including sausagelike links and thin tubes as long as three feet. They are available suffused with flavors, including spicy, smoked, barbecue, and cheese. Customarily, the tubular snacks are

called sausage, contain pig meat, and are more tender, like salami, whereas the tile-shaped snacks, sold as beef *jerky* (and closer in texture to genuine air-dried beef or pemmican) are tough and rugged. The Wisconsin Bar Brand Quality Snack Food Company ("the Snack Food People") packages a deluxe seven-inch beef snack side by side with an equal-length, yellow piece of aliment described on the package as a cheese-flavored stick.

The Cadillac of beef snacks is Slim Jim Gold, made without filler or soy protein and a minimal amount of poultry. When *Meat Processing* magazine visited Slim Jim's maker, GoodMark Foods of Raleigh, North Carolina, in August 1984, it described the grueling inspections all Slim Jim snacks must undergo, including a shear test to measure chewiness, a color inspection to affirm their rich mahogany luster, a taste test performed by panelists selected from the ranks of Slim Jim employees, and microbiological inspections to ensure a shelf life of eight to twelve months. There are thirty varieties of Slim Jim, including Big Jerk, Big Slim, Super Jerk, Giant Jerk, and Tabasco-flavored Super Slim. GoodMark also makes pickled pigs' feet and knuckles, sold mostly in taverns and from displays adjacent to the beer coolers in convenience stores, where one promotion invited customers to "Pig Out for 25¢!"

208

MIME

Long ago, after humans started walking upright, they learned to speak. Speaking was an excellent invention, enabling everybody to make helpful statements such as "Watch out—don't step in that hole" or informative ones such as "I am sleepy." Speech also aided people in expressing more complex and compelling thoughts: e.g., "I love you" or "Help! I can't swim." Before there was talking, all these things could be signified only by grunts or complicated gestures: frantic pointing and pretend tripping to warn about the hole; yawns to express tiredness; moony faces and the rubbing of one's heart to show affection; puffing cheeks and wild paddling as signs of drowning.

Mimes behave as though speaking had never been invented. They act dumb, oddly enough, to *communicate*. But the idea is to use the marvelously expressive human body and grimacing face instead of a voice. According to mime logic, exchanging speech for gesticulation is a way of revealing greater truth. That is why mimes paint their faces white—to become Everyman instead of an individual, and thereby express universal things. In her instructional book *Mime: A Playbook of Silent Fantasy*, Kay Hamblin suggests that aspiring mimes looking for a routine "try the 'Biggies'—evolution, birth and death, love and rejection, crime and punishment, pollution and ecology, Armageddon or epiphany."

Even if they are not doing the Biggies, mimes are seldom simply funny. There is usually some higher purpose to their exhibition. If you see a mime portray a seed growing into a flower (a toe or little finger will sprout first), or act out the familiar "prisoner in a box" routine, you are seeing parables about Life and Freedom. Like those seriocomic clowns who strive to deal with profound issues by playing the fool (Red Skelton, Emmett Kelly, Jerry Lewis), mimes act out melodramas that may or may not be funny but are certainly maudlin, and almost always painfully sanctimonious.

Although they cannot yell at onlookers, mimes are extremely aggressive performers, especially if they do what is known as "street theater" in public places, as opposed to a performance on stage before voluntary spectators. Part of the street performer's job is attracting attention, and because mimes are masters of manipulating space, they are usually able to intrude into other people's space enough to capture their gaze. Don't dare make eye contact with a street mime on the prowl for an audience; if you do, he or she will *own* you for the length of the performance. The mime (whom we will refer to as "it" in honor of the quest for universality) will demand you figure out what it's doing (tugging on an invisible rope, peeking around an imaginary wall), and if you don't figure it out, or don't care to try, it will then force you to watch it portray sadness and hurt.

Mime as we know it burst into blossom in the 1960s. Before that, it was a rather elegant kind of European burlesque with roots in Théâtre des Funambules in nineteenth-century Paris. That was where Jean Gaspard ("Baptiste") Deburau transformed mime from the slapstick of the Italian commedia dell'arte into a more serious exercise in theater (an event portrayed in Marcel Carné's movie *Les Enfants du Paradis*). The tradition was elaborated by the great twentieth-century mime Marcel Marceau, a Frenchman who perfected a sad-sack character known as Bip. Bip's poignant struggles with life's injustices were the inspiration for the undying mime cliché of the sensitive soul trying to grapple with a harsh world.

Bip and his struggles were abstract and poetical. Activist performance artists of the sixties wanted to make mime relevant. That was when R. G. Davis founded the San Francisco Mime Troupe because he believed that mime's broad theatricality was an ideal way to combine theater and politics and to break down the then much-maligned barrier between performer and audience.

The San Francisco Mime Troupe didn't only do pantomime. They sponsored didactic puppet shows in support of LSD; they staged silent playlets on Haight Street, blocking traffic; they dressed up like dwarfs from the Middle Ages and danced in the park tooting penny whistles as a means of raising people's consciousness. The first rock-and-roll show at the Fillmore auditorium was a benefit for the Mime Troupe, whose enigmatic and aggressive (but nonviolent) performances seemed to be a perfect example of the New Age nonverbal communication that hippies liked so much. One faction of the (always quarreling) San Francisco Mime Troupe spun off and became the Diggers, a theatrical social-service group at the heart of the hippie movement. The Diggers' leader, Eugene Grogan, changed his name to Emmett Grogan in homage to silent clown Emmett Kelly.

Along with rock and roll and psychedelic posters, mime was one of the essential hippie arts. Unlike music and posters, however, which have both evolved with the times, mimes have maintained a strong countercultural aura, which is evident in their clothes. Earlier on, mime fashions had changed from the flowing white robes of the commedia dell'arte's Pierrot to Marcel Marceau's high-waisted white pedal pushers, toe shoes, and rumpled top hat; but the fashion evolution stopped in the Age of Aquarius. Most mimes on today's city streets have the same basic happy-vagabond look of broad-striped shirt and bell-bottom trousers with suspenders or work shirt and leotard. Because of the way they dress, as well as what they do, it is important to be aware that the sighting of a mime can result in an alarming sixties flashback.

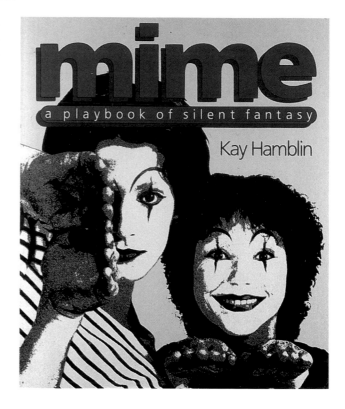

MINIATURE GOLF

The appeal of miniature golf is its freakishness. Like the teenie-weenie bicycles clowns ride around the big top, or a flea circus you can watch only through a magnifying glass, pixie golf offers the weird thrill of experiencing things that are dramatically out of scale. The annals of bad taste brim with attractions that are grotesquely big (the world's largest impacted human intestine, on display in Philadelphia) or abnormally small (carnival midgets riding Shetland ponies). Miniature golf is an especially gratifying example of the delights of haywire scale because it not only takes the actual game of golf and cuts it down to size, it also caricatures the pomp and pretense sometimes associated with it. With names such as Hutsie Putsie (Deposit, New York), Par-King (Chicago), Sir Goony (Chattanooga), and Wacky Golf (Myrtle Beach, South Carolina), most courses are a rowdy parody. There can be nothing effete about a game whose object is to knock a little ball past a spinning windmill into the mouth of a concrete clown. No special golf clothes are required; there are no club dues and few rules that cannot be bent or broken.

Amazingly, miniature golf began as couth as croquet. John Margolies's comprehensive book *Miniature Golf* shows pictures from the 1920s of people in formal wear playing midget golf on beautifully landscaped courses that resemble English formal gardens. Before the stock market crash of 1929, there were over a hundred rooftop courses on Manhattan skyscrapers, where the high-riding new class of stockbrokers and office workers went to unwind at lunch or after hours.

Shrunken golf courses were a novelty enjoyed by the well-to-do until Garnet and Frieda Carter universalized the game in 1929. They were proprietors of the Fairyland Inn in Lookout Mountain, Tennessee. To add to the magic aura of their resort, they designed an especially fanciful set of links, which they thought would amuse the children of their wealthy guests. The Carters decked the tiny course with statues of woodland elves and built each hole around an obstacle, making the kiddies putt through a

hollow log or up a steep incline. They discovered that parents liked the wacky game as much as children. So they named it Tom Thumb Golf, got a patent, and in September 1929—a month before the stock market crash—began installing roadside Tom Thumb courses around the country.

The Great Depression was a boon to miniature golf, which at twenty-five cents a game was cheap entertainment. Miniature golf became a widespread American obsession, and by mid-1930 there were fifty thousand courses around the country. Movie studios forbade their contract players from being seen on them: They were worried that nobody would go to movies if the game got any more popular. It wasn't just affordability that made Tom Thumb Golf such a hot phenomenon. In her book *The Colossus of Roads,* Karal Ann Marling suggests that "the muslin banners [advertising miniature golf courses] along the highway were a frontier between a somber world of hard times and getting by, and a fantasyland of swaggering panache, a place where the player literally called the shots."

The original woodland fairy-tale theme of the Carters' Tom Thumb course was surpassed by silly and exotic scenery that surrounded players with African jungles, mysterious shrines of the Far East, or the Seven Wonders of the World. Entrepreneurs built links indoors and out, in former movie theaters and on vacant lots; an enterprising lady in California planned a course in a cemetery, using gravestones as obstacles. "Half of America is bent over," Will Rogers said. Within a year, however, the nation's enthusiasm vaporized. The mania for little links proved to be just the latest of the shooting-star fads that had electrified the twenties. *Miniature Golf* reports that by late 1931 *Miniature Golf Management* magazine editorialized, "Every course that opens from now on is just one more too many."

Miniature golf, however, did not die. After much attrition in the thirties and forties, the postwar move out to the suburbs (and the great highway-building boom that went with it) gave vest-pocket golf a fresh start. In 1954 Don Clayton of North Carolina founded Putt-Putt Golf and began to sell franchises along roads near shopping centers and adjacent to driving ranges and full-size courses. Putt-Putt, based more on skill than on gimmicks, engendered a Professional Putters Association that sponsors championship tournaments with $250,000 in prizes every year. (Nonprofessional Putt-Putters win an orange ball for a hole-in-one.) *Popular Mechanics* offered plans to suburban homemakers for turning old tires and potato-chip cans into a basement miniature golf course for the kids. And as theme parks grew up in the wake of Disneyland, miniature golf became a necessary adjunct to any roadside attraction that purported to offer family fun. In 1989, miniature golf returned to New York City when Donald Trump financed a course in Central Park; its hazards included no classical windmills or dinosaurs, just famous pieces of local architecture.

Developments in fiberglass foam-sculpting techniques have allowed modern course designers to create fantastic life-size (and larger) animals, such as the pink elephants and car-size walleye pikes constructed by Dave Oswald of Creative Display in Sparta, Wisconsin; but purist linksmen prefer the old-fashioned concrete-and-chicken-wire techniques, as used by T. J. Neil of New Hampshire's World of Concrete Sculpture to create such venerable goofy hazards as the boxing reptile known as Ali Gator (putt beneath his pedestal) and the three-holed pink Princess Tuna, both of which lord over the links at Putter's Paradise in West Yarmouth, Massachusetts.

MOBILE HOMES

Straight from the factory, a mobile home looks naked. Some stay that way—doomed to be nothing more than a grubby temporary office on a construction site, or to fester as a hillbilly shack on a stack of cinder blocks in a weedy field behind a factory. But many mobile homes inspire their owners to heights of decorative creativity never seen in and around an ordinary home on a foundation. In the proper hands, the mass-produced, prefabricated cubicle technically known as a manufactured home (because most are so cumbersome they are barely mobile) can become a veritable Taj Mahal in crimped aluminum.

You want landscaping? Where but around a mobile home will you find conservatories of perpetual plastic topiary; pastel pompons and pink flamingoes on sticks; statues of elves, gnomes, jockeys (white and black), lazy barefoot Mexicans with their donkeys; gurgling electric fountains; spinning clotheslines; lawn balls on Doric pedestals; AstroTurf putt-putt pads; and brightly colored satellite dish antennae? The urge to adorn is partly a matter of necessity: Mobile-home dwellers must create attractive surroundings because even the largest mobile homes tend to induce claustrophobia. Therefore, people who live inside spend a lot of time outside. Perhaps the most beloved activity of mobile-home owners is sitting outside in housecoats or Bermuda shorts on webbed chairs under the awning, listening to the local Tradio Swap 'n' Chat program. "The patio porch is our pride and joy," wrote John L. Scherer in *All About Mobile Homes*. "There is nothing that can equal the quiet evening hours we spend there after the sun has gone down. To us, it is the high point in a lot of happy days."

Until the fifties, there were no mobile homes. There were house trailers—made to be pulled by an ordinary car, and generally marketed as supplements to people's first homes, like portable hunting cabins. Some poor and/or peripatetic people, however, found it convenient to live in them, and even to park them semipermanently where they could enjoy such comforts as mail delivery and electricity. About the time of the New York World's Fair of 1939, futurists predicted that someday all Americans would live in portable trailers, and nobody would have an address. The problem was that mobile-home communities attracted the wrong kind of people. FBI director J. Edgar Hoover, never one to avoid an opportunity to discover depravity, wrote an article called "Camps of Crime" for *American Magazine* in 1940, describing trailer parks as "dens of vice and corruption, haunted by nomadic prostitutes, hardened criminals, white slavers, and promiscuous college students."

During World War II, to house military personnel and construction workers, clusters of these semipermanent mobile homes "began to erupt all over the nation like smallpox," according to trailer pioneer Wally Byam, writing in *Trailer Travel Here and Abroad*. "The high esteem which the smart little travel trailer had earned through its service to vacationers, sportsmen, and tourists faded in the squalor of slum camps," Byam grieved. The reputation of mobile-home communities sank so low that by the early fifties, when an estimated 1.5 million people lived permanently in trailers, many states were passing legislation forbidding a trailer to stay in any one place for longer than ten days. Even now, most communities have laws that do not allow mobile homes on ordinary building lots, lest real estate values plummet. In many people's minds, a mobile home suggests occupants from a John Waters movie (Divine lived in a mobile home in *Pink Flamingos*) or halfwit hermits in the woods surrounded by junked cars. Few mobile-home parks are located in the part of town known as the Miracle Mile.

In 1955, Welburn Guernsey of Florida decided to upgrade mobile homes' wretched image. He pioneered the concept of a deluxe park —landscaped, with a communal pool, with wide, palm-lined streets among the neatly lined-up homes (all of which were required to have skirting and patios). His Guernsey City in Tampa featured a security booth to keep out undesirables and an air-conditioned recreation center, and it excluded anyone who wasn't over fifty years old or retired. It also had what park aficionados know as ''attractive signage,'' meaning no ugly billboards letting people know how cheap it was to live there. Guernsey was the first to conceive of the double-wide home—two modular units bolted together to form a twice-as-wide living space. This concept reached an apotheosis in the mid-sixties with Guernsey Mansionettes, complete with three doors each, attached steps, and surrounding sidewalks.

A modern mobile home is definitely *not* a

travel trailer or a camper built for recreation. Once it is blocked (mounted on piers and secured by a hurricane anchor) and skirted with brick-look vinyl or corrugated plastic to hide the undercarriage, it is ready for such luxurious additions as an attached carport, a patio, a mini-deck, a Florida room, and canopies for doors and awnings for windows. As for interior amenities, they are one of the particular attractions of mobile homes to young moderns who have no possessions. Most of them come fully loaded, with everything from wood-look vinyl interior walls and soil-resistant carpeting to color-coordinated drapes, valances, and linen, French provincial furniture, and impressionistic oil-look paintings of picturesque fishing boats and Paris streets on the walls. The only thing lacking in brand-new manufactured homes is the decorative plate for the wall that says ''God Bless Our Mobile Home''; but that is available in souvenir stores everywhere.

If ever a modern mobile home does have to be moved, it is a traumatic experience for the owners, for the frail home itself, and for everyone in its path. Between ten and fourteen feet wide and up to seventy feet long, preceded by a signal car with a flashing emergency light supposed to frighten other vehicles out of the way, the WIDE LOAD whips beyond its lane as it shimmies and flexes on sets of little bouncing tires like some demented dinosaur that might crush anything around it just by accident. Cheerful as it may seem when surrounded by lawn ornaments on its lots in a mobile-home community, a mobile home in transit is sheer highway terror.

See also **MOTOR HOMES AND CAMPER/ TRAILERS; VANS**

MONSTER TRUCKS

Take a regular-looking pickup truck and replace its tires with Alaskan tundra treads that are eight feet tall and four feet wide, put ten shock absorbers on each wheel, give it an engine of about a thousand horsepower, and you've got a monster truck. Strap on a kidney belt, climb into the cab, gun the unmuffled engine, and you are ready to make your monster truck do what it was built to do: drive on top of ordinary cars, crushing their roofs and making their windshields pop and doors bulge.

Why are there monster trucks? *Pulling Power* magazine asked precisely that question, to which it gave two answers: They fulfill everyone's desire to get through traffic by running over all other cars on the road; and they are huge. "We Americans like things big and these trucks are just that!"

Monster truck driving is a sport. Enthusiasts fill fairground tracks and indoor arenas to watch races in which pairs of monster trucks with names like Nitemare II, Wild Hair, Lethal Weapon, and Coors Brewser sprint side by side at speeds of up to fifty miles an hour. The contestants run a short course, accelerating toward a pair of uphill dirt ramps that propel the speeding fifteen-thousand-pound trucks high into the air. They crash down onto piles of automobiles, whose tops they drive upon until they reach the finish line. This kind of basic straight-line car crush lasts eight to ten seconds. On occasion, the action will be spiced by putting the ramps and junk cars on a curved or even figure-eight course or by making the monster trucks run through axle-deep mud holes.

Mud is what originally inspired monster trucks. The concept of a powerful vehicle raised up on gargantuan tires with snaking tread lugs was developed to meet the real-world needs of off-road sportsmen who wanted to motor from cabin to fishing hole to hunting lodge in muddy backwoods regions. They needed what they called gumbo mudder tires to gain traction in the soupy swamps; and the higher up their cab, the

less likely their chances were of getting mired. Back in 1974, Bob Chandler of Hazelwood, Missouri, built a concept truck around these principles to advertise his auto/truck parts business. It was a blue Ford with four-foot-tall tires and a souped-up engine sticking out through its hood—small potatoes by today's standards, but the beginning of the monster truck era. Chandler called his vehicle Bigfoot (not because of its big tires, but as reference to his reputation as a leadfooted driver). He took Bigfoot around to county fairs, where he demonstrated its might by driving up to piles of junked cars, shifting into stump-pulling low gear, and simply *driving over everything in his path!* Spectators thrilled to the sight, and Bigfoot became a vehicular celebrity, boasting thirty thousand members in its fan club.

Bigfoot begat bigger Bigfoots, a compact monster truck known as Ms. Bigfoot, and a monster van called the Bigfoot Shuttle. And naturally, Bigfoot started attracting competition, mostly in the form of big-tired Chevrolets. By the early eighties, monster truck exhibitions had become regular attractions at county-fair tractor pulls and weekend drag races. Monster trucks got fancier, some growing as high as fifteen feet, featuring four-wheel steering and flame-thrower chrome exhaust pipes, and costing $150,000.

It wasn't long before someone got the idea to race monster trucks; and in 1987 Bob Chandler started the MTRA—the Monster Truck Racing Association—in an attempt to standardize track size, junked-car-pile size, and safety rules. He has even dabbled in monster truck water racing, having discovered that huge tires with thick lugs are workable sources of marine propulsion. One of Chandler's Bigfoots (he now has ten) beat a paddle-wheel boat in a match on the Chattahoochee River, and his rivals, the Breen brothers (who drive Chevies with ''Have You Driven Over a Ford Lately?'' on their tailgates), have a monster pickup truck that regularly takes passengers for ferry rides on the Lake of the Ozarks. Chandler flouts water racing, however, as a short-lived fad. He knows that the real thrill of monster trucks is watching cars get squished.

MOOD RINGS

Sophia Loren made tabloid headlines in 1975 when she halted a press conference in a sudden state of shock. She looked down at the ring on her hand. It had turned black! Everyone in attendance knew what that meant: Miss Loren was wearing a mood ring, which changed color to fit the wearer's emotional state. Happy people's rings were blue; dull people's turned greenish yellow; grouches' were brown. If a mood ring turned black, it meant its wearer was shrouded in gloom, despair, and downright evil karma. With the stage presence of a consummate performer, Miss Loren rallied: She concluded that her ring must be defective, threw it away, and bought a hundred more to send to her friends and family in Italy.

Mood rings were one of the biggest, silliest, and shortest-lived fads of the seventies. What gives them a place of honor in the annals of gaucheness beyond trivial novelties such as the hula hoop or Pet Rock is how thoroughly they reflected the colossal self-absorption of what Tom Wolfe called the Me Decade. Imagine the chutzpah of assuming the world really wants to be made aware of your exact emotional state as it changes! Mood rings were such a big hit in the summer and fall of 1975 that they inspired mood nail polish, mood shoes, and mood panties, all of which changed color to advertise the wearer's inner self to whomever was watching.

The technology of the mood ring was not new. Inside their "quartz" stones were heat-sensitive liquid crystals chemically synthesized out of grease extracted from sheep's wool—the same material that had long been used in certain kinds of hospital thermometers, some 3-D movie glasses, and even in an obscure line of jewelry that a Pittsburgh designer had tried to market (with no success) in the early seventies.

What made the mood ring unique was its association with the psychospiritual mumbo jumbo of its time. This was the doing of Joshua Reynolds, a Wall Street dropout who had discovered biofeedback (modulating your own brain-wave emissions) in a search to overcome his anxieties. He started a meditation center in New York called Q-Tran ("Tran" for tranquillity), which offered customers the opportunity to relax by getting hooked up to a complicated biofeedback machine. The problem was that the machine was expensive and broke often. So Reynolds took the same principle and designed a "portable biofeedback aid," the mood ring, using about a dime's worth of liquid crystal. He hired a press agent, got the cosmetic company Fabergé to back him, and suddenly mood rings became the story of the year and one of the biggest lifestyle embarrassments of the seventies, right up there with platform shoes and disco.

Syndicated columnist and astrology buff Eugenia Sheppard wrote glowingly about mood rings. The first day they went on sale at Bonwit Teller in New York, a thousand sold at $45 each. By December, fifteen million mood rings had been gobbled up, ranging from $5 knock-offs to $250 fourteen-karat-gold models sold by Neiman-Marcus. They were worn by such New Age superstars as Paul Newman, Barbra Streisand, and Muhammad Ali (who wrote a poem about his). The fact that the rings were actually responding to temperature rather than mood didn't seem to concern anybody; however, it was not uncommon for unscrupulous players of mind games to figure out they could keep their rings in the refrigerator (where they turned black) or warm them in a toaster oven (until bright, happy blue) and thereby maintain mastery of their projected mood.

Within months, the fad passed, Q-Tran went bankrupt, and mood rings were dead. However, their wizardry lives on in flea markets and job-lot bazaars throughout the world, where fifteen-year-old charms are sold for prices ranging from sixty-nine cents to twenty dollars. Although the liquid crystal material that made Mr. Reynolds' mood rings work tended to lose its zest after a year or so, causing the rings to turn a permanent moribund black, there are some non-Q-Tran variations (the Persona Ring, the Tattletale Stone) made of stronger stuff that seems to have the power to render their chameleon magic in perpetuity.

MOTOR HOMES AND CAMPER/TRAILERS

A motor home is *not* a mobile home. Whereas mobile homes are generally planted in one spot and stay there, a motor home is an extremely expensive luxury vehicle that you, John or Jane Q. Citizen, can drive from one place to another along almost any highway. Motor homes are for roaming, and although they may have all of the comforts of a house with a foundation, the real purpose of a motor home is not to live cheaply but to indulge yourself, to be carefree and have fun!

The advantage of going places in a motor home is that you can take everything you need wherever you go. Families lumber down the road in their Free As the Wind Country Coach Cruiser with bicycles and all-terrain vehicles hanging on the back, a Mr. Turtle pool tied on top of the roof-mounted storage pod, and a compact car on a Kar Kaddy tow dolly jouncing along behind. The man behind the wheel of a forty-foot, triple-axle, corrugated-aluminum Xplorer is like some traveling potentate of the ancient world, accoutered with everything necessary to create his own dominion wherever he encamps.

Although modern motor homes make life on the road indistinguishable from—if not better than—life at home, there was a time when going places in a camper involved ingenuity and adventure. This was long before campers became *motor homes*. In the twenties, well-to-do people in search of novel recreation (now that they were blasé about train travel) vacationed in custom-made ''house cars'' equipped with cots and primitive cooking equipment. One such foursome was Henry Ford, Thomas Edison, Harvey Firestone, and John Burroughs, who traveled with a custom-made Ford-built generator and Edison bulbs to light their campsites. In his book *Travelers,* Horace Sutton wrote, ''Wherever they went, these early campers-for-fun made a lasting impression on the people of the community and were sometimes woven into the local folklore for a number of years thereafter.''

Most ramblers built their own rigs, but by the mid-twenties, a cottage industry had arisen to make ''tent-trailers'' with such names as Prairie Schooner and Auto-Kamp to tow behind a car. As early as 1923, a book called *Autocamping* contained advice for bolting tents to running boards and installing a sleeper that converted a car seat to a bed. ''The immense popularity of motor camping is easy to understand when one realizes that this pastime is romantic, healthful, educative, and at the same time economical,'' declared intrepid vagabonds John D. Long and J. C. Long in their book *Motor Camping* in 1926.

The hardships of Depression nomads took a lot of the glamour out of outdoor camping; but the idea of a travel *trailer,* whose occupants were protected from wayfaring bums and coddled in homelike luxury, had great appeal to travelers with money and a hankering for adventure. Among those tinkering with the idea was Wally Byam, who would soon become the dean of American trailering. Byam tried attaching boxes, tents, and trailer bodies to Ford Model T chassis; and in 1937 he took cues from aircraft production and contemporary aerodynamics and built a trailer out of riveted, lightweight aluminum. He called it the Airstream. It was a beautiful silver teardrop with a pointed tail, outfitted with furniture and amenities. ''Stepping into a modern travel trailer is like stepping into your own home if it were shrunk to, say, 8′ × 26′ dimensions,'' Byam later observed.

Despite the luxuries they liked to boast about, trailer people retained an intrepid reputation, as suggested by the tribulations of Lucille Ball and Desi Arnaz in Vincente Minnelli's hilarious movie *The Long, Long Trailer* (1954). After establishing Airstream as the Rolls-Royce of travel trailers, Wally Byam spent the fifties leading expeditions of Airstreams around the world. Like invading armies, hundreds of caravaners hauled their silver trailers en masse to Mexico and Canada, parking each night like wagon trains, meeting local mayors and tribal chiefs by day. In 1956, they shipped their trailers, and V-8 Cadillacs to pull them, to Cuba and to Europe; and in 1959—60, they spent eighteen months caravaning through Europe into Africa, where they were greeted by Emperor Haile Selassie in

Ethiopia and witch doctors in Uganda. This was the zenith of trailering, when pulling a trailer meant excitement and discovery.

John Gartner's *All About Trailers* (1956) offered these reasons for vacationing in a trailer instead of staying in a motel, hotel, or cabin: You never have to worry about a "No Vacancy" sign; you can sleep in your own bed every night; you can eat whenever you want to eat; anytime a place becomes obnoxious, you can drive away; women—such as wives—like trailers much better than camping in a tent or a cabin with mice and rats in it.

By the late fifties, mobile homes and travel trailers were heading in two different directions. Mobile homes got bigger and less mobile; they were made to be hauled to a lot, put down, and lived in. Travel trailers grew bigger, too, but they were not aimed at the cheap-housing market. They were for wanderers with money, as

suggested by such luxury trailer names as Airflyte and Va-Ka-Shun-Ette. In the early sixties, the travel trailer begat a new kind of recreational vehicle: the self-contained "motor home," patterned after a bus, that was easier to maneuver than a trailer and allowed people to enjoy leisure time in the home *while traveling.* (Trailers are uninhabitable while being towed.)

The halcyon days of motor homes were the late sixties until the gas crisis of 1973—a time when former hippies as well as many in the silent majority craved to experience then-popular myths of discovery and communion-with-America along the open road. Love children did it in rattletrap vans and converted school buses. For establishment types, there were Winnebagos—

the capacious, flat-fronted recreational vehicle introduced in 1966, which accounted for one of every three motor homes sold by 1971. Retired people with no particular place to go sunk their savings into motor homes and became "snowbirds"—gypsies who travel south in the winter and spend their summers parked in the driveways of their children's homes. Even the Back-to-Nature Barbie doll, introduced in 1972, includes a Winnebago-shaped camper with "LOVE" and daisy decals on the side.

Amazingly, titanic recreational vehicles survived the oil shortages of the seventies (partly because Winnebago and others diversified into smaller vehicles and vans); and as of the late eighties, the Family Motor Coach Association had over sixty-thousand members, who can always spot each other by the little numbered oval plaque, called a "goose egg," on the side of their vehicle. Today's luxury land yachts, which sell for several hundred thousand dollars each, are as much a status symbol among the family-value set as seagoing yachts are among snootier levels of societ

Convenient they may be and romantic wanderlust they may serve; but there is no getting around the fact that motor homes are ugly. Wherever you spot one, on the road or in camp-

grounds, the beige slab-on-wheels is so immense, and often so covered with bumper stickers ("We're Spending Our Grandchildren's Inheritance") and decals (from the Good Sam Club or Six Flags Over Texas), that it seems to actually drain color from the surrounding scenery the way a black hole in space sucks in light. Because they usually have a spare tire hung on the back, spare-tire covers have become personalized billboards that drivers stuck behind them on a two-lane road are forced to look at for miles: "Here Come the Kapinskys" or "Chasin' a Rainbow" or "Kenny Rogers Is Our Man." Motor homes' small-fry cousins, the aluminum "caps" or teetering outhouselike boxes that fit on the back of pickup trucks, are even more ghastly eyesores.

When you pass a mobile home bounding down the highway and look in its picture window at the floor-bolted pedestal card table littered with bags of Double-Stuff Oreos, at the flickering VCR, yelping dog, somersaulting children, Fussball and Nintendo games, you suddenly appreciate the clean efficiency of an automobile with its streamlined shape and forward-looking seats. And you marvel at the audacity of the drivers of these bloated shoeboxes who in their quest for freedom on the open road have chosen to carry their entire households, including toilets with waste to be disposed of and frost-free freezers packed with frozen pigs-in-blankets, wherever they roam.

See also **MOBILE HOMES; VANS**

MUSCLE CARS

Muscle cars are medium-size American coupes with great big engines. You will find them cruising the main drags of all small towns and cities where rednecks live, and idling outside 7-Eleven stores while their driver goes in to buy a seventy-two-ounce Big Gulp and a pack of smokes. You will be able to identify a muscle car by its jacked-up rear end and big tires, by the outsized decal of a gigantic warlike bird across its hood (a Firebird), or by the wealth of dangling junk hanging from its rearview mirror. No muscle car is complete without a clod of graduation tassels, bandannas, rubber shrunken heads, baby shoes, fluffy feathers, crystals, and roach clips swaying back and forth in the middle of the windshield. Before you see a muscle car you will likely hear it, courtesy of a head-pounding sixteen-speaker sound system that carries John Cougar Mellencamp's lyrics into the next county. Drivers of muscle cars were described by *Breakers (The Ultimate Spring Break Magazine)* as ''the young and the restless . . . in touch with street ethics, teenage angst and rock and roll.''

Wonder in awe at the never-ending popularity of these white-trashmobiles. There is no convincing way to argue their automotive merits. They do not match up to any known standard of classical automotive beauty or function. They are extremely cramped and uncomfortable, with room for only two legless people in the backseat. They are not especially well-made, and their value depreciates fast. They are overweight and handle poorly. Judged by almost any measure of aesthetic beauty, even the warped standards that prevail in most auto showrooms, they are monstrous. To understand their tremendous appeal you have to sit behind the wheel, find a stretch of straight road without any bad curves or bumps, and press the accelerator to the floor. The tires squeal on the pavement, making a lot of noise and a rubbery smell, and the car goes very fast.

Another way to appreciate the cachet of a muscle car is to drive one up to any video arcade or poster shop. See the respect it gets from clerks and customers. What Porsches are to stockbrokers and lawyers, muscle cars are to graduates of cosmetology schools and the boys down at the plant. If Bruce Springsteen were a machine, he would be a muscle car.

Muscle cars were born as part of the fun-seeking youth culture that blossomed in the pre-Beatles sixties. It was the golden age of twist parties, surfing, spring break, and car songs in which guys like the Beach Boys and Jan and Dean crooned happily about 409s, Little Deuce coupes, and GTOs that could shut down any challenger. In 1964 a young Pontiac engineer named John Z. De Lorean designed the GTO (its name taken from the Italian *gran turismo omologato,* meaning a touring sedan) to appeal to the newly discovered youth market. The GTO packed a triple-carbureted 348-horsepower V-8 engine into Pontiac's sedate mid-size Tempest, with explosive results. David Davis, Jr., of *Car and Driver* magazine wrote that his first ride in a GTO left him ''with a feeling like losing my virginity, going into combat, and tasting my first beer all in about seven seconds.''

By the next model year, nearly every manufacturer had a muscle car for sale. There were Cyclones, Chargers, Challengers, Demons, Barracudas, and Javelins. They had bucket seats and four-on-the-floor; many sprouted power bulges in the hood (for air induction scoops or to make space for big engines); nearly all the muscle cars were heavily tricked up with decals to signify their brawn, such as angry bumblebees, Road Runners (from the cartoon), and hissing cobras. Dodge's advertisements for its top muscle car, the Charger Daytona, boasted that it ''has a snout that strikes out a country mile in front and an adjustable spoiler that looks two stories tall in the rear, and it idles like a coffee can full of rocks.''

The early seventies nearly killed the appeal of muscle cars, because manufacturers cut back on power to improve gas mileage and reduce pollution, and added uncool safety features; but the impotence was only temporary. Gas became plentiful again, and in 1976 muscle cars got their biggest boost since Ronny and the Daytonas' top-ten hit ''GTO'' in 1964: Burt Reynolds drove a Pontiac Trans Am in the movie *Smokey and the Bandit.* In fact, three Trans Ams were destroyed while shooting *Smokey,* in which the powerhouse car leaps rivers, smashes through barricades, and flummoxes cops in four states. Dozens of similar movies followed, many of them featuring Burt Reynolds piloting a speeding Trans Am, elevating Pontiac's muscle car to the status of a folk hero. (One of *Smokey and the Bandit*'s Pontiacs is on display in Nashville's Country Music Hall of Fame and Museum.) Similarly, the General Lee, a personality-plus muscle car featured in the long-running television show ''The Dukes of Hazzard,'' made many a young man wish for a big high-powered hog that could outrun the sheriff and the deputy.

By definition, a muscle car is powered by a big V 8 with enough torque to pull a house off its foundation. Only a few coupes today can be bought with that kind of bulging power: Ford's Mustang, Pontiac's Firebird Trans Am, and Chevrolet's Camaro (which is essentially a Trans Am in Chevrolet sheet metal and decals). Because of its starring role in so many good-old-boy-outrunning-the-cops movies, the Trans-Am is the one most beloved by the young and the vulgar. It is true to the heritage of the original American muscle cars: bulky, unwieldy, uncomfortable, impractical, unsightly, and neck-snappingly fast.

MUZAK

Muzak is meant to be heard but not listened to. Using fifteen-minute medleys of innocuous instrumental selections in which the tempo sneakily accelerates from song to song and the instrumentation grows more complex, it gives listeners a subliminal lift that causes them to work harder or to buy more. While the subject is slouching at a desk mid-afternoon in a cubicle at work, or dragging through a wearisome shopping mall, his brain is infiltrated by the pleasant sounds even though he may not even be aware that there is music playing; somehow, suddenly, he feels eager to tackle that stack of paperwork or to walk into Florsheim's and purchase a pair of Imperial brogues. Muzak is also intended to reduce jitters and feelings of aloneness in public places such as airlines terminals and hotel lobbies, thus forestalling anxiety attacks and psychotic outbursts and ensuring that everyone behaves the way they are supposed to behave.

It is a proven fact that Muzak does what it is designed to do: Thanks to it, factory workers produce more, stores make more money, and clerical workers complete 13.5 percent more paperwork. In one study, supermarket shoppers bought 38.2 percent more groceries when Muzak-style easy listening was played, although one-third of them had no idea they had heard anything while breezing through the aisles and filling their carts. It has even been claimed that cows give more milk if Muzak is piped into their barns and caged parrots are more likely to mate if they hear easy-listenin' versions of "Indian Love Call" and "Red Sails in the Sunset."

The one thing Muzak programmers seem never to have tested is the irritating side effect of the surreptitious musical stimulant: the way its flaccid melodies insinuate themselves into people's minds and get stuck there for hours, sometimes days. For example, you walk out of an elevator cheerfully humming the Monkees' "Pleasant Valley Sunday," and you find the chipper tune running around in your skull for the rest of the day no matter how desperately you try to consign it to oblivion. You have no idea how it got there: Muzak has worked its magic all too well.

Several companies program what is known as background music (as opposed to foreground music, which is meant to be listened to). Muzak, now called Muzak Limited Partnership, was the pioneer, supplying psychologically soothing programs to companies beginning in the thirties, via power-modulated radio lines. The name Muzak, chosen as an allusion to Kodak—a big and respected corporation—has become synonymous with "elevator music" and is a symbol of relentless triteness, as typified by the company's bland interpretations of "The Hawaiian Wedding Song," "Gigi," and "Born Free." Selections change with the times (Mantovani is no longer part of the repertoire), but songs are always chosen because they can be made into a mellifluous cloud of consonance to which no one pays attention. Some popular musicians—Bruce Springsteen and Boz Scaggs among them—have refused to let their work become Muzak; the Beatles, Paul Simon, and Michael Jackson have collected handsome royalties by allowing such tunes as "Michelle," "Sounds of Silence," and "Billie Jean" to be made into pap. When Muzak buys a song (they record about a hundred every month and pay $4 million in royalties each year), it is re-arranged and recorded by Muzak musicians using stringed instruments and mellow horns and much electronic polishing and enhancement. In an article for *Smithsonian* magazine, Jeanne McDermott called the results "like the Boston Pops on an austerity budget."

Now headquartered in Seattle (in an office building saturated by the soothing melodies), Muzak sends what it likes to call "environmental music" via satellite and FM subcarriers twenty-four hours a day to more than 150,000 locations, reaching fourteen countries and approximately one-third of the population of America. The music plays in fifteen-minute segments separated by short pauses and always goes uptempo from ten to eleven in the morning and three to four in the afternoon, when people require extra stimulation.

NEHRU JACKETS

Many stupid fashion fads come and go and are forgotten. The Nehru jacket came and went in 1968, but it was so funny that it has become one of the unforgettable fashion bloopers of modern times.

Credit for starting the fad belongs to its greatest proponent, Sammy Davis, Jr., who in the early sixties went shopping on the King's Road in London, where he found a white, button-front, lapel-less jacket with a small stand-up collar in one of the boutiques. He bought it, and because it came from India he called it his guru coat and just for fun wore it to a party in Paris. Pierre Cardin, who had recently been to India himself, got wind of what Davis was wearing and—remembering how popular the Beatles' lapel-less jackets had been—decided to pattern a design of his own after the style originally popularized by Jawaharlal Nehru, prime minister of India. In America, the same idea began appearing in late 1967, made by small clothing manufacturers and worn by hippies who were, at the time, discovering the grooviness of India.

It was a moment in time when men's fashions were erupting, and nobody knew what was right or proper; but a lot of guys wanted desperately to be hip. All things oriental, but especially things Indian, were glorified by the counterculture, because conventional wisdom deemed that Indians had figured out the love-and-peace thing long ago. Nehru himself was the best-known symbol of peaceful resistance after Gandhi. From patchouli oil to paisley printed shirts to heavy mandala medallions, accoutrements of orientalia became necessary accessories for the long-haired rebel who wanted to advertise the mellow trip he was on.

Nehru jackets had it all. Not only were they Indian but they were also less uptight than ordinary sports coats, because they were worn on top of a turtleneck rather than a button-down shirt; and instead of a tie, they required a medallion, a peace symbol, or a similarly meaningful amulet. Furthermore, the Nehru jackets' notched collars bore an unmistakable resemblance to the clerical collars worn by priests, giving them a vaguely religious air perfectly suited to the foggy evangelistic sanctimony of the drug culture. Prototypical Nehru jackets, as worn by such groups as the Strawberry Alarm Clock, were known as meditation coats.

In the last months of 1967, the Nehru jacket emerged as a fashion statement symbolizing a kind of earnest, harmless impertinence—irreverence but not rebellion. It suited groovy cats who wanted to show their disdain for neckties and all the social constrictions they represented but who nonetheless wanted to look well groomed (i.e., not like a wild and naked hippie). "The style horrifies restaurant

STEREO

SAMMY DAVIS JR.
I'VE GOTTA BE ME

Sears

Spring through Summer 1969

Children's apparel from our
Winnie-the-Pooh Collection
Pages 18-25

headwaiters,'' *Time* reported; but maverick football player Joe Namath wore his Nehru all around town, and the Smothers Brothers wore theirs on TV. Eddie Belmonte, known to fellow jockeys as ''the Puerto Rican hippie,'' helped popularize a sleeveless Nehru jacket, which he wore over a chromium-yellow shirt and bell-bottom pants. Sammy Davis, Jr., ever on the cutting edge of men's wear, became famous for his closet full of Nehrus in cool pastel colors, which he wore draped with pounds of chains and medallions when he performed in Las Vegas. At Martin Luther King, Jr.'s funeral in 1968, he wore a tweed Nehru jacket unbuttoned to his midriff and a black arm band.

As fast as it had been embraced by love-and-peace guys, the Nehru surged into the mainstream. Early in 1968 *Playboy* predicted

''a revolutionary array of tunic-type innovations, from pajamas and bathrobes to overcoats and rainwear,'' showing a model in a white linen tunic shirt with gold-plated medallion; and in October it featured a fall fashion forecast that included one male model sucking on a hookah pipe while wearing a ''cotton tapestry tunic with fabric covered buttons, stand-up collar, and deep center vent''—i.e., a Nehru jacket. Johnny Carson wore one on television. Sears's 1969 summer catalogue featured a boy on its cover wearing a Perma-Prest Rajah Nehru sport coat from the Winnie-the-Pooh Collection, ''styled like big brother's'' with notched collar, five bright buttons, and three flap pockets.

The naturally long and lean look of the Nehru was incongruously adapted by manufacturers of portly apparel; and because crudely made versions required very little tailoring, cheap Nehrus flooded into discount stores. Suddenly, even faster than it had appeared as the hippest thing on the rack, it was transformed into the squarest thing a man could own, sure proof that the wearer was trying to be hip but was months behind the times.

Counterculture fashion abandoned its mid-sixties fascination with foppery and turned to a more ascetic Jesus-in-a-bedsheet look, and finally to functional blue-jean grubbies. By the end of the decade, hippies themselves were becoming a joke; and the idea of hippie-inspired semiformal wear seemed positively grotesque. Clothiers were stuck with such an oversupply of Nehru jackets that one company sewed on collars and tried to remarket old Nehru jackets as slender-cut Edwardian topcoats.

NEIMAN, LEROY

He has executed his paintings between commercial breaks during ABC-TV sports events, and he makes millions of dollars selling lithographs and etchings. Critics might forgive him those things, but Leroy Neiman is guilty of the ultimate sin in the art world: He is popular among people who don't know art.

Neiman splatters gobs of paint on canvases that are meant to create brilliant impressions of things: the swirl of the flags at an Olympics tournament, the swell of water and billow of sails as yachts race, the smeared blood and sweat of a prize fight, a dalliance over champagne and roses on a balcony in Cannes. His style is explosive and purposely slapdash, designed to convey mood and energy, so you can look at one of his paintings and think that you really feel the experience of being there, in the bright sun, in the action, on the waves or the playing field, or close enough to smell the suntan oil on a bathing beauty in a pink bikini. It's like a trip through Disney World's Magic Mountain, but in some way even more extraordinary, because the vicarious feelings are conveyed by nothing more than paint on canvas.

Neiman is condemned by professional art critics for making over-the-couch art—''grim, abstract-expressionistic slather,'' according to Robert Hughes. When another critic called his oeuvre ''hotel room paintings,'' Neiman retorted, ''What's wrong with paintings in hotel rooms?''

Boxing promoter Don King explained to *Sports Illustrated* why sports fans like Neiman's work: ''Leroy strives for excellence and makes it par excellence. When Neiman does a tennis ball, it's a tennis ball personified. A Neiman is alive, it has a pulse and a heart. His magic wand profounds and astounds.''

His art is perfectly suited for hanging in rec rooms or places where guys and gals gather to watch sports on TV, but even small prints cost many hundreds of dollars, and serigraphs even more. You have to be a movie producer, an owner of a sports team, or otherwise really rich to afford an original painting, which can cost more than a hundred thousand dollars if it is a major work.

Neiman began his art career in the fifties in Chicago as a fashion illustrator. He met Hugh Hefner, who asked him to contribute to his new magazine, *Playboy*. The assignment shot Neiman high into a life-style that most readers of the magazine only fantasized about. For fifteen years, the man known as "our nomadic artist" roamed the world's pleasure centers, beaches, and night spots, creating a series of paintings *Playboy* called "Man at His Leisure," which were often printed on extra-heavy, foldout double pages, along with small sketches and scenes to round out the visual flights of fancy. The paintings were designed to be magical invocations of the good life, *Playboy*-style. In bright chromy colors and with an impatient brush, Neiman hurled onto his canvas the glint of the sun on a pair of skis at Gstaad, the curve of a suntanned bottom on the sands at the Côte d'Azur, a mane of perky blond hair above a smear of bright red lipstick glowing out from the shadows of the bar at P. J. Clarke's in Manhattan.

The paintings were always captioned at length by *Playboy* staff writers spinning out the sybaritic alliterations for which the magazine was famous. When Neiman "limned the sophisticated frenetics of Gotham's in-est discotheques" (as *Playboy* put it) in January 1967, the accompanying commentary advised readers that Ondine "appeals to the madly Mod set," while Yellowfingers "is a chic showcase for high-fashion models who boogaloo nightly in bell-bottoms or mid-thigh miniskirts, their eyes hidden by space-age sun visors."

Neiman often contributed poetic and artistic ruminations to the captions, noting in the disco story that "clothes may not make the man, but apparently they help make the woman. Today's young blade tends to be as modest about his out-of-sight Mod outfit as a peacock is about his plumage." The sketches include just such a blade in a white Edwardian jacket, white-on-blue polka-dot shirt, blue-on-white polka-dot tie, and long black Beatle boots, nuzzling close to a busty bird in lavender bell bottoms. When he painted "surfers and surf birds" for the July 1967 "Man

at His Leisure," Neiman noted that "the boards and costumes create a symphony of colors."

Neiman himself is a blade, appearing on television to create his paintings of sports events as they happen while wearing his own symphony of colors, or his familiar white trousers, open shirt, and broad-brimmed hat, or (if outdoors in cold weather) an extravagant coronation-length fur coat. He has honed himself into an established caricature by cultivating a Salvador Dali waxed and upturned mustache and always carrying a big cigar (which Dali himself advised him to do because it made him instantly recognizable).

Recently, he spread his creative wings to write *Monte Carlo Chase*, a forty-three-page work of fiction accompanied by paintings and sketches. It tells of a mustachioed, sensual, well-known, and well-respected sports artist tracking down an art counterfeiter known only as "M. Renard" during race week in Monte Carlo. The prose and pictures create a saturated picture of Neiman's pleasure-seeking world, crowded with princes and princesses, mysterious gamblers, glittering roulette wheels, and topless girls on the beach. As the book concludes with the mountebank Renard unmasked, the narrator says

Behind me, the star-emblazoned curtain of night has dropped over Monte Carlo, the self-perpetuating Principality of Pleasure with all its masques and baroque behavior. It's now time for this knave Renard's reentry into the real world. In this mecca of chance, I have performed my task to my own artistic satisction, nonviolently overtaking this contemptible rascal and beating him at his own game. And the wheels of fortune spin ever onward.

Road and Track gave *Monte Carlo Chase* a complimentary review, calling it "a handsome book with an elegant style of typeface, loads of color, and fine coated paper."

NODDING-HEAD DOLLS

The best place to see a doll with a nodding head is a car dashboard or the shelf beneath the car's rear window. Touch its loose-jointed cranium, or simply let the bumps in the road work their magic, and watch its tiny noggin merrily bob side to side and up and down.

Nodding-head dolls, or "nodders," as aficionados know them, have been favorite car and desktop accessories since the fifties, but they have an ancestry that goes back to long before they joined fuzzy dice and leopard-skin seat covers as fundamental expressions of gaucherie in automotive-interior decor. The first nodders were made in China in the mid-1800s. They were little dolls made of high-quality porcelain or bisque, or in some cases papier-mâché, that had not only moving heads but moving arms, too, making them appear to wave hello or goodbye. None of the early dolls used metal springs or rubber bands to hold their heads to their necks; rather, they relied on a fragile balancing pin as a connector, which created a gentle rolling effect when the head was tapped.

By the end of the century, the dolls were a popular knickknack in Europe, where the better manufacturers of pottery in France, Germany, and England produced their own. The most popular one was an imitation of the original Chinese dolls, depicting a seated, smiling mandarin in traditional robe and slippers. By the early twentieth century Japan began making nodders, copying not China but European imitations of the Chinese dolls. Japan also began adding new nodders specially designed for the American marketplace: caricatured black people and round-eyed, impish white boys and girls. As the dolls grew less refined, they also became cheaper and were soon available in novelty and automobile-customizing catalogues.

Nodders became popular midway prizes at carnivals and bingo nights. The mandarin and cherub motifs were joined by dogs; and by the late forties, many a Pontiac convertible sported a lolling-headed German shepherd or a whinnying palomino horse glued to its dashboard. The original attraction of fine china was gone, and

realism was now the goal of nodding-head manufacturers; most animal nodders were manufactured with coats of sprayed-on flocking material to give them a fuzzy feel, as well as glued-on glass eyes. Similarly, the finely tuned pin mechanism that joined the head and neck on the early nodders was replaced by a resilient spring better able to withstand the shocks of the road.

Thanks to the Beatles, who were famous for bobbing their heads as they sang, group nodders became a hot novelty item in the sixties. Quartets of wiggle-headed John-Paul-George-and-Ringos clustered together shaking their spring-powered heads on dressers in teenage bedrooms and as decorations on sweet-sixteen birthday cakes. Like most nodders, Beatles dolls are about four inches high and have disproportionately outsized heads. Group nodders have since become passé (although nodding Beatles are worth twenty dollars or more to both Beatles collectors and nodding-head doll collectors); the recent trend is back to single statues with an emphasis on cuteness: trolls, hula girls, and adorable, fat-cheeked children patterned after Hummel ware.

NOSE JOBS

In her head-to-thigh (hair transplant to lipolysis) analysis of image enhancement, *Cosmetic Surgery for Women* (1988), surgeon Paula A. Moynahan wrote, ''While the nose may be less expressive than the eyes and mentioned in less poetic metaphors, it is a crucial and highly prominent feature, one that precedes us wherever we go, an inch or so in advance of the rest of the face.'' It is the ''or so'' in Dr. Moynahan's observation that causes trouble. People with big noses, women in particular, sometimes feel they should have them made small by the surgical procedure called rhinoplasty.

Nose jobs, which generally cost between one thousand and five thousand dollars, are useful not only to reduce the size of a jumbo proboscis. People with dorsal humps, such as Cher used to have, get nose jobs that turn their once-lumpy snoots into isosceles triangles. Nose jobs can also shave bulbous tips, abbreviate nostrils, and transform witchlike hooks into pert bobs. For people with homely noses that are a constant source of laughter or derision, surgery can make life a lot easier. Nose jobs enter the realm of the absurd, however, when they are used to turn relatively normal noses into grotesque caricatures of beauty.

When a fabricated nose clearly doesn't fit the face it's on, or when it appears as a perfectly formed protuberance on an otherwise misshapen human being, the poor person carrying the nose around may as well wear a blinking neon sign on his face that says ''LOOK AT MY NOSE JOB!'' In extreme cases, when too much cartilage is removed, a nose job results in the condition known as ''pinched tip,'' now suffered by both Michael and LaToya Jackson, whose shrunken schnozzes are reminiscent of Lon Chaney's in the original *Phantom of the Opera*—little more than tip and nostrils.

The idea of reshaping noses is not modern. Gaspere Tagliacozzi of Bologna, Italy, who wrote the first textbook of plastic surgery in 1597, described how chopped-off or otherwise disfigured noses could be fixed by using skin grafts from forearms. (Historically, adulterers have had their noses cut off as punishment, and nose tips were a frequent casualty in sword fights.) The difficulty of Signor Tagliacozzi's technique was that for the graft to work, the patient had to keep his arm pressed up against his nose for a month.

The modern era of aesthetic nose surgery was made possible in 1887 when John Roe of Rochester, New York, described a technique for making inside incisions, enabling the surgeon to remove bone and cartilage without leaving scars. The procedure was perfected by Jacques Joseph, a German doctor who became famous for his work on disfigured soldiers after the First World War. In the twenties, his flair for reshaping noses made him the first internationally celebrated plastic surgeon and won him the nickname ''Dr. Nosef.'' Biographer Dr. Paul Natvig rejoiced, ''There was hardly any part of the human face and body which he could not reconstruct and enhance.'' His last operation was performed in 1934 on a sixteen-year-old Jewish girl named Adophine Schwarz whose nose he bobbed so she could look more Aryan. A month later Dr. Joseph, who was himself Jewish, died of a heart attack at his home, a villa he had built and into the wet concrete foundation of which he had pressed a bottle with a poem inside. The poem said: ''And when under the green grass / He finally reposes, / Know that the house of Joseph / Was built from noses.''

Modern rhinoplasty is a subtle art, but it is not a grueling procedure. It requires no more than a half-hour (twenty minutes more if you throw in the chin). Over 90 percent of all people who elect to have it done are women, the goal being cuteness. On those rare occasions when men get their noses reshaped, the aesthetic ideal is different. ''[The nose] is traditionally left in larger proportion to the face in the male, even when a reduction is done,'' Dr. Moynahan advises, explaining, ''The male nose is a phallic symbol.''

See also **FACE-LIFTS**

NOVELTY WRESTLING

The Milwaukee Hustlers, the first team of professional lady mud wrestlers to tour the United States, were sent forth by Bruce Rosenbaum of the Rosenbaum Talent Agency of Catawiffa, Pennsylvania, in the early seventies. "It was all in good fun," Mr. Rosenbaum wistfully recalled about the origin of novelty wrestling in America. "But before we knew it, mud wrestling turned into a cheap sex show."

In fact, well before Mr. Rosenbaum got to it, mud wrestling was a cheap sex show. Along with wet-T-shirt contests and teeny-weeny-bikini competitions, the spectacle of two women pinching, pulling, squeezing, and poking each other in an arena full of muck had been a hallmark of sleazy bars in all the bad parts of town across America for many years. The appeal of the sport was to watch the mud blur the line between the women's skin and their stingy swimsuits, thus making them appear naked. Mr. Rosenbaum, who says he was horrified by the reputation of the

game, racked his brains trying to figure out a way to make it into wholesome entertainment. In 1985, he had his breakthrough when he converted his act from mud wrestling to mashed-sweet-potato wrestling at the Allentown, Pennsylvania, fair. Since that date, grappling in sticky foods, which Mr. Rosenbaum has copyrighted as Novelty Wrestling, has flourished.

"We will not work a nightclub or any place alcohol is being served," he explained. "And no one enters my ring unless they abide by the dress code." Women must wear a one-piece swimsuit; and if it is cut too low, they are required to top it with a T-shirt. Men are allowed to be bare-chested and wear traditional wrestling trunks. Fanciful costumes are permitted.

Proclaimed by the *New York Times* to be "the latest in good clean family fun," Novelty Wrestling is staged in high schools and county fairs as a way of raising money for worthy causes. Instead of a car wash to pay for band

uniforms or a bake sale to send the senior class to Colonial Williamsburg, a school might hire Mr. Rosenbaum to organize a *mano a mano* battle royale in creamed corn between the principal and the phys-ed teacher, or among members of the student council. During a summer 1989 trip through Pine Grove, Pennsylvania, we were lucky enough to catch a chocolate-pudding wrestling match staged by students of the middle school; the four-dollars-per-head admission went to an ''Alternatives to Drugs and Alcohol'' support group.

Although the company is headquartered in Pennsylvania, Novelty Wrestling matches have taken place from Maine to Florida and as far west at Texas; there are plans to sell franchises on the West Coast. ''It's catching on in Japan,'' Mr. Rosenbaum declared. ''We're going national, then international.'' According to *People* magazine in a 1987 article about the phenomenon, ''wrestling in comestibles has gone mainstream.''

Mr. Rosenbaum's company provides the ring, the music, and an emcee and prepares the wrestling medium du jour. As there are only a few professional Novelty Wrestlers, it is up to whoever stages the event to provide contestants.

The major choice that must be made by anyone putting on a Novelty Wrestling match is an appropriate substance to wrestle in. In addition to mashed sweet potatoes and chocolate pudding, bouts have taken place in oatmeal, creamed spinach, spaghetti with marinara sauce, smooth peanut butter, and vanilla ice cream with cherries and bananas. In 1987 in Jersey Shore, Pennsylvania, Mr. Rosenbaum staged what he described as the world's first two-course wrestling tournament: It started in Jell-O and ended in pudding.

The code of Novelty Wrestling demands that the substance wrestled in be absolutely edible, just like you would serve at the family dinner table. Lime Jell-O is by far the most popular substance, mixed in five-gallon batches and chilled with ice to a consistency somewhat looser than anyone would want it for dessert, but firm enough to stick between contestants' toes and in the ears and nostrils. To add variety to matches and to make the substance more familiar-looking, Mr. Rosenbaum explained, he often mixes cans of fruit cocktail or chunks of pears and peaches into the Jell-O. A full evening's card requires approximately twelve hundred   pounds.

NUDISM

For those of us who like wearing clothes, nudism is a strange spectacle. We do not mean getting undressed, which even the most modest people must do from time to time, nor are we referring to the occasional naked stroll from bedroom to kitchen in search of a snack. Real nudism is a way of life in which stark-naked people (sometimes wearing shoes or carrying a pocketbook) play volleyball, go to the beauty parlor, shop for food, and ride motorcycles.

At best, nudism is about sleek, tanned bodies lying on chic European beaches. At worst, it's about Mom and Pop sitting outside their trailer home on web-strapped lawn chairs, roasting weenies on the grill, and wearing nothing but pincurls and vinyl house slippers.

What makes nudism so puzzling is its incessant striving for normalcy. Put a horde of sweaty naked bodies together and most of us could think of something more exciting to do than have a sing-along. But not nudists, who are determined to show the world what an average life they live. They are, they insist, just as boring as everybody else, except with better tans.

Modern nudism is divided into "nudists" and "naturists." Naturists have a New Age mentality that says nude is natural and therefore good, and they want to make beaches and parks "clothing optional"; nudists are more old-fashioned, and prefer to confine their nude time to private weekend gatherings where they engage in such immemorial nude-person activities as volleyball, outdoor calisthenics, and making human totem poles while swimming. Like artists, lepers, and ants, nudists have traditionally separated themselves from the rest of the world as "colonies" (a term they want to replace with the more innocuous "clubs") at which they engage in all kinds of organized group activities and grade-A hokum, from nude talent shows and an undressed version of "The Newlywed Game" called "The Nudelywed Game" to nude dancing to music from the album *Music for Skinnydippers* (the lyrics of which include, "Everybody take off your clothes / Jump in the water and hold your nose"). Nudists buy their kids the *No Clothes Coloring Book,* consisting of line drawings of naked people praying, cooking, and making beds; and if the cold doesn't bother them, they go on invigorating nude backpacking expeditions through the rugged snow-covered mountains of New Hampshire.

Nudists are high-minded. They advocate nudism for its physical benefits (vitamin D from the sun); and they cite the original Greek Olympics' nude competitors, noting that modern scores would almost certainly be improved, especially in swimming, diving, and track and field, if athletes weren't encumbered by clothes. When not engaging in healthful physical activities, nudists have nudist literature and art to appreciate, such as Aileen Goodson's book *Nude Psychotherapy* (''Removing the mask of clothing broke down barriers to inter-personal honesty''); Fred Foldvary's article ''Nudity in the Bible'' in the magazine *Clothed with the Sun* ('' 'And Ham, father of Canaan, saw the nakedness of his father': *Genesis 9:22''*); and the videotaped *Winter Fantasies* ballet that features an earnest but very chilly couple doing arabesques and pliés in a snow-covered patch of forest, accompanied by jungle drums and the humming of a ghostly voice.

Although Adam and Eve were the first nudists, nudism as a philosophy started early in the twentieth century in Germany, where *Nacktkultur,* or naked culture, was seen as a way to turn the tide on the poor physical condition of

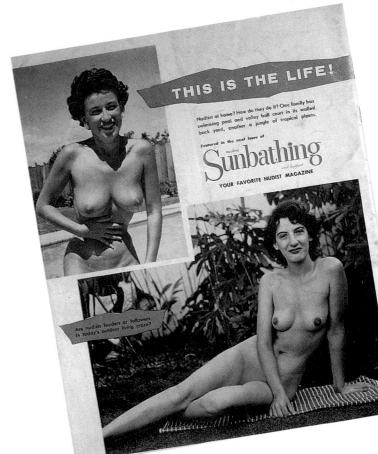

the general population, who bathed little, ate poorly, and lived in unsanitary conditions. As the German Youth movement blossomed after World War I, encouraging boys and girls to walk through the woods, bathe in cold streams, and get back in touch with nature, nudism and Nazism followed similar paths. The striving to create muscular blond supermen and superwomen was a shared ideal. The raised-arm salute of ''Heil'' was in fact revived first by the Wandervögel, a nature-worshipping youth league that had been founded in the 1890s and believed the ancient gesture to be a more natural form of greeting than the popular military clicking of heels. The *Naturheilbewegung,* or natural healing movement, was a cult that advocated heliotherapy, a fancy name for lying in the sun to fight such postwar plagues as TB and rickets.

These proto-nudist activities were an amalgam of health, philosophy, and politics. The Confidential Lodge for the Friends of Rising Light in northern Germany insisted all members be blond, blue-eyed, nonsmoking vegetarians. Equally ominous was the Nudo-Natio Alliance, formed by Professor G. Hermann of Berlin, which established four nudist colonies, bearing the names Naked Lodge, Swastika, Valhalla, and Hellas. These people did not lounge around or dance the charleston. They did calisthenics and followed strict diets; they took medicinal baths, massages, and purges to cleanse their bodies of modern life's impurities.

By 1930, nudism in Germany was thriving. Adolf Koch, a socialist and gymnastics teacher who advocated the hygienic efficiency of being without clothes for young people, claimed a following of sixty thousand socialist-nudists. The same year, in Frankfurt, the first International Nudist Conference attracted devotees from around the world. It was estimated that three million people in Germany practiced nudism. However, when Adolf Hitler became chancellor in 1933, he banned nudism. The Führer was a prude; besides, no matter how rigorous its calisthenics, and despite many adherents' belief in strong Aryan bodies, nudism was a way of life too free for the Nazi state. After the war, Germany's interest in nudism revived. Freilichtpark, which had opened in 1903 as the first nudist resort in the world and was the subject of the profoundly influential 1930 picture book by Americans Mason and Frances Merrill, *Among the Nudists,* continued as a nudist mecca until 1981.

It was the rigorous Germanic brand of nudism that arrived in America in 1929 when immigrant Kurt Barthel banded together with a small group of other sun worshipers from the Old Country and formed the American League for Physical Culture; they took off their clothes for the first time on American soil on Labor Day in an isolated wooded spot on the Hudson River north of New York City. Barthel's calisthenic-crazed eight-member League for Physical Culture eventually became the American Sunbathing Association, a nationwide group of thirty thousand nudists whose life-style has mellowed considerably from the cold-shower, prune-eating era into a fun-loving philosophy of feeling good about your body, and letting everybody see it, whatever you look like.

Organized nudism has adherents around the world and from Maine to California, but oddly enough it is most popular in those parts of the United States where the weather is inclement, especially in the northeast. Inveterate sun-worshippers like to say that they represent all levels of society and all walks of life, but Lee Baxandall, founder and owner of the Naturist Society of Oshkosh, Wisconsin (where the doormat to his office requests, ''Please Undress Before Entering''), estimated that nearly one-half of the people who attended the Tri-State Sun Club's Naturist Eastern Gathering in the Poconos in 1989 were computer programmers. ''It makes sense,'' he explained, ''because when you work with computers you learn to think rationally. Nudity is the rational choice, much more than the choice taken by clothing-compulsive people.''

THE NUDIST PICTURE NEWS

modern

Sunbathing

SEPTEMBER 1955 50c

THE WORLD'S NUDEST STRIP...
The NAUGHTY LADY Of Sandy Lane
1955 REPORT ON VIRTUE

HOW TO GET A BOOT OUT OF YOUR DAY OFF

PANTY-HOSE CRAFTS

Could there be any less likely inspiration of creativity than a used pair of panty hose? Panty hose aren't all that lovely even fresh out of the box, with their shriveled nylon legs hanging from a baggy cloth-crotched panty. As for old, smelly, torn ones: Well, it takes a certain type of genius to find beauty in them waiting to be released.

You may think you have never seen panty-hose crafts, but if you've ever been to a country crafts emporium, gift shop, antique mall, or flea market you've undoubtedly encountered them. Soft-sculpture panty-hose dolls are a booming craft from coast to coast, as evidenced in a profusion of life-size grannies and grampas and crying babies with distended nylon heads the size of basketballs. The strange texture of the beige stocking material gives these figures a disturbingly lifelike skin, with faces reminiscent of embryos, or of the half-formed pod people in *Invasion of the Body Snatchers.*

The dean and doyenne of panty-hose crafts are Ed and Stevie Baldwin, a husband-and-wife team from Tulsa, Oklahoma, who write a syndicated newspaper column called "Makin' Things." Like many people who don't like to throw out stuff that still might have some use, the Baldwins just hated it when a pair of Stevie's otherwise perfectly good panty hose developed a giant-size run. So they figured out a few hundred wonderful ways to recycle the lingerie-drawer discards—as dolls' skin, footstool coverings, Christmas wreaths, fantasy flowers, puppets, draft stoppers, and boot stuffers (for packing into boots like shoe trees so the boots don't bend over in the closet). To let others in on how much fun it was to make such panty-hose crafts, they wrote the two seminal books on the subject, *The Great Pantyhose Crafts Book* and *More Great Pantyhose Crafts.*

For most panty-hose items, all the craftsperson needs are a sharp needle, glue, and polyester fiberfill—plus lots of old panty hose. Regular weave and thick winter hose in various shades of beige or taupe, nurse's white hose, the occasional pair of knee-highs, and extra-roomy queen-size panty hose (for monumental projects) are helpful for the artist who wants to work with a full palette.

With a rag bag full of such cast-offs, even a beginner can make a life-sized soft-sculpture doll like the one the Baldwins call "Aunt Goldie," who sits in a wing chair wearing a calico bonnet and a shawl, holding in her mesh-covered fingers a pair of knitting needles and a half-finished muffler. "She's a life size, livin' doll," say the Baldwins. We say she looks like Norman Bates's mother with a pair of panty hose over her head.

The great thing about making panty-hose dolls is how pliable they are. Even after the head is stuffed and tied off, its features can be manipulated to create smiles, frowns, smirks, protruding foreheads, warts (for witches), whatever is required. Fiberfill is malleable, and panty hose will stretch, but many overenthusiastic beginners stuff the head with far too much material, resulting in a lolling,

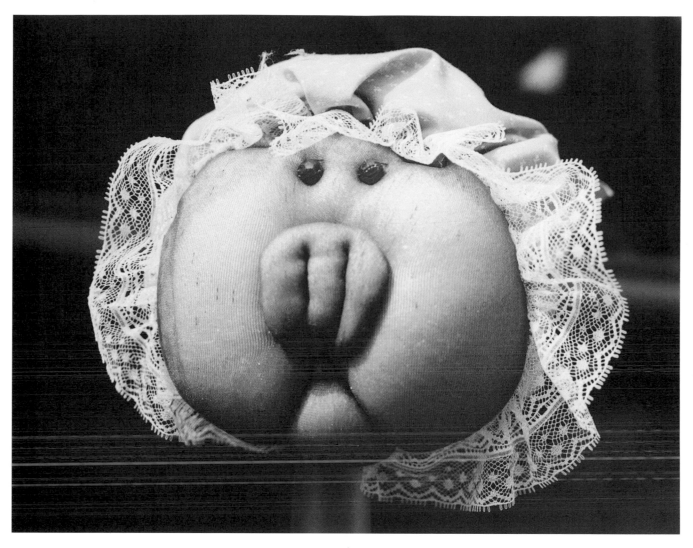

spherical pumpkin head impossible to mold. Another mistake novices often make is the inappropriate use of support hose, which is fine for ''Katie T. Cozy'' the tea cozy but makes baby dolls with rhinoceros skin.

All panty-hose dolls are designed to be adorably cute or adorably ugly. The Baldwins offer patterns for ''The Gork'' (a household elf), ''Christi Christmas Witch,'' ''Three Men in a Tub,'' and a family of ''Sock-Its'' with donut-shaped panty-hose faces attached to tube-sock bodies designed to hold money or marbles.

Lovable dolls are the soul of panty-hose crafts, but there are many other cute things to make, too. The Baldwins suggest a ''Magical Unicorn'': ''Unicorns are very special animals that spread their magic wherever they go. Just looking at him it's hard to believe that he is made from cardboard and nurses white pantyhose.'' One especially practical project is the Baldwins' ''Casserole Carrier,'' which ''will carry your contribution to the potluck dinner in style'' and is made from opaque blue knee-highs, which form a two-part cozy for the steamy tuna du jour. Another culinary project, recommended as a thank-you gift to friends, is a ''Hot Pad, Drink Coaster, and Napkin Ring'' set made of heavy brown panty hose and white knee-highs. Who could resist a meal presented on a hot pad made with the hose you wore to work last winter!

239

PARTON, DOLLY

I t's a good thing I was born a woman," Dolly Parton once observed, "or I'd have been a drag queen." Barely five feet tall, the country girl with the trilling, honey-sweet voice is known for towering blond wigs, for makeup so thick that the Minneapolis *Tribune* wrote, "You could carve your initials in her face and not draw blood," for sequined gowns and frilly blouses with zeppelin bust lines, and for stiletto heels and two-inch magenta-colored fingernails. Massively bosomy with an eighteen-inch waist, she has always had a tendency toward an unbelievably voluptuous plumpness, fueled by a voracious appetite for Velveeta cheese, white bread, and Doodleburgers.

One of eleven children raised in a two-room tar-paper shack in Sevierville, Tennessee, she learned to pick and play as a child and appeared on local television at age ten in 1956. Two years later, she debuted at the Grand Ole Opry; and she moved to Nashville the day after graduating from high school. It was there as an ambitious teenager that she devised her exaggerated image by studying local prostitutes. "I always liked the look of our hookers," she told *Ladies' Home Journal*. "Their big hairdos and makeup made them look *more*." After cultivating her own slutty look, for which she encumbered her head with architectonic wigs and encased her body in tight, rhinestone-encrusted gowns, she had her first hit song in 1967: "Dumb Blonde." Although there was a sophisticated irony in her lyrics, Dolly's cheap appearance, a preposterous caricature of femininity, ensured that many did perceive her as a bimbo.

Like those of that other not-so-dumb blonde Jayne Mansfield, Dolly's oversize bosoms have been the source of many well-publicized mishaps, such as when she drove through Beverly Hills with one breast exposed (she said she was only trying to flash a friend) and the time both breasts erupted out of her dress at a Country Music Awards ceremony. "You shouldn't try to put fifty pounds of mud in a five-pound sack," she noted.

As a singer, she began as pure country, making her name as the featured female in Porter Wagoner's country music show in the late sixties, singing solos and duets with Wagoner, who was himself known for a stupendous blond pompadour and jewel-crusted wardrobe. It was an inspired pairing; as Wagoner's protégée, she became one of country music's favorite queens. But by 1974, Dolly wanted more; and Wagoner thought her ambition unseemly for a woman. After an ugly separation, complete with lawsuits, Dolly rocketed to success beyond country music with her song "Here You Come Again." She wowed television viewers with appearances on "The Tonight Show" in which Johnny, Ed, and other male guests on the couch made much ado about her bust; and she starred with Jane Fonda and Lily Tomlin in the hit movie *9 to 5*.

She has been successful on the pop charts as a crossover artist despite the attacks of country-pure critics, one of whom lambasted her as "slicker'n a greased pig." But Dolly's show-business career after *9 to 5* has had its problems, notably the movie *Rhinestone,* in which she played a nightclub headliner who tries to turn lunkheaded cab driver Sylvester Stallone into a sequin-bedecked country singer. "I don't think people want to see Stallone with his shirt on,'" she said to explain the movie's failure. She received $44 million from ABC-TV to star in a variety show called "Dolly" in which she performed as host and singer and played a compassionate waitress in an ongoing sketch that took place in a hillbilly truck stop from which seriocomic wisdom was dispensed each week. Dolly dieted down to a skeletal hundred pounds that left little more than hips, bosoms, hair, and makeup, but the show was cancelled after one truncated season in 1987—88.

The problem with movies and television is that they seem small and pale when they have to contain the glittering burlesque that is Dolly. "I look like the girl next door," she once remarked, "if you happen to live next door to an amusement park." And sure enough, her greatest nonmusical triumph has been the $20 million hillbilly theme park named Dollywood in Pigeon Forge,

Tennessee—just miles from Dolly's once-sylvan girlhood home in Sevierville. Unless you drive deep into the woods, however, you will see little evidence of the Smoky Mountain beauty that Dolly sometimes sings about, because Pigeon Forge has become one of the most densely developed strips of factory outlets, fudge shops, and miniature golf courses in America. At one point Dolly wanted to purchase the actual home she was raised in, upheave it from the woods, and move it to Dollywood as an attraction. But the headstrong mountain folks occupying it refused to sell; so visitors must settle for an exact reproduction in an exhibit called ''Tennessee Mountain Home.'' Dollywood also features the Smoky Mountain Rampage rubber-raft ride, the Thunder Express roller-coaster trip through what a brochure calls ''some of the Smokies' most breathtaking wilderness,'' Aunt Granny's Dixie Fixins restaurant, and the Dolly Parton Museum wig collection.

See also **BREASTS, ENORMOUS; SMOKY MOUNTAINS**

PEPPER MILLS, HUGE

One of the silliest rituals of dining out is the ceremonial grinding of the pepper. After your salad or entree is set before you on the table, the waiter appears with a colossal pepper mill and asks if you want some. If you say yes, he grinds until you tell him to stop. In soigné restaurants, the pepper mill is handled with utmost finesse as it glides in a circle above the plate and the waiter twists the knob with aplomb; in establishments that are less deluxe but nonetheless have sufficient delusions of grandeur to maintain an outsized pepper mill, waiters tend to wield the instrument like a baton or juggler's club, swirling it over the food as the freshly ground spice sprinkles out, then slapping it up into their armpit in order to free their hands to carry dirty hors d'oeuvre dishes back to the kitchen. Either way it happens, a huge pepper mill looks ridiculous—the height of obsequious pretense masquerading as elegance.

There is a dim historical logic to the practice of doling out pepper like gold. It was one of the rarest, most sought-after spices in Europe in the Middle Ages, so valued in England that peppercorns were accepted as legal tender. Christopher Columbus set off for America in hopes of discovering, among other things, new supplies of pepper; and in fact he and the explorers who followed him were so eager to vindicate their exploration of the New World they named nearly all the hot spices they found "pepper," when they were actually cayenne and chili, which are different kinds of plants altogether. Pepper was still a dear commodity in the seventeenth century, when a Yankee clerk named Elihu Yale made a fortune in the Indian pepper trade and donated his profits to a young Connecticut college that thanked him by changing its name to Yale College.

Venice had always been the center of Mediterranean pepper commerce; and in later years, after the business had been wrested away by the British and Dutch East India companies, it remained customary in many northern Italian restaurants to honor the heritage by keeping a great wooden pepper mill on hand to dispense the honored spice with the respect it deserved and to ensure that the supply of pepper was controlled by the house. In some cases the mill was an imposing, carved wooden instrument, part of the decor of the restaurant, kept on display near the hearth.

No one knows how the custom came from Italy to America's showy restaurants; we guess it might have happened about the same time Chianti-bottle candle holders and spumoni were discovered—when GIs returned home after World War II. Unlike those quaint little affectations of friendly Italian restaurants, however, the ceremonial pepper mill worked its way into the upper echelons of arrogant American dining rooms of all ethnic persuasions.

Should you desire to dispense pepper at home with all the pomp of a snooty restaurant, the mill you want to choose is the Italian-made Giant Corona Premium: thirty-two inches of hand-lathed, mahogany-stained beechwood with five coats of urethane and a brass base and dome. The one problem you must consider before purchasing a thirty-two-inch pepper mill is that, unless you have the arms of a gorilla, you will be unable to put pepper on your own plate without standing up, possibly on a small footstool.

PERKY NUNS

Soldiers, policeman, and nearly all members of a uniformed special brigade can be said to display impeccable taste: Livery bestows the wearer with an invincible majesty that transcends the vagaries of personal style. So it used to be with nuns. No matter what they really looked like, all nuns were stunning in their black habits, as their unpainted faces, framed by yards of starched white linen, glowed with the distant pain of heavy laced shoes and tight-corseted underpinnings. Their behavior was mesmerizing, too. They glided instead of walked; they spoke with hushed voices; they went through life with downcast eyes.

In 1963, Sister Luc-Gabrielle of Belgium recorded a clever little folk song called ''Dominique.'' It was a pop music phenomenon, and it toppled nuns from their pedestal. Suddenly the world was faced with an epidemic of kooky, perky, goofy nunnish antics. Sister Luc-Gabrielle —dubbed ''the Singing Nun''—appeared on ''The Ed Sullivan Show'' with a guitar she named Sister Adele. Her life was retold as a movie starring Debbie Reynolds in which the merry sister rides about on a gay blue Vespa motor scooter and plays rough-and-tumble games with orphaned children in the schoolyard.

Prompted by such lighthearted antics, nuns joined the go-go age. The pale, prayerful hands of sisters everywhere developed guitar calluses as somber masses were traded in for hootenanny versions of ''Michael (Row Your Boat Ashore)'' and ''He's Got the Whole World in His Hands.'' The fad produced the Singing Nuns of Jesus and Mary from Hyattsville, Maryland, who recorded ''The Happy Wanderer,'' and Sister Adele (named after Sister Luc-Gabrielle's guitar), who tried (unsuccessfully) to climb to the top of the charts with ''Savez-Vous Planter les Choux?'' (''Do You Know How to Plant Cabbages?'')

Playful nuns saturated movies and TV sitcoms, saying ''Sock it to me'' and ''Would you believe?'' right along with everybody else. Button-nosed novice Hayley Mills battled it out with Mother Superior Rosalind Russell in *The Trouble with Angels;* and a muscular Sidney Poitier grew

adorably exasperated by the demands of the sisters in *Lilies of the Field.* Lovable freckle-puss Sally Field got into a habit and played Sister Bertrille in ''The Flying Nun,'' a TV show that showed her playing poker with the guys at the local casino, strumming her guitar, getting sunburnt, and flirting with Carlos, San Juan's most eligible playboy. And whenever a strong gust of wind kicked up under her extra-wide cornet, she just sailed away into the cloudless blue Caribbean sky.

Nuns were now certifiably good for a laugh and a double take. Disco dancers in nun's habits cut as high as miniskirts did the frug on television's ''Laugh-In.'' Mary Tyler Moore co-starred with Elvis Presley as Sister Michelle in the 1969 movie *Change of Habit,* about a trio of plainclothes nuns loose in a red-hot ghetto. The credits of the movie roll over a scene in which the audience is treated to the spectacle of Sister

Michelle doing a slow striptease as Elvis sings the title song. Limb by limb she unrolls her black nun's stockings and wiggles out of her dowdy habit to don the raiment of a streetwise sister: a double-knit A-line frock, with her hair styled into a neat bubble bouffant.

Even more distressing than the movie and TV images of perky and sexy nuns was the reality of modern-thinking nuns who shed their classic habits in favor of contemporary duds. Dress rules were relaxed in many convents, and the full penguin getup became an anachronism. Up-to-the-minute nuns wore polyester pantsuits with a short hairdo and a large crucifix pendant similar to those favored by Las Vegas lounge singers. Nuns no longer looked mysterious; they were simply drab and dumpy. Nowadays, when you see six women bunched together in a gray, no-frills Chevy driving slowly down the road, it is impossible to know if they are sisters or merely dowdy souls on their way to K Mart.

PET CLOTHING

All wild animals and most pets go through life in their birthday suits. Horses get saddles and saddle blankets; pet cats and dogs might get a flea collar or a leather collar or possibly even a harness, but none of these articles of clothing do much to hide their bodies, and none makes a meaningful fashion statement.

Although naked is normal, there are some pets who find themselves wearing clothes. They are dressed by the people who own them for one or more of three reasons: (1) out of shame, so their private parts aren't exposed; (2) because their owner is extremely fashion-conscious and feels embarrassed by a dog or cat who wears the same coat as all others of its breed, day after day; and (3) as a joke. Whether the reason is prudery, fashion, or wit, pet clothing is always ridiculous. The only animals that have a legitimate need for it are tiny short-haired chihuahuas and even tinier hairless Peruvian Inca Orchid Powder Puffs, who can shiver to death if not protected; but these dogs, because they are so grotesquely miniaturized to begin with, are ludicrous even before they get coddled in a chinchilla muffler.

Nearly everyone likes to anthropomorphize his or her pet, and clothes are one of the most effective ways to do it. Put a sombrero on your parrot or a Santa Claus suit on your Siamese cat, and it is all the more enjoyable to talk baby-talk and treat the little creature as a member of the family. And let's be honest: Some long-lived pets, particularly those who don't have good personalities, can become rather boring to have around the house over many years. Sporty T-shirts, scarves, eyeglasses, and funny hats are a good way of putting some life back in the pet-owner relationship, just as old married couples sometimes dress in costumes to revivify their sex lives.

The pet-fashion business is 90 percent sweaters and rain slickers, which are the apparel that comes closest to being practical and has been available in pet shops for years. Counterculture dogs have been wearing bandannas, which are more liberated-looking than collars, since the sixties (at which time a British firm marketed bomb shelters for pets, buried underground adjacent to the human family's shelter); but according to Vincent Rienti, buyer for Macy's pet shop in New York, the high-fashion trend in pet wear began in the early eighties.

Now most well-equipped pet boutiques sell clothing and accessories for dogs that include a full line of active wear such as jogging suits, swimsuits (one- or two-piece),

Every Night, Josephine!

Jacqueline Susann

How does it feel to be owned by an almost human poodle? A report from the other end of the leash and running shoes or cowboy-style boots. For around the house, there are pajamas and sleeping caps, as well as futon doggie mats and designer sheets for dog beds. Silk-N-Satin of New Jersey is a specialty company run by Patricia Henderson, who calls herself "the Dior of Dog Fashion." Ms. Henderson makes sequined jumpsuits and fancy denim duds. She has taken special orders from customers who need dog clothes to match their own; she has made a mink coat for a parrot who recites Chaucer; and she has even had requests for marriage outfits for male and female dogs who were about to be bred.

One of the most complete lines of dog apparel is merchandised by a wholesaler called Pet Smarts of New York. They offer Burberry-style raincoats, bright red raincoats for lady dogs with white lace collars and lace appliqué heart, op-art raincoats in rainbow, polka-dot, and zebra-stripe patterns with adjustable belts and Velcro closures, sporty snoods for long-headed hounds such as salukis and afghans, one-size-fits-all bibs for sloppy eaters, and fun-fur jumpsuits in leopard skin or lambskin. They also sell T-shirts with such slogans as "I've Licked the Best," "4 on the Floor," and "Preppy Puppy" (with rampant lion shield and crest).

If there isn't a pet boutique near you that carries these items, Pet Smarts has the answer: Order merchandise from them wholesale, then stage parties at home, at the office, at church, or in a local diner at which you sell sequin stretch collars, "pet sweats," and paw socks to your guests. "Your friends will beg to have the next party at their house," Pet Smarts promises. "Don't be a Tupperware Party Person—Be the Puppurrwear Party Person of Pet Fashions!"
See also **CHIHUAHUAS; POODLES**

POLYESTER

Suffocating, dull-witted, rubbery, cut-rate, and liable to melt into a viscous wad of petrochemical poison if touched by a lit cigarette—this is the image polyester had attained by 1983 when designer John Weitz declared that "polyester created a whole world of bad taste: Polyester people. Polyester towns. Polyester hotels."

It was a bum rap. Polyester did not deserve such ill repute. It was what had been done to polyester in the seventies that branded the fiber —composed of synthetic molecules melt-spun out of ethylene glycol and terephthalic acid—as a loathsome symbol of irredeemable vulgarity.

Before the seventies, no one thought badly of polyester. No one thought badly of any man-made fibers. Rayon, created in the twenties out of natural cellulose using a process that mimicked the way silkworms feed on leaves, was the basis of brightly colored, affordable sportswear, such as Hawaiian shirts. Nylon, a noncellulosic (i.e., completely artificial) material first produced in 1939, became one of the war's most precious commodities; women lined up around the block to buy nylons when they became available again in New York department stores after 1945.

In Great Britain after the war, J. T. Dickson and J. R. Whinfield of the Calico Printers Association figured out how to spin molten polymers (giant molecules created by combining elements from coal and petroleum) into threads, creating the first polyester fiber. In 1950, Du Pont purchased the patents. In 1952 it coined the term "wash and wear" to describe a blend of cotton and acrylic. And in 1953, polyester fiber was first produced in mass quantities. The golden age of man-made fibers had begun.

It seemed a miracle. "Homemakers Aided by New Synthetics" headlined the New York Times, offering tips for washing and drying such marvelous new materials as modacrylic, Acrilan, Dynel, Orlon, and Chromspun. The earliest polyester fiber was spongy and impenetrable and had problems holding dyes; but as technology improved, it was refined into a hundred different forms that mimicked down, wool, suede, silk, or rubber, depending on how the chemicals were spun, curled, and combed. As dryers replaced clotheslines, irons and ironing boards seemed ever more old-fashioned; and in the seventies, knit polyester fibers, which held their shape and color eternally, seemed to offer the ultimate convenience.

The problem was that by the mid-seventies, when the word "natural" had attained a status of inviolable goodness among many consumers, industrial-sounding "polyester" connoted the opposite of all that was good. Fabric makers masked it with trade names such as Kodel, Fortrel, Crepesoft, and Golden Touch. But soon there would be no combatting the hideous image

BET YOU NEVER SAW WALKING SHORTS THAT FIT SO GREAT or looked so super, or stayed so neat . . that's because these are ribbed-textured DOUBLE-KNIT DACRON* POLYESTER *PERMA·PREST* SHORTS with natural 2-way stretch. And the trim smooth line is in to stay . . they shun wrinkles, won't shrink or stretch out of shape. Just machine wash, warm, not even touch-up ironing needed when tumble-dried.

DACRON

The polyester fiber in shorts is DACRON *DuPont reg.

1 Quality-detailed with a handy side-seam pocket; Ban-Rol® interlined waist-band that stays in place; non-snag nylon back zipper. Misses' sizes 10, 12, 14, 16, 18, 20. *Please state correct size.*
7 A 5494F—Medium turquoise blue
7 A 5499F—True red
7 A 5495F—Pearl gray
7 A 5498F—Medium yellow
7 A 5496F—White
7 A 5497F—Navy blue
Shipping weight 8 ounces $6.97
*Reg. DuPont T.M.

PRINT PANT-TOP
2 Cued to all the shorts in a mix of red, yellow, navy and turquoise blue on gray and white. Pullover style, in nylon jersey, has a bateau neckline. Hand wash.
Misses' sizes S(8-10);
M(12-14); L(16-18).
State S, M or L. Shpg. wt. 7 oz.
7 A 2240F $4.97

ORDER YOUR USUAL SIZE
If in doubt, see pages 586 and 587

★ Wear Sears PERMA·PREST* for great no-iron, wrinkle-resistant performance . . that's what NEATNIKS wear

Sears 235

★ PERMA·PREST® fine line Twill Casuals

498 Sears

of double-knit polyester garments, which became so popular in 1974 that manufacturers could not meet the demand for polyester.

Texturized polyester clothes were originally a big hit not only because they were convenient but because they seemed rakish. Polyester pantsuits, leisure suits, slacks, and shirts were made to be fun, in crazy textures and bright colors; in most cases they were tailored to project a sporty, informal image. Knit-look powder-blue pants flared into grotesquely wide bells; qianalike shirts were made in patterns of fluorescent flowers; ladies' pantsuits of nubby sienna-red polyester knits were available with matching globe-head caps and jumbo pocketbooks: The world was filled with outrageous clothes that never needed pressing. But polyester's glory days were numbered. Discount bins at Korvettes as well as racks in swank department stores grew overcrowded

with polyester apparel, much of it poorly designed and cheaply made. The aggressive informality of most designs, combined with the fact that pure polyester clothes did not breathe— causing the wearer to perspire profusely— suddenly made polyester appear to be far from stylish. It became the fabric of cheap, sweaty boors.

Then along came disco fashions at the end of the decade to put a stake into polyester's heart. The look that John Weitz called ''neo-Italian, West Coast cowboy,'' personified by John Travolta's shiny white, skin-tight suit (worn with open-collar black shirt) in the movie *Saturday Night Fever,* gave polyester a reputation as not merely boorish but downright sleazy.

No doubt about it—by 1980, polyester equaled bad taste. ''Bid for Better Polyester Image,'' the *New York Times* announced in 1983, describing how America's six top polyester makers were planning a campaign to make it stylish again. Results were not forthcoming, despite a brochure called ''The Polyester Touch,'' which featured swatches of polyester next to swatches of natural fiber, showing how alike they were, and a Man-Made Fiber Producers Association's production of *Man Made Fibers: The Video.* The rest of the world had come to love it (it was the fastest-growing fabric in Asia in the late eighties, according to the Polyester Council), but in America polyester remains a fiber with an ugly past it cannot live down.

See also **DISCO; HAWAIIAN SHIRT; LEISURE SUITS**

POLYNESIAN FOOD

Polynesian food is the most nature-loving cuisine in the world. In a good Polynesian restaurant, everything about a meal suggests natural elements: fire, leaping out of the Sterno can in the middle of the pu-pu platter appetizer tray; water, gurgling in the recirculating joy fountain near the cash register; vegetation, in the form of plastic palm fronds on the walls, thatch umbrellas, and lifelike yucca-pole palm trees. The back-to-nature feeling is reinforced by the distant sounds of island drums thumping on a sound system, by flickering colored pagoda lamps on tables, and by brightly colored flower-print Hawaiian shirts and pretty plastic leis on the waiters and waitresses.

The food itself is meant to sweep away all mundane thoughts of meat-and-potatoes or Whoppers-with-cheese and carry your imagination to a breezy isle in the South Pacific. With names like Kilauea Purple Passion Pork and Tuna Ono Niu (tuna casserole in a coconut), it is never simply plopped down on a table. It arrives from the kitchen stuck with sparklers or marshaled on monkeypod trays around an iridescent flame. As for the taste of the food, that, too, is something more exotic than any known civilized cuisine, heavy with the elemental tastes of sugar and oil, and glowing with the lustrous hues of unadulterated food coloring. It is food with the strength of a volcano, an earthquake, and a tidal wave: dizzyingly sweet and sour, fried and refried, soaked in coconut milk and larded with sugary concentrations of pineapples, bananas, and maraschino cherries.

Although there really is a place called Polynesia—a group of islands including Hawaii, Samoa, Tahiti, and the Maori Islands of New Zealand—the Polynesian food we speak of is not eaten there. Real Pacific-island cooking is a great melting pot into which have gone pigs brought by European explorers, beef jerky and salted fish introduced by American missionaries and whaling men, Chinese rice and stir-fry cookery, Korean *kimchi,* Filipino fish sauce, and even scones brought by Scottish sugar-cane technicians. But none of these foods have much to do with the gooey pressed ducks and glutinous spare ribs on the menu of every Polynesian restaurant in North America, and many all over the earth.

In the Polynesian lounges and dining rooms of the civilized world, authenticity is no more an issue than it was when Cecil B. De Mille made a movie: The point is not to slavishly copy reality but to create a magical experience that transcends reality. In this kind of *faux* Polynesian restaurant, the process of suspending disbelief is aided by tropical drinks, which customarily combine anesthetic amounts of high-proof rum

and gin with fruit juices that disguise the liquors' potency and are served in totemic mugs shaped like skulls, coconuts, the head of Fu Manchu, or the Moai heads from Easter Island. The mugs are garlanded with tiny paper parasols, lifelike orchids and gardenias, and colored plastic pics skewering bright-colored fruit slices.

The man to thank for Polynesian food and drink is "Trader" Vic Bergeron, a restaurateur who started his career in the food business in the early thirties at a beer joint named Hinky Dink's in Oakland, California. Mr. Bergeron was famous for his bar tricks—such as stabbing an ice pick into his wooden leg and flipping skillets full of ham and eggs high into the air across a ceiling

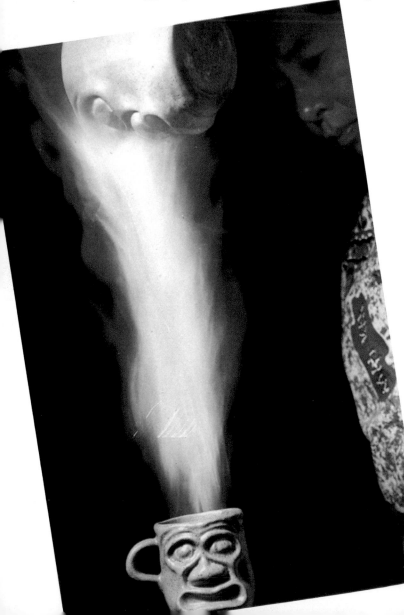

beam. He was also known for mixing odd and potent libations with whimsical names such as Frankenstein, Tongo Punch, and his most notorious invention, a blend of orange curaçao, rums, lime, and rock candy, the Mai Tai (named when a Tahitian friend tasted it and proclaimed, "Mai Tai—Roa Aé," meaning "Out of this world —the best"). The place was a dump, and the food was plebeian—steak sandwiches, roast chicken, and bowls full of olives and herring.

In 1937, Bergeron visited a restaurant in Hollywood called Don the Beachcomber's, where the Zombie and the Missionary's Downfall had first been mixed. The dining room had tropical decor, and the menu offered dishes from Hawaii. Bergeron was inspired. He returned to Oakland and changed the name of Hinky Dink's to Trader Vic's. He tore down the old deer horns and moose heads and covered the walls with green, grassy fabric and bamboo. "The Trader," as he now liked to be called, had always loved San Francisco's Chinese food, so he decided to make Trader Vic's a Chinese restaurant. But it would be Chinese cooking with a twist, incorporating underspiced and innocuous versions of dishes the peripatetic Trader discovered during travels to the South Pacific and Caribbean, as well as his own inventions, such as owl hoot crackers (mashed, baked slabs of Parmesan cheese). However exotic his sources, nothing the Trader served was frighteningly foreign, and that was the secret of his—and Polynesian food's— success. Trader Vic civilized savage cuisine. "I didn't want a fish coming with its eye staring at you or funny cuts of meat," he said.

Trader Vic's business boomed during the fifties. He moved to San Francisco, then opened branches in Hilton and Western hotels throughout America and Europe, all the while augmenting the tropical atmosphere with fishnets, fiberglass canoes, war masks, and other primitive native artifacts that were so fashionable at the time.

By the early sixties, when Trader Vic's was synonymous with Polynesian cookery, Americans were hungry for worldly sophistication. Earnest gourmets discovered French cuisine; playful ones embraced the Trader's brand of Polynesia, which seemed exotic but tasted familiar (like the Chinese food you eat on Friday night), and was served with festive, sugary potations rather than tart, sugarless wine. The Polynesia Pavilion at the 1964 New York World's Fair featured two longhouse buildings—one for dance and drum recitals, one for eating South Seas food. Every customer was greeted with a colored plastic lei. The Beach Boys got on the bandwagon with their first record, ''Surfin','' in 1961, the B side of which was a song called ''Luau,'' about how much fun it is to have a Polynesian picnic in your own backyard.

In fact, the great success of Polynesian food in the sixties wasn't only in elaborately decorated restaurants with names such as Hu-Ke-Lau and South Seas Lanai; it was in people's homes. Because it is a whimsical cuisine, and because eating it in the proper setting demands a bit of decorative ingenuity, Polynesian became a choice motif for patio parties and suburban potluck suppers. A 1961 recipe pamphlet issued by the Stitzel-Weller Distillery of Kentucky, called ''Let's Have a Patio Luau,'' advised readers that ''with a bit of imagination, plus a few props, you can glamorize and dramatize your next patio party to the admiration of all your friends. Simply make it a delightful LUAU instead of an ordinary cook-out.'' Stitzel-Weller's suggestions for a successful luau include:

- Have the KANES (men) dress as beachcombers; the WAHINES (women) as hula sirens. Sarongs, flower leis, grass skirts, straw beach hats, aloha shirts, and tattered pants all lend a picturesque flavor.
- ''Atmosphere'' is a prime requisite. This can easily be accomplished by an abundance of greenery including ferns, palms, philodendrons or similar potted plants, combined with a profusion of fresh flowers and fruits.
- Put some Hawaiian platters on the record player or dig out that old ukulele.

As for food, the great thing about a luau was that you could throw basically any old thing on the backyard grill, add chunks from a can of pineapple, and it became Hawaiian! ''Let's Have a Patio Luau'' admits that ''the traditional luau calls for a pit-roasted pig. But who has a pit and who has the heart to roast a pig!'' Instead, the booklet suggests giving the meal a Polynesian flavor by adding soy sauce instead of salt to hamburgers, and serving lots of cook-it-yourself hibachi appetizers such as rumaki, anchovy-stuffed shrimp, pickle-on-a-stick wrapped with Canadian bacon, marinated sardines, and bourbon-soaked prunes stuffed with cheese and ham.

Time was not kind to Polynesian food. As culinary snobbery became a sure method of achieving status in the upwardly mobile seventies, the frivolity of such delicacies as bongo-bongo soup (made with oysters and baby-food spinach) and banana chicken with grape-juice-flavored rice seemed ever more déclassé. The fevered decor of most Polynesian restaurants looked gauche in contrast to the new-money look of dove gray and muted pastels affected by fashionable eateries. Like Hawaiian shirts before them, Polynesian restaurants and the bright, sticky food they serve became outlandish symbols of vulgarity.

POODLES

Poodles are not sissies; they aren't even French. But it's easy to understand how they got their reputation if you see one in full dress clip. It is a stunning sight, like topiary shrubbery but able to beg, fetch, roll over, and play dead. To gaze upon a standard (full-size) poodle in a "Miami Sweetheart" cut with centered fur hearts on hips and back, pantaloon legs sculpted lathe-smooth, tassel ears, a Van Buren mustache drooping from its muzzle, a ribboned topknot, and a wagging pompon tail, parading along the boulevard in a rhinestone collar at the end of a jeweled lead, is to see an animal that has become a walking, barking work of art.

Poodles have been known erroneously as "French" poodles since the nineteenth century, when they won fame as the great trick dogs of the French circus. Extraordinary intelligence and an uncanny sense of humor fated them to become the clowns' clowns, in which capacity their coats were sheared into plumes and ruffles, and they were dyed bright colors to add to the merriment as they jumped through hoops, walked around the circus ring on their two front legs, and balanced duckpins on their noses. Such talents subsequently made them renowned in American vaudeville shows and on Ed Sullivan's television program in the 1950s and 1960s.

The idea of shearing and clipping poodles was not originally clownish. Before the Frenchification of poodles by the circus, they were well-respected European gun dogs, and their coats were clipped by hunters as a means of improving their performance. In fact, the most familiar fey poodle look, known as the "lion" cut, was developed to help them slog through rugged swamps. Poodles needed their thick coats for warmth in the cold water, but it was a hindrance when they swam fast, and it caught on brush; so only the hindquarters were sheared, with cuffs left around the ankles and hips to protect against rheumatism. Even the gay ribbon tied around the topknot had a purpose: Each hunter marked his dogs' heads with his own colors, allowing groups of hunters to tell their dogs apart.

In postwar America, where poodles went from the twenty-fifth most popular breed in 1946 to number one in 1960, the full possibilities of poodle extremism were realized. It was an era when perspective and scale in all forms of decoration went haywire; and so it made perfect sense to take the most decorative of dogs, the poodle, and breed it in tiny sizes guaranteed to be even more amusing than the normal one. As standard poodles rose in popularity, miniatures (under fifteen inches tall) and toys (under ten inches) zoomed. Shrunken poodles had been around for nearly a century, but "the rise of the miniature poodle was meteoric in the years after World War II," wrote Harry Glover in *Pure-Bred Dogs*.

In this same spirit of making cute things cuter, the poodle's ordinary colors (a wide range, including blue, gray, silver, brown, café-au-lait, apricot, and cream) were supplemented by vegetable dyes that could turn them more shades than nature ever knew. The Vitacoat company made "Marron" to make beige poodles a lovely chestnut brown and "Silver Sheen" to cause silver-coated poodles to sparkle. But the serious poodle colorist started with a white-coated dog, which could be tinted with pastels as pretty as those of a Coupe de Ville. "Women like to make them the same shade or a contrasting shade, to go with their wardrobes," observed "Miss Cameo" (Kay Waldschmidt), the great poodle stylist of the fifties, who worked in St. Louis and Tucson. Miss Cameo also advised coloring poodles for Easter or Christmas, suggesting pink, orchid, and green as especially becoming. Tinting poodles was an exacting craft, using a bucket of dye and a ladle to bathe the dog in its chosen hue, but always being careful that one area didn't get too much dye and become darker than the others. Shaved parts, such as the stomach and face, were colored with cotton swabs.

Along with Cadillacs and Harry Winston diamonds, poodles became one of the preeminent symbols of wealth and luxury as well as ostentation in the fifties. Nearly every glamorous movie star had one, or at least got

253

herself photographed with one: Joan Crawford had a toy poodle; Jayne Mansfield (who also had Chihuahuas) had a couple of standard poodles that she regularly dyed pink to match her home. In the Douglas Sirk comedy *Has Anybody Seen My Gal?* (1952), a movie about a nice middle-class family that suddenly inherits a fortune and becomes obnoxious, the change is expressed when they abandon their loyal old mongrel in favor of a brace of high-bred, snooty French poodles. That same year, Doris Day played an American chorus girl who has to pass for a diplomat at a Parisian art show in a musical called *April in Paris.* To promote the film and signify the pretense of the masquerade, she appeared on the cover of *Collier's* holding a sextet of clipped and dyed poodles: two pink, two aqua, one green, and one gold.

The remarkable thing about poodles as a status symbol is that they were a symbol available to nearly everyone. That is because they symbolized something bigger than just money. They were *chic;* they stood for modernity and sophistication, which anyone could shoot for, whether they were rich or just wanted to appear à la mode. Teenage girls wore stylish poodle skirts decorated with felt appliquéd French poodles wearing rhinestone collars; ladies bought handbags with embroidered poodles on the side and decorated their powder rooms with wallpaper that had pictures of poodles strolling down the Champs-Elysées.

For something to be labeled French in America in the fifties and early sixties usually meant that it was as soigné as it could be. French cuisine was the epitome of high style; in the world of high fashion, Paris was still le dernier cri. Poodles were now commonly known as French poodles, and vast numbers of them got named Fifi, Gigi, and Pierre. They appeared alongside Parisian-looking fashion models in hundreds of advertisements for products from perfume to washer-dryers in hopes that their elegance would convince consumers to buy. And as they grew in popularity, that aspect of them that was considered the most French—their ridiculous haircuts—was even more exaggerated.

Miss Cameo's *Poodle Clipping Book* in 1962 was the first encyclopedic survey of poodle-grooming styles, featuring step-by-step instructions and such chapters as "Your Clipper and Blades," "Basic Round Head Styles," and "Mustaches." In a revealing chapter called "Why Your Poodle Should Be Well Groomed," the answers to the rhetorical question include:

1. An ungroomed poodle doesn't look like a poodle at all!
2. It will bring you prestige in many ways.
3. When you go on vacations or trips, you will be able to take him with you, because most motels and hotels do not object to a clean, well-groomed poodle, even though they have a "NO DOGS ALLOWED" sign posted.
4. He is a thing of beauty and should be kept that way.

In the instructional section of *The Poodle Clipping Book,* Miss Cameo takes the reader from basic "Puppy Trim," "English Saddle," and "Continental Clip" (the only cuts permissible in the show ring) to such stupendous styles as the "Bell Bottom Banded Dutch" cut (with a rounded head like a cossack's hat), the "Scottsdale Exquisite" (puffs on legs and hocks, tasseled ears, and pointed head), and the "Triple Puff Sweetheart" (heart-shaped puffs on jacket and hips, double puffs on back legs, single puffs on front legs).

In her preface to her magnum opus, Miss Cameo (who was also a founder of the Chihuahua Club of St. Louis) says she knows that publication of the *Poodle Clipping Book* will permit other professional poodle stylists to pirate her work. But she is not disturbed. She concludes her remarks, "As long as poodles look better, I will have my reward."

Collier's

August 9, 1952 • Fifteen Cents

Can the POLITICAL POLLSTERS Predict This Year's Election?

ALL EYES ON DORIS DAY

POP-TOPPING

Ermal Cleon Fraze of the Dayton (Ohio) Reliable Tool and Manufacturing Company went on a picnic in 1959 but he forgot to bring a can opener. He had to use the edge of a car bumper to break into his can of beer. Fraze was so disturbed by the experience that he invented the pull-tab can opener, which was patented by 1963 and became known informally as the pop top. By the end of the sixties, nearly every can of beer or soda was equipped with one. Can openers were suddenly passé: To open a can you simply grabbed its ring and yanked. Off came the ring—about finger-sized—along with its attached pliable aluminum flap, leaving a neat oval hole in the top of the can. The ring and flap were useless, and until Mr. Fraze invented the prepuncturing pull tab of today, with a pop top that stays attached, many people just heaved their pop tops onto the street or grass like cigarette butts. It was a real mess.

Flash back now to 1970, when the original pop tops were in style: San Juan, the night before a big Tom Jones concert. Gonzalo Chavez and his friend have tickets to attend, but Mr. Chavez is in a panic. "I *had* to have something really outstanding to wear," Chavez wrote. So he used his imagination and made two vests, one for himself and one for his friend—completely out of pop tops! They looked like medieval chain mail. "We arrived at the stadium in our pop-top vests and created an immediate sensation," said Chavez, describing crowds of people demanding to know where the fabulous pop-top vests could be purchased. When Tom Jones arrived on stage, he was eclipsed by the pop-top vests. At least that's the way Mr. Chavez remembers it in his autobiographical and instructive crafts book, *Pop Topping!*, published in 1975. "One poor lady, who was leaning far out over a balcony to look at us, lost her wig. It fell to the tier below, but she didn't seem to notice. She kept right on staring at us."

Gonzalo Chavez suddenly knew his destiny. He changed his name to Pop-Top Terp, gave up a career as a professional knitter and Greenwich

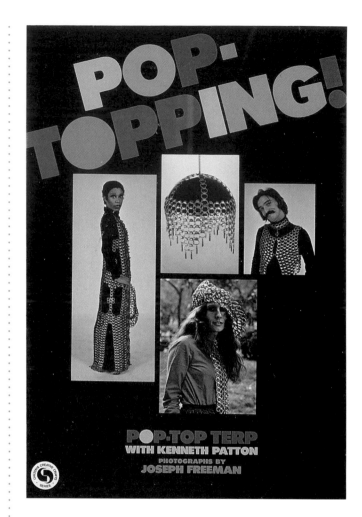

Village flower shop owner, and made it his business to teach the world how to create glittering attire out of rings torn off aluminum cans. Appearances on "To Tell the Truth" and "What's My Line?" didn't quite make Pop-Top Terp a household name; but there was no doubt that pop-topping's time had come.

Terp set up shop in San Juan, where he found all the pop tops he needed in rubbish heaps behind the local bars. At first the going was slow; it took him a whole day to make one vest from six hundred rings, which he sold for sixty dollars. As he picked up the pace, Pop-Top Terp began making other garments, some even more demanding then the vests, such as the 2,800-ring maxi coat he priced at $350. He quickly realized that the art of pop-topping was not only in the craftsman's hands but also in the quality of material used. Not all pop tops were equally fine. In an interview with *Time* Terp said that Budweiser rings were the best for soft garments, while Pepsi rings, which were heavier, were preferred for stiffer ones. For the silkiest smooth feeling, he liked Miller High Life pop tops best of all.

Pop-topping tapped into one of the most popular ideas of the early seventies—recycling. It was an ecologically inspired fashion statement with a motto, "Help Keep Mother Earth Clean," which Pop-Top Terp preached wherever he went: "Whenever you open a beverage can you have in your hand an item that can either litter the environment or be used to create stunning articles of clothing and useful home decorations." Terp called things made out of pop tops "eco-art"; and in response to his personal message of hope, twenty-two hundred New York City students collected sixty-five thousand pop tops in May of 1974 and made enough clothing out of them for a fashion show.

Mr. Terp was a mentor to eager pop-toppers everywhere. He had a charismatic style and a long history of imaginative craft making—such as the bedspread he once created for his water bed from a heap of cast-off baby-bottle nipples. Who could resist the lure of pop-topping after seeing, at the front of his book, the portrait of Mr. Terp titled *The Blessing*, in which he rises out of a heap of 150,000 unused pop tops wearing a full metal pop-top robe and a shoulder-length pharaoh's headdress of silver rings, his arms outstretched like a prophet?

The variety of what could be made from the tops of cans was unlimited. Mr. Terp appeared at the Craft Materials and Equipment Show in New York in 1974 showing a "Zingy Child's Vest," a Garbo cloche, wall hangings, miniskirts, and adjustable hats. *Pop Topping!* includes plans for a "Doggie Toggie," modeled by Ruby, a dachshund who appears none too delighted to be encased in a tube of metal tops. In a chapter called "Dazzling Decor for Your Pad," Terp suggests a "Fringy Lamp Shade," a "Swingin' Garden" hanging plant holder, and napkin rings made of pop tops. He even offers instructions for making pop-top curtain valances and tiebacks as a dramatic addition to formal silk draperies.

About the only thing wrong with pop-topping was that it clashed with another fad of the same period, which was toplessness. Pop-Top Terp lamented to one reporter that a topless go-go dancer had worn one of his vests on stage and gotten her right nipple stuck in a ring.

Now that cans are no longer made with disposable pop tops, no one will ever be able to go pop-topping again. Because they were fragile to begin with, precious few specimens of Mr. Terp's brash couture remain. Pop-topping has joined scrimshaw as a vanished American craft.

PROFESSIONAL WRESTLING

Professional wrestling is melodrama with muscles. It is less a test of athletic skill than it is a giddy morality play in which good guys whop the stuffings out of bad guys, something that doesn't happen often enough in the real world. The script is simple and unchanging: The bad guys cheat, but the good guys win.

Lest there be any confusion, professional wrestling has nothing to do with Greco-Roman wrestling—a real sport with real rules and a history going back to the emperor Commodus, who claimed to be the incarnation of Hercules and loved to wrestle both humans and wild animals in public. Many countries have a wrestling tradition, from Japan's sumo to the legendary strong men of Russia, India, and Turkey; but no contest based on mere brawn and skill could possibly approach professional wrestling—booked into most arenas as an "athletic exhibition"—in boorishness, flimflam, burlesque, and all-around bad taste.

Before television, wrestling wasn't exactly respectable, but it did have a certain athletic cachet as a kind of poor man's boxing; and it seems that opponents sometimes actually went into the ring not knowing how the match would end. It was hugely popular in many parts of the country, especially in cities with big populations of immigrants, who could root for grapplers of

ZUMA—Man from Mars
SEPTEMBER 2, 1950

their own ethnic group. As early as 1908 a crowd of ten thousand people came to Chicago's Dexter Park Pavilion to watch Frank Gotch take the heavyweight title from George Hackenschmidt. Hackenschmidt was a by-the-rules wrestler from Europe; Gotch was a farm boy from Iowa, known for strangleholds, head butts, and eye pokes, as well as for a body so oiled up that no opponent could grasp him.

The first televised wrestling matches came out of Los Angeles's Olympic Auditorium in 1945. The programs were so well received that within a few years it was possible in Los Angeles, and in most American cities, to watch live pro wrestling on television every night of the week. Television made wrestling an American obsession; and wrestling was the reason many people bought their first television sets. It was not unusual in the late forties for appliance stores to display new TV sets in their windows with pictures of pro wrestlers pasted on the screen. One wrestler in particular captured the public's fancy. He was a villain, an odious fop who demanded the ring be sprayed with perfume before he set foot in it. His name was Gorgeous George.

George Wagner was just another ring nobody until he reached for the bleach bottle and transformed himself into Gorgeous George, "the Human Orchid," affecting a platinum page-boy hairdo and a satin-and-lace wardrobe designed to

GORGEOUS GEORGE
MAY 20, 1950

drive the blue-collar Blutos in the audience mad with rage. George was the greatest bad guy in ring history, a heel fans loved to hate, and wrestling's first nationally known celebrity. He cheated, he sniveled and begged for mercy when hurt, he cried when opponents mussed his hair, and he carried a little mirror into the ring so he could periodically gaze at himself and primp.

Outside the ring he stayed in character. When he met a lady, he gave her his famous Gorgeous George kiss, in which he would lift her hand, chivalrously bend down to kiss it, but reconsider at the last moment and kiss his own instead. When he went into turkey farming to supplement his ring salary, he dyed his turkeys lavender and installed lavender velvet curtains in their lavender cages. At the 1951 National Turkey Show, he brought his valet, who as always was dressed in formal attire, to spray the birds every two minutes with his favorite scent, Chanel Number 10. ("Why be half-safe?" George said.)

In Gorgeous George's wake came throngs of other peroxide skunks such as Nature Boy Buddy Rhodes, Freddie Blassie, Johnny Valentine, and this year's model, Ric Flair, but few have equaled George's virtuoso showmanship. It was he who was the first to fully realize that wrestling—especially wrestling on television—was show business, not athletics. There was another important lesson wrestlers learned from

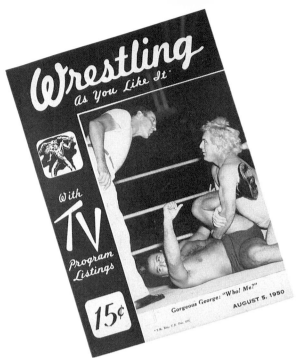

Gorgeous George: "Who! Me?" AUGUST 5, 1950

Gorgeous George: It's the villains that make it exciting. "It's hard for customers to work up a fever week after week cheering some nice guy," said former ring villain George Lenihan in the book *Whatever Happened to Gorgeous George?* "But the world never seems to run out of boos."

Boo though they may, fans have always loved the bad guys more than the "baby faces" (wrestling's terms for heroes) because the point of wrestling is to see the bad guys be bad, then get their comeuppance. For this plot to work well the bad guys have to be *hugely* bad—like 601-pound Haystacks Calhoun, who wrestled in a pair of overalls and delighted in turning opponents into "human pancakes" by jumping off the ropes and landing on them. Villains who make the ring into a little geopolitical morality play are especially delicious to hate, and as the times change, so do they. Cunning sheiks, sneaky orientals, drug-crazed hippies, mean hillbillies, highfalutin noblemen, and mad Russians have all been cast as the loathsome brute of the moment in the ring. And of course there have always been hateful slews of monocle-wearing, goose-stepping Germans such as Baron Fritz Von Raschke and the sneaky Count Zuppie. Some bad guys have regional followings. Fidel Castillo, the cigar-chomping commie, was hugely popular (i.e., hated) in any city with Cuban immigrants.

Recent wrestling rats have included the Iron Sheik, who wears a burnoose and a sour

Mildred Burke—World's Champion Wrestler
SEPTEMBER 9, 1950

expression; Preacher Man, who sobs bogus tears of piety like Jimmy Swaggart; and an overweight Elvis clone called the Honky Tonk Man, complete with an evil manager known as "the Colonel" in tow. Today, most of wrestling's good guys started as bad guys and earned their tough reputations when they were hateful. Conversely, it often happens that good guys who get too boring have a change of character and become evil. Or they remake their identities completely by turning into masked unknowns or bandage-swathed mummies.

Other than villainy, the thing that can make a wrestler famous is deformity. Nearly all pro wrestlers have abnormal bodies—overmuscled or obese—but certain freakish body types have always done especially well in the profession. Uglies like the Swedish Angel, the French Angel, and the Polish Angel ("Old Prune Head")—all sufferers of the feature-distorting disease acromegaly—were popular ring attractions for years, as were grotesquely fat boys such as Man Mountain Dean, the Blimp, and Hillbilly Jim. Midgets such as Sky Low Low and Lord Clayton Little-brook, and oversized oddballs like Andre the Giant, Baba the Giant, and the latest sensation, Kamala the Ugandan Giant, have always been fan favorites.

Although it would seem that there was no level of taste beneath professional wrestling, it did take some time for female wrestlers to be fully accepted into the ring. "Men shouldn't be the only ones allowed to get hurt," argued female wrestler Betty Niccoli, and by the mid-fifties "ladies' wrestling" was part of the program nearly everywhere (it wasn't legal in New York until 1972). Recently, Sylvester Stallone's mother, Jacqueline, has been promoting a new breed of women wrestlers, known as the GLOW girls (Golden Ladies of Wrestling), for syndicated television. GLOW girls slam each other in the breadbasket wearing scanty outfits that provide full views of their well-muscled buttocks.

In the early eighties, a remarkable thing happened to professional wrestling. For a short time it made the leap from being the favorite freak show of adenoidal fourteen-year-olds, lowbrows, and demented grandmas to being culturally fashionable. The catalyst was an event known as the "Rock 'n' Wrestling Connection," a smart piece of music-video merchandising that meshed the colorful personalities of rock star Cyndi Lauper ("Girls Just Want to Have Fun") with ring rats like Captain Lou Albano and the Fabulous Moola. Rock and wrestling seemed to be a perfect marriage: both rude, both loud, both about pomp and attitude.

But rock fans, new to wrestling, did not cotton to the bloated middle-aged physiques of veteran wrestlers such as Dusty ("the American Dream") Rhodes and Greg Valentine. No one in rock and roll, except maybe guitarist Leslie West, was that fat. So wrestling promoters tapped for stardom a tower of muscle from Venice, California, named Hulk Hogan. A body builder, "the Hulkster" was closer in looks to Arnold Schwarzenegger than to a load of suet in trunks. He started as a villain, made an appearance in *Rocky III*, then turned virtuous and was a sensation as wrestling's new Golden Boy. His superhero image inspired not only a line of kiddie toys but a cartoon on Saturday-morning TV. Meanwhile, jaded rock fans have drifted away from wrestling as the fad of the moment, leaving it once again to the loving embrace of its addlepated followers.

RECLINING CHAIRS

When Edward Knabusch and Edwin Shoemaker started the Kna-Shoe Company in Monroe, Michigan, in the 1920s, they had bad luck right away. Everybody who heard them say the name of their business thought they manufactured new shoes. "Kna-Shoe" was scrapped in favor of Floral City Furniture Company. In 1927, the two cousins had what would turn out to be the best idea of their lives: a chair with a seat that moved forward as the back reclined.

Like the company name, the flexible chair wasn't exactly right at first. As designed by Mr. Knabusch and built by Mr. Shoemaker, it was a Spartan piece of lawn furniture made of hard wood slats—a sales dud until Arthur Richardson, a buyer from the Lions Store of Toledo, Ohio, said he might be able to sell jointed chairs if they had upholstery. The two Eds returned to the

workshop in Monroe, where they garnished their simple, functional design with a padded seat and backrest, fringed manchettes, ornamental feet, and Victorian floral-patterned fabric. The reclining easy chair, every modern home's most comfortable place to loaf, was born. A new level of consciousness, or, more accurately, semiconsciousness, was born, too: the blissful, slack-jawed stupefaction so suitable for listening to the radio (then) or watching television (now).

The La-Z-Boy Chair Company (renamed in the late forties) was not alone in its quest to put American buttocks in a fitting seat. In the thirties, a tinkerer named Dr. Anton Lorenz had come up with a scientific-seeming concept for a chair that held its occupant in the "floating on water" position: head back, legs up, arms held limp by

the sides, the whole body stretched out in such a way that no muscle was taxed. Lying this way, Dr. Lorenz contended, was the best way to alleviate stress. His project came to fruition when he met Edward Barcalo. Barcalo was a visionary man, known as "the Father of the Coffee Break" since 1902, when he first allowed employees at his Buffalo, New York, bedding factory to take a mid-morning recess. In furniture circles, he was also known as the father of the New York State Bedding Law (1933), which required all mattresses to be tagged with dire warnings, called Law Labels, about what will happen to you if you tear one off. In 1941, Barcalo licensed Dr. Lorenz's design, and soon he sired yet another modern wonder, the BarcaLounger.

After World War II the pursuit of comfort became an ambition at least as driving as good health. Many Americans heading for the suburbs aspired to dream homes with cozy, wood-paneled dens; and in those dens, of course, there would be a chair appropriate for the man of the house: a big, soft one where he could smoke his pipe and pet his dog and spend each evening reading the sports pages. BarcaLoungers sold so well that the trademarked name became many people's generic term for any chair that reclined, rocked, and pivoted or massaged its occupant. Contour, Inc. ("the relaxing miracle"), patented a similar but nonarticulated design, eventually adding "Viveration" (a vibrating motor) and "Thermonic Heat" and offering Contour Cuddler Chairs big enough for two, which they now advertise as using "the same basic design used by space engineers when designing seating to support our Astronauts for days in space!" By the fifties, dozens of low-grade manufacturers were counterfeiting the medically inspired BarcaLounger and the well-built La-Z-Boy, offering hideous vibrating "TV recliners" in shades of chartreuse and metal-flake bronze, stuffed with rubberized hair and slipcovered in easy-wipe Vinelle or acetate. As a result, reclining chairs—which had begun as a vaguely therapeutic curiosity—developed an indelible reputation as the sign of an uncouth home.

Their image problem was inevitable: With their heavy padding and big, blocky frames (to conceal the mechanism), recliners look oafish—suitable, at best, for the rumpus room in the basement, certainly not for company. Besides, etiquette demands that polite people sit upright while in the company of others. Lying flat on one's back in the living room, or even tilted forty-five degrees with one's feet raised in the direction of everyone else present, is good form only for invalids or babies.

La-Z-Boy and BarcaLounger have struggled tirelessly to elevate the reputation of what the furniture industry knows as "motion chairs" from their ignominious status as uncouth den-and-rec-room furniture. In its crusade for respectability, La-Z-Boy hired celebrities known for being relaxed to be company spokespeople, including Bing Crosby, Joe Namath, and Jim Backus as Mr. Magoo. Backus recorded fifteen thousand La-Z-Boy commercials—a feat listed in *The Guinness Book of World Records*. In the sixties, BarcaLounger gave the ugliness dilemma to Ramond Loewy, the esteemed industrial designer responsible for the Studebaker Starliter Coupe, and Dorothy Draper ("the Grande Dame of interior designers," according to company literature). The result was a line of "designer recliners": svelte and fashionable, so like a normal chair that guests of delicate sensibilities never needed know there was a reclining chair in the room.

BarcaLoungers are available today in four different varieties: the classic Lounger, the Wall Lounger (which can be positioned within three and a half inches of the wall), the Rocker Recliner (with Swivel Option), and the Low Profile Lounger with Pop-Up Headrest. La-Z-Boy has become the third-biggest furniture manufacturer in America, offering over one hundred models, including Reclina-Rockers, La-Z-Boy Rockers ("the chair that breaks its back for you"), La-Z-Sleepers, Lectra-Loungers, and Motion-Modular groups that can fill a living room with sumptuous banks of furniture that allow whole groups of families and even friends to lie in formation—feet up, mouths agape, remote control at the ready.

Edward Knabusch,
Edwin Shoemaker, and
the first La-Z-Boy recliner

RICKIE TICKIE STICKIES

Flower power blossomed in 1967. Flowers were symbols of niceness and happiness and sunshiny good cheer. Hippies wore flowers in their hair and painted them on their bodies and on their vans as their way of announcing to the world that they were joyful people who believed in peace. Don Kracke, a Los Angeles inventor, was driving along a freeway one day when he saw three cars driven by hippies one after another, each decorated with flowers. The designs were scrawly and amateurish, but they made Kracke smile; and he noticed other drivers smiling, too. Kracke was so inspired that he went home and invented Rickie Tickie Stickies: brightly colored daisies made of vinyl so flexible and adhesive that you could slap them onto nearly anything and they would stick forever.

Kracke began selling his invention in August, giving it a silly name as his own personal protest against the harsh, one-syllable names used by the big corporations that manufacture detergents (Fab, Duz, etc.). The Kracke family stuck Rickie Tickie Stickies on their station wagon, their garbage can, and their mailbox. Neighbors' kids appeared at the Krackes' door wanting some for themselves. And much to the surprise of Kracke (who had assumed Rickie Tickie Stickies would be bought only by the hippie fringe), the kids' mothers wanted them, too—for their own station wagons, for the refrigerator, to enliven the brown wood paneling in the den, and to give their garage doors a clever sixties look.

By mid-1968, Rickie Tickie Stickies were selling at a rate of more than a million a week, in America and throughout the world. Knock-off "Funky Flowers," available in shades of Mellow Yellow and Out of Sight White, entreated buyers to "turn on with mini-flower power!" Artist Peter Max sold psychedelic stick-on fluorescent flowers, birds, and butterflies called "the Cosmic Spring Group" at the astronomical price of $9.95 per set. (Rickie Tickie Stickies went for twenty-five cents apiece.) *Cosmopolitan* magazine advised readers with decrepit old bathrooms that Rickie Tickie Stickies were the cheapest and most adorable way to brighten up tubs and sinks suffering from unsightly cracks or worn-out enamel.

And that is the place where Rickie Tickie Stickies got stuck in the time warp: as a slapdash patch for disguising unsightly bathroom fixtures. Hippies and flower power faded from popularity, as did the smiles automatically generated in 1967 by the sight of a flower stuck on a car or mailbox; but stick-on bathtub patches at twenty-five cents apiece were just too practical an idea to go the way of Nehru jackets and love beads. It required only a small stretch of the imagination to design nonskid appliqués, thereby giving them safety value as well as beauty. Adhesive cheerfulness with that bright-as-a-daisy sixties spirit is still available in low-rent discount stores and at flea markets everywhere. And millions of aging bathtubs around the world are stuck with faded white Rickie Tickie Stickies that no amount of scrubbing can remove.

After making it into a multimillion-dollar business, Don Kracke sold Rickie Tickie Stickies, Inc., but went on to distinguish himself as the marketer of Snappy Patches (for ironing on blue jeans), Parent Protest Posters (like hippie posters but reversed—featuring slogans such as ''Mom Wants You to Clean Up Your Room''), the Little Lumpsie Doll, and the Neat Garage (a system of modular, prefabricated interlocking storage cabinets designed to hang on walls). In 1977 he revealed the secrets of his success in a book called *How to Turn Your Idea into a Million Dollars,* which concluded with these encouraging words: ''It *can* be done. You *can* have a million-dollar idea. Do it! Get out there and be another Gary Dahl.'' (Gary Dahl is the man who invented the Pet Rock.)

ROLLER DERBY

Roller Derby combines the hysteria of professional wrestling with the ferocious team spirit of ice hockey and the thrill of seeing athletic women and men on roller skates beat one another up. It is fast and fierce, and although it has rules against tripping, punching, head blocks with elbows, and straight-arm face smashing, the fun of a game comes when the rules are broken: Blood flows, referees are mercilessly kicked and battered, players scream at each other, punch it out, ''eat track'' (have their face smashed onto the wood boards and their head stomped with a skate-shod foot), and get carried away on stretchers.

The game is played by two teams of five players on an oval track, each team bunched together in a pack. To score points a team starts a ''jam,'' which means sending its swiftest skater up ahead of the pack in an attempt to pass members of the other team. For every one passed, one point is earned. Five points is a ''grand slam.'' No jam can last more than ninety seconds. Defense is everything. To prevent the other team's jammer from passing, skaters use knee checks, head slams, elbows in the solar plexus, and flying cross-body dunks, all while catapulting around the oval track at speeds up to thirty miles per hour.

Roller Derby shares the honor of being one of only three sports truly native to the U.S.A. (Baseball and volleyball are the other two.) It began as a variation of the roller-skating marathons of the depression, which were like dance marathons except that participants skated around tracks until they dropped. To spice up the action, spectators placed bets on skaters for individual laps; and the skaters, who often had a piece of the action, used violence to keep others on the track from getting ahead. In 1935, a Chicagoan named Leo Seltzer, who had promoted walkathons emceed by the then-unknown Red Skelton, invented Roller Derby. He trademarked the name and organized teams that traveled by bus from city to city in the Midwest, slugging it out each night until the climactic championship games in Chicago at the end of the summer.

Roller skating suffered from boot and skate shortages during World War II, and so did Roller Derby; but when the war was over, skating's golden days began. Plush new rinks were built around the country. Guy Lombardo recorded ''The Roller Skating Song.'' Mickey Rooney starred in the 1950 Roller Derby movie, *Fireball*. On opening night of the Roller Derby World Series in 1950, 16,234 customers packed Madison Square Garden. Like bowling and wrestling, Roller Derby was basking in fame won on television. It was perfect for TV—cheap to produce, with plenty of thrills, it starred take-charge players that sedentary television viewers could deify as gods. The prime-time program ''Roller Derby,'' given extra punch by Ken Nydell's rousing commentary, became the most popular show on ABC's schedule in 1950—broadcast three nights a week.

Television made household names out of track superstars such as Anne Calvello (who dyed her hair and painted her fingernails to match her uniform and had five lion tattoos, three visible when she was uniformed), bad boy Bob Woodberry (who was famous as the target of fans' chairs), Sandy (''Watch my elbows!'') Dunn, Charlie (''Mr. Roller Derby'') O'Connell, and Bob

(''the Bald Eagle'') Hein, who although injury prone was known as one of the meanest men on skates. The game's greatest star was Joanie Weston of the Bombers, a big, jut-jawed blond bombshell beloved by fans because she took no crap from anyone, especially not from her archrival, Marge Laszlo, a former model who was an absolute terror on the track.

There was always something deliciously déclassé about the antics of Roller Derby (''as much a piece of Americana as aluminum-sided diners and pink lawn flamingos,'' proclaimed New York's *Village Voice*). In the early seventies, when the media suddenly became fascinated by the grotesqueries of middle America—in TV's ''All in the Family'' and the movie *Joe*, for example— Roller Derby was ripe for a major leap in status. Raquel Welch starred in *Kansas City Bomber*, playing a derby-demon sex goddess. James Caan played ''Jonathan E.'' in the futuristic *Rollerball*, which envisioned Roller Derby remade into a murderously violent sport featuring motorcycles as well as skates. Jerry Seltzer, Leo's son, produced a cinema-verité movie, *Derby*, about a young player (Mike Snell) trying to break into the game. Somehow, none of these efforts was able to tap into the raw frenzy of the real thing, which continued to attract big crowds and big TV ratings.

After its peak in the early seventies, Roller Derby plummeted in popularity. Blaming falling attendance on the gas shortage and stung by the failure of *Derby*, Leo Seltzer shut down the original Roller Derby circuit in 1973. The gauntlet was taken up by a group called the International Roller Skating League (the IRSL), who tried to revive interest by fielding midget teams and staging games refereed by clowns. Many of the top players sat out the shenanigans in disgust. Joanie Weston resigned; Judy Arnold, one of the most beloved derby stars, hung up her number— but not her skates—to become ''the Original Holy Roller,'' an evangelist who skates among the pews while delivering her sermon. ''Today's game has gone stale,'' mourned Joseph Valerio

ROMANCE AND PAIN ON THE BANKED TRACK

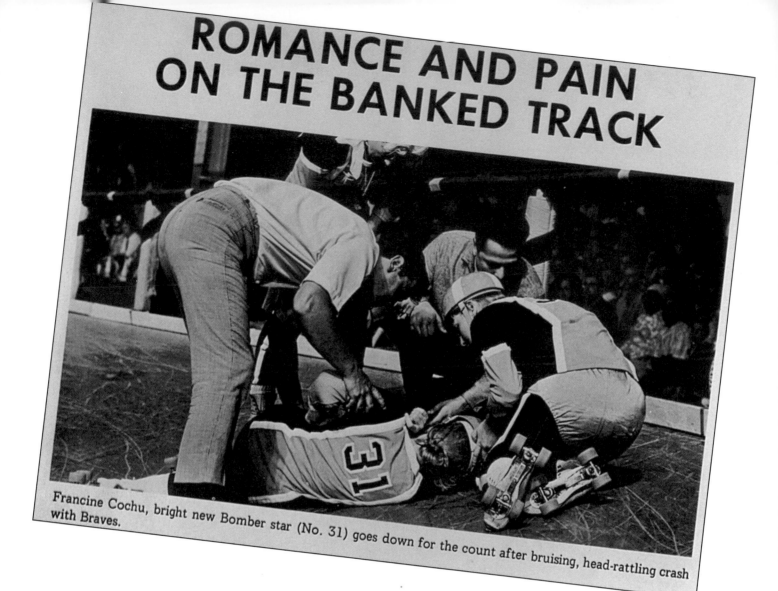

Francine Cochu, bright new Bomber star (No. 31) goes down for the count after bruising, head-rattling crash with Braves.

of the New York *Post* in 1975, observing that the thirteen thousand fans who came to see Roller Derby at Madison Square Garden came ''out of curiosity rather than religiosity. And they come only once a year.''

Encouraged by the fabulous successes of professional wrestling, Roller Derby tried but failed to stage a comeback in the eighties as ''Rollermania'' (named after ''Wrestlemania''). It offered such alluring spectacles as wheel-to-wheel full-contact grudge-match races and plenty of prematch hype, bluster, threats, and pushing and shoving among the combatants. Even golden girl Joanie Weston put aside her work as an embroidery-supply salesperson to rejoin the sport as captain of the

Bay Bombers and dean of the world's only Roller Derby training school in Hayward, California. Tuition at Ms. Weston's school is four dollars per lesson; the faculty includes Jackie (''Super Gnat'') Garello; and lessons are given in falling, slamming, elbowing, and ducking.

Modern-day Roller Derby stars include the T-Birds' gorgeous Darlene Langlois de la Chapelle, a 36-25-36 blonde known for her hard-hitting hips, and 367-pound Robert (''the Icebox'') Smith, who can eat twenty-four Big Macs and four tacos in a single sitting and who explained his love of the sport by saying, ''I strive for pain—mine or anybody else's.''

RONCO

Late one Friday in Chicago in 1964, sleepy television viewers watched a miracle. As the programming day neared its end, their screens filled with salad. "It slices, it dices, it chops, it juliennes!" ranted a burp-gun voice as a white plastic canister gobbled up whole vegetables and extruded vegetable shreds. The voice didn't stop for breath as the food mounded up in piles: ". . . French fries, carrot sticks, pepper red, pepper green, onion thin, onion chopped (don't cry!); shave slaw; snip a radish; cut a cuke. Can you beat these beets?" The miracle was the Veg-O-Matic food slicer, and the most miraculous thing about it was, according to the frenzied voice, "IT REALLY WORKS!"

So began a new era in hard-sell television advertising. Produced for $550 and broadcast during desolate TV time bought for $7.50 per minute, the stupefying commercial launched the sale of nine million Veg-O-Matics. Its producer, the Ronco company, hollered through the next twenty years selling such equally amazing household contraptions as Steam-A-Way (no more wrinkles, no more dry-cleaning bills!), Miracle Broom, Miracle Sander, Bagel Cutter, Record Vacuum, Sit-On-Trash Compactor, Cellutrol+ ("Here's beautiful help for buttocks!"), Glass Froster ("Frosted drinks anywhere!"), Seal-A-Meal, Hula-Hoe ("The weeder with a wiggle"), Electric Whisk (doubles as a flashlight), London Aire Hosiery (which was assailed on camera by Brillo pads and nail files, but stayed run-free), Mr. Dentist ("Clean your teeth the professional way"), and the immensely popular Mr. Microphone ("Put your voice on the radio") as well as Mr. Microphone II (the "Executive Model," in stereo).

Ronco's hyperthyroid sales pitch was imitated by many companies, including Krazy Glue and hundreds of special TV record offerers; and many of its products were copied by other manufacturers (Ronco claims to have been the first to sell hosiery with panties attached, as well as Teflon frying pans); but there was a wry style to its low-budget advertising and a

demoniac genius to the best of its products that established Ronco as the undisputed king of thunderbolt salesmanship. In the early days, Ronco made television viewers privy to a special deal, assuring them that the products were "not available in stores." By 1984, when Ronco declared bankruptcy after taking a bath with its CleanAire machine, the gadgets were familiar sights on shelves of job lot outlets and down-market department stores, where they were announced with the exclamatory sign "AS SEEN ON TV!"

Ron Popeil, the brains behind the flying flapdoodle, started his illustrious career as a teenage pitchman for Popeil Brothers, an appliance company founded in 1939 by his father and uncle. Working the crowds in Chicago's

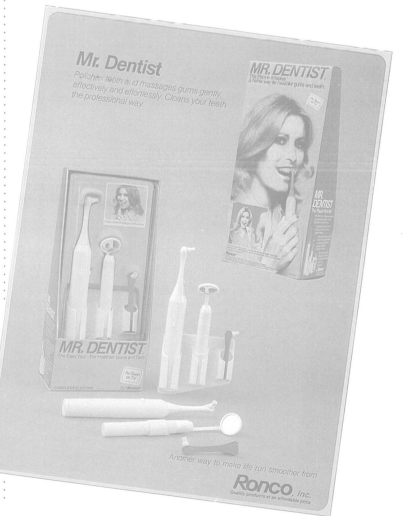

269

outdoor Maxwell Street market and at state fairs, he did stand-up demonstrations of Popeil Brothers' Chop-O-Matic, Mince-O-Matic, and Dial-O-Matic—all precursors of the Veg-O-Matic. "My hands always smelled like onions," he recalled. Beets were part of every demonstration, so that when he cut a finger—as he inevitably did chopping fifty pounds of onions a day—he could use the beet juice to camouflage his blood. A Chicago newspaper, observing him sell Chop-O-Matics in a local Woolworth's, called the young Popeil "a silver-tongued orator."

Before he formed Ronco in 1964 to market the Veg-O-Matic on TV, there had been plenty of late-night television ads for miracle slicers/dicers/choppers. But Popeil didn't have the money to buy fifteen minutes as the other companies did. So he compressed his entire sales pitch down to thirty- and sixty-second volleys, editing the sound tracks to cut out dead space between phrases and mechanically speeding up his voice until it verged on Mickey Mouse's pitch. "You have to introduce a product, show how a problem exists without the product, show how the problem is alleviated by the product, tell the price and how to get it—all in thirty seconds," he said.

Problem solving was the key to Ronco's success; most Ronco products were devised because Ron Popeil found himself facing a problem for which there was no known solution. "The problem with buttons is they always fall off," he said, explaining the invention of Buttoneer, "the five-second button attacher." When he got a grease burn cooking bacon, he came up with the idea for Ronco's Spatter Screen. When his father, Sam Popeil, got poked in the eye by a friend's fishing pole, Popeil's compact Pocket Fisherman was the logical result. (Two million Pocket Fishermen were sold within a year of their introduction in 1973.)

The problems solved by Ronco products are not always obvious. For instance, the French toast problem: As a child, Ron Popeil hated the albumen in eggs, especially when an imperfectly scrambled egg meant that there might be streaks

of runny egg white sticking to a piece of his French toast. So as an adult, he created the Inside-the-Shell Egg Scrambler, a small cup with a bent needle sticking out. Impale a raw egg on the needle, turn on the machine, and the insides are thoroughly scrambled in just five seconds. "You are rid of the slimy aspect of the egg!" Popeil exulted to a crowd while demonstrating the product in Chicago in 1984. When doubting Thomases in the audience interrupted his sales pitch by asking why it wouldn't be just as easy to scramble an egg with a fork or whisk, Popeil shot back a question no one could answer: "How else are you going to get a hard-boiled egg with a perfectly blended yolk and white?"

See also **HOME SHOPPING NETWORK**

SHAG RUGS

A shag rug has cut pile two to three inches deep, made of twisty, pill-resistant nylon or polyester strands that flop into organic sculptural effects when walked on. When they were popularized in the fifties and sixties, shag rugs were not explicitly sold as dirt repositories; but their ability to secret vast amounts of dust, hair, crumbs, and fingernail clippings proved to be the secret of their success. Sure, they were kinky fun because of the exaggerated pile and the wacky colors they came in; but the really good part was that you never had to clean them. "Shaggy texture Camineau has long, cut loops that give an informal appearance and conceal dirt well," advised Ray and Sarah Faulkner in their book *Inside Today's Home*, first published in 1954 before the term "shag rug" was known, and before shags were made of slippery synthetic fibers.

Prior to the development of the cheap shag rug, long-pile carpet was a soigné novelty, particularly in the form of wavy-textured throw rugs in streamlined homes. Many fluffy carpets had a Scandanavian quality, as in the popular long-haired Finnish "rya rugs" that decorators hung on walls to provide a fuzzy contrast to sleek teak and low-slung Danish modern furniture. The *Color Guide to Home Decorating*, published in 1956, showed an ideal contemporary bedroom in which a satin-grained blond wood desk and smooth, natural wood floor are brought together with a rough brick wall and an avocado plant by the use of a hairy green scatter rug. The *Better Homes and Gardens Decorating Book* (1956) showed a wood-floored living-dining room done all in shades of bronze, green, and gold, including what is described as a "shaggy textured rug to pick up the colors of the scheme." These weren't yet called shag rugs, and they were made of natural fibers in tasteful colors, but they suggest how long carpet pile was growing.

At Monarch Carpet Mills in Dalton, Georgia, which has specialized in throw rugs since 1947, advances in the use of nylon and polypropylene and in vulcanized backing in the fifties made inexpensive twist-pile "scatter rugs" available for use as an accent for bedrooms and rumpus rooms.

And yet even as it became more affordable, thanks to synthetic fibers and automated tufting machines, all carpeting retained an aura of luxury; the more of it there was, the more luxurious a setting seemed. *Home Decorating Trends* (1960) announced that the trend was "towards greater depth and density of pile—factors that make for increased richness." The book marveled at "piles that are one, two and even three inches high!"

Not only was carpet getting longer, but it was being put places no carpet had ever been before. It was a bold and sybaritic decorating statement to carpet a conversation pit or a kitchen floor. "Interior designers have taken to cutting a lot of capers with carpet, and these are showing up in all the better places," exulted Dorothy Wagner's 1967 book, *What You Should Know About Carpet*, marveling at the dazzling modernity of whole walls that are extensions of the carpet on the floor and "a charming sleeping alcove completely lined in carpet—quite provocative!" In 1963, the Borg Frickson Corporation astonished the bathware business by introducing a bath scale with a platform covered with a long-pile "fur fabric" shag.

All of these developments set the stage for the shag rug explosion of the late sixties. Just about the time men's hair went wild, shag rugs did, too, sprouting long and unkempt in groovy colors. Unlike close-cropped level loops and formally sculpted multilevel tip-sheared carpets, shags were *liberated!* You could roll around on them and squish bare toes among the strands. They expressed a floppy joie de vivre, like furry sheepdogs and mop-top Beatles (in fact, proper shag rug care required regular combing with a coarse-tined rake); they were fun and fuzzy and friendly and free. In 1967, Sears devoted a page of its fall and winter catalogue to the "sumptuous shag attention-getter," available for as low as $4.99 per square yard (good carpet was $10.49), rejoicing, "The more it's mussed up, the better it looks!"

Planning Your Bathroom, published in 1968, recommended shag rugs for a "living look" in a luxury bath, suggesting also that "bathroom sounds, often embarrassing, can be confined within bath walls in several simple ways.'' Because thick shag rugs were terrific soundproofers, they appeared not only in bathrooms but stapled to the walls of makeshift recording studios and rehearsal garages for amateur bands —where their decrepit remains can occasionally still be found today. The ability of shag rugs to disguise dirt ensured also that they became a favored material for covering motel floors; now, an aging shag rug, with years of who-knows-what fallen deep into its nap, is surely one of the most horrific sights to encounter when checking into a room.

By the early seventies, shag rugs and fun furs were both at the peak of popularity. Each in its own way was part of the general infatuation with wide, distended, elongated shapes (sideburns, bell bottoms, platform shoes). In fact, in some cases it was impossible to differentiate between a shag rug and a fun fur. For toilet-seat covers and bathroom hampers, for hirsute vests and boot trim, or for covering the dashboard of a custom van, a few hanks of polyester shag rug were every bit as serviceable as (and likely more colorful than) Glenarctic hi-pile imitation llama fur. Even Charles Manson used shag rugs to soften the surfaces on his armor-plated dune buggy, so when the revolution came, he and his family of psychopaths could shoot it out with the pigs in comfort.

Because it demonstrated a sense of exaggerated luxury, shag was the covering of choice in the homes of sybarites—on floors, and stairs, running up wood-paneled walls, and affixed to the sides of basement cocktail counters. Install enough shag rug, and it was practically inevitable that you (and your inamorata) would soon wind up rolling around with sensuous abandon among the thick pile. One of the most profligate of all pleasure seekers,

Elvis Presley, relished shag rugs so much he installed them (along with fake fur) throughout Graceland: bright red shag in the bedroom, fluffy white flotakis (like the pelt of some Arctic llama) in the halls, olive green on the floor, walls, and ceiling in the Jungle Room. The King's taste for voluptuous surroundings, however, may have been a dangerous one. His stepbrother, Rickey Stanley, one of the last people to see him alive, is certain it was a shag rug that killed him. Elvis had an especially sumptuous one on the floor of his bathroom. The night he died, Stanley suggests, Elvis was sitting on the toilet, he dozed off, fell forward off the seat, and landed face-first in the rug, which was so thick it smothered him to death.

Shag rugs were available in all the up-to-the-minute colors: the murky geological hues of the seventies, such as avocado and copper-bronze, as well as leftover yellows, reds, and pinks from the pop-op sixties. ''Gold is the color of the sun and probably the happiest color of all,'' advised *What You Should Know About Your Carpet*. Sears shag rugs were available in fifteen colors, including Blue Rhapsody, Inca Gold, and White Satin.

As awful as all those hues may have been when they were new, years of wear and tear and accumulated grime had a devastating effect on them. The greens and blues faded to sickly umber. Pure white flotakis soon turned from lustrous snowy white to dingy. And the strands of pile, once so gaily mussed and tangled, got mashed down onto the backing like a million little polyester worms flattened on a rubber road. Worst of all, an old shag rug can never truly be called clean. If it is small enough you can put it in a washing machine, or you can pressure-squirt it with a carpet cleaner; but you will never know for sure if those repulsive, twisted cords have given up the filth they have accumulated in the many years that have passed since the rug was fashionable.

See also **FAKE FUR**

SMOKY MOUNTAINS

The last human home owner in the Smoky Mountains died in 1984 at the age of ninety-five. Lem Ownby was born in the Smokies and was one of a few mountain people who refused to sell their family land when the government began buying up the mountains in 1934 to turn them into the Great Smoky Mountains National Park—800 square miles of majestic forest, blazing azaleas and rhododendron, meadows carpeted with wildflowers, and purple mountains' majesty.

Now that Mr. Ownby is gone, the Smokies have reverted to what they were hundreds of years ago, before the settlers came, with the added distinction of being graced by the world's largest cuckoo clock, Ripley's Believe It or Not Museum (with a replica of Christopher Columbus's *Santa Maria* made entirely of chicken bones); Ronald Reagan in wax; Sheriff Buford *(Walking Tall)* Pusser's charred death car; Dolly Parton's four-hundred-acre Dollywood theme park; a three-dimensional rendering of Leonardo da Vinci's *The Last Supper,* complete with swelling chorale music and banqueting sound effects; the Dixie Stampede Dinner Theater (''Non-Stop Action and Non-Stop Eating''), in which spectators from the North and the South sit on opposite sides of the arena where pigs race and cowboys ride Brahman bulls; an exhibit of Elvis Presley's bathroom amenities, including electric razor and fur-covered scale; and the largest concentration of factory outlet stores in Tennessee.

Everything any tourist ever wanted is on the rim of the Smokies. Cherokee, North Carolina, at the southern entrance of the park, and Gatlinburg

and Pigeon Forge on the Tennessee side have more things to do and buy than any other tourist attraction in America.

Route 441, which runs between the towns, is the best place to see nature in the raw, without so much as a fudge shop, water slide, or miniature golf course to obstruct the view. You will have vast amounts of time to appreciate the great outdoors as you drive through, because on any nice day, the line of cars, vans, recreational vehicles, and touring motorcycle gangs clogging Route 441 through the verdant forest is bumper-to-bumper, seldom allowing speeds greater than 10 miles per hour. There are many areas for naturalists to pull off the road and (if a parking space can be found) enjoy the sight of people taking pictures of trees. For those who don't know what to take a picture of, Mountaineer Photo Adventures offers a guide service that leads aspiring shutterbugs to the most scenic spots and points them in the right direction.

Despite signs warning of bears, it is not likely that you will encounter one anywhere near the road or hiking trails now that Great Smoky Mountains Park garbage cans have been outfitted with bear-proof lids. Don't despair, though, if it's bear you've come to see; because in the towns on either side of the park there are bears galore, not only at Chief Saunooke's Bear Park in Cherokee (which boasts an oil painting of Victor the Rasslin' Bear posing with Ed Sullivan) and Ober Gatlinburg's Municipal Bear Habitat but also in many roadside entrepreneurs' exhibits of single adult grizzlies and cubs, panting on hot concrete floors in pits and cages, where their keepers have trained them to get up and dance on command, and where paying customers can throw things at them without fear of being mauled. Another attraction for people who like to see incarcerated animals is Cherokee's "Bird Brain," where chickens and ducks in glass boxes are made to hop and pound their beaks on miniature piano keys whenever customers put coins in slots.

While a good many of the souvenirs to be bought and things to be seen in the Smokies can also be found around such other well-worked natural wonders as the Wisconsin Dells and Old Faithful, the Smoky Mountains attain a special level of gaucheness because they market not just nature but a loutish, ersatz version of bumpkin life. The place to get the most concentrated dose is the immense Hillbilly Village and Craft Center, where the merchandise includes hillbilly fudge and taffy, hillbilly hand-dipped candles and freshly blown glass, and hillbilly whoopee cushions and miniature cedar outhouses for desk and den.

At the southern entrance to the park, it's Indians, not hillbillies, who are the big draw. Centuries ago Cherokees named the Smoky Mountains "the land of a thousand smokes," and in the town of Cherokee, the actual center of a modern reservation, the red men are in full feather. To help visitors feel the injun spirit, Cherokee has dozens of stores (such as the Tom Tom Shop and Pow Wow Shop) selling rubber tomahawks and giant wooden salad tongs, as well as low-priced cigarettes by the carton. It is the place to see the Indian Wax Museum and the live, 130-character *Unto These Hills* drama depicting the entire history of the Cherokee nation. In addition to Indian things, Cherokee is loaded with Christmas merchandise at the Four Seasons Christmas Shop and Santa's Land Village, which are perennially stocked with artificial trees, wreaths, ornaments, and epigrammatical Yuletide samplers. Outside of most of Cherokee's stores stand living Indians, dressed in buckskin fringe and feathered war bonnets, ready to pose with tourists for three dollars per picture, five dollars for two.

See also **DEATH CARS OF FAMOUS PEOPLE; PARTON, DOLLY**

SNO-GLOBES

Like the sunset or a gentle spring rain, a big winter snow can be a memorable, even romantic event. One difference among these natural occurrences is that mankind has figured out a way to neatly package the winter snow and the feelings that come with it, so that anytime you want to see swirling white flakes and think of sleigh bells and a cozy hearth, all you need do is pick up a sno-globe and shake. Sno-globe, snow-dome, water globe, snow shaker: Call it what you will; nearly everybody is familiar with the clear round ball containing a submerged winter scene and enough white particles to create a miniature blizzard on demand.

The traditional sno-globe contains wintry scenes, such as Santa and his reindeer; but souvenir makers' ingenuity being what it is, sno-globes offer many dioramas of less-likely subjects trapped in eternal snowstorms, from pink flamingos to big black mammies and skylines of nearly every city in the world.

The earliest ones, made as paperweights during the 1920s in Germany and in America by the Atlas Crystal Works, were leaded glass spheres set atop cast ceramic bases. They contained small unpainted china figurines of elves and animals associated with Christmas, as well as a Kewpie-doll-type character known as a snowbaby. Atlas also made sno-globes with china renderings of New York's sleek new buildings—Radio City at Rockefeller Center and the Empire State Building—as well as a sno-globe containing the "Statue of Liberty, America's Symbol of Liberty and Freedom."

Visitors to the 1939 New York World's Fair needed keepsakes to remember the occasion; and several manufacturers made sno-globes filled with the fair's emblems, the Trylon and Perisphere. By 1941, when Orson Welles began *Citizen Kane* with a scene in which the dying Charles Foster Kane looks into a sno-globe and recalls his childhood, sno-globes had already become a convenient symbol of cheap sentimentality.

After the war the sno-globe industry began to flourish in both Germany and Italy, each country offering a distinctive style. A German manufacturer named Koziol pioneered a revolutionary change in the original crystal-ball shape by designing the first flat-bottomed sno-globe dome, a style still popular today. Nancy McMichael, sno-globe advisor to *Warman's Americana & Collectibles,* reports that the new design was meant to replicate a winter snow scene as viewed through the back window of a Volkswagen. Italian sno-globes, often with a papal or religious motif, tended to be more ornate, their bases encrusted with sea shells.

American sno-globe manufacturers produced favorite tourist scenes, such as Niagara Falls, the Wisconsin Dells, and the giant redwoods of California; and in the fifties they also

FLORIDA

made sno-globes filled with movie and television stars. Davy Crockett and the Lone Ranger were both available. They were, in fact, identical figures, just wearing different clothes. The Driss Company of Chicago made one globe that featured an American flag in the center of a whirlwind of red, white, and blue snowflakes. Many sno-globes were made as advertising giveaways. The *Warman's* guide lists values for vintage sno-globes such as Crown Termite Control ($35), Jimmy Wilson Jr. Van Lines and Storage Warehouses ($35), and Jell-O ($10).

If you see a new, well-finished sno-globe for sale today, it was probably manufactured in Austria, where they are still made of glass with a tasteful black or white base, sometimes hand-painted. Most sno-globes—the ones sold in roadside souvenir shops—are made in Hong Kong. The ball-on-pedestal shape is increasingly rare, having given way to the flat-bottomed, domed Volkswagen window and the square bottle-on-its-side. Accoutrements, a wholesale novelty company in Seattle, offers several models in the dome style, featuring flamingos or exotic plastic fish. There is also one called TV Waterglobe on a four-inch base, depicting a family sitting on a couch watching a television with rabbit-ear antennas. "Shake it and it snows!" crows the catalogue. "What an extraordinary object it is. You can't live without it." (Be that as it may, Accoutrements will not mail it to you in the winter. "They freeze during shipment in the winter, they crack, they leak. What a mess!" says the catalogue. "Once the freezing weather starts in the Rockies in late September we cannot ship them to you no matter how much you beg us! . . . P.S. We can ship through the winter to most of Washington, California, and Hawaii. BUT THAT'S IT AND WE MEAN IT.")

What to do if the liquid leaks out of your sno-globe? If it's a Progressive Products sno-globe from the forties or fifties, which were filled with oily liquid and glitter flakes, there is no hope. Similarly, the *Warman's* guide cautions that bottle-on-its-side sno-globes are permanently sealed and cannot be refilled. However, any model with a plug can be opened and replenished with distilled water; and *Warman's* suggests that "dirty snow can be caught in a handkerchief, washed and put back." We have opened up some of our own sno-globes (not because they were leaking; we were just curious) and discovered that like human fingerprints, each style of globe is different, and each has its own unique kind of snow. The flakes in the 1964 World's Fair *Pietà* dome (in which Michelangelo's work is improved by the addition of lifelike red blood pouring from Jesus' wounds) were tiny white plastic nuggets with a rough texture. We swished them around in dishwashing detergent, returned them to the globe, and the *Pietà* was once again blanketed with flakes as fresh as those on a Vermont hilltop in January.

SPAM

Spam is ground pork shoulder and ground ham combined with salt, sugar, water, and sodium nitrite, stuffed into a can, sealed, cooked, dried, dated, and shipped. You can slice it, dice it, fry it, eat it raw, or bake it. Its advantage over ham is that it needs no refrigeration. It will keep in its can until the end of time. It makes ideal provender for emergency meals such as those eaten by foot soldiers or inhabitants of bomb shelters who find themselves stuck underground for decades after a nuclear holocaust. Modern Spam comes smoke-flavored, low-salt, traditional, or with pasteurized processed American cheese chunk implants.

When Spam was introduced by the Geo. A. Hormel Company in 1937, ham was being touted as health food. "It plays a large part in the transformation of food into physical strength by gently exciting a sufficient flow of the digestive juices," explained the Armour Meat Company (Hormel's rival) in its booklet extolling "The Ham What *Am.*" Hormel, which got a leg up on the competition by inventing canned ham in the twenties, introduced Spam as "the Miracle Meat" because it tasted as good as or better than ham, it was cheaper, and it was so much more efficient and convenient than a twenty-pound Smithfield.

An early magazine advertisement: The man of the house wakes up, wondering, "What's that sizzling sound I hear?"

"Get up! It's Spam and eggs, my dear!" answers his cheerful wife.

She shares a secret with her girlfriend: "Here's a lunch that's good and quick . . . Hot cheese Spamwich does the trick!

At dinnertime she wonders, "What can I cook without much fuss?"

"Spam bake would tickle all of us!" her family answers.

Hormel had sold only twenty thousand tons

277

of Spam when World War II started; it was during the war that Spam, like S.O.S. (dried chipped beef on toast, known to soldiers as ''Shit on a Shingle''), became notorious. Spam was a lend-lease staple, sent in such abundance to Allied troops that Nikita Khrushchev later credited it with the survival of the otherwise starving Russian army. In England, where beef was severely rationed, Spam was the only meatlike matter many families ate for weeks. Hawaii, staging ground for the war in the Pacific, fell so in love with Spam that to this day, Hawaiians eat an average of four cans per person per year, far more than in any other place on earth. Because it was unaffected by meat rationing, Spam was eaten on the American home front in record quantity, too.

After the war, Spam enjoyed a popularity that can explained only by the Helsinki syndrome, that paradoxical condition in which captive people come to feel affection for their captors. Forced to live with Spam during the war, many soldiers and civilians didn't want to give it up. Aspiring gourmet housewives, eager for any kind of convenience food and for a bit of exotic culinary adventure, too, embraced Spam as the basic ingredient for vast numbers of Polynesian-

and Cantonese-flavored casseroles, in which the luncheon meat gets chunked, then combined with maraschino cherries, grape jelly, soy sauce, cans of bamboo shoots, and corn starch. By 1959, a billion cans had been sold.

To celebrate its product's fiftieth anniversary in 1987, Hormel released these interesting facts:

If all the cans of Spam ever eaten were put end-to-end, they would circle the globe at least ten times.

In the USA alone, 3.6 cans ''are consumed every second'' (assuming Spam is eaten round the clock, 365 days a year).

Senator Robert Byrd of West Virginia (where the fried balogna sandwich is the state dish) eats a sandwich of Spam and mayonnaise on white bread three times a week.

Nowhere on earth is Spam more exalted than in Korea, where it is sold in stylish presentation gift boxes (nine cans to the box), and where there is a booming black market in Spam (spirited away from army PXs). In 1989 the *Wall Street Journal* reported that Koreans love to fry it with *kimchi,* their traditional pickled cabbage; they roll it with vinegared rice and seaweed to create elegant Spam sushi rolls known as *kimpap;* and when they cannot get their hands on a prized can of the real thing, they eat the locally concocted imitation Spam, which goes by the brand name of Lo-Spam. Next to spit-roasted dog meat, Spam is just about Korea's favorite delicacy.

SURF 'N' TURF

Trying to live life to the hilt can present some real dilemmas. For instance, when you go to a restaurant with all good intentions of ordering the fanciest thing on the menu, what on earth are you supposed to do when you discover that the king-size filet mignon and the twin rock lobster tails are equally expensive? If you are lucky, the restaurant has considered this predicament already, and will offer a meal that is even more expensive than either steak or lobster, because it is both: surf 'n' turf. You get a smaller queen-size fillet, and just one lobster tail instead of two, but at least you have the satisfaction of knowing that you have left no luxury unsavored. Surf 'n' turf is an example of the voracious rapture that defines much classic kitsch: adding two swanky things together in hopes of doubling their value, and in fact winding up with a flatulent faux pas.

Surf 'n' turf configurations vary. Often the lobster tail is stuffed, thus augmenting its lavishness by heaping the tail meat onto a clump of flounder or wads of wet crab-flavored bread crumbs. Even unstuffed tails are usually presented with great panache, using a technique in which the chef manages to extract the rubbery lobster from its shell in one bouyant piece, then to *reattach* it to the outside of the exoskeleton, thus using the shell as a pedestal for the precious white meat. Lobster tails from Antarctic waters, not whole lobsters, are the traditional "surf" half of the dish. They are always prefrozen, and always plenty chewy, with a nice, innocuous flavor that only hints at briny seafood. The good thing about lobster tails is that they require no work to eat. They allow total indulgence, with no such unseemly manual labor as sucking meat out of legs or hammering or picking at the carcass. A lobster tail is all laid out for you, ready to ingest, as if you were Lucullus.

The same is true of the traditional "turf" half of the meat, which is usually filet mignon—the cut of steak that is the blandest, and the easiest to slice and to chew. It comes as a big cylinder of meat with no bones, no fat, no gristle, so tender you can practically sever a piece by pressing hard with the side of a fork. Traditional garnishes include a giant mushroom cap affixed with a toothpick, and occasionally a single fried onion ring.

Since the point of surf 'n' turf is to maximize hedonistic extravagance, in a full presentation both surf and turf are gilded. For the lobster there is a dipping cup of melted butter, and for the steak there is hollandaise sauce, thus allowing the diner to enrobe the food in even greater richness while also camouflaging any overly coarse meat or fish flavors.

Apocryphal stories attribute the origin of surf 'n' turf to a clumsy busboy at Delmonico's who accidentally dropped a lobster onto Diamond Jim Brady's steak; but there is no need for so clever a twist of plot to explain it. There were increasing numbers of nouveau-riche people in late-nineteenth-century America; and one common way to show off money was to be an imprudent gastronome. While the old-money upper crust tended to go in for elaborate French cuisine, arrivistes liked to spend their fresh cash at showy restaurants known as lobster palaces, where the portions were prodigious, and where Brobdingnagian meals frequently included lobster and steak (and fish and lamb and capon, too). By the twenties, however, such conspicuous consumption was passé (put to final rest by Prohibition); and the parvenu's favorite combination, surf 'n' turf, did not become popular again until the early sixties—as the top-of-the-line item on the menus of steak houses and deluxe continental dining rooms.

One of the first modern restaurants to serve it was the Eye of the Needle, the spinning restaurant atop the space needle at the Seattle World's Fair of 1962. Surf 'n' turf 'n' spinning restaurants all fit a new era of culinary profligacy that honed a sky's-the-limit attitude toward the pleasures of the world. Gourmet dining once again became a way for people to show they were rich and sophisticated sybarites, seeking ever more prodigal ways to please their palates.

There are now many more recondite preferences that prove a person's culinary savoir faire, but surf 'n' turf is still a well-received item on menus in restaurants that cater to weekend gourmets intent on having nothing but the best, and plenty of it. We have noted these variations on the theme: steak and duck ("cow 'n' cooter"), steak and quail ("heifer 'n' hen"), and chicken and fish ("pullet 'n' mullet").

T-SHIRTS

Since prehistoric man first fashioned grunts and whistles into talking, free speech never had such an amenable accomplice as the T-shirt. Traditional free speech—that is, talking with one's mouth or writing words—generally requires the ability to formulate a thought. T-shirts are not so demanding. To express yourself with a T-shirt, all you need do is give money to the clerk in the T-shirt store, in exchange for which you receive a shirt with a thought already on it. Just about any thought you could imagine is available, from cheerful ones such as ''Have a Nice Day'' and ''I'm So Happy I Could Shit'' to ''Fuck Housework'' and ''Life Sucks, Then You Die.'' T-shirts let people know where you spent your vacation, what kind of beer you drink, and if you like to party naked. If you already have a thought and somehow cannot find it on a ready-made shirt, every vacation spot, honky-tonk strip, blighted urban neighborhood, and flea market has a place selling ''tees'' with an airbrush or iron-on artist ready to put your thought on a shirt so you can wear it and let everybody know what is on your mind.

Imagine: Less than a century ago, nobody wore clothes that made personal statements. Seventy-five years ago, there weren't any T-shirts in America! It wasn't until World War I that doughboys discovered T-shirts, which soldiers brought back from France because their soft cotton was more comfortable than the usual itchy underwear. T-shirts were strictly underclothing: Nobody but soldiers, sailors, and sloppy workingmen would ever wear one exposed. They could be funny (Art Carney wore one as Norton in ''The Honeymooners''); they were sexy (Marlon Brando playing Stanley Kowalski in *A Streetcar Named Desire*); they were rebellious (Brando again, in *The Wild One*, wearing a T-shirt under his leather jacket, and James Dean in *Rebel Without a Cause*); but they did not usually carry explicit messages.

There were rare examples of message T-shirts before the sixties—for political campaigns, such as ''I Like Ike''; from the movie *The Wizard of Oz*, in which some Munchkins wore shirts with the letters ''O-Z'' stitched on the front; and for extraordinary marketing efforts on behalf of such popular cash cows as Roy Rogers, Davy Crockett, and Elvis Presley.

The ascendance of the T-shirt as an individual's own bulletin board occured when pop art (which hybridized advertising and personal expression) and activism came together and eradicated ideals of modesty and dignity in clothing. Suddenly it was okay, even fashionable, for people to make themselves into walking billboards not only for their own ideas (against the Vietnam War, in favor of marijuana) but for a favorite rock-and-roll band. At the same time, Ed ''Big Daddy'' Roth, the West Coast car customizer, began producing a line of what he called ''Weirdo T-shirts,'' featuring movie monsters, hot-rod cars, and tattoolike outlaw motorcycle slogans such as ''Born to Lose'' and ''Mother Was Wrong.''

In the early seventies, when handcrafted clothing such as patched blue jeans and macramé floppy hats seemed to be at the vanguard of what was then called ''street chic,'' T-shirts had their finest hour. They provided do-it-yourself clothiers vast front-and-back tableaux for silk-screen, tie dye, batik, iron-on messages, scratch-'n'-sniff pictures, and hand-painted designs. This

was the era of amusing trompe l'oeil shirts that masqueraded as tuxedos, naked chests, or thoracic organs. Some people earned instant wealth for shirts that captured the imagination, as happened in 1971 when Mary Anne Wyman and Virginia Anderson of Virginia created a T-shirt covered with pictures of clouds and sold tens of thousands of copies up and down the East Coast.

By 1973, *Women's Wear Daily* declared T-shirts the ''number one counter culture status symbol.'' Poet Rod McKuen became known for wearing a different T-shirt every day and for amassing so many he never wore the same one twice. In 1975, Anheuser-Busch had an ingenious idea. During springbreak, they gave away T-shirts emblazoned with the Budweiser beer logo to vacationing students in California and Florida. To return to school with a Bud shirt became a supreme status symbol among party animals. It became apparent that there was no need to give the shirts away: People would gladly pay to advertise not only Budweiser but Coors and Colt 45 and just about any other favorite product. ''It looked like the t-shirt had sold its soul to advertising,'' lamented a paperback how-to crafts book called *The Great American T-Shirt* in 1976.

Today nearly every business has its own promotional T-shirt, as do movies, popular (and unpopular) musicians, tourist attractions, religious denominations, and every known hobby and profession. Like matchbooks used to be before butane lighters, T-shirts have become so familiar that no one pays them much attention anymore. Just because a person walks by in a shirt that says ''Plumbers Do It With Their Plungers'' does not mean he or she is a plumber or a plumber's spouse; nor does ''I Can't Believe I Ate the Whole Thing'' necessarily imply that the person inside the shirt is either a glutton or an oral-sex aficionado.

Evidence of T-shirts' ignominy in the modern world is a bitter, self-referential sentiment found on ''tees'' sold in all vacation gift shops. We found this example at the T-Shirt King store (''Central Florida's Largest T-Shirt Kingdom, 5 for $9.95—NO LIMIT''): ''My Grandparents Went to Orlando and All I Got Was This Lousy T-Shirt.''

THREE STAGES OF A MAN'S SEX LIFE: TRI-WEEKLY TRY-WEEKLY TRY-WEAKLY

TATTOOS

"**D**ermagraphics is an expression of the inner self," observed Christine Natanael, writing in the fall 1989 issue of *Tattoo* magazine about the tattoos on the music group Circus of Power—"Rockin' Rebels with a Cause." Miss Natanael noted that "each member has his own idea and approach to the tattooing process, yet the results are the same—lasting expressions of individualism."

The most heavily tattooed member of the band, Alex Mitchell, expresses his individuality on a right arm covered with pictures of people jumping out of windows ("a statement on materialism," he explains). His left arm features a slashed wrist spouting blood, skulls, peyote buttons, cacti, lizards, and a bird. On his torso are a swastika ("An Indian swastika, not the Hitler one," he says) and the masks of comedy and tragedy. He has a snake on his neck and a devil on his ass. "Skin prejudice is the worst form of prejudice," Mitchell says, explaining that people who put down tattoos are "just jealous because they haven't got the balls to get one."

The question of skin prejudice notwithstanding, the acquisition of a brazen tattoo or, even better, many tattoos is a surefire strategy for violating most people's ideas of good taste. Unlike other forms of rebellious behavior, a tattoo is permanent; it shows serious commitment to the cause of blasphemy. Although some "tattoo artists" and their apologists have championed tattooing as an ancient and respected means of body beautification, in the modern world it is not the Beautiful People who get themselves tattooed: it's skinheads, heavy-metal rock groups, and motorcycle outlaws.

Tattooing wasn't always déclassé. In 1691, when British mariner William Dampier brought "the Painted Prince" from Mindanao in the South Pacific and exhibited him naked in London so everyone could see the serpents, flowers, and geographical maps that covered his body, the idea of colorful scarification for cosmetic purposes captivated fashionable society. The art had been practiced for centuries in Japan and in the South Seas (where the word *tattaw*, meaning to knock or strike, comes from), and although full-body tattoos as on the Painted Prince or on Herman Melville's Queequeg in *Moby Dick* have always been considered primitive, it became perfectly acceptable in certain stylish circles to beautify one's skin with a tasteful little bird, butterfly, or cameo.

The grand master of tattooists, George Burchett, who practiced his craft in London from the 1890s through the 1950s, credited the Prince of Wales—later King Edward VII—with establishing the fashion for artistic tattooing by getting the Cross of Jerusalem on his forearm, then serpents on his torso. Edward's son King George V acquired a slew of risqué tattoos while a young midshipman—most of which Burchett was later able to "improve" at Queen Mary's behest. Winston Churchill's mother, Lady Randolph Churchill, had herself tattooed to commemorate the coronation of King Edward VIII,

and liked it so much she had her limbs adorned with a half-dozen additional decorative vignettes. Burchett was renowned for his ability to redden ladies' lips and cheeks with the blush of youth, and to shade their eyelids and outline their eyes. He was also able to give baby-faced men a permanent, manly five o'clock shadow. In the twenties, when fashion-conscious society went mad for all things Egyptian, Burchett specialized in tattooing English women with tiny scarabs.

Although famous for his patrician clientele, Britain's great tattooist did not hesitate to create dermagraphic freaks. In his *Memoirs of a Tattooist* he catalogued a grossly fat gourmet whose stomach he covered with a picture of the glutton's favorite meal (duck with gravy, roasted potatoes, mixed vegetables, and a baked jam roll with custard); an Australian actor who had his entire body tattooed forehead-to-ankles to resemble a swathed Egyptian mummy; women who requested Clark Gable, Gary Cooper, and Bing Crosby on various body parts; and J. P. Van Dyn, known to prison wardens from Sing Sing to Devil's Island as "the World's Worst Man," whose face and shaved head were completely covered with dainty hearts, butterflies, and flowers. Burchett died in 1953, just weeks before the coronation of Queen Elizabeth, whose portrait —suitable for chest, back, or arms—was his last design.

Americans didn't begin to get tattooed in large numbers until World War II, when many sailors, especially those stationed in the Pacific, returned home with "Mother" or the Marine motto "Death Before Dishonor" on their arms. Because in those days the dyes were punched into the skin with big, primitive needles that hurt like hell, it was customary to get rip-roaring drunk first. Frequently, tattoos were "accidents": a sailor got drunk, then awoke the next morning to discover that in his stupor, he had gone and had a picture of a clipper ship permanently implanted in the skin of his chest.

Military men popularized many of the still-traditional subjects: fierce animals such as bulldogs, snakes, and panthers; exotic parrots in fancy colors; hearts and bleeding hearts; Jesus on the cross or wearing his crown of thorns; and hoochie-coochie girls that shimmy when the muscle underneath them is flexed—plus, of course, names of sweethearts and proudly waving flags.

These traditions were carried on and elaborated by motorcycle outlaws. Because they liked to accentuate the negative, bikers favored skull-and-crossbones, bloody daggers, and such mottoes as "Born on a Mountain; Raised in a Cave: Bikin' and Fuckin' Is All I Crave," as well as the spread wings of the Harley-Davidson motorcycle eagle emblem. When they began rubbing up against hippie culture in the sixties, their tattoo repertoire grew to include the Zig-Zag man (whose likeness appeared on packages of cigarette papers used to roll joints), the "Keep on Truckin'" big-foot motif from R. Crumb's *Head Comix*, and the triple-leaf marijuana plant.

Because bikers were fashionable among hippies, and because hippies fancied themselves akin to primitive peoples and sought ways to prove they weren't part of straight society, some flower children started getting tattoos, too. They were petite ones, to be sure, nothing like what the bikers wore. Janis Joplin got a small red heart on her left breast. Peter Fonda had a frolicking dolphin put on his shoulder. Cher, Joan Baez, and Grace Slick all got polite little images of such gentle things as butterflies and sunbursts.

By the early seventies, tattooing had become something of a fad among what remained of the counterculture. New India inks in rainbow colors and the development of high-speed, multiple-needle dye injectors made tattoos prettier and less painful. Needle artists such as Lyle Tuttle (who was covered neck to ankles with his art) and Spider Webb became celebrities. Webb produced series of special-edition motifs that were marketed to tattoo parlors around the country as Woodstock, Woodstock II, Woodstock III, and Woodstock IV, with fanciful images of Pegasus, flowers, hearts, doves, and beautiful naked chicks having orgasms.

The short-lived fad for allegedly tasteful tattoos faded away in the mid-seventies, although as recently as 1989 *Esquire* magazine suggested that ''serious'' artists were joining the ranks of tattooists, and that some of these virtuosos are so refined they refuse to tattoo anybody who is drunk or to apply racist or obscene messages. Such politeness aside, the art of tattooing has basically returned to its familiar vulgar and fetishistic reputation as the insignia of society's dregs. Modern conventions such as the Am Jam Tattoo Expo held in Schenectady, New York, each year attract what appears to be approximately the same demographic group as a biker rodeo. (In fact, many bikers were in attendance in 1989.) Events include leather fashion shows, contests among male and female ''collectors,'' as heavily tattooed people like to call themselves, and displays of tattooing's ancillary art, body piercing.

Always crude, tattoo imagery has broken any remaining barriers of good taste thanks mostly to the bikers and punks for whom it has become emblematic. At the Am Jam Tattoo Expo the skin on display included a man with pictures of bosoms up and down his arm, a woman whose bosoms were ringed with pictures of stars and planets, and a man with a tattoo on his stomach that showed the naked hindquarters of a woman with her legs spread in such a way that his belly button appeared to be the tattoo's vagina. The latest catalogue from Spaulding & Rogers, leading purveyors of tattoo equipment and designs, features images of naked Oriental women being raped by skeletons and a picture of a body builder peering out from the skin with a dialogue balloon above his head reading ''Eat Shit,'' his arms outstretched with a steaming pile of feces in his hands.

See also **BIKERS; HEAVY METAL**

TAXIDERMY

Don't confuse taxidermy with mummification. Mummies are whole bodies—including the bones and meat, but usually not including the organs—that are embalmed. Taxidermized things use just the fur of the animal or of one of its parts (the head, leg, backside), or in the case of fish, the skins and scales, which are stripped off, treated, then put back on an animal-shaped frame, dressed up with glass eyes, and mounted on a plaque or in a diorama depicting nature. Mummification and its modern descendants such as cryonics (freezing), preservation in fine wine or herbal tea, and the pickling of whole human heads, including brains (Timothy Leary's chosen means of interment), are generally thought of as a way to beat death and come back later. Taxidermy is a decorative art; although its goal is usually to create specimens that are lifelike, it is a celebration of death: a trophy proving the hunting or fishing skills of whoever it is killed the taxidermized animal.

(There are some modern taxidermists who freeze-dry beloved household pets and animals for museums because freeze-drying is considerably cheaper than gutting, tanning, and mounting. The process is a kind of hybrid between taxidermy and mummification: Organs, eyes, and some of the fat are removed; but the meat stays, bolstered by straw stuffing, and is injected with preservatives and pesticides. What remains of the animal is then freeze-dried, just like instant coffee or blood plasma. An improperly freeze-dried specimen, however, can shrivel and shrink, and rot until the smell is unbearable. Tradition-bound taxidermists pooh-pooh the process as slapdash.)

Taxidermy dates back to the Middle Ages, when techniques were developed by alchemists who needed ways to keep small totemic animals such as frogs, owls, and lizards handy for magic rituals. Bigger-game techniques were well developed by the sixteenth century, when the oldest existing specimen, a rhinoceros now in Florence, Italy, was stuffed. The craft flourished in America during the age of the robber barons, for whom hunting was a gentlemanly adventure.

The home-decorating needs of these rich men were served by the now-defunct Society of American Taxidermists, who turned the big game they killed into trophies, which were a way to prove one's masculinity and derring-do.

Now that bagging big game is immoral and hunting of any kind has become a dubious activity, the display of parts of dead animals has taken on a seedy, not to mention gruesome, cast. The common image of the taxidermist has sunk from that of a civilized craftsman to that of an antisocial ghoul in the tradition of Norman Bates of the Hitchcock movie *Psycho*, who taxidermized his mother (but clearly skimped on the tanning agent, causing her face to wrinkle).

Like hunters, taxidermists justify what they do as a way to express their love of nature. *Home Taxidermy for Pleasure and Profit,* published in 1944 but still available by mail from A. R. Harding Publishers in Ohio, urged its readers to never let a dead animal go to waste. "Dry skins have their value, perhaps, to the museum or naturalist," wrote author Albert B. Farnham, professional taxidermist, "but a well-mounted skin is a pleasure to all who see it."

If you agree with taxidermist Farnham, don't just think you can blithely gut the next animal you see and stuff it with straw. Do that and you'll be lucky to wind up with an animal-skin bean bag. Taxidermy is a demanding craft and requires such supplies as pickling crystals (to prepare the hide for tanning); black dye, so the nose and paws don't turn gray; skin-relaxing compound (especially for birds, so their skins don't become as crisp as a fried chicken's crust); and a substance known as Critter Clay, to rebuild parts of the animal that may have been shot off when it was killed. For fish, you'll need fish eyes and paint to paint them, and if mounting the trophy medallion-style (just half the fish on a board or a plaque of imitation pebbled upholstery leather), clothespins to clamp the fins away from the mounting surface. When mounting lizards and reptiles, it's essential to have a bottle of Reptile Tan on hand to keep the skin pliable.

The most important element in the process

is the form on which the skin is stretched. Let's say you've got a squirrel pelt. Do you want the finished exhibit to appear to be sitting, climbing, jumping, sleeping, attacking, arching its back, or looking backwards? For prices between three and ten dollars in any taxidermist's catalogue, each of these postures is available. Deluxe forms have enough flex in the limbs, tail, and neck to allow the taxidermist to customize the position.

If you've gunned down a bobcat and want to remember the drama of the occasion, you might want to use the "Fighting Bobcat" form made by the acclaimed taxidermy sculptor LeRoy Martinez, its paw raised for the kill, its back arched and mouth open and snarling. Not only is the "Fighting Bobcat" flexible, but for only $5 above its regular $47.75 price it is available with preset, socketed eyes from the Van Dyke Taxidermy Supply Company of Woonsocket, South Dakota. For a dead deer, you'll likely want its skin glued on Wendy Christensen Senk's running and leaping white-tail buck, described in the Van Dyke catalogue as showing "the most exquisite detail of muscle and veining . . . to create the most life-like results possible."

A lot of people who hunt don't have the space to keep all of everything they kill, so many just have the heads, or sometimes just the antlers, mounted on simulated-wood-grain plaques small enough to hang on the wall of any house trailer or modest backwoods shack. That leaves the rest of the animal to dispose of. "Thousands of feet are thrown away each year," worries the Van Dyke catalogue, suggesting attractive uses for amputated hooves and legs of deer, elk, moose, bison, and cape buffalo that

would otherwise go to waste. There are forms to bend their legs and make them into gun racks, forms for lamp stands (one- or four-footed), forms to make footstool feet, and forms for a dangling leg with a indoor-outdoor thermometer inserted in the shin.

What with all these good body parts and pieces of pelt floating around the taxidermist's studio, it was inevitable that some nature-loving animal stuffer would get creative. And so it came to pass that the jackalope was born in 1934, when Ralph and Doug Harrick, taxidermists in Douglas, Wyoming, based a form on a small two-point mule deer and covered the form with jackrabbit skin. They sold their gag animal to a local tavern keeper, who put it up above the bar. The Harricks' horned rabbit eventually became such a hit that Douglas, Wyoming, declared itself "the Jackalope Capital of the World" and erected a man-sized jackalope statue on Center Street. Now the town boasts of the West's finest selection of jackalope postcards, jackalope hunting licenses, and genuine mounted jackalope heads made by the thriving local community of taxidermists.

Jackalopes became such a great practical joke that the idea spread beyond Douglas; you can sit on mule-sized jackalopes at the Wildlife Exhibit in Dubois, Wyoming, and at Wall Drug in Wall, South Dakota. In fact, this region of the country—known as the badlands—has become a rich lode of mutation taxidermy, including such entertaining examples as the fur-bearing trout covered in leopard skin like Howdy Doody's plush pal, the Flubadub, and the flying jackalope (with pheasant wings).

By the way, if you are not a hunter and not interested in purchasing someone else's kill, most of the better studios in the badlands also specialize in taxidermy's allied arts, including leather tooling, photo lamp shades with pictures of elk and moose on them (or your own vacation photo), and log-slab clocks made of a slick lacquered cross-section of walnut or pine with clock numbers around the circumference and

a hole in the middle big enough for a clock movement and hands. The most up-to-date taxidermists will be able to tell you all about the newest wrinkle in the craft: *synthetic taxidermy*, which uses artificial hides to create fun-fur rugs and trophies as well as pseudobionic curiosities such as taxidermized bean-bag chairs, tiger-skin footstools shaped like toadstools, and toilet-tank covers with antlers.

TELETHONS

There are many grueling fund-raising events broadcast on television, but there is only one Jerry Lewis; and his telethon, on the air every year since 1956, is television's crowning supplication. It wheedles, begs, scolds, shames, entertains, and counts money all night and all day; it is guaranteed to leave any viewer wrung out, agog, and aghast.

It is a pageant of wrenching emotional highs and lows unknown in any other form of programming, we daresay unknown in any other medium. With wheelchair-bound kids and crippled adults as the centerpiece, in struts Wayne Newton in his sequined Las Vegas torero jacket and glittering thunderbird belt buckle to belt out "Danke Shoen" and Lola Falana in slit skirt kicking up her curvy gams—all in the hopes they can coax viewers to dig deep into their pockets. And now a quiet moment as the nervous little man from the firemen's association presents Jerry with a check from all the guys and gals at the firehouse. And now money from the healthy kids who ran around their school a thousand times to raise cash for kids who cannot run. And always, there is the tote board of contributions with Ed McMahon keeping score as it climbs higher with each roll of the timpani.

The heart and soul of it is master of ceremonies, founder, and star, Jerry Lewis: biting his lower lip to fight back tears, telling jokes, berating friends and viewers, sweating, singing, talking silly, walking goofy like a spastic, chain-smoking cigarettes (until he quit after a heart attack in 1982), humiliating himself in any way he knows how if he thinks it will pull more money from the audience, yet so proud his ego lights up America from coast to coast.

It is a dizzying fusion of sanctimony and sincerity that, like all aggressive comedy—from tickling to sick jokes—makes the audience squirm, giggle, and beg for mercy. The telethon chews up, swallows, and regurgitates all the nice standards and practices that make everything else on TV seem bland. It feels almost dangerous to watch because it is in some tormented way an insane experience—swinging madly from show-biz banter and goofy jokes to grievous personal tragedies, and from Jerry's mawkish warmth to his ferocious anger when the money isn't coming in. How agonizing it is to see people parade their afflictions in order to solicit money—but the mendicancy works. It turns your stomach to see celebrities outdo each other's pandering—but they haul in millions to help sick people, which makes you feel great. It is aggravating, but it is hypnotic; who can watch the telethon without worrying about a slow-moving tote board and rooting for it to top last year's figure? Who can see the afflicted, known as "Jerry's Kids," and not feel the urge to help?

Telethons have been part of TV's repertoire from the beginning: Milton Berle did the first one in 1948, shortly after making his earth-shaking debut as host of the "Texaco Star Theater." The supercharged entertainer known as "Mr. Television" worked twenty-four hours straight, sweating under hot klieg lights and sustaining himself with cold sandwiches and black coffee, and raised a hundred thousand dollars for New York's Damon Runyon Memorial Cancer Fund. Two years later, the brightest comedy team in show business, Dean Martin and Jerry Lewis, drummed up a million dollars' worth of pledges in their telethon for the New York Cardiac Hospital. In 1952, Bing Crosby made his television debut teamed with Bob Hope in a telethon to raise money to send the U.S. Olympic Team to the Helsinki games.

In 1956 *Radio-Television Daily* announced that dozens of charities were "jumping on the telethon bandwagon." Although a vice-president at NBC said that the network had deemed the format unsuitable for the medium (as not cost-effective) and the New York *World-Telegram* fretted that the gimmick had worn thin, Dean Martin and Jerry Lewis were busy planning the biggest one yet. Scheduled to run from ten in the morning on Friday, June 29, to seven o'clock Saturday night, the show was broadcast from the studios of New York's WABD and featured an entire television production team imported from Hollywood by Martin and Lewis at their own

THE JERRY LEWIS LABOR DAY TELETHON

expense. The beneficiary of the show was the Muscular Dystrophy Association, which had been founded in 1950 to help find treatments and cures for kids with muscular dystrophy and other muscle and nerve diseases.

In 1957, the comedy team of Martin and Lewis split up. The Muscular Dystrophy Telethon became Jerry Lewis's alone; and for the second annual broadcast (on November 30 and December 1), Jerry modernized the format. Instead of broadcasting from a stage in a theater, he set it in the Grand Ballroom of the Roosevelt Hotel, giving the event what Bob Salmaggi of the New York *Herald Tribune* called "the air of a spontaneous party."

In the early years the die was cast and all the great telethon traditions were begun, including Jerry's bathetic rendition of "You'll Never Walk Alone" at the end of the show, the introduction of his family and family dog in the audience, and the almost ghoulish thrill of watching Jerry stagger to the conclusion without any rest— hoarse, sweaty, collar loosened, eyes puffy, hands trembling. "People watch the show to see if I'm going to make it," Jerry said in 1977. "Last year I went without sleep for seventy-seven straight hours before and during the show. It's not humanly possible, but I did it." Jerry's superhuman stamina has always been one of the program's greatest attractions; in 1976, he was off-screen a mere nineteen minutes during the entire twenty-one-hour broadcast.

The MDA telethon hit the one-million-dollar mark in 1966, topping itself every year through 1981 ($31.5 million). By the mid-eighties, the take was in the $35 million range; and the telethon, carried on over two hundred independent stations across America that Jerry called "the Love Network," originated from Caesars Palace in Las Vegas.

Snooty arbiters of good taste have always delighted in making fun of the Jerry Lewis telethon. "Institutionalized kitsch" proclaimed Cliff Jahr in *New York* magazine. But influential people have supported it, and not only for its

good works. "Every TV critic takes an unspoken oath that at some point in his professional life he will write a column trashing Jerry Lewis for the way he conducts his annual Labor Day show," wrote Tom Shales of the Washington *Post* in a 1988 article that went against the critics' oath and praised the telethon for its hopefulness, and as "television's living museum of American vaudeville . . . a glimpse of entertainment as it was in the pre-rock era, when it seemed kinder and happier."

Like good melodrama, the telethon has triumphed over many obstacles. In 1981, antitelethon complainers found a substantial ally in Evan J. Kemp, Jr., of the Disability Rights Center, who wrote an editorial for the *New York Times* condemning the event because it "reinforces a stigma against disabled people," and suggesting that instead of appealing to viewers' pity the telethon ought to "show disabled people working, raising families, and generally sharing in community life.'' Jerry's answer was to parade forth dozens of ailing children and adults and their families, who all testified about how much they have been helped and how much they need the telethon to continue. Nonetheless, the 1982 telethon was the first in history to rake in less money ($28.4 million) than the previous year's. Jerry Lewis had a heart attack and nearly died.

The telethon is one of the most riveting pieces of entertainment on television because it is live, and something goofy always happens. In 1973 a young phone volunteer in Gainesville, Florida, was slipped a brown paper bag containing ten thousand dollars collected by the ''Gainesville Marijuana Dealers Association.'' In 1976 viewers were treated to a surprise reunion between Dean Martin and Jerry Lewis, engineered by Frank Sinatra. Dean looked drunk and Jerry looked like he was ready to kill.

Most of all, the telethon is a way to be awestruck by the invincible Jerry Lewis, a man who has battled critics his whole career. The heart attack, bypass surgery, and kicking a decade-long addiction to Percodan, like the naysayers, were only trivial obstacles in his path. ''I don't have all that much time left,'' he said in 1986. ''I have got to beat this thing once and for all. I don't care what I have to do to accomplish it —whether it's writing, begging, pleading, crying, or standing naked before one hundred million people on Labor Day.''

The big question is *why?* Why does Jerry Lewis do it? The obvious answer is that it is a good thing to do. But there is another, more specific explanation, and Jerry has told it to only one person, his press agent, who died in 1976. During one telethon in the late seventies, a Texas millionaire said he would give a half million dollars if Jerry revealed his real motivation, but Jerry refused (and got only fifty thousand). When a cure is found for muscular dystrophy, he said, he will disclose the answer.

TREASURES FROM TRASH

Some people throw out trash. Others make it into treasure. You can see the results of the treasures-from-trash school of recycling at nearly all church bazaars and local crafts fairs. They include wind chimes made from the tops of coffee cans and Christmas angels fashioned by adding colored felt (wings) and an old scouring pad (hair) to an empty Ivory Liquid dishwashing detergent bottle. Among the most commonly seen treasures are modernistic sculptures, such as a "spool bouquet" created by some demonically inventive soul who figured out what to do with a hundred empty thread holders, a handful of dowel sticks, and a chipped flowerpot.

The drive to turn refuse into useful or pretty objects gathered momentum around 1970, when the idea of recycling was new and exciting. Suddenly it was very groovy to see beauty and purpose in what the rest of the world regarded as junk. For more than ten years artists such as Robert Rauschenberg and Richard Stankiewicz had been using old rags, pipes, and trash to make "assemblages" for hanging on gallery walls; the next step was to do something useful with the rubble. In the late sixties, commune dwellers of Drop City, Colorado, attracted massive media attention by their clever reuse of old automobile parts as geodesic dome housing. Hippies wore cast-off army uniforms and ratty old boas, creating fashion from flea market pickings and Salvation Army store bargains.

This fad jumped quickly from art galleries and counterculture crash pads to Mr. and Mrs. Average's rec room. By the mid-seventies many handy suburbanites and small-town creative types had eagerly adopted the idea of making something from nothing because it segued perfectly into the same pecuniary values that encouraged them to join their local save-a-buck club back in the fifties. And it also provided them something that middle Americans have always relished: new hobbies.

To help the inventive recyclers in their quest to make something from nothing and have a heck of a good time doing it, crafts books were published by the score, including such classics as *How to Make Something from Nothing, Something From Nothing Crafts, Junk Shopping with Sari, Creating with Cattails, Cones, and Pods*, and *Treasures from Trash*. All these books were built upon the same basic principle: Nothing is so ugly or misshapen that it cannot be transmogrified into a nifty new thing. The kind of arts-and-crafts projects once reserved for schoolchildren and patients in mental asylums were now approved handiwork for happy homemakers looking to show their decorative cleverness. With a touch of paint, a few pipe cleaners, and a snippet of nylon netting, any commonplace Spam can, jelly glass, or pair of panty hose could become the makings of a hair-curler tree or vacuum-cleaner cozy.

One of the loopiest books in the genre is *Fun with Junk: Making Funny Figures out of Odds and Ends,* which advises that a discarded object such as a teapot should be meditated upon until

classic ''something from nothing'' headgear, a sportsman's hat, using empty beer cans crocheted together with bright orange yarn. Nowhere will you find cuter critters made from old thread spools (pop tops for ears, scrap wool for hair) or a prettier example of a mint dish made from an empty Crisco can.

How to Make Something from Nothing, by Frank B. and Rubye Mae Griffith, offers a hundred fascinating ways to ''turn boo boos into items for a boutique.'' The enticing dust jacket promises to show readers ''how to turn a dog-food box into a lingerie hamper, an oven roaster into a candle sconce, an egg poacher into a portrait frame. Prune jar lids become coasters before your very eyes, shin bones wind up as necklaces, salad dressing bottles masquerade as candle holders and egg shells appear as glittering knights.''

Apparently stimulated by their previous books, *How to Live with a Horse* and *My Best Friends Speak in Whinnies,* the Griffiths fill *How to Make Something from Nothing* with an awe-inspiring array of crafts made from the bones of dead farm animals. Especially creative is the fun centerpiece they suggest for children's parties, a sculpture called ''Giraffes Gossiping,'' made from two cow ribs in a base of modeling clay.

See also **CANDLE ART; DRIFTWOOD; MACRAMÉ; PANTY-HOSE CRAFTS; POP-TOPPING**

it suggests novel ideas, such as ''an elevated elephant, a whistling boy, Voltaire, or a pomeranian with water wings.'' It is also the most artistic of the volumes, since it does not limit its repertoire of tricks to simple decoration of old bottles and boxes. *Fun with Junk* encourages readers to use whole heaps of household garbage as the superstructure for coats of dripped wax, finger paints, and washes of polymer lacquer. As an example, a beautiful and serene ''Infanta'' sculpture is made from an unwanted upside-down goblet onto which has been poured an avalanche of candle wax, the statuette completed with two bright beads mashed into the wax to make the infanta's eyes.

Anne Orth Epple's *Something from Nothing Crafts (Raid Your Wastebasket and Join the Fun!)* contains the last word on how to make the

TROLL DOLLS

The first troll doll was carved from wood in the 1950s by a Dane named Thomas Dam, who made it as a birthday gift for his teenage daughter. It was a homely little imp with a spray of wooly white hair, a flaring nose, jug ears, big black eyes, a toothless grin, and spatulate, four-fingered hands—an effigy of the mythical Scandinavian elves visible only to children and childlike grown-ups. If one of these pixies is ever captured, he is supposed to provide his captor with a lifetime of good fortune.

A Danish toy-store owner encouraged Dam to manufacture more of them. Known as Dammit Dolls, his comical gnomes arrived in the U.S.A. in the early sixties, at a time when cuteness of all sorts was glorified—from the Singing Nun with her lilting ballad ''Dominique'' and the adorable mop-top Beatles to 1963's number-one television show, ''The Beverly Hillbillies.'' In the fall of 1963, college coeds began adopting troll dolls for their dorm rooms and carrying around miniature ones in their purses. Suddenly, they were a phenomenon. That same year, the belief that a troll doll provided its owner good luck was attested to by Betty Miller, the daredevil pilot who retraced Amelia Earhart's long-distance flight with only a troll doll as her copilot. Troll dolls soon became the second-biggest-selling doll of the decade, after Barbie.

Original trolls were naked, but as the fad caught on, they were sold in tunics, diapers, aprons, and sports jackets and with hair in kicky, mod colors. There were baby trolls, Grannynik and Grandpanik trolls (old ones with wrinkles), trolls on motorcycles, troll piggy banks, a complete troll wedding party in formal wear, a superhero troll in a black cape and mask, animal trolls (cows, giraffes, monkeys), and trolls to dangle from rearview mirrors in cars. At the height of the fad, a rumor spread that if you put a troll doll in the freezer overnight, its hair would grow. Montgomery Ward's 1966 Christmas mail-order catalogue offered a troll village complete with cave, rocks, trees, and fourteen prehistoric 1¼-inch-tall troll villagers.

Because there is no way to patent cuteness, other manufacturers joined the fun, creating Dam Things, Wish Niks, Norfins, Warm Fuzzies, Two-Headed Trolls, and hippie-haired Dawks (who came with picket signs protesting vanilla ice cream)—most of whom shared the original doll's stubby frame, oversize head with big eyes, cute-ugly smile, and pudgy hands. To collectors, the only genuine troll dolls are Thomas Dam's Dammits. Rare ones, such as 1964 Long Troll Turtle, are worth $100 today.

After the boom of 1963–64, the personality of many troll dolls underwent a gradual and distressing change—from mischievous and magic forest elves to maudlin emotional sponges, existing not so much to bring good luck as to give their owners something to cuddle. Soon sold by every truck stop and novelty store in the land, trolls became icons of institutionalized adorability and/or impishness, often manufactured with grating modern epigrams attached, such as ''Ve Get Too Soon Old und Too Late Shmart'' or ''I Hate Housework '' The classic such figurine is the fuzzy doll designed for secretaries' desks, its arms outstretched looking for hugs, a sign on its pedestal broadcasting ''I Love You This Much.''

TUNA CASSEROLE

Like all things in life, food gets ranked by status. Some foods are definitely high class, such as caviar and filet mignon. Quiche and kiwi fruit were prestigious for a while but soon became clichés. Anchoring the low end of the culinary hierarchy, with no hope of upward mobility, is the tuna casserole, a dish of such unmitigated cloddishness that no one concerned about his reputation as an epicure would dare admit to eating it.

Smell those lumps of hot, oily tuna interspersed with pale green peas that only a diner junkie could love. Taste that beige emulsion of condensed cream soup so salty you can imagine crystalline saline deposits forming on parts of the casserole dish where the soup has germinated overnight. And look at the coup de grace: The surface is crowned with a garnish—if "garnish" could possibly be the word for taking a fistful of potato chips, squeezing hard, then scraping the crumbs off your palm onto the top of the casserole. Is it any wonder it is among the most disrespected foods in the land?

There was an optimistic moment in kitchen history when tuna casserole was not at the bottom of the culinary barrel. In fact, it was pretty spiffy. This was in the fifties, when it seemed that the drudgery of cooking was about to be eliminated, and housewives freed. The instrument of their liberation was convenience food: cans of soup, gravy, fish, chicken, stew, and beans; bottles of salad dressing; boxes of cake mix, packaged rolls, Jell-O, and macaroni dinner. The strategy was to mix, match, and combine two or three or four of these items in a unique or novel way. The result: a "creative" meal, using convenience foods as its ingredients, requiring no more thought or effort than a bologna sandwich.

Tuna casserole was, if not the ultimate, among the easiest of the convenience formulas. The basic recipe, on soup cans and in hundreds of housewife-helper brochures, calls for a can of tuna, a can of soup, peas (canned or frozen), and a bag of potato chips. In addition, the cook is required to measure milk and—here's the tricky part—hard-boil and slice two eggs. Tuna casserole was especially convenient because by the 1950s tuna was a standard ingredient on every home's emergency shelf—the requisite supply of foods so boring that you'd never eat them if there was something good in the house, but you *could* eat them if the refrigerator was bare. It was also handy for Catholics, who were forbidden to eat meat on Fridays.

So much tuna casserole was eaten in the fifties and early sixties that by 1967 *The Co-Ed Cookbook* listed it as "Old Time Tuna Casserole," suggesting it as a wonderful thing to serve the first time you invite a boy to dinner, because it was inexpensive and might provide him with happy memories of his childhood.

In fact, the idea of tuna casserole *does* go way back to before the great convenience craze. As early as 1917, *A Thousand Ways to Please a Husband* suggested a casserolelike tuna loaf as the perfect thing to serve at a "Rainbow Announcement Luncheon," given to celebrate a friend's engagement. At the time, canned tuna was a clever novelty, available only since 1903, when sardines mysteriously vanished from waters off the California coast and local canners and fishermen needed a replacement. As meat grew scarce in World War I, canned tuna filled in. During the next war, Florence Brobeck's *Cook It in a Casserole* (1943) gave a low-ration-point recipe that combined canned tuna fish with cubed potatoes, peas, cheese, and a white sauce to make a casserole that could have been a prototype for the familiar recipe that housewives with can openers discovered as even easier if they had condensed soup in the cupboard.

By 1953, *Tuna As You Like It,* published by the Tuna Research Foundation, announced that tuna had become the best-selling canned fish, bought at least once a month by two-thirds of all American homemakers. "Open a can of tuna and you open a tale of adventure," the foundation rhapsodized, suggesting such exotic variations on the theme as a tuna corn chip casserole, tuna Romanoff casserole with cottage cheese and sour cream, and a tuna confetti casserole with corn and mushrooms.

The most popular modification on the formula is adding cooked egg noodles or elbow macaroni to make *tuna noodle casserole.* This gives it more heft and helps dilute the sodium double-whammy of the tuna and the soup. Other creative variations include changing the soup (try cream of mushroom or cheddar cheese) and substituting canned French fried onion rings, corn flakes, or crumbled Ritz crackers for potato chips. There is no limit to the culinary merriment one can have with tuna casserole. The *Favorite Brand Name Recipes Casseroles* cookbook lists recipes for curried tuna casserole, corny tuna casserole, oyster cracker tuna casserole, tuna casserole Florentine (with frozen spinach and spaghetti sauce), and tuna sunflower casserole (with salted, roasted sunflower nuts). In 1956 Mrs. Herbert Ward Whitney of Dallas entered the Ninth Pillsbury Bake-Off with a recipe for Tun-au-Gratin, which was tuna casserole put into a pie shell and beautified with a cheese and pastry-crumb top. Mrs. Whitney's recipe won the Bride's Second Prize.

CLASSIC TUNA CASSEROLE

1 10¾-ounce can condensed
   cream of celery soup
¼ cup milk
1 7-ounce can tuna, drained and flaked
2 hard-boiled eggs, sliced
1 cup peas, cooked
½ cup crumbled potato chips

Preheat oven to 350 degrees.
Combine soup and milk in one-quart casserole. Stir in tuna, eggs, and peas. Bake 30 minutes. Stir. Top with potato chips. Bake 5 minutes more.
Yield: 4 servings

TUPPERWARE

To buy Tupperware, you must attend a Tupperware party. At the party, customarily given in a neighbor's home, the Tupperware salesperson explains how Tupperware storage devices make life good, and whips guests into a frenzy of enthusiasm for new ways to squirrel away provisions. You never knew there were so many kinds of containers and so many different foods that need containing. When you make your purchase, you become a Tupperware person, with a lifetime guarantee against chipping, cracking, breaking, or peeling.

Tupperware people are happy people. Their Tupperware prevents sadness and frustration by keeping the Nut 'N' Honey cereal crisp and the nondairy creamer dry and the tacoburger casserole in the freezer from absorbing the smells of old ice cubes. It solves problems that non-Tupperware people probably aren't even aware of, such as the distress of chasing a pickle around in its glass jar: Store your pickles in the Tupperware Pick-A-Deli, and you can lift them up and out of the garlicky brine and never suffer the embarrassment of fingernail odor. Or the dilemma of the half-eaten block of Kraft Velveeta cheese: Wrapped imperfectly, it hardens; and it is well-nigh impossible to slice without smearing cheese food on the cutting block. Stored in a Tupperware Velveeta Keeper, a two-pound loaf keeps soft and fresh, and pulls out on a sliding tray conveniently marked to designate quarter-pound segments for slicing.

Tupperware people love their Tupperware because it has a personality. Not only is it limitlessly convenient, it is fun. It comes into your life in a fit of jubilation when it is chosen at a party—a delirious, enchanted party if the Tupperware hostess is good at the "icebreaker game" phase of the evening. Then, if it is deployed the way the Tupperware dealer advises —as the regimenting principle of a Modular-Mated Custom Food Center—it brings order and calm to a home, vocalizing its airtight perfection with a gaseous burp every time you seal it closed.

Tupperware is nothing less than a way of life, or at least a symbol of a way of life in which housewifery has reached perfection. In the world of Tupperware, nothing is wasted, nothing spoils. Everything in the pantry has been decanted from its mismatched, helter-skelter supermarket boxes and bags and put into clearly labeled, proper-sized containers with color-coded lids on shelves divided into the Breakfast Center (cereals), the Beverage Center (Tang, coffee, Kool-Aid), the Baking Center, the Carbohydrate Center (pasta, beans, rice), and the Snack Center. All food in the freezer is kept in Tupperware Freezer Mates. In the refrigerator are formations of Modular Mate Rounds, Ovals, and Squares, Tri-Jel Molds for Jell-O, Snak-Stor flats for luncheon meat, and Square-A-Ways for ready-made sandwiches. On the table there are pitchers, tumblers, and Multi-Mugs, egg trays (for deviled eggs), and Serve-It-All pedestal sets for chips and dips.

The polyethylene empire began with one seven-ounce bathroom tumbler. It was molded in 1945 by former Du Pont chemist and self-described "ham inventor" Earl Silas Tupper of Farnumsville, Massachusetts. Tupper called his material Poly-T (a more salesworthy name than generic polyethylene); the cup was manufactured in heretofore unseen frosted pastel colors; and it was remarkably supple. When Tupper turned his attention to bowls the following year, it was Poly-T's flexibility that made it unique. He designed the bowls with a tight-fitting lid that could be flexed in such a way when it was closed that air inside was audibly burped out and a vacuum was created, thus keeping what was inside fresh. He called them "Poly-T Wonder Bowls" and tried advertising them to housewares stores as "the Tupper Millionaire Line."

Store sales were lackluster. In 1946, Tupper devised a plan to sell the Millionaire Line directly to consumers, but without the stigma of door-to-door salesmen. He created the Tupperware party, at which local distributors sold the bowls to groups of neighbors in the living room of a

The Tupperware Museum of Historic Food Containers, Kissimmee, Florida

"Tupperware Hostess" who received a free bowl for the use of her home. The results were so successful that retail sales were abandoned by 1951. During the next quarter-century, Tupperware parties became one of the most bewitching rituals of suburban life; and by the late seventies, a hundred thousand Tupperware ladies were selling over nine hundred million dollars' worth of Tupperware every year.

Sales of Tupperware slowed in the eighties. One former party goer told *Business Week* in 1985 that she and her friends had bought so much they were "all Tuppered out." The home-party formula had become cumbersome in an era when more women were away from home working, and dozens of similar plastic containers were available for less money in hardware stores. Ever ingenious, the Tupperware Company (now owned by Premark International) invented what *Time* magazine called the Yupperwear party—twenty-minute sales pitches given at health clubs, play groups, or during lunch hours in offices. New products were added, including Tuppertoys and a plastic portable desk for

travelers. And by 1988, 3 percent of the sales force were men.

All Tupperware products can be admired in a lifelike setting at the Tupperware International Headquarters in Kissimmee, Florida. Visitors attend a mock Tupperware party and get a free seven-ounce Modular Mate and two free postcards of the Tupperware Friendship Fountain. The tour concludes in the Museum of Historic Food Containers, where ancient vessels are displayed in glass cases and Tupperware is out in the open —stacked and martialed in rows with military precision under halos of lights. The museum is staffed by women with a deportment that can only be described as that of a Tupperware dignitary: smiling and efficient, but with the stinging hauteur of a person who has more Tupperware than you could ever dream of owning. Furthermore, the women are blemish-free; their hairdos and makeup are outstanding; and they are so adept at their jobs you want to beg them to take you to their homes so you can look at their pantries, which are undoubtedly some of the best-systematized in the world.

TV DINNERS

Imagine a world so primitive that if you want to eat a turkey dinner with all the fixins you must roast a turkey, mash potatoes, bake dressing, simmer gravy, boil peas, and turn cranberries into sauce. So it was until 1954, when the Swanson Frozen Foods Company of Omaha, Nebraska, invented the TV Dinner.

Sure, there were already plenty of canned and even frozen foods to make life easier; Swanson itself had been making frozen pot pies since 1951. But it was nothing less than a culinary epiphany when they began manufacturing an *entire dinner* in one partitioned aluminum tray that went from cardboard box to oven to table, requiring no pots and pans or serving bowls, no mixing or slicing or mashing, no thinking about what goes with what, no plates, no dish washing, not even a mom to make it.

Swanson called its product TV Dinner because television symbolized the modern world. Everybody wanted a television. It meant instant fun. Likewise, TV Dinner meant instant eating, and so it was packaged in a box designed to look like a television console. The border of the cardboard container resembled a wood-grain frame with knobs on one side (where the price was put). In the center of the frame was an oval space meant to be a television screen, where a picture of the dinner appeared, as if on TV. Although no early advertising suggested that TV Dinner was supposed to be eaten *while watching TV,* the aluminum-clad meals were ideally suited for fold-up TV trays, and for people too busy watching their favorite programs to bother cooking, and too comfy in the den to leave it for the dinette or dinner table.

The initial TV Dinner was turkey, Swanson's logic being that turkey was a festive meal, eaten by most folks only on holidays. A freezer stocked with TV Dinners meant that anyone could have a fancy dinner any day. The first ones came with whipped sweet potatoes, but there were problems with them turning watery, so mashed potatoes were substituted almost immediately. There was magic about TV Dinners in their early days. It was a thrill to peek under the foil of a frozen one and see the whole rock-hard meal in its compartments, a pat of butter in the spuds; then, forty-five minutes later, to peel back the foil and behold a steaming holiday feast with a square indentation oozing viscous rivulets of yellow where the butter pat used to be. All the early TV Dinners were designed as special-occasion meals. Roast beef and fried chicken soon came on the market, then ham with raisin sauce.

Housewives were freed from kitchen drudgery! An early television advertisement showed the lady of the house wearing her mink stole, about to go out on the town. "What about feeding the kids?" the announcer asks. "I'm not going to worry," Mom replies, then gets in her car and drives away. Inside the house, her two teenagers are jitterbugging in the kitchen while their TV Dinners bake.

TV Dinners flourished during the convenience-crazed sixties; but by the end of the decade, a lot of trendsetters had begun to disdain anything prepackaged or convenient as "plastic," favoring health foods and labor-intensive back-to-nature cookery instead. Swanson dropped the name TV Dinner in favor of the more generic Frozen Dinner. In 1972, the same year Nixon and Agnew won a landslide based on their appeal to the silent majority, Swanson introduced Hungry Man Dinners with jumbo quantities of meat and starch in them, appealing to the same bedrock values. Hungry Man Dinners were aimed at gluttons for whom mass quantities of red meat and second helpings of potatoes equaled good eating. By the end of the seventies, it was that class of eater that many people associated with frozen dinners, known to nearly everyone by the now-generic term TV dinner. As the eighties began, the culinary world seemed divided between effete francophilic gourmets and lumpen square-meal eaters, and TV dinners were definitely food for the latter—enshrined along with bowling shirts and plastic-covered furniture as a quintessential symbol of lowbrow life.

Frozen dinners lost some of their stigma when they were reborn in the eighties as chic food for yuppies on the go. In 1982 Swanson came out with a line called Le Menu, offering beef stroganoff instead of salisbury steak, and a list of suggested wines to accompany what *TV Guide* called the new "designer dinners." Other manufacturers offered portioned-out gourmet and low-sodium health-food frozen meals, ready to microwave. But the classic TV Dinner, containing its old-fashioned meat-and-potatoes feast in a no-fuss aluminum tray, will always be a symbol of the industrial magic that once promised to make every day a holiday.

TWINKIES

The most famous snack cake was named after a shoe. In 1930, during the Great Depression, Jimmy Dewar, manager of Chicago's Continental Bakery, was looking for a way to use the company's "Little Short Cake Finger" pans year around, instead of only during strawberry season. On a trip to St. Louis, Mr. Dewar saw a billboard advertising Twinkle Toe Shoes. No one remembers if the gigantic shoes were depicted filled with feet or empty, but the vision inspired Mr. Dewar. "I came up with the idea of injecting the little cakes with a filling," he recalled; and he named his invention Twinkies. Once the recipe was perfected, Mr. Dewar ate three a day for half a century. "I have twelve great-grandchildren, all of them eating Twinkies," he boasted in 1981, shortly before he died at the age of eighty-eight.

The original filling was banana creme (*creme,* not cream), and the cakes were hand-filled, one at a time. During the forties, banana creme was replaced by vanilla creme; and in 1988, strawberry-creme-filled Twinkies were introduced. Modern bakeries can fill 52,000 per hour, and although Twinkies have stayed the same size and shape, the cool, sticky tubes have gotten softer and prettier thanks to food-manufacturing technology.

Few gourmets and even fewer nutritionists appreciate their charisma, but Twinkies are edible Americana. They were Howdy Doody's favorite petit four (touted on television by the inhabitants of Doodyville, including a cowhand named Twinkie the Kid). Archie Bunker demanded them in his lunch box on "All in the Family." To celebrate Superman's fiftieth birthday in 1988, DC Comics gave the Man of Steel a party in New York with an eight-foot-tall cake made of Twinkies, at which Mayor Edward Koch is reported to have feasted. Reviewers have credited singer Tom Jones's success to a bulge in his pants that resembles a Twinkie.

Twinkies are so important-seeming that they took the blame for driving former San Francisco city supervisor Dan White insane. After he murdered Mayor George Moscone and Supervisor Harvey Milk in 1978, White's lawyers successfully used what jurisprudence now knows as "the Twinkie defense" to convince a jury that their client was suffering "diminished mental capacity" because he ate a diet of Twinkies and candy bars. White got off on a lesser charge and subsequently committed suicide. "Nobody knows what's going on inside of me," he said, neither blaming nor exonerating Twinkies for his condition.

Twinkies have had startling effects on animals as well as humans. In Sarasota, Florida, when an elephant refused his normal diet after surgery, the attending veterinarian prescribed Twinkies. The elephant recovered and grew strong. In 1976, in Kings Mill, Ohio, runaway baboons were recaptured with bait of Twinkies and bananas.

It is easy to take Twinkies for granted: They are always piled on the store counter, ready to be ingested whenever the whim for sponge cake and creme filling strikes. But you don't have to only eat them plain. Creative chefs, flouting all rules of epicurean propriety, have invented many ways to use Twinkies as the star ingredient in baroque desserts such as "Twinkie Pie" (layer them with custard, whipped cream, and chocolate chips). Ourselves, we are proud to claim authorship of a dessert known as "Undescended Twinkies," for which they are floated like depth charges in a gelatinized mixture of 7-Up and vanilla ice cream.

Other products made by Continental Bakery under the Hostess label include Sno Balls (creme-filled cakes shrouded with marshmallow and coconut), Suzy Q's (oblong creme-filled sandwich cakes in either banana or devil's food flavor), Ding Dongs (creme-filled chocolate cakes wrapped in chocolate candy), Ho Ho's (rolled chocolate with white creme filling), Hostess O's (jelly rings surrounded by doughnut), Pudding Pies, and Choco-Bliss cakes filled with chocolatey (not chocolate) creme (not cream). Continental Bakery also makes Wonder Bread.

UNICORNS AND RAINBOWS

If you believe in unicorns and rainbows, you are an interesting person. That is the message broadcast by the several billion variations of both these themes available on cigarette boxes, wall plaques, bumper stickers, T-shirts, baby-crib mobiles, stuffed animals, and wallpaper for little girls' bedrooms. Keeping the image of a unicorn and/or a rainbow nearby provides steady reassurance that you are not a mundane individual who leads a drab life. Unicorns and rainbows mean hopes and dreams. So many people crave that kind of spiritual reassurance that unicorns and rainbows have virtually obliterated the happy face from gift shops across America.

The rainbow and the unicorn had a long, slow march to their present popularity. Rainbows first became popular with hippie freaks in the late sixties. They were hip because they were natural, and their primary colors had a childlike simplicity; plus, being ephemeral, they suggested groovy mythical connotations best appreciated by people who were into mind expansion. They were even appropriated as New Age names, their enchanted spirit enhanced even more if the spelling was changed in a creative way, such as "Rainbeaux." The spectral visions sometimes induced by the drugs LSD and mescaline made rainbows extra groovy, so hippies painted their crash pads with rainbows and appliquéd them onto tattered jeans and denim jackets; they painted their vans with rainbow-colored psychedelic patterns; then, when they got older and more respectable, they put tasteful rainbow decals on their cars' windows, or on the bumpers in the form of a cheerful iridescent sticker.

By the seventies anything with the word *rainbow* in it had countercultural reverberations. Jesse Jackson soon formed the Rainbow Coalition, signifying people of all colors coming together, while New Age space cadets who did not want to let the sixties die banded together for an annual convention of alternative life-stylers known as the Rainbow Gathering, which still takes place. The mainstreaming of rainbows was exemplified by Robin Williams's character Mork on the television show "Mork and Mindy." Mork was a funny guy from the planet Ork who wore pants held up by rainbow-colored suspenders. His relentless cuteness and street-mime wardrobe marked the beginning of the end of rainbows as a symbol with anything other than commercial resonance.

The fact that the unicorn wound up in tacky gift shops and as the subject of wall tapestries in biker bars is a strange twist of fate, given its high-flown lineage. Although mentions of a one-horned beast go back to ancient Greece and the Bible, the unicorn's first big wave of popularity was in the fifteenth century, when it was carved, painted, and woven into tapestries (e.g., *The Hunt of the Unicorn* at the Cloisters in New York City) as a powerful figure that embodied forbidden sensuality as well as the redemption of the spiritual world. The unicorn became a stylish way to represent Christ until the Council of Trent in 1563 forbade all unusual portrayals of the Savior.

The unicorn revival of the twentieth century rests on the mythical beast's reverberations as a lonely symbol of belief in sorcery in a world that desperately needs it. Laura Wingfield keeps one in her collection in Tennessee Williams's *The Glass Menagerie* (its horn gets broken off, along with her hopes). Nancy Hathaway's book *The Unicorn,* published in 1980, speculates that the unicorn has special appeal because he "reminds us of a time when good existed." Unlike the powerful and even ferocious unicorns depicted in the Middle Ages, most modern unicorns are like Laura Wingfield's—fragile and sad, like a fuzzy little troll doll in need of love.

Unicornmania got a big boost and a fast black eye when the Barnum and Bailey Circus came to New York City in 1986, promoting a real live unicorn. It was quickly exposed as a horse that had a horn transplanted surgically to its skull. In fact, *faux* unicorns are nothing new. In 1933, Dr. W. Franklin Dove of the University of Maine made one by transplanting the horn buds of a day-old calf closer together to make them grow as one. It worked, but the resulting animal had none of the charisma of the mythical beast. He simply looked like a big, stupid bull with a cone on its head.

For a short while in the waning afterglow of the happy delirium of Woodstock Nation, unicorns had a smidgen of nonconformist cachet. Like rainbows, they signified that their owner wanted to be ''different.'' That's probably still true; but the fact is that so many people like to see themselves as different in precisely the same way, they're the same, and a huge gift and novelty industry mass-produces rainbows and unicorns to supply them.

Today, when you see a rainbow or a unicorn on an office desk or on a magnet stuck to the refrigerator, do not be surprised to learn that its owner also keeps a crystal hanging from her or his car's rearview mirror, thinks Shirley MacLaine is deep, and swoons at such symbols of modern romance as a single rose, pink champagne, and Julio Iglesias on cassette crooning in the back of a white stretch limo hastening toward a dinner of shrimp cocktail and all the prime rib you can eat.

VANITY LICENSE PLATES

It is not enough for some people to express themselves in conversation or in the kinds of clothes they wear; nor do they find it sufficiently satisfying to limit their self-expression to the company of friends and associates. Some individuals like to broadcast themselves at every possible moment, to everyone. One of the most blatantly vulgar ways to do so is to get a vanity license plate.

Instead of a random assortment of numbers and letters, vanity plates display a combination chosen by the owner of the car: sometimes a simple monogram, but often a word, words, or cryptogram that other drivers and parking attendants are supposed to read and enjoy, spend time deciphering, or be impressed by. A person who wants to be sure everyone knows he is rich might have MYCADDY, EGOTRIP, or LOTABUX. A Hollywood agent announces DEALS on his Mercedes. A Beverly Hills shopper gets BUYIT. Patrons of designer merchandise hope to secure plates that announce their affiliation: GUCCI, BIJAN, POLO, even LLBEAN.

Vanity plates don't display only money lust and materialism. A brainy guy might get PROF, or LEPROF if he speaks French. Personalized license plates can be a way of showing ethnic pride (AFROGUY, WHITEY) or gender pride (IAMWOMAN, MACHOMAN); making toasts (LKHEIM, SALUT); flaunting sexuality (XRATED, KISSME, DUIT2ME); or displaying nonsense mottos (OINK, AEIOU). A driver in California used to have IVNIK8, until authorities realized that

reading the "IV" as a Roman numeral could cause drivers to see the word "fornicate."

Vanity plates were first made available to the public in Connecticut in 1937, when the state decided to allow motorists with spotless driving records to design their own four-character plates (for a fee), which they could then pass along to other members of their family. Scatology was forbidden, although Connecticut did issue MERD to the proprietor of the Raymond Dairy, who said it stood for "Milk, Eggs: Raymond Dairy." For years, the idea was to have a very low number (signifying a fine old family) or a tasteful set of initials. It was assumed in Connecticut, as in other states where personalized license plates were issued in special cases, that having a low number or your initials meant you were the governor, a state senator, or at least very powerful and rich.

In the sixties, vanity accelerated in Washington, D.C., where the quest among status seekers had always been for the lowest number. In 1965, motor vehicle commissioners began allowing any five-character combination. The plan (for which motorists paid an extra twenty-five dollars) was an instant success, because in those days a personalized license plate still implied that its owner was somebody important.

When California began allowing vanity plates in 1970, the possibilities for self-expression were explored with zeal by movie stars and moguls eager to announce themselves wherever they went, as well as by hundreds of thousands of

other ordinary citizens of the Me Decade hungry for ways to spread their egos far and wide. Within a year of the creation of the PLP (Personalized License Plate) division of California's Department of Motor Vehicles, Commissioner Irene Ridenor had rejected GAYLIB, HOMO, SEX, LOVE69, and LSD. She also revealed that she used a mirror to check requests, lest a backward message such as 3M TA3 slip by her.

Now the proliferation of vanity plates in many states has caused problems for ordinary, nonvain motorists who just happen to get letter or number combinations that might be mistaken for their choice. In 1973, when New York went to three-letter-and-three-number combinations on ordinary (nonvanity) plates, the state Department of Motor Vehicles specifically eliminated from the list of possible combinations FAT, OAF, JEW, WOP, JAP, POT, SIN, PIG, ODD, FEM, DYK, and FAG. In Kansas City, Tonya Turnbull had to go to Federal Court to get her license plate changed. The Missouri Department of Revenue had issued her CPG-666. But because 666 is given as the number of the devil in the Bible, she said, her license plate was causing her to be ''shunned as the anti-Christ.''

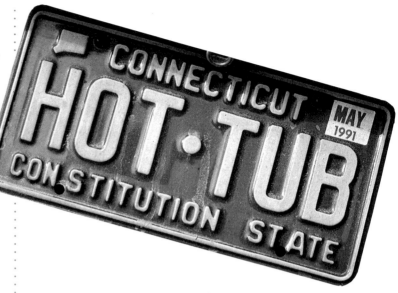

VANS

A van is a boxy truck big enough to provide its occupants nearly all the comforts of a bus-size motor home in a vehicle that is actually not much bigger than a sedan. Activities you can do in a van include watching television, playing Nintendo games, serving cocktails, microwaving a casserole, vibrating in a reclining chair, having sex on a water bed, and cavorting in a hot tub. Not every van is so well equipped, but they all share what Joseph Bohm, writing in *Hanley's Buyer's Guide to Van Conversions,* described as "an atmosphere that allows people to relax and socialize at will."

In addition to amenities reminiscent of a honeymoon hotel in the Poconos, deluxe vans exhibit an extravagant decorative style, inside and out, that, in Mr. Bohm's words, reflects "each individual owner's very explicit taste." Specifically, this means such ornamental touches as windows shaped like hearts and airbrushed mythological murals on the exterior panels starring unicorns, gnomes, muscular superheros wearing wide leather wristbands, and well-stacked women dressed in shredded cave-dweller hides. On the back, the spare-tire cover is where van owners display their personalized credo: "The Dream Team from DeKalb," "We Believe in Unicorns," or "Retired and Loving It."

The inside of an exemplary van is spongy with tuck-and-roll Naugahyde and royal-purple fake-fur-encased hassocks or acres of crushed velvet upholstery. In many older models, smelly old shag rugs are stapled to the floor, ceiling, walls, and dashboard, with cheap wood paneling wherever there are no rugs. Modern refinements include wood-grain pedestal dinette tables with built-in cup holders and capacious sunken ashtrays, flocked drapes on the windows, captain's chairs and couches to sit on, and refreshment stations complete with blenders for making peach daiquiris and Fuzzy Navels. Dashboards are done in wainscoted oak or cherry wood, ordinary steering wheels are replaced by spoked varnished ships' wheels, and rows of Lexan skylights or fiber-optic constellations twinkle in the ceiling.

Conceived as a pleasure palace on wheels, a well-equipped van makes its occupants feel like royalty when they go on a family vacation or simply drive to the videotape rental store. Whatever the whim or need of its passengers, a van can fulfill it, thus engendering the same illusions of mastery and control provided by an obsequious dog or an expensive home-entertainment center.

Thirty years ago, vans were utilitarian vehicles—plain, windowless, bare-inside variations of the traditional panel truck, used mostly by small businesses to deliver merchandise when a full-size delivery truck was too large or too commercial-looking. By the mid-sixties, when Doyle Dane Bernbach's advertising campaign for Volkswagens (using irony rather than Detroit's customary flimflam) had begun to popularize the ugly, unstylish Beetle, itinerant hippies needed a vehicle that was big enough to sleep in, and even to live in if they arrived in a city and no suitable crash pad could be found. Volkswagen had just the ticket: the "Type 2" station wagon, also known as the Microbus. It was spacious, cheap to operate, easy to repair; and because of those eccentric advertisements, it had a credibility among iconoclasts that American-made vehicles (vans especially) did not have. In addition, it had been imported in ever-larger numbers since the mid-fifties, so there were plenty of used ones available at bargain prices.

The Volkswagen bus became America's prototypical van, and the unofficial vehicle of the love-beads set. Hippies painted them with swirling psychedelic designs, draped the interiors with paisley cloths and beaded curtains, and piled in en masse for tribal journeys inspired by Ken Kesey (who had campaigned around the country in 1964 with his Merry Pranksters in a full-size International-Harvester bus). Once a Microbus broke down beyond repair, it was often recycled as a makeshift shelter in hippie communes such as Drop City, Colorado, where all the housing was created from parts of cars.

As hippies made the oddball Volkswagen Microbus their own, another subculture discovered hulking American-made vans. Surfers needed to transport their boards up and down the California coast to where the waves were breaking; and while their traditional favored car was an old wood-sided station wagon, a few life-style pioneers among the wave-riders began to realize that vans were bigger and afforded wonderful tableaux for customization. Surf culture and car culture were intertwined, so it wasn't long before car-conscious surfers began turning Dodge Econolines and Chevy Greenbriars, originally designed strictly as commercial delivery vans, into the choicest way to appear at the beach.

Surfers were partiers; and surfer vans, with either no windows or curtained windows, provided complete privacy as well as plenty of room for the most gymnastic kind of sex in comfort. As the seventies' singles culture grew out of the remnants of the sixties, vans were a part of it—sin bins equipped with most of the appurtenances a swinging guy on the make would want in his penthouse, with the added attraction of mobility.

It wasn't only horny swingers who discovered the advantages of carrying one's own cold beverages and bed wherever one went. Increasing gas prices made bloated Winnebagos, motor homes, and forty-foot trailers prohibitively expensive to operate, so many vacationing families learned to downscale their recreational

travels into relatively economical, fully outfitted vans. The image of the swinger in his water-bed-equipped sin bin became a joke, and as sixties people matured and developed life-styles built around the pursuit of leisure, an industry was born to meet their needs: the van conversion business.

Nearly a thousand different companies, most of them located in northern Indiana, are in the business of taking plain factory-made vans and converting them into comfort-laden, glamorously decorated multipurpose vehicles fit for self-indulgent families on the go. Contemporary Coach of Goshen, Indiana, turns Chevrolets into "Marques Ltd." with solid oak trim and recessed windows; International Vehicles of Bristol, Indiana, makes Chevies or Fords into Sport Top

Horizons with full-featured kitchens and marine toilets; Dealer's Choice of Elkhart specializes in remote-control overhead entertainment centers with color television, VCR, CB radio, radar detector, Nintendo games, and private sound systems for every passenger.

However gaudy they get, none of the factory-made van conversions can compete in ostentation with vans tailor-made by their owners. Nearly any handyman with a spray gun, a can of paint, and masking tape can put "custom graphics" on the sides of a van, turning it into a jumble of lines, shadows, boxes, and artistic patterns. Some of the favored stylistic motifs include cobwebs, ''vreebles'' (Metalflake Company's patented name for a crackly mosaic finish), ''freak drops'' (globby snowflake patterns), spaghetti stripes (thin geometric lines in an apparently random pattern), and the ever-popular flames, clouds, and fish scales.

Advanced do-it-yourselfers use a paint called Eerie-Dess, another Metalflake Company product, and while it is still wet, daub it with aluminum foil to create a crystalline effect. Then, too, there are the classic garish candy, pearl, and Metalflake finishes with their iridescent sheen. The weirdest of these chromatic aberrations is known as Flip-Flop pearl because it seems to change color as the viewer moves around it: excellent for murals with spiritual or religious overtones.

Many vans are completely thematic, with murals on both sides, back, and front, as well as complementary interior decor. Nearly every van-customizing shop has a resident muralist who can cover the sides with J. R. R. Tolkien characters, Grateful Dead motifs, jungle animals, distant planets, and atomic bomb explosions. *The Art of Custom Painting* by Carl Caiati, who is known in the custom-van world as ''the Psychedelic Psycho,'' suggests van motifs of spooky caverns, mountain lakes, and cartoon cuties.

The most dramatic murals are self-referential, showing the very van on which they are painted riding through futuristic or outer-space landscapes, driven by a raging Conan the Barbarian look-alike accompanied by a barely dressed Wagnerian siren in the passenger's seat. Such fantasies might have a tantalizing effect if you find yourself parked next to one in a Burger King lot, unless and until the real occupants of the van waddle out looking for a trash can into which to heave their Whopper wrappers.

VELVET PAINTINGS

Bright paint on black velvet creates an image so plush it makes you want to touch it, or maybe even wriggle your naked toes against the part of the painting's fuzzy pile that isn't covered by paint. The drama of lustrous brush strokes on a raven field is visually thrilling no matter what is in the picture, but the reputation of velvet painting does not come from bravura technique alone. Tradition demands powerful subjects that are sentimental, dramatic, or ennobling. It is rare to see a still life or landscape; on the other hand, there are plenty of ferocious jungle beasts, tearful big-eyed tots sitting on the potty, Elvises sweating with microphones in their hands, clipper ships braving stormy seas, and matadors dodging angry bulls.

Not all classic velvet paintings are exciting action scenes. Many of the most popular works of oil on velvet take advantage of the magical luminescence of the medium and portray heroic or godly characters in an uplifting way. No roadside display (which is where the majority of velvet paintings are sold) is without such idols as Jesus Christ, Martin Luther King, Jr., John F. Kennedy, John Lennon, Sylvester Stallone as Rambo, the deceased *Challenger* astronauts, and most recently, Lucille Ball (au naturel or in clown makeup). The traditional way to paint these effigies is to leave plenty of untouched black velvet all around the subject and use nearly phosphorescent pigments for the highlights on their skin, making them appear bathed in a spotlight. For around the heads of Jesus, JFK, and Martin Luther King, a halo or starburst effect is sometimes employed to emphasize their goodness.

One genre of velvet painting that is always in great demand is the inspirational ethnic stereotype. These are pictures of racial ideals, listed in velvet-painting catalogues by such titles as *African King* (a scowling black man holding a dagger while sitting on a leopard-skin throne), *Aztec Warrior* (a musclebound Hispanic man protecting a swooning maiden from an attacking pterodactyl), and *Indian Maiden* (a serene squaw wrapped in a serape with eagle feathers in her braids). There are no such Caucasian ideals (a bespectacled man in suspenders working on a spreadsheet in his cubicle?), but white people who want a universal image of their own kind for the wall will discover that most well-stocked velvet-painting displays do carry erotic portraits of nude white women, sad clowns in whiteface, and perhaps even a replica of Gainsborough's *Blue Boy*.

Although painting on velvet began in late-fifteenth-century Italy, today it is the specialty of Mexican border towns Juárez and Tijuana. The paintings are made in factories by groups of artists who have precise specialties such as charging bulls, glorious sunsets, or Afro hairdos. The better artists pride themselves on painting the old-fashioned way, using brush and pallet knife rather than a spray gun or (in the lowest-level factories) an inked press to apply the entire painting to the velvet in a trice. In top-of-the-line velvet-painting workshops, the master artist signs his work, and each painting is furnished with a genuine wooden frame. Nearly every supplier of velvet paintings makes each image in several sizes, so customers with grand living rooms can buy their *Bandido with Cigar* in a two-by-three-foot model, and those with only a little space above their dinette can get the same fierce-looking *Bandido* shrunk to twelve by eighteen inches.

From the manufacturers, velvet paintings are shipped to huge repositories in the U.S. (The biggest cocaine bust in history, in Los Angeles in 1989, took place at Adriana's Pottery Warehouse, which purported to be a velvet-painting distributor. The drug dealers were caught, however, after fashion-conscious citizens observed that the alleged velvet-painting merchants were far too well dressed for their trade.) From the warehouse, paintings are shipped to truck-stop gift shops or put on consignment in motel lobbies. Some go directly to individual entrepreneurs who use a van to carry the art to a choice location in a mall parking

lot or near a highway exit ramp each weekend, where it can be displayed alongside plush animals to attract passing motorists.

If you cannot find a painting you like, but do know a velvet-painting ''gallery'' that you believe will be around for several weeks, you may want to inquire about one of the most fascinating services offered by a few of the elite velvet painters—custom work. You supply them with a clear color picture of a loved one, a pet, or a favorite saint; and within six to eight weeks, you receive the cherished image in a hand-carved wooden frame, immortalized on black velvet with the artistic panache that only a factory in Mexico can provide.

WALTZING WATERS

U.S. 41 south of Fort Myers, Florida, offers a throng of malls, mini-malls, and fast-food franchises to service your every need, plus one place that serves no purpose other than to bring beauty into the world and make audiences gasp in wonder: Waltzing Waters. Billing itself as "the most elaborate water, music, and light production in the world," Waltzing Waters outdoes all other fountains that spout in tune to music or are lit with colored lights. In an otherwise ordinary auditorium, six hundred hydraulic spouts are marshaled behind the curtain line on a watertight stage. The lights dim, and a svelte prerecorded voice, teetering on the edge of breathless hysteria because of the joyful wonderment about to transpire, booms forth from loudspeakers to explain what will happen: "Get ready to tap your feet, as we all get hooked on the classics!"

The voice fades, and the spouts pump massive jets of water high up toward the proscenium. The hundreds of geysers arc, leap, wave, shimmy, and sway in formations as precise as sine waves while colored lights make the patterns glow with rainbow hues. Every nuance of the water's flight is synchronized note by note to passages from familiar classics such

as *Swan Lake,* the *1812* Overture, and "The Ride of the Valkyries." Then come modern favorites, starting with "Stranger in Paradise," all the way up to theme songs from television's "Entertainment Tonight" and "M*A*S*H" (the latter synchronized with water jets that are blood red).

After the classics and TV themes come show tunes: passages from each and every song in *My Fair Lady.* Then the climax: a patriotic medley that salutes America by having the water waltz to a titanic melody composed of fifty—count 'em, fifty—different musical passages, one for each state. For one hour and ten minutes you sit in a dark auditorium watching illuminated water squirt out of a sprinkler system and tapping your feet to an agitated synopsis of the history of music since the eighteenth century and a musico-geographical pilgrimage through all of America.

To understand how uncanny the show is, you must imagine the booming music and disembodied voice of the narrator nearly drowned out by the incessant din of gallons of water falling back onto the aquatic stage. It is overwhelming and exhausting, fraught with the kind of relentless obsession that breeds (and is bred by) hysteria. ''Most folks applaud. Some folks sing along. A few folks even cry,'' the Waltzing Waters brochure advises.

When the concept of Waltzing Waters was devised in thirties Germany, there was actually a man who ''played'' the sprinkler system, manipulating the water nozzles while an orchestra played the music. Michael Gunter Przystawik, proprietor and copyright holder of Waltzing Waters in America since the sixties, uses computers. Early on, he replaced the fountainmeister with a white-suited ''conductor'' who stood at the front of the auditorium and only seemed to direct the waters' movements. In recent years, however, the conductor has been done away with altogether. The show now is just the audience, the water, the music, the lights, and the prerecorded voice.

If you attend Waltzing Waters in the evening, you can go outside afterwards and experience an entirely different outdoor show in a covered amphitheater at nine p.m.; and as encores for those who cannot get enough of this zestful place, Waltzing Waters of Fort Meyers also features a Hanging Gardens Beauty Walkway, a Rainbow (miniature) Golf course, and one of the largest gift shops in southwestern Florida. The brochure for Waltzing Waters in Fort Meyers describes it as the ''global headquarters'' of water-and-light ballets, but there are other Waltzing Waters theaters in Gatlinburg, Tennessee, and Branson, Missouri.

WATER BEDS

Swept up in the Love Generation's search for Nirvana, furniture designer Charles Hall spent the late 1960s trying to make a chair that would suspend its occupant in a state of bliss. Bean-bag furniture (rubber or vinyl sandbags in the shapes of chairs, couches, and ottomans) was popular at the time, but too unyielding. Inflatable furniture filled with air was too springy. Hall thought he had the answer when he designed and built what he called the Incredible Creeping Chair, which was made of vinyl and filled with three hundred pounds of liquid starch, designed to gradually creep up around the occupant and lull him or her into cosmic contentment. The starch was too stiff, so he tried colored Jell-O inside see-through vinyl; but the Jell-O turned lumpy. Realizing that it was the chair's shape as much as its contents that was giving him problems, Hall abandoned his quest for the perfect chair and created what many people at the time celebrated as truly the perfect bed—the water bed.

No starch, no Jell-O, no difficult armrests to keep in their proper place: Hall simply filled a vinyl mattress-shaped rectangle with water. It seemed perfect until he slept on his invention and reported, "I woke up with my bottom feeling like ice." Hall designed a heater for his bed, and by early 1969 his crusade was done. He gave a water bed to a friend who described sleeping on one like returning to the womb—the highest compliment anything could get in those mystic days on the cusp between the Age of Aquarius and the psychobabbling seventies. Hall considered calling his invention the Bedwomb, but stuck with "water bed" (a term in use since 1853 to describe water-filled mattresses for invalids) when it went on sale in August 1970, in department stores from coast to coast.

Within months, America went water-bed crazy. "I got a vision," water-bed promoter Michael Valentine Zamoro told *Time*. "I saw a wave of blue water like a breaker. On the wave in golden script was written: The World Wants Water Beds." Zamoro made a fortune selling them, as did dozens of manufacturers with such names as Innerspace Environments, Joyapeutic, and Wet Dream. Water beds were the focus of thousands of kooky news stories. *Good Housekeeping* published warnings about the two-ton beds crashing through floors and about leaking ones shorting out electrical circuits. In California, an escaped water bed, set in motion by a man test-filling it on a slope in his backyard, was reported to have gathered momentum going downhill and to have flattened everything in its path like a runaway elephant. Water beds were great novelty attractions in stores, where everybody had to try one at least once. Kids jumped up and down on them like trampolines; department store customers lay down for a test nap and were lulled into deep sleep by the rippling tides.

There was something psychedelic about water beds' sloshy motion, and they were instantly associated with the watery-headed hippies of the sixties who were bent on finding a higher state of consciousness. "You can't fight the water," inventor Hall coached novice water-bed buyers, parroting Timothy Leary's instructions about taking a LSD trip. "You have to go with it." It was a popular assumption that most water beds were bought by people who lay on them in naked communal groups while watching their Lava Lite, smoking dope, making love, and listening to sitar music.

But hippies were already on their way out when water beds were coming in; it was the burgeoning singles culture that made water beds a preeminent sex symbol of the early seventies and gave them a lewd and tasteless reputation the modern water-bed industry is still trying to shake. There was, after all, something undeniably provocative about a bed that rocked and jiggled. "Two things are better on a water bed," teased an advertisement by Aquarius Products, Inc. "One of them is sleep." Dr. HIPpocrates, the syndicated medical columnist, recommended water beds to women who had trouble having orgasms. Hugh Hefner, the world's most eligible bachelor, supplemented his famous round motorized bed with a king-sized water bed

covered with Tasmanian opossum fur. The water bed showroom at Bloomingdale's in New York became a notorious meeting place for singles on the make.

Guys looking to turn their pads into bona fide sin bins bought a model known as Pleasure Island, made by Innerspace. It was eight by eight feet with built-in color television, stereo system, wet bar, and mood lighting, and was surrounded on all sides by contour pillows. It cost $2,800. Although $45 would buy a spare bare-vinyl bed with a wood-fiber box around it, most of the models sold in the seventies were in the Pleasure Island mode: significant pieces of furniture with multimedia headboards that transformed the bed from a private place to sleep into an invitation for revelry. Such beds were often sold with built-in

footboard cabinets, too, designed to hold large-screen projection televisions that could be watched while undulating on the mattress. One popular model known as the Aquarius had a footboard that contained a four-foot-tall illuminated fish tank (fish not supplied).

Many of these behemoths came in bed frames made of distressed or darkened thick-grain #2 pine, sanded and shellacked to the same glassy polyurethane finish seen on crafts made by inmates in penitentiary woodworking programs. It was in this painfully primitive form that water beds joined the sad ranks of other leftover Aquarian emblems such as carved teak hash pipes, Aubrey Beardsley posters, and gloppy, rainbow-colored shades for Tiffany-like lamps.

WAX MUSEUMS

Wax museums often advertise themselves as educational because they present important scenes from history, but the big attraction at almost all of them is seeing dead and dying people with their guts hanging out. No wax museum is without gape-mouthed heads fallen into guillotine baskets, scalps being severed from pioneers' heads, partially dressed beautiful women being tortured, savage battle scenes, gruesome movie monsters, and famous mass murderers. The brochure from the Royal London Wax Museum explains, ''Whether we like it or not, our chronicle is scarred with man's inhumanity to man, with villains and murderers, and it is the business of the Wax Museum to depict life in all its many aspects.''

The ancient art of wax modeling made butchery its leitmotiv during the French Revolution, when Marie Grosholtz, briefly imprisoned as a suspected royalist, was put to work making death masks of noble heads lopped off by the guillotine. Mlle Grosholtz was suited to the task, as her uncle Dr. Philippe Curtius had taught her wax-modeling techniques he had perfected in the 1760s in Switzerland. Dr. Curtius had learned his trade because fresh cadavers were hard to find, so he started a business making wax limbs and organs for medical demonstrations. His talents were so re-

nowned he set up waxworks of famous people in Paris, including La Caverne des Grands Voleurs (the Cavern of Great Thieves), where Marie became his apprentice.

After the revolution, Marie met and married François Tussaud. In 1802, Monsieur and Madame Tussaud left the Paris waxworks behind and went to England with seventy of their finest death masks and effigies. For thirty-three years, their gory gallery of famous and infamous mannequins toured throughout the United Kingdom; and in 1835, at the age of seventy-four, Madame Tussaud found a permanent home for the collection on Baker Street in London. Its descendant, on Marylebone Road, today features death masks of Louis XVI and Marie Antoinette, as well as the actual blades that beheaded them, plus an Elvis that talks, a David Bowie with hair that seems to move, and a chamber of horrors with Adolf Hitler and Charles Manson.

George L. Potter opened America's first wax museum in St. Augustine, Florida, in 1949. Potter's is still in business, promising figures ''created in England by leading European artists after painstaking historical research,'' and gives visitors the opportunity to have their picture taken standing next to Napoleon Bonaparte. Almost every big tourist attraction in America now has a wax museum somewhere nearby, including such specialty waxworks as Ripley's Believe It or Not Odditoriums, featuring shrunken heads and the human unicorn.

Most exhibits are timeless, such as Pocahontas pleading for Captain John Smith's life or Marilyn Monroe standing above the subway grate in *The Seven-Year Itch* with her dress being blown above her waist; but some featured attractions do go out of date. In the late sixties, nearly every popular waxworks had Faye Dunaway and Warren Beatty as Bonnie and Clyde; a decade later, John Travolta in his disco suit from *Saturday Night Fever* was immensely popular. Most Bonnies, Clydes, and Travoltas have been melted down and remade into Indiana Joneses, Batmans, and Jokers by now.

According to Gene Gurney, author of *America in Wax,* the most enduring of all wax-museum displays is Leonardo's *The Last Supper.* Comparisons of two-dimensional reproductions of paintings alongside three-dimensional reproductions of the subjects are always a popular theme—e.g., a wax figure of the Mona Lisa sitting in a chair and a wax figure of Leonardo painting her, and an exact reproduction of the canvas on his easel. This enables the viewer to see how well Leonardo has captured the wax model's smile in his painting. Paintings are popular also because they provide an opportunity to fill the wax museum with lifelike nudes—the "models" used by Botticelli or Rubens, or that gorgeous gal who posed as the Venus de Milo, who looks even better as a wax effigy, because her arms and head are intact.

Although modeling techniques haven't changed much since Madame Tussaud's time, there have been improvements in material. Dorfman Museum Figures of Baltimore ("Select from more than 700 already-sculpted heads or have heads sculpted to your own needs and exacting specifications") uses a mixture of resin and plastic rather than the traditional beeswax. Once a head is created using a plaster mold, real human hair is implanted follicle by follicle (and facial stubble may be implanted on a male who needs it, such as Richard Nixon), glass eyes are inserted, and dentures are put in the mouth. After a head is made, it must be cleaned like any human head: the hair shampooed and combed, the teeth brushed, the brow dusted. Similarly, a wax-museum figure's clothes must be laundered and pressed from time to time.

Scrupulous attention to detail and the finest artistry cannot overcome the inherent flaw of a wax figure, which is that it almost always looks disappointingly small. Many wax museums try to explain the diminution by the fact that the human race has been getting bigger over the years, but the real problem is the figures' immobility. Because their clothes just hang on resin torsos, every exhibit in a wax museum tends to look shrunken and drained, engulfed by its wardrobe, no matter how robust its features.

Nude exhibits do not have this problem, which is one reason Adam and Eve in the Garden of Eden (as at the Natural Bridge Wax Museum) is so popular. On the other hand, it is a major problem if one figure is clothed and the other one is nude, as was the case in the exhibit of Hugh Hefner at home with a Playboy bunny in the buff that used to be on exhibit at the Underground Wax Museum of Atlanta. The bunny, lying naked on a white fur rug (but tastefully facing away from the viewer) looked voluptuously waxy. Hef, sitting smoking his pipe and wearing mod checked pants and a sweater, appeared to be half her size, like a ventriloquist's dummy that someone had tossed onto an easy chair.

319

WEEKI WACHEE MERMAIDS

Weeki Wachee is a fathomless natural artesian spring forty-five miles north of Tampa, Florida, in which mermaids stage an underwater pageant three times a day, every day of the year. Their performance takes place in a theater sixteen feet below sea level, behind panoramic glass windows. The audience watches the mermaids through the glass from a four-hundred-seat air-conditioned auditorium.

What do mermaids do when they put on a show? Like the roller-skating cockatoos and kissing macaws in Weeki Wachee's exotic bird show (above sea level), they do everyday things. The fact that they are underwater and wearing zip-on tails is what makes them remarkable. They toss a Frisbee back and forth. They drink soda pop from bottles. They eat, actually swallowing, apples and bananas. One lies down on a rubber-ribbed lounge chair and applies lotion to her arms, as if she expects to get a tan. Another swims out with a rake and pretends to scrape up leaves from the ground. If it weren't for the long manes of hair hovering weightlessly up and around their heads, and a periodic suck on the air hose that each mermaid carries (and sometimes wields like a whip), you could almost forget they are underwater: They look like lovely lunatics dressed in fish tails who happen to have been stunned into slow-motion stupor by a heavy dose of Thorazine, and for whom these everyday activities are a considerable challenge.

Being a mermaid is a challenge in many ways. Staying underwater for a half hour, three times a day, is itself a taxing occupation. Anyone prone to ear infections or dermatological disorders could never make the cut. Once a girl is selected, she undergoes two to three months of training and practice before joining the twenty-mermaid squad. One of the most peculiar things she learns is how to apply waterproof makeup. A nice blushing pink complexion above the surface looks sickly pale sixteen feet below. Using color research done by fishing-lure companies, Weeki Wachee mermaid trainers have devised makeup strategies that give the girls a glamorous radiance in the deep. Out of water, however, a mermaid in her makeup is a harsh, shocking sight.

The most impressive part of the show is the mermaids' underwater ballet: sets of acrobatic adagios that would be impossible on any air-bound stage. ''The adagio is the trademark of Florida's Weeki Wachee,'' a promotional brochure advises—meaning not that Weeki Wachee has trademarked slow ballet but that the image of one mermaid effortlessly holding another aloft is Weeki Wachee's emblem, rendered most majestically in an all-white classical sculpture at the top of a tall Grecian pillar in the parking lot.

Mermaid shows at Weeki Wachee began in 1947, when former navy frogman Newton Perry bought the spring and came up with the idea of breathing through a garden hose supplied with air from a compressor. Perry's first mermaids performed in a canvas tank outfitted with small portholes through which audiences watched them reenact ballet poses. It was a winning combination of cheesecake and culture, with the added attraction of nature appreciation—of Weeki Wachee's miraculous 72.4-degree, crystal-clear water. A year after opening, Weeki Wachee was featured in the movie *Mr. Peabody and the Mermaid*. Esther Williams swam in the springs in *Neptune's Daughter* (1949) but required professional mermaid Mary Zellner to double for her in the underwater scenes (Zellner knew how to breathe through a hose). Weeki Wachee's last brush with Hollywood glamour occurred in 1964, when it was the site of the world premiere of *The Incredible Mr. Limpet*, starring Don Knotts as a man who becomes a fish.

WELK, LAWRENCE

Wouldn't you like to visit a land where everyone is polite; a place brimming with accordion music, polka bands, sunbonneted bathing beauties twirling parasols, and men in straw hats singing barbershop tunes. Add a tear-jerking Irish tenor, four hymn-singing sisters with lace mantillas on their heads, a mustachioed violinist named Aladdin, and a machine that spouts merry soap bubbles without end. This was "The Lawrence Welk Show," sponsored by Geritol, Sominex, and Aqua Velva.

Lawrence Welk was born in 1903 to German immigrant parents in Strasburg, North Dakota, and did not learn to speak English until he was twenty-one. But he was practically poetic when he described the reason for his success: "The farmers come in from their hard day milking the cow and tending the crops and they want to put their feet up and drink beer and listen to the polkas."

For sixteen years on ABC and eleven more in syndication, he was able to give his viewers exactly what they wanted, because it was what *he* wanted: girls who didn't show too much leg; boys with neatly cut hair; blithe, bouncy tunes that nice people could tap their toes to. As the sixties ran amok, testing all rules, Welk created a world without controversy or questioning, where nothing shocking happened, and where events were as happy and bland as white-meat-only Thanksgiving turkey dinner.

As a teenager in Strasburg, Welk found his musical ambition first roused when he heard an accordion recital by a traveling musician named Tom Gutenberg. In exchange for four years' work on the family farm, his parents gave him his first professional instrument: a rhinestone-studded accordion. He played polkas and waltzes at weddings and barn dances; then in 1924 he went to the big city—Bismarck, North Dakota— and eventually formed a dance band known as the Hotsy Totsy Boys (or sometimes the Honolulu Fruit Orchestra). Radio station WNAX of Yankton, South Dakota, hired him to play on the air for the first time; and suddenly Welk was a local sensation. Despite their immediate success,

some of the band members quit, complaining that Welk bounced around the stage as if he were at a barn dance and that he spoke embarrassingly poor English.

Welk traveled around the country with "America's Biggest Little Band," including Leo Fortin, who was famous for playing two trumpets at the same time, and Terry George, who could play "Nola" on trombone using his right foot to operate the slide. Welk dropped the Hotsy Totsy—Honolulu Fruit names in favor of the more dignified "Lawrence Welk and His Champagne Music Makers" when he saw a roadside billboard advertising Miller High Life beer as "the Champagne of Bottled Beers."

For ten years Welk and his orchestra were a fixture at Chicago's Trianon Ballroom; then in 1951 he went west and got his first television show on a Los Angeles station. Four years later "The Lawrence Welk Show" debuted on ABC as a summer replacement for "The Saturday Night Fights." From the start, he was his own harshest censor. Sponsors wanted the show spiced up, suggesting a line of chorus girls and a racy comedian. Welk was horrified and threatened to walk out unless everything met his moral specifications. He won his battle and set the tone for three decades of unchallenged wholesomeness. "Nobody's going to pull the wool over my head," he announced, and he meant it.

The mannerisms that endeared "the Guy Lombardo of the Corn Belt" to his fans were a gold mine for comic parodists. His peppy "Uh-one, an' uh-two" cue for the orchestra, and the "Wunnerful! Wunnerful!" he exclaimed when the Lennon Sisters sang a favorite tune such as "The Lady in Blue Taught Me How To Pray," became as recognizable as Ed Sullivan's "really big shew." Furthermore, he was a master of the malaprop; he referred to feminists as "womens ad-libbers" and was known on more than one occasion to tell an appealing woman she was "appalling." Once after a rough plane flight he said, "I saw my whole life pass between my eyes"; and when he heard of a politician who

had been cited for doing a good deed, he observed, "That's a real feather in his head."

Although he was sensitive to the jokes made at his expense, it never distracted him from the real aim of his job: figuring out what his audience wanted. This was made easy by legions of fans who saw the people on the show as an extension of their own kin, and believed Welk when he referred to them as his "musical family." Welk scrutinized fan mail, tallying pro and con letters for each performer, featuring those who were liked and excising the ones who bothered too many viewers. When one elderly lady wrote to protest Welk's own appearance dressed in lederhosen, explaining she was offended by his knees, Welk took the criticism seriously. From that time on, it was rare to see him on television without a jacket and tie. Once in the late sixties, he violated this code and appeared on stage at a live concert dressed as a hippie wearing a sleeveless bearskin vest, a flowered green shirt, and a shoulder-length black wig. The audience grew deathly quiet. Welk recalled that even after he removed the wig, things did not go back to normal for the rest of the show.

Other members of the cast were allowed to have a little fun with their wardrobes, appearing in Gay Nineties bathing trunks or Easter Bunny suits or Uncle Sam top hats to match that week's theme. There were Christmas shows, Easter shows, St. Patrick's Day shows, shows that featured only songs that had the word "baby" in the title, and "battling accordion" shows that pitched Welk against resident squeeze-box meister Myron Floren.

Lawrence Welk was the king of his kingdom of schmaltz, and the Champagne Lady was his queen. Champagne Lady was the position of penultimate honor in the show's hierarchy. She was chosen for her talents as a charming female sidekick and for her ability to sing and do a graceful waltz and polka with Welk. The first to hold the title on television was Alice Lon, who appeared on Welk's first televised show from the Aragon Ballroom in Ocean Park, California, to sing "Love Me or Leave Me," and got as big an ovation as Myron Floren's frenzied accordion rendition of "Tico Tico." She served as Champagne Lady until July 1959, when she left the show in a hail of rumors that ranged from creative differences to chronic bleeding hands. In fact, Welk fired her because she had sat down and crossed her legs, revealing a knee. "Cheesecake does not fit our show," he told her. After a year and a half of substitute Champagne Ladies, Welk hired Norma Zimmer, who at first didn't like the title because it reminded her of beer, whiskey, and other unladylike beverages. He convinced her that "Champagne Lady" meant only a "bubbly personality and bubbling music."

Bubbles were the motif of every show. As the Champagne Music Makers played, cascades of bubbles rose up and filled the stage. They were an essential part of Welk's happy mise-en-scène, but they drove set designer Charles "Chuck" Koons crazy for years. In the book *Champagne Music: The Lawrence Welk Show*, he recalled that

the bubbles caused me nothing but twenty-seven years of problems! Bubbles are greasy. You had to protect the floor or somebody would slip. Through the years, we had them behind the orchestra, and had a bank of eight or nine fans to try to keep the bubbles blowing straight up. They'd get on the violin strings and the bow would slip. They'd spot the brass. They got on the heads of the drums. Cal Tech tried to make a bubble solution that wasn't greasy. They gave up.

Being old-fashioned, Lawrence Welk felt that it was unseemly for the female regulars on the show who were "in a family way" to flaunt their pregnant bellies. And it was just his luck to have a cast of highly fertile, mostly Catholic stars who made pregnancy a perpetual problem. Dozens of solutions were devised to protect viewers from blatant displays of fecundity. Ragtime piano player Jo Ann Castle was dressed in a chicken costume and made to sit in a huge half-egg that came up to her waist. The highly reproductive

Lennon Sisters, who tended to get pregnant en masse, were posed behind all manner of potted palms, pianos, telephone switchboards, and other bulky props. To further conceal their bulges they were costumed in blue chiffon dresses known to cast and crew as "tents."

The lovely Lennon Sisters—Kathy, Dianne, Janet, and Peggy—became almost as famous as Lawrence Welk himself, and symbolized values of hearth, home, and family. They originally met the maestro when Welk's son, who attended the same school as they, was so impressed by their sunny singing voices and wholesome attitudes, he brought them home to meet his dad. Welk's first memory of the Lennons, who ranged from nine to sixteen when he met them, was that they were "fresh-faced and glowing, very sweet and lady-like—the kind of girls I have always liked." They first appeared on his TV Christmas special show in 1955, then joined the musical family.

For thirteen years, the Lennons reigned as Middle America's sweethearts. They were on the cover of movie and TV fan magazines as frequently as Liz Taylor and Jackie Kennedy. *Silver Screen* reported that Peggy Lennon often had discussions with Welk about the teaching of St. Thomas Aquinas, while *Screen Stories* ran the headline, "What the Lennon Sisters Can Teach Lynda and Luci About Love," and a story in which Dianne Lennon brags that she married a guy who works for the phone company and not a playboy like George Hamilton (who was dating President Johnson's daughter Lynda at the time).

When the Lennons grew dissatisfied with their role in Lawrence Welk's family and quit in 1968 to build their own careers, fans wept in their hankies as if their own daughters had walked out on them; and Lawrence Welk, who in public had only kind things to say about the girls, was reported to have stated in private that by leaving the show the Lennon Sisters "were digging their own funerals."

When ABC canceled "The Lawrence Welk Show" in 1971, it was not for lack of an audience. It was because the audience was too old, and youth-pandering advertisers needed young people to buy their products. Welk continued taping his show and airing it in syndication, often pulling in ratings higher than the network competition. The last "Lawrence Welk Show" was taped in 1982, but reruns are carried in nearly every television market, and watching a rerun of a "Lawrence Welk Show" is even better than watching it the first time: It's proof that bubbles are forever.

See also **ACCORDION MUSIC**

WHITE LIPSTICK

With occasional exceptions—such as eighteenth-century French women who ate arsenic wafers to give their skin a fragile pallor—makeup has almost always been used to create an appearance of good health: to give cheeks a cheerful glow, to outline eyes so they sparkle, and to make lips appear rosy. One of the most frightening modern exceptions to this rule is a peculiar style of macabre makeup developed in the early sixties, which makes its wearer look deceased. The appearance is achieved by applying enough dark eye shadow and eyeliner to turn the sockets into skeletal holes, whitening the face, then applying white lipstick. The lipstick gives the mouth a gruesome ashen hue so devoid of color that even the cleanest white teeth look yellow by comparison.

It began as a chic European look, first spotted on the solemn faces of some alienated heroines of *nouvelle vague* movies and Antonioni art films such as *Red Desert*. The cadaverous complexion was customarily combined with a bouffant hairdo and a sack dress, and was emblematic of a woman who, rather than present a perky face to the world, wanted to announce her soul-corroding angst. Like the bouffant, the ghastly look trickled down fast to vulgarians hungry for glamour. Beginning as high fashion worn by the likes of Princess Luciana Pignatelli, movie star Virna Lisi, and long-limbed model Verushka, it was grabbed by precocious high-school girls who loved it for its drama.

Teenage cosmetics enthusiasts had been perfecting a white-lipped look of their own for several years. White lips became a vital component of the insouciant vulgarity so many teen girls tried to cultivate, using Elizabeth Taylor (in her *Cleopatra* getup) and the kids on "American Bandstand" as their guide. As there was not yet any good white lipstick on the market, they figured out that they could use a product called Erace, which came in a lipsticklike tube but was designed to erase dark circles under women's eyes. Smeared on lips as a way of "whitening down" a color, or as a noncolor all by

Priscilla Presley,
December 1963

itself, Erace achieved a breathtaking spectral effect. Then in 1959, Max Factor consummated the trend by introducing a line of lipsticks called Iridescent Magic, including white Essence of Pearl and Golden Frost. Advertisements suggested using both in combination with ordinary red, pink, or coral to give them pizzazz; but the truly exciting look was to use an iridescent shade alone, creating white or gold lips that appeared electrified with an eerie black-light glow.

You would think that a fashion so bizarre would vanish as quickly as platform shoes; but along with the towering bouffant it complements so well, white lipstick and its frightening mien remain a stylish look among beauty queens for whom femininity includes a whiff of horror—in the form of a face made up to resemble a living corpse.

See also **BOUFFANTS**

WINKING EYES

In the annals of cheap thrills, few scientific wonders are as daft as a winky. Also known as a flicker, a winky is a picture that seems to wink at you as you wiggle it in front of your face or walk back and forth staring at it. Actually, not all winkies wink; in some of them, other things move. There are many winkies of the Beatles on which they bob their heads or jump in the air; there is Elvis with a shaking pelvis, a Mona Lisa who smiles and frowns, and hoochie-koochie girls who bump and grind and sometimes strip. Probably the most popular subject of winking-eye pictures is Jesus, who is usually shown on the cross fluttering His eyelids or in more elaborate three-way winkies opening His eyes, looking out at the viewer, then looking up at God, then closing His eyes again. Another Jesus winky postcard shows the Savior laying hands on a blind boy, who opens *his* eyes when the picture pivots.

Winkies illustrate the two-for-one principle of bad taste: Instead of getting one picture, you get two, plus the tireless fun of watching (for example) a dog lift his leg against a fire hydrant over and over as many times as you wiggle it before your eyes. The idea of a picture that shows two aspects of the same scene has an antecedent in the work of Charles Allan Gilbert, a Hartford, Connecticut, illustrator at the beginning

of the century who made a lithograph called *All Is Vanity*. His picture shows a woman sitting at a vanity table in front of a mirror; but if you look at it long and hard enough, another image takes shape. What you thought was a woman and a mirror is also a grinning skull; and thus you are forced to contemplate the folly of vanity. There is no winkylike mechanical trickery in Gilbert's (much imitated) picture; but his memento mori has become classic kitsch for its brazen combination of melodrama and morality.

Winkies were manufactured in the forties and fifties by a company named Vari-Vue in Mount Vernon, New York, which produced everything from key chains with winking pinup girls to suitable-for-framing vistas of great moments in history (Lee's surrender; the Pilgrims' landing; the signing of the Declaration of Independence). The last great winky era was the psychedelic sixties, when stoned hippies blew their minds contemplating abstract spiral winkies and peace-sign winkies that turned into rainbows. In 1968 the Rolling Stones put a winky on the cover of *Their Satanic Majesties Request*: Careful wiggling revealed all four Beatles secreted among a bunch of flowers.

What makes winkies work is a plastic ribbing fastened on a picture that is actually several pictures. Depending on your angle of view, the ribbing brings one or another of the pictures below it into focus, thus creating the illusion of movement as your angle of view changes. The identical technology is used to create autostereoscopic 3-D pictures, which don't require glasses. In a 3-D picture, instead of having an open eye and a closed eye below the plastic ribbing, you have the same scene several times, but photographed at slightly different angles. The 3-D effect is created when you bob your head back and forth looking at the picture: As in reality, things in the foreground appear to move more than things in the background. Traditional 3-D pictures include Leonardo's *Last Supper* and close-ups of Jesus on the cross with blood and/or tears that not only stand out from His face but also appear to roll down His cheeks.

President and Mrs. Richard M. Nixon Visit to China, February 1972

WONDER BREAD

There are many brands of spongy factory-made white bread, but the spongiest and biggest-selling bread of all is Wonder. Wonder, as well as all the lesser-known cottony-soft loaves made from bleached white flour, is gastronomy's unfailing litmus test to divide the snobs from the slobs.

How you feel about Wonder Bread announces your attitude about eating, your self-image, and to a great extent your philosophy of life. To scorn it is to announce that you are a sniveling sophisticate; you reject common people's tastes. To sport a couple of giant loaves of it in the shopping cart runs the risk of other shoppers suspecting you will likely go home to eat bologna and Miracle Whip sandwiches while yelling at the professional wrestling match on TV and lounging in your recliner wearing an undershirt or housecoat.

Bread has always been a symbol bigger than itself, but for the last hundred years, since millers began extracting the germ from wheat to make the grinding more efficient and bleaching flour white to make it prettier, it has been the flashpoint for food fights among the gastronomically self-righteous. Early defenders of mass-produced white loaves said that not only did homemade bread waste valuable time, it was too heavy and therefore impeded digestion. Furthermore, the puffy loaf was elegant, and a fine way to elevate one's table above the coarseness and vulgarity implied by thick-crusted, rough-grained peasant loaves. The Reverend Henry Ward Beecher, on the other hand, condemned white bread in 1871 as soulless: "What had been the staff of life for countless ages [has] become a weak crutch."

Sixty-three years later, the battle was still raging when a 1934 booklet called "Vitality Demands Energy" (published by General Mills) took up the cause of white bread by crediting it with nothing less than America's survival. "An abundant supply of bread has meant a well nourished, satisfied people, the bulwark against revolt," it said, reminding readers what had happened in countries where the bread was black: "Weakened nations have succumbed." "Vitality Demands Energy" contains these other encouraging facts:

- White bread is the source of movie star Sylvia Sidney's "soft, glowing beauty."
- Emily Post says that all the well-known signs of an elegant hostess, such as olives, celery, radishes, and salted nuts, "are like nose veils or slipper buckles," i.e., mere frivolities. White bread, she says, "is like dresses, hats, and shoes—in other words, essential."
- Dr. Lafayette B. Mendel of New Haven deplores "the misguided (or perhaps even malicious) efforts in some quarters to detract from the undeniable value of breadstuffs."
- Raymond Hertwig of the American Medical Association says that "white flour is a wholesome food and has a proper place in the well balanced, adequate diet."

Anti-white-bread people never lost their skepticism about mass-produced bread, an attitude that won new converts as the health-food craze evolved from nuttiness to a socially acceptable point of view. Since hippie days, virtually all white foods (white rice, mashed potatoes, white sugar, even milk) have been on the list of suspiciously corporate, potentially carcinogenic evils; whereas dark foods (brown rice, honey, bran) are automatically considered honest. "Read the label on that ghastly cloud of chemicals that passes for the staff of life in America today," scoffed John and Karen Hess, food writers who wondered in 1977, "How shall we tell our fellow Americans that our palates have been ravaged, that our food is awful . . .?" Waverly Root and Richard de Rochemont, also worrying about the rape of the American palate, concluded their book *Eating in America* by saying that "the poor will continue to buy the inflated white loaf" but that "some young households will get around the problem by baking their own bread, with a few of them grinding their own wheat and grains in little kitchen mills."

Enlightened loaves, however, will never win

favor among Wonder Bread eaters. When Mike and Gloria Stivic, Archie Bunker's daughter and son-in-law in "All in the Family," brought a loaf of seven-whole-grain bread to the table, kindly Edith complained that "there wasn't even one grain of tastiness in it" and said that even the neighbors' dog Pug didn't want any part of the kids' health-food loaf.

One amazing historical fact to consider is that the original Wonder Bread, introduced in 1920 by Taggart Baking Company of Indianapolis in the newly popular one-and-a-half-pound size, was sold *unsliced*. Can you imagine what an unsliced loaf of Wonder Bread must have felt like? Perhaps like a balloon? Probably so, because the name "Wonder" came about when a Taggart executive was watching a balloon race, and the balloons apparently reminded him of the bread. Because they also filled him with wonder, he put the two thoughts together and realized he had a name for the company's new product. The package was almost the same as it is today,

covered by pictures of balloons, which gave Wonder the nickname by which many still know it, "Balloon Bread."

Wonder Bread was bought by Continental Bakeries, who made it a national brand; and in 1930—the same year they introduced Twinkies—they started selling Wonder Bread in pre-sliced loaves. Wonder was the first bread to be available sliced, an innovation that carried it to the number-one position it holds today. (During World War II, when bread slicing was considered a waste of national effort and bakeries returned to selling unsliced loaves, the expression "the greatest thing since sliced bread" became popular.)

Despite the best efforts of the nutrition police and the good-taste patrol, Wonder Bread continues to be America's most popular bread, and the only really correct stuff for lunch meat, for sponging up barbecue sauce, and for peanut-butter-and-jelly sandwiches.

ZOOT SUITS

Few fashion statements are so offensive they get banned by official decree of the United States government, but that's what happened to zoot suits in 1942. The rationale was that zoot suits were so big and baggy that they wasted cloth essential for the war effort. In fact, it was the vulgarity of zoot suits as much as their wastefulness that got them outlawed. They symbolized irreverent youth, dirty dancing, and the threat of "licentious" black culture as seen by protectors of the status quo.

Zoot suits were, and still are, an astounding sight—the all-time high-water mark in audacious apparel. For a full-bore model, the coat has extra wide draped shoulders, dramatically flared lapels, a high, girdle-tight waist, and a long flare nearly to the knees. The pants are cinched far above the waistline, double-pleated so they bloom out around the hips; but then they taper to a pegged ankle so small that in the most extreme cases they cannot be put on by men with big feet. Classic zoot suit material contains a vertical zig-zag stripe; and the requisite accessories include a fat, satin-finish tie, an unfolded handkerchief protruding from the breast pocket, a dangling-below-the-knee key chain, cufflinks as big as jaybird eggs, pointy-toed shoes, and a pancake-brimmed hat.

There was a precedent for this kind of exaggeration in the long coats and pegged trousers worn by collegiate dandies in the early 1900s; but no one was prepared for the shock of the zoot suit as it began appearing simultaneously in Harlem and Los Angeles in the early forties. The style was the mark of black hipsters who needed the leeway afforded by baggy pants and a long coat to "shuffle along" (the hep cat's way of walking down the street using slow, elongated steps—pioneered by zoot-suit—wearing Cab Calloway) and to jitterbug on the

MEN!
"HEP"...
AND HOW!

ZIPSTER FLY FRONT!

24 INCHES AT THE KNEE!

17-INCH CUFFS!

HI-WAIST "PEG" TROUSERS $2.98

Sensational 4-star Hollywood hit. And here's why! Full 24-inch knee tapers to a neat 17-inch bottom, the last word in "hep" styling. Swank high French waistband. Smart drape pleats. Zipster fly closing. Fine quality dressy striped worsted-like Cotton Suiting. Green, Blue or Brown, each with stripes. Sizes: 28 to 36 waist; 28 to 34 inseam. Ship. wt. 2 lbs........$2.98
18 T 887—Green, Blue or Brown, each

dance floor. The name was coined as a way to say *suit* with a twist of jive, the dialect that favored rhymes and paired words for emphasis. *"Zoot!"* was a neologism shouted by members of the audience to hot swing bands in Harlem nightclubs.

The fashion vaulted from the black subculture to young white fashion pacesetters, which is when it began to bother America's taste wardens. The War Production Board issued its anti-zoot suit proclamation after a dance in a Washington, D.C., hotel, at which zoot suits and juke coats (the female counterpart) were required attire. "The classy-cut scandalously wasteful zoot suit is doomed," declared *Life* magazine; of course the interdiction only made zoot suits a cause célèbre among restless teenagers, hipsters, hoodlums, and juvenile delinquents. Although it soon lost the aura of immediate danger and disappeared as a controversial issue in its own right, its effrontery, outsized lines, and outrageous fabrics reverberated in all manner of profane apparel through the fifties. Billowy, loud clothes became the mark of a dangerous outsider —ranging from overdressed bad guys in television's "Superman" to Elvis Presley wiggling his pelvis under rakish double-breasted jackets in bawdy hues.

Now, amazingly, the zoot suit has returned and been adopted as an emblem of a new style of impertinence among low riders, for whom it has the same bloated opulence as a big, chromed, and fur-lined 1960 Chevrolet. For these self-styled fashion renegades who flap along the boulevard in eye-popping "zoot suits with reet pleats," the fifty-year-old ensemble has become a delicious way to thumb their noses at straitlaced ideas of proportion and poise. No mere article of clothing, the zoot suit has proven itself a powerful weapon in bad taste's relentless war on propriety.

See also **LOUD TIES; LOW RIDERS**